Palgrave Studies in Prisons and Penology

This is a unique and innovative series, the first of its kind dedicated entirely to prison scholarship. At a historical point in which the prison population has reached an all-time high, the series seeks to analyse the form, nature and consequences of incarceration and related forms of punishment. Palgrave Studies in Prisons and Penology provides an important forum for burgeoning prison research across the world.

More information about this series at
http://www.palgrave.com/gp/series/14596

Stanton Wheeler · Hugh F. Cline

The Scandinavian Prison Study

Edited by David J. Armor

Foreword by Marcia Chambers
Preface by David J. Armor
Afterword by Thomas Mathiesen with Flemming Balvig, Aarne Kinnunen and Henrik Tham

palgrave
macmillan

Authors
Stanton Wheeler (Deceased)

Hugh F. Cline (Deceased)

Editor
David J. Armor
Schar School of Policy and Government
George Mason University
Arlington, VA, USA

Palgrave Studies in Prisons and Penology
ISBN 978-3-030-26464-2 ISBN 978-3-030-26462-8 (eBook)
https://doi.org/10.1007/978-3-030-26462-8

This Palgrave Macmillan imprint is published by the registered company Springer Nature Switzerland AG
The registered company address is: Gewerbestrasse 11, 6330 Cham, Switzerland

Foreword by Marcia Chambers

A reader might wonder why this research on the Scandinavia Prison system, conducted by my late husband Stanton Wheeler and Hugh "Tony" Cline between 1960 and 1975, is being published at this time. This story began long before I met Stan when he, his first wife Mary Lou, and his three young children went to live in Norway where Stan was going to study the Scandinavian prison system under a Fulbright Fellowship.

Stan had a passion for prisons. It started early on when he was a jazz musician and met any number of men who had prison backgrounds. He believed in rehabilitation long before it became fashionable. He wrote his doctoral thesis at the University of Washington on the prison at Walla Walla in Washington. He studied every sixth prisoner and how he lived and coped with prison in life. Over the course of his life he never let his commitment to the study of prison, in Scandinavia, and in the United States, leave his side. It was always part of our conversation over the years of our marriage.

When we first married Stan took me to his house in Manchester Vermont. It was the summer and he piled cartons of papers into the trunk. He said he had work to do on this prison study. That was in the early 1980s. And he did, on occasion, return to the partially completed manuscript. But only on occasion. Other projects intervened as well as his love of sports, especially golf. Given the choice of a beautiful Vermont day sitting inside working on a prison study and taking four or five hours to play 18 holes, well, the choice was no choice at all.

He was confronting any number of realities, he said, about this manuscript. One it was aging. More than twenty years had passed since he first conducted the research. And while one article based on Tony Cline's Ph.D. dissertation was published, the full manuscript, all 12 (planned) chapters, had not been.

Another issue was how data compilation was collected and analyzed in the 1960s versus the 1980s and onward. A computer-driven universe was emerging and daunting. Indeed this manuscript was not digitized until preparation for this book.

Between 1967 and 1977, Stan and Tony were both at the Russell Sage Foundation. With the help of Susan Shapiro, they made a lot of progress writing many chapters of this book. After Tony left Russell Sage work was more intermittent, but Stan was enthusiastic about revisiting and working to publish. At the Yale festschrift, in 1998, everyone returned to Yale, including Thomas Mathiesen. Photos were taken of Thomas, Stan, and Tony holding a mock-up of the SPS. That was twenty years ago.

A few years after Stan passed away, I contacted Tony about finishing the book, and we worked collaboratively, reaching into the archive boxes that we both had. We were both pleased to find so many of the chapters in final form. After Tony's death his wife, Hilary Hays, had all his boxes shipped to my home. And then David Armor came here and combed through the files and data.

It was exciting to be in my basement unearthing this historical study and bringing it to light for future researchers.

After Tony's death I felt at a loss of who I would turn to help me get the study edited and published. I contacted the Russell Sage Foundation, I contacted Susan Shapiro and to my surprise, the person who told me of Tony's death, David Armor, turned out to be a perfect man for the job.

Susan Shapiro was a key player in bringing the study from research data and rough drafts to the final manuscript. She was one of Stan's students at Russell Sage and had since gone on to become a Research Professor at the American Bar Foundation. She was helpful in discussing and reviewing this project and in my conversations with her she was helpful and insightful in bringing this project forward to publication.

I am a reporter. An independent full time employed woman my whole life. As Stan lay dying I made him a promise that SPS would someday be published. But I was a working journalist (and still am) and it took much longer than I thought.

From the 2016 Stan Wheeler Memorial Concert at Yale School of Law

For those of you new to this event I want to tell you a little bit about Stan. He grew up in Pomona, California and started his trumpet lessons as a teenager in Los Angeles, studying with the legendary cornet player Herbert L. Clarke, the lead soloist in the great John Philip Sousa Band. Clark died in 1945 and Stan, at age 15, was one of his last students.

In his late teens and early 20s Stan gravitated to the segregated 1950s jazz clubs of Los Angeles. He once said he was drawn to sociology because "through music I had become deeply concerned with race relations." It was a topic always close to his heart and thoughts.

He was a pioneer in the integration of law and social science, a scholar who conducted studies on delinquency, prisons, sentencing, state courts, white-collar crime and sports. He wrote widely in these areas, all the while mentoring hundreds of students on the graduate level.

Dean Koh once said that over the course of his life Stan Wheeler was a scholar, a teacher, a college master, a musician, a mentor, a sportsman.

He headed the Yale faculty committee on athletics for years and he was the first president of the Amateur Athletics Association of Los Angeles, the beneficiary of the 1984 Olympics. He was in many ways a citizen of Yale who applied his side interests to his academic life. It is no accident that he taught his hobbies, Sport and Law and Music and Law. But he was also a person who had what he termed "side interests." In fact, he kept a file entitled: "The social organization of side interests." He had many.

Golf was a lifelong passion and sports of all types were never far from his mind. Indeed, if the Masters tournament were this weekend instead of next, well, he might well have taken a break from his horn to watch the last nine holes.

He defined side interests "as an activity that at least for most persons—in time—cannot equal that of the work place, but is an activity that has come to occupy a crucially important role in one's life."

Playing jazz, playing trumpet, cornet or flugelhorn, was a crucially important part of Stan's life. He maintained a thirty-year association with the Yale Jazz Ensemble as a member of the trumpet section until the time of his death; jazz moved his soul. He spoke often about double lives, a life he knew well as both an academic and a trumpet player.

I am indebted to Tom Duffy, who was the director and conductor of the Yale Jazz Ensemble, a jazz group now on hiatus. We deeply miss the Jazz Ensemble in this room today and we hope they will return when the music building reopens.

Tom Duffy, a dear friend and the inspiration for these concerts, took the jazz ensemble all over the world. We were all together in Bermuda in another era of the Jazz ensemble when Stan and I became engaged. We traveled to France and England with Duffy's re-incarnated Glenn Miller band on the occasion of the 50th anniversary of D-Day.

Stan played Harry James, an inner dream come true, he said. Without Tom, we would not be here today.

And then there is Reunion the Reunion Jazz Ensemble, so named because as Stan would say it was always a reunion when the group got together, whether in Vermont, or New Haven, at Morse College, in Short Beach or today.

They all came together to celebrate their long friendship, which began in the mid-1970s when a number of Reunion's players were undergraduates here at Yale, playing with the Yale Jazz Ensemble. This weekend they return to the place where they began their friendship more than 35 years ago. (Editor's Note: Marcia Chambers passed away unexpectedly in July 2018).

Branford, CT, USA

Preface by David J. Armor

Introduction

The data for the Scandinavian Prison Study (hereafter SPS) were collected nearly 60 years ago by Stanton Wheeler when he was an Assistant Professor at Harvard University. The data were analyzed and a manuscript written over the next fifteen years by Wheeler with the help of Hugh F. "Tony" Cline, Stan's research assistant at Harvard who continued as a major collaborator. Wheeler went from Harvard to the Russell Sage Foundation and Yale in the mid-1960s, while Cline went from Harvard to UC Santa Barbara and then to Russell Sage at about the same time. Cline served as President of the Foundation from 1972 to 1976.

The manuscript was nearly completed by the mid-1970s when other projects and obligations interfered, and the draft languished for the next 30 years. Stan became ill and passed away in 2007. Tony wanted to finish the book after he finished another project, but he passed away from an unexpected illness in 2016 before he could restart work on the SPS. These events were unforeseen but nonetheless unfortunate because the SPS was the first study of its kind—a large comparative study of 2000 prisoners in 15 prisons across four Scandinavian countries.

My reasons for offering to complete and edit the SPS manuscript are twofold. First, I was good friends with both authors, and I was especially close to Tony Cline. Second, I had known about the SPS for many years and, although criminology is not one of my specialties, I have taught enough public policy courses to appreciate the value of a unique prison study.

Tony and I met in 1961 as first-year graduate students in the Department of Social Relations at Harvard, and we became best friends soon after. During that first year we took a seminar on social deviance from then Assistant Professor Stan Wheeler, who had just finished collecting the data for SPS. We both enjoyed that course and took an instant liking to Stan and his family, not only because he was an outstanding teacher, but also because he immediately welcomed us and other graduate students to social occasions in his home. Tony became even closer to Stan after he became one of his research assistants, doing major portions of the quantitative analyses for the SPS. Tony's time in Stockholm and his natural gift for languages made him especially valuable for the Scandinavian study. His Ph.D. dissertation utilized the SPS data to examine important questions about the normative order in prisons.

Although Tony and I came to Harvard with different backgrounds, he with a Masters Degree from Stockholm University and me with a Bachelor's Degree from UC Berkeley, we nonetheless had similar outlooks on the world and our field of sociology. We both enjoyed the interdisciplinary program at Harvard, we were interested in policy as well as theory, and we took an instant liking to computer-based data analysis, which we practiced throughout our graduate years and well beyond. Equally important, we had the same sense of humor; we had wives who got along well; and within a year or two, we both had daughters and sons about a year apart in age. Over the five years we were together at Harvard, our families vacationed together on Cape Cod, and that tradition continued long after we left Harvard and pursued academic careers in different parts of the country. It continued after Tony's first wife, Pat, passed away and he married Hilary Hays in 1990, also a close friend from the Harvard days.

After getting his Ph.D. from Harvard, Tony accepted an Assistant Professor position at UC Santa Barbara, but he was there only three years before accepting a research staff appointment with the Russell Sage Foundation in 1967. Stan had joined the Russell Sage Foundation as a full-time staff member in 1964, so the stage was set for a resumption of their collaboration on the SPS. Although Stan accepted an appointment as a Professor of Law and Sociology at Yale a few years before Tony became President of the Russell Sage Foundation (1972), Stan continued consulting for Russell Sage and the collaboration continued. By the time Tony left Russell Sage in 1977, they had finished drafts of nine chapters of their planned book on the SPS. Only a couple of chapters remained to be written, according to the book plan discussed in Chapter 1.

After Tony left the Foundation to join the Education Testing Service as a senior research sociologist, work on the SPS book either slowed or stopped altogether. It is not clear why the work slowed, but obviously both Stan and Tony had acquired other research interests and demands on their time, including Stan's growing interest in the Sociology of Law and related topics. Stan wrote extensively on criminology subjects between 1970 and 1994, including books on juvenile delinquency and white-collar crime.

As long as I knew them, Stan and Tony always planned to complete and publish the SPS, but as more time passed it became increasingly difficult for them to resume work on the project. In the early 2000s Stan developed some serious heart problems, finally succumbing to that illness in 2007. After that Tony did not discuss the SPS very much, but he was working on numerous studies at ETS as well as his major contribution to sociology, a book on technology and society (*Information Communication Technology and Social Transformation*) which was finally published by Routledge in 2014.

In late May of 2016, my wife, Marilyn, and I visited Tony and Hilary in Princeton, and he was quite excited because Stan's wife, Marcia Chambers, had recently been in touch about finishing the SPS and getting it published as a tribute to Stan. She had sent him the first six chapters, and on rereading those chapters, he was surprised that they were in such good shape. He told me that he was looking forward to starting this project and perhaps getting a final manuscript during the summer and finally getting the book published.

Not long after that visit, Tony was hospitalized suffering from a serious and fast-acting respiratory illness. Shocking to all his friends and family, he was gone by July 4. Hilary asked me to undertake the sad job of writing Marcia that Tony was gone, commenting about Tony's excitement over resuming work on the SPS and finally finishing the book. I told Marcia that in memory of both Tony and Stan, I would be happy to help finish putting the book together, depending on the status of the remaining chapters. She sent me all the draft chapters from the study, and after reading them, I felt they represented the main topics that Stan and Tony had planned to cover, and that they would constitute an informative report on Scandinavian prisons. Marcia had also been in contact with Thomas Mathiesen at the University of Oslo, who volunteered to write an Afterword that would discuss current issues in Scandinavian penology, assisted by several other criminologists from the Scandinavian countries. Tragically, Marcia also passed away shortly after I delivered the final edited chapters of the SPS, but not before she had written a helpful Forward that explains how this book came together.

Purpose and Content of the SPS

Before reviewing the editing plan and specific editing issues, some discussion of the objectives and content of the SPS are in order. This topic is covered by the authors in Chapter 1, in some detail, but a short discussion here will help set the agenda for this preface and also underscore the strengths and limitations of this volume. As the authors state in Chapter 1,

> We are not primarily concerned with an immediate input to social policy, either with reference to the particular institutions we studied or to others… Our hope is to learn something basic about the nature and structure of prisons, about the effect of that structure on individual prisoners, and on the other factors that may influence the way they respond to confinement.

The authors felt that some of their findings might have relevance to prison policy, but their main purpose is to offer more basic descriptions and explanations of prison "phenomena" using the tools of social science research. Their theoretical framework is presented in Chapter 2.

Because the SPS involves nearly two thousand inmates in fourteen prisons, the authors propose two primary levels of analysis. Chapters 3 and 4 focus on the prison as the unit of analysis, and the social climate of the prison becomes the basis of outcomes measures. One of the authors' major outcomes is an index of social deprivation measured in terms of amount of contact inmates have both inside and outside the prison. Explanatory variables include a variety of institutional measures, such as the age and configuration of the prison and various aggregate characteristics of staff. Some of the important findings in these chapters are the discovery of strong relationships between various prison characteristics, such as its age and configuration, and the overall level of social deprivation.

In Chapters 5 and 6 the emphasis shifts to the inmate as unit of analysis, and the authors turn from social organization to the social psychology of individual inmates. A number of theoretical issues are evaluated in these chapters, including a theory of Emile Durkheim which evolved from his classic study of suicide and its causes. Durkheim's theory of "anomie" holds that individuals' psychic well-being is influenced by their degree of social integration. Although Durkheim used his theory of anomie to explain variation in suicide rates, less serious outcomes can be postulated. The SPS investigates whether the total amount of contact both inside and outside the prison affect various prisoner attitudes. One of the most important outcomes throughout these chapters is "attitudinal conformity" to staff (as opposed to inmate) norms. Attitudinal nonconformity is an outcome similar to what other prison studies have referred to as "prisonization" (see below).

Another investigation in Chapter 6 is Edwin Sutherland's theory of differential association, in which the type and content of the interpersonal contact influence various outcomes. The authors state that Sutherland's theory underlies Clemmer's concept of "prisonization," whereby the more contact an inmate has with other prisoners, the more likely that inmate will take on anti-social beliefs and behaviors. The "prisonization" concept was studied extensively in many prison studies conducted between the 1960s and 1980s. To test Sutherland's theory, various behaviors and attitudes are combined into several independent variables or indicators, and then these indicators are related to a series of outcomes. For example, the SPS finds a solid relationship between the pattern of contacts inmates have with other inmates and their feelings of being harmed by imprisonment or their degree of attitudinal conformity.

Chapter 7 combines the social organization concepts of Chapters 3 and 4 with the social psychological behaviors from Chapters 5 and 6 to investigate whether the various relationships among prisoner behaviors are impacted by aggregate characteristics such as national or institutional differences. That is, is there is an interaction between relationships among interpersonal measures and institutional context? Such multi-level relationships can only be studied when one has large samples of individuals across a sizeable number of institutional settings. This chapter offers the most complex analyses in the SPS, and the authors point out that the various relationships found might be the most tentative in the study. It is nonetheless groundbreaking research because at that time there had been no prison study that encompassed both a large sample of inmates and a large sample of prisons.

Regarding the issue of research findings with policy relevance, the most likely candidates are found in Chapter 8, which examines "considerations of justice in the sentencing and treatment" of inmates. The authors are candid about the limitations of their data on this issue, because findings are based on inmate responses to only two questions on justice—whether inmates feel they have been justly sentenced and also justly treated. By the time this chapter was written (in the mid-1970s, according to dates on drafts), a series of prison riots had occurred in the United States, most notably the Attica prison riot in New York in which numerous prisoners were killed. They acknowledged that more questions would have been included on this issue if data collection was occurring at the time of writing. However, the authors believe that responses and relationships were sufficiently consistent to offer some meaningful conclusions about the perceived justice of treatment in Scandinavian prisons.

Chapter 8 also mentions an unexpected finding, that preventive detention prisons—which had more psychiatric than custodial staff—tended to have the lowest levels of perceived just treatment. According to the authors, this finding would be discussed in "the next Chapter." This would have been Chapter 9, but no draft of this chapter was ever written. Chapter 1 states that Chapter 9 would deal with "the effect of adopting a psychiatric approach within the confines of a custodial prison."

It is possible that this unwritten chapter would have said more about the policy implications of the "unusual" findings concerning just treatment in preventive detention prisons. The unusual finding was that prisoners in these prisons reported especially high levels of perceived unjust treatment despite the fact that they tended to have lower levels of guard power and coerciveness, no doubt because the staff was more treatment-oriented than regular prison guards. Additional comments about this issue, including a description of some new analyses added by the Editor, are found in the editing notes for Chapter 8.

Approach and Methods for Editing

A few comments about the editing process are in order. The amount of editing depended on certain sections of the manuscript. Accordingly, I have divided the editing description into three sections: The first six chapters, Chapter 7, and finally Chapter 8.

Editing for Chapters 1–6

The editing for Chapters 1–6 was the most straightforward, because the drafts for these chapters were the most complete and were in near final content and format. Editing of the text consisted primarily of correcting typographical errors, occasional grammatical corrections, and completing footnotes wherever possible. Some footnotes did not have sufficient information to identify a specific paper or book; for example, just the last name of an author who has published widely in the field of criminology with few clues as to which work was being referenced. In these cases, the footnote includes only the information from the original footnote.

In the case of tables with numerical results, extensive editing was required to put them into a proper Excel format required by most publishers. The same labeling was used as much as possible, but sometimes table titles were shortened to fit one row of a page. In the case of figures, for the most part these had been prepared by hand, and my decision was to leave them as prepared by the authors in the original text. Some of the figures were color-coded, and these colors have been left as-is; in some of the later chapters only black-and-white copies were available, and these have also been copied as-is, although some have been reduced in size.

Editing for Chapter 7

Unlike Chapters 1–6, Chapters 7 and 8 were not final drafts, and there were several notes in each of the manuscripts indicating missing material or topics that needed more discussion. Accordingly, the editing tasks were more extensive and require more explanation.

According to Chapter 1, the goals for Chapter 7 and 8 were to "put together…two levels of analysis, attempting to say what we can about the extent to which individual inmate responses to the prison are a function…of the type of prison in which he is confined." At some point, a decision was made to have Chapter 7 discuss not only the four types of prisons but also the country where the prison was located, a topic originally planned for Chapter 10 (whose title was "Cross-national Differences"). The end result was an overlap of materials in the original drafts of Chapters 7 and 10.

My editorial decision was to take non-overlapping sections from Chapter 10 and fold them into Chapter 7, removing a section described as an analysis of "contextual effects." The analyses of contextual effects were rather difficult to follow, and this difficulty was compounded by the absence of a summary or discussion of what the analyses demonstrated. Thus Chapter 7 includes most of the content in the original Chapters 7 and 10 with the exception of these contextual effects.

Editing for Chapter 8

Chapter 8 takes up the topic of justice, namely prisoners' feelings about the justice of their sentences and also the perceived justice or injustice of their treatment in the prisons. The authors are quite open about the limited number of questions they asked on this topic, given the many issues of prison reform and prisoner unrest that developed around the world in the late 1960s and early 1970s, such as the prison reform movements KRUM and KROM in Scandinavia and the 1971 Attica riots in the US.

Against this backdrop, the single questions about justice of sentence and justice of treatment do seem a bit thin. However, the authors felt that responses were reasonable and relationships with other variables offered important insights to prisoners' evaluations of justice, and thus they proceeded to write the chapter. As such, it is a chapter that had more potential policy implications than the other chapters.

One finding surprised the authors, which is best illustrated in their Fig. 8.1. They were struck by results for the preventive detention prisons which had relatively low levels of just treatment, despite considerably lower ratings of guard power, relative to other prisons. Indeed, the authors' noted they formed a subgroup that was set apart from all other prisons. Similar results occurred for other prison conditions, although the phenomenon was most clearly illustrated in Fig. 8.1. This result could have had important policy implications at that time. Apparently preventive detention prisons became controversial and have changed considerably since that time, and they have changed appreciable since.

Because of the finding for preventive detention prisons in Chapter 8, I have taken liberties to add a few of my own observations, consulting with some of the authors of the Afterword. Although we have no way of knowing for certain, Wheelerand Cline might have added comments like these if they had completed the book in contemporary times.

The SPS and Contemporary Prison Studies

Given that the SPS data was collected in 1960 and the writing of the SPS manuscript (and supporting data analyses) took place over the next 15 years, it is reasonable to ask how this work relates to prison research over the next 40-plus years. It would be both presumptuous and inappropriate to claim a comprehensive review here. Presumptuous because prison research is not one of my fields of expertise (although I have taught criminal justice policy as one topic in graduate public policy courses), and inappropriate because it would take this Preface too far from its purpose. It is possible, however, to offer some context for this "re-discovered classic" by summarizing some of the major themes of prison research during the 40-plus years since the final draft of the SPS was written.

While this brief review includes prison studies in the four Nordic countries, its scope includes major studies other countries. While the SPS includes only Nordic prisons, the substantive issues addressed are not unique to Nordic countries. Indeed, the theoretical models developed in Chapter 2 could be applied to a prison in any country. In Chapter 1, the authors offer a rationale for selecting these prisons: "[they] provide a very wide range of institutional designs and programs, including what are regarded as some of the most innovative developments in penology throughout the world."

At the outset, it is noted that while the full SPS findings were not published as a book, some papers and a book were published during the 1960s that discussed or presented data from the SPS. A paper by Clineand Wheeler used SPS data to test different theories explaining levels of anti-staff social climate in prisons; the analyses were similar to some of those found in Chapter 6 of this volume.[1] Wheeler discusses similar data in a later paper about socialization processes in prisons, and the Cline-Wheeler findings are also mentioned here.[2]

The noted Norwegian criminologist Thomas Mathiesen collaborated with Wheeler during the SPS design and data collection phases. Simultaneously, he conducted his own independent study of Ila, a preventive detention prison, based primarily on participant observation

[1]Cline, H.F., and S. Wheeler, "The Determinants of Normative Patterns in Correctional Institutions," in *Scandinavian Studies in Criminology*, ed. N. Christie, Vol. 2. (Oslo: Universitetsforlaget, 1968.

[2]Wheeler, S. "Socialization in Correctional Institutions," in *Handbook of Socialization Theory and Research*, ed. D. Goslin, (Rand McNally, 1970).

and interviews.[3] Mathiesen also analyzed SPS questionnaire data for Ila and Botsfengslet, a more conventional custodial prison. For example, he shows tables for the "just treatment" questions that are discussed in Chapter 8 in this book. Because Mathiesen's results are based on just these two prisons, it is not possible to see the pattern of relationships discussed Chapter 8 that are based on all 14 prisons. Mathiesen's current views about developments in Norwegian prisons are presented as an "Afterword" to this volume.

There are, of course, many other writings on Scandinavian prisons during the 1960s, but English translations are not available for most of them. One study by noted Danish criminologist, Flemming Balvig, is of special note here because of its comprehensive discussion of Danish prisons and prisoners, and it also discusses some of the SPS findings.[4]

Rounding out this early research on Scandinavian prisons, in 1970 Ulla Bondeson conducted a major study of 13 prisons in Sweden.[5] Her study had some similarities to the SPS but also some major differences. Like the SPS, she administered questionnaires to about 1000 inmates from a cross section of Swedish prisons, and no doubt the questionnaire approach was influenced by the SPS research design. In fact, she cites a 1963 mimeographed paper by Wheeler summarizing some of the methods and findings of the SPS.[6]

There were two major differences between the SPS and the Swedish prison study. First, Bondeson operationalized the prisonization concept by constructing scales of "criminalization," which assess favorable attitudes toward criminals and criminal behavior, including identifying oneself as a criminal. Moreover, unlike the SPS, Bondeson also conducted a 10-year follow-up study to measure recidivism. In this way, Bondeson could test the relationship between criminalization attitudes and later criminal behavior. She did not find a significant effect of criminalization on recidivism.

[3]Mathiesen, T., *The Defences of the Weak.* (London: Tavistock, 1965).

[4]Balvig, F., et al., *Fængsler og fanger.* (Jørgen Paludans, 1969).

[5]Bondeson, U., *Prisoners in Prison Societies.* (Transaction Publishers, 1989).

[6]Wheeler, S., *A Preliminary Report on a Scandinavian Prison Study.* N.d. (mimeographed), 1963.

The most important publication from the Bondeson study is her book, *Prisoners in Prison Societies*, published nearly 20 years after the data was collected. However, many of her findings were published in earlier papers, including a summary in English published by the US National Institute of Justice (Bondeson, 1974).[7] This paper includes the following summary:

> Results were obtained on the following factors: the informal social system, the impact of imprisonment, negative effects of institutionalization, positive effects, political attitudes of prisoners, socialization in prisons, and the inmate subculture. The author concludes that institutional treatment fails not only to fulfill its official therapeutic function but even militates against rehabilitation.

Perhaps the most notable development in the late 1980s and 1990s was the growth of new strategies and concepts for prison sentencing, and in particular promoting the concept of "incapacitation" as a major goal of incarceration in addition to (or even in place of) rehabilitation, at least for the "career" or "dangerous" criminals. This idea received considerable attention when it was proposed by noted US political scientist James Q. Wilson.[8] The idea received support from several quarters, and not many years later it was being endorsed by a wide spectrum of experts in criminology, in both academic circles and among policy practitioners. Although support was strongest in the United States, it was embraced to some extent in the UK and other English-speaking countries.

For example, a study by the Rand Corporation in the early 1980s offered some evidence that "selective" incapacitation was a cost-effective policy for reducing the rates of certain types of crimes.[9] The idea of selective incapacitation was endorsed for "dangerous offenders"

---

[7]Bondeson, U., *Socialization Processes in Training Schools, Youth Prisons, Prisons, and Internment Centers*—Summary, (P.A. Norstedt & Soners Foerlag, 1974).

[8]Wilson, J.Q., *Thinking About Crime*, (Basic Books, 1975).

[9]Greenwood, P.W., *Selective Incapacitation.*, (The Rand Corporation, 1982) R-2815-NIJ.

by a group of criminologists from the prestigious Kennedy School of Government at Harvard University.[10]

The Rand Corporation did some additional cost–benefit studies for the state of California, and soon after California became the first state to adopt a "Three Strikes and You're Out Law," meaning a third conviction for a felony would lead to a mandatory long sentence (25 years to life). Similar laws were adopted in approximately two-thirds of the states, and as a result the number of prisoners in the United States more than tripled from 1980—already high by European standards at 220 per 100,000—to an incredible 685 per 100,000 by 2000. In that same period the number of prisoners increased from 85 to 125 per 100,000 in the UK and from 59 to 113 per 100,000 in Australia.

These developments have been explained and defended by some criminologists but strongly criticized by others. For example, Feeley and Simon describe these trends as reflecting a "new penology" that "shifts away from a concern with punishing individuals to managing aggregates of dangerous groups".[11] No doubt some persons involved in criminal justice systems have this viewpoint, but even a cursory reading of the literature shows great diversity in experts' theories of crime and the effectiveness of different types of punishment.

As rates of incarceration increased during the 1990s, many experts became highly critical of the trend and its implications. One prominent and consistent critic of these increasing rates of incarceration was Thomas Mathiesen, a contributor to the SPS. His book, *Prison on Trial,* offered a strong critique of incarceration, even including policies in his own country, Norway, which has maintained relatively low incapacitation rates for many decades, especially when compared to the US.[12]

---

[10]Moore, M.H., Estrich, S.R., McGillis, D., and Spelman, W. *Dangerous Offenders*, (Harvard University Press, 1984).

[11]Feeley, M.M., and Simon, J., The New Penology: Notes on the Emerging Strategy of Corrections and Its Implications. *Criminology* 30(4) 449–474, (1992).

[12]Mathiesen, T., *Prison on Trial*. (Waterside Press, 2006).

Mathiesen was not the only strong critic of this trend. Others include John Pratt[13] and Loïc Wacquant. In one essay, Wacquant compared US prisons to urban black ghettos.[14] In another essay, Wacquant described "the American carceral boom" as the "great penal leap backward."[15] There is a growing literature in the United States which criticizes the very high proportions of African Americans in prison populations. A good example is a critique by an American historian who sees the war on poverty transitioning to the war on crime, with African American men the primary victims.[16] Other prominent US criminologists take a less critical approach, arguing that some of the increase in prison sentences can be explained by increased rates of crime, but he also questioned the effectiveness of long prison sentences for drug crimes.[17]

In 2002 Wacquant wrote another influential article, "The Curious Eclipse of Prison Ethnography," arguing that the ethnographic approach might be most useful during a period of expanding incarceration, particularly in the United States where "carceral exceptionalism" suggested an urgent need.[18] Many criminologists seemed to agree with this analysis, because the ethnographic study of prisons grew substantially over the next decade, particularly in Europe. It might be fairly stated that it became the predominant methodological approach in European criminology after 2010.

The ethnographic study of prisons was not a new technique; indeed, some of the classics such as those by Clemmer and Sykes are based on qualitative approaches that might be reasonably classified as

[13]Pratt, J., Brown, M., Hallsworth, S., and Morrison, W., *The New Punitiveness*. (Willan Publishing, 2005).

[14]Wacquant, L., The New 'Peculiar Institution': On the Prison as Surrogate Ghetto. *Theoretical Criminology* 4(3):377–389, (2000).

[15]Wacquant, L., The Great Penal Leap Backward: Incarceration in America from Nixon to Clinton. In *The New Punitiveness*, ed. Pratt, et al. , (Willan, 2005).

[16]Hinton, E., *From the War on Poverty to the War on Crime*, (Harvard University Press, 2016).

[17]Blumstein, A., (2004).

[18]Wacquant, L., "The Curious Eclipse of Prison Ethnography in the Age of Mass Incarceration", *Ethnography* 3(4), 371–397, (2002).

ethnographic.[19] A classic ethnographic study of a prison-like institution was carried out by Goffman who studied a mental hospital, an "asylum", which he described as a "total" institution with unique characteristics.[20] Especially notable was the near total control of every aspect of an inmate's behavior and environment.

The decline of ethnographic methods and the rise of quantitative methods during the 1970s, 1980s, and 1990s might be related to the evolution and spread of computers and the availability of statistical software that made it relatively easy to analyze data on hundreds, even thousands, of individuals. In the United States, most graduate schools with Ph.D. programs in the social and behavioral sciences emphasized quantitative and statistical methods. They stressed the importance of "objective" quantitative analysis to verify hypotheses derived from a formal theoretical foundation. The SPS and the Bondeson studies fall into this category of research.

The ethnographic method differs considerably from the quantitative approaches illustrated in the SPS and Bondeson studies. In contrast to formulating hypotheses, operationalizing concepts, collecting information via questionnaires and structured interviews, and then testing these hypotheses using statistical analysis, ethnographic studies approach a prison population as a self-contained society or culture with unique sets of values, assumptions, rules, a power hierarchy, and even a vocabulary. Ethnography originated in the field of anthropology, where its goal was to understand a new and unfamiliar culture on its own terms. These methods and concepts have been expanded and refined over the years, and they can be applied to a prison population conceived as a "society" with a unique "culture." Documenting and understanding this society and culture requires an ethnographic approach and methods. Without question, many if not most ethnographic studies represent not just a

---

[19]Clemmer, D., *The Prison Community*. (Reissued 1958. New York: Holt), Rinehart & Winston; Sykes, G. (1958). *The Society of Captives. A Study of a Maximum Security Prison*, (New Jersey: Princeton University Press, 1940).

[20]Goffman, E., *Asylums. Essays on the Social Situation of Mental Patients and Other Inmates*, (New York: Doubleday, 1961).

different methodology, but a different goal—to humanize the prisoner and change the discourse from punishment to recovery.

Good examples of modern ethnographic research in prisons include Crewe's study of a medium security in Britain,[21]Ugelvik's study of Norway's largest prison in Oslo,[22] and Rhodes' study of "supermax" prisons in Washington state.[23] In contrast to the SPS or the Bondeson works, in these ethnographic studies no questionnaires are distributed, no classifications of behavior are put forth, there is no counting of various types of behaviors, and no quantitative analyses are presented. In fact, one does not see any numbers at all, except (perhaps) the number of prisoners or staff who have been interviewed or observed. Instead, there are transcripts from interviews, descriptions of prison scenes, quotes from statements made by prisoners and staff, and of course interpretations as to what this information means and how it might be used to improve the conditions of human life in a prison environment.

The resurgence of ethnographic research is highlighted by publication of the "Handbook of Prison Ethnography" edited by Drake, Earle, and Sloan.[24] The chapters are drawn from a symposium on prison ethnography which, as the editors acknowledge in their introduction, was a response, in large part, to the Wacquant essay about the "eclipse" of prison ethnography. This volume illustrates many different approaches and applications for the ethnographic approach to prison research, and it offers descriptions of prison conditions in many different and less studied countries such as Russia, India, and Uganda.

The resurgence of ethnographic research does not mean that quantitative prison research like the SPS is in decline; it is still going strong in US sociological studies. For example, the topic of "prisonization," as investigated in the SPS, is still studied in the United States. A recent doctoral dissertation and book by Gillespie conducts a quantitative assessment of the prisonization thesis drawing on data collected in

[21]Crewe, B., *The Prisoner Society: Power, Adaptation, and Social Life in an English Prison*, (Oxford: Oxford University Press, 2009).

[22]Ugelvik, T., *Power and Resistance in Prison.*, (Palgrave Macmillan, 2014).

[23]Rhodes, L.A., *Total Confinement*, (University of California Press, 2004).

[24]Drake, D.H., Earle, R., and Sloan, J., *The Palgrave Handbook of Prison Ethnography*, (Palgrave Macmillan, 2015).

several prisons in Tennessee, Kentucky, and Ohio.[25] Popular textbooks in criminology also discuss quantitative research and testing of formal theories.[26]

Even a brief review of recent prison research would not be complete without mentioning some of the comparative research on prison policies and practices in the Nordic countries vs. the English speaking ("Anglophone") countries like England, Australia, and the USA. John Pratt coined the term "Scandinavian Exceptionalism" to describe the very low rates of incarceration in Scandinavia as compared to many European countries, which he attributed to relatively homogeneous egalitarian values and the related welfare state. In a companion paper, he expressed concerns about threats to these values and policies posed by forces such as immigration.[27] In a later study, he contrasts Scandinavian exceptionalism to Anglophone "excess" by discussing the very low rates of incarceration in Norway, Sweden, and Denmark as compared to the much higher rates in the Anglophone countries of England, Australia, and New Zealand.

Finally, had not the term "exceptionalism" been applied to certain American values and institutions in a positive sense, it might have been applied pejoratively to its incarceration rate, which reached remarkable levels over 700 per 100,000 before tapering off. Criticism of the high rates of incarceration in the United States finally led to a National Academy of Science study which was critical of many of the assumptions behind incarceration, especially that incapacitation was the most effective way to manage crime. The report also called for revision of criminal justice policies to "…significantly reduce the rate of incarceration…".[28] It remains to be seen if this view is adopted by American states, particularly those in the South, which have the highest rates of incarceration.

Arlington, VA, USA

---

[25]Gillespie, W., *Prisonization*, (LFB Scholarly Publishing).

[26]Blomberg, T.G., and Lucken, K., *American Penology*, (Routledge, 2017).

[27]Pratt, J., Scandinavian exceptionalism in an era of penal excess: Parts I & II. *British Journal of Criminology*, 48(2) 119–137 & (3) 275–2920, (2008a, b).

[28]National Research Council, *The Growth of Incarceration in the United States: Exploring Causes and Consequences*, (Washington, DC: The National Academies Press, 2014).

Acknowledgements

Writing acknowledgements for the SPS is a major challenge, because authors Stanton Wheeler and Hugh (Tony) Cline did not draft one, and I had limited knowledge about the SPS during the 1960s and early 1970s when they were doing their major research and writing. I apologize to any contributor to the SPS who is not mentioned here.

I believe Stan would offer special thanks to Nils Christie, who he mentioned many times when he discussed the SPS. I believe Nils helped in the early stages of study design as well as data collection in Norway. Thomas Mathiesen was a graduate student when he worked on the SPS, visiting prisons and collecting data in Norway, which he used for his doctoral dissertation and later in his book, Defenses of the Weak. While Stan and Tony were at the Russell Sage Foundation in the early 1970s, Susan Shapiro did major work on earlier drafts of the manuscript.

Of course, this book would not have happened without the substantial support of Stan's wife, Marcia Chambers, who sadly passed away just as the editing was being completed for this volume. Her assistant and executor, Beth Rosen, helped finalize legal arrangements for authorizing publication. Tony's wife Hilary Hays delivered study materials to Marcia and offered encouragement, and my wife, Marilyn, was very supportive as I added this unexpected book project to an already-full agenda.

Finally, I wish to thank Ben Crewe and Thomas Ugelvik, who read and made helpful editing suggestions to various portions of the manuscript, and Lynn Cline who proofed the copyedited manuscript.

Warrenton, VA, USA
2019

David J. Armor

Contents

1	**Scandinavian Prisons in Perspective**	1
2	**Research Design and Methods**	19
3	**Social Change and the Prison**	41
4	**The Social Climate of the Prisons**	79
5	**Personal Background and Response to Incarceration**	113
6	**Patterns of Social Involvement and Inmate Response to Incarceration**	157
7	**Personal Response in Divergent Prison Environments**	205
8	**Considerations of Justice in the Sentencing and Treatment of Scandinavian Prison Inmates**	223

Afterword 279

Appendix I: Prison-Level Data Collection Methods 295

Appendix II: Inmate Data Collection Methods 301

Appendix III: Figures for Chapter 8 (Figs. 8.6–8.13 and Figs. 8.1'–8.5') 325

Index 337

List of Figures

Fig. 3.1	The relationship of prison age to social deprivation ($r = -.77$)	66
Fig. 3.2	The relationship of prison age to inmate association with other inmates ($r = .63$)	72
Fig. 4.1	The balance of power between guards and treatment staff	84
Fig. 4.2	The balance of understanding between custody and treatment staff ($r = -.10$)	87
Fig. 4.3	The relationship of total power to total understanding ($r = .58$)	89
Fig. 4.4	The relationship of the balance of power to the balance of understanding ($r = -.25$)	90
Fig. 4.5	The relationship between two items reflecting coerciveness of the prison regime	91
Fig. 4.6	The relationship of coerciveness to balance of power ($r = .66$)	93
Fig. 4.7	Relationship between coerciveness and total understanding of prison staff ($r = -.68$)	94
Fig. 4.8	Balance of pressure between inmates and staff ($r = .53$)	96

Fig. 4.9	The relationship between balance of power and balance of pressure (r=.84)	99
Fig. 4.10	The relationship between private and perceived conformity (r=.69)	104
Fig. 4.11	The relationship of perceived norms to the gap between perceived and privately expressed norms (r=.62)	107
Fig. 4.12	The relationship between perceived nonconformity and the balance of pressure between staff and inmates	109
Fig. 4.13	The relationship of the gap between perceived and privately expressed norms to the balance of pressure between staff and inmates	110
Fig. 5.1	Relation between age, attitudinal conformity, and feelings that prison will help them	130
Fig. 8.1	The relationship of justice of treatment to guard authority (tau=−.16)	234
Fig. 8.2	The relationship of justice of treatment to guard understanding (tau=.33)	236
Fig. 8.5	The relationship of justice of treatment to total pressure (tau=−.47)	237
Figs. 8.6 and 8.7	Relationship of justice of treatment to age and marital status	326
Fig. 8.8	Relationship of justice of treatment to social experience favorable to crime	327
Figs. 8.9 and 9a	Relationship of justice of treatment to criminal experience and prior incarcerations	328
Fig. 8.10	Relationship of justice of treatment to sensitivity to authority	329
Fig. 8.11	The relationship between attitudinal conformity and justice of treatment	329
Fig. 8.12	The relationship between behavioral conformity and justice of treatment	330
Fig. 8.13	The relationship between perceived effect of incarceration and justice of treatment (Gammas: Overall −.30; Context 1 −.26; Context 2 −.30; Context 3 −.31)	331
Fig. 8.1'	The relationship of justice of treatment to guard authority (r = −26)	332

Fig. 8.2'	The relationship of justice of treatment to guard understanding ($r = +.42$)	333
Fig. 8.3'	The relationship of justice of treatment to coerciveness ($r = -.38$)	334
Fig. 8.4'	The relationship of justice of treatment to staff pressure ($r = -.65$)	335
Fig. 8.5'	The relationship of justice of treatment to total pressure ($r = -.70$)	336
Diagram 2.1	The organizational level of analysis	22
Diagram 2.2	The individual level	25

List of Tables

Table 1.1	Demographic inidicators for Scandinavia	13
Table 1.2	Economic indicators for Scandinavia	15
Table 1.3	Consumer indicators for Scandinavia	17
Table 1.4	Political and social welfare indicators of Scandinavia	17
Table 2.1	Institutions and number of inmate respondents (see Key for prison type)	34
Table 3.1	Structural correlates of modernity in prison regimes	63
Table 3.2	Relationship between structural features and interaction patterns	73
Table 4.1	The relationship between staff social climate indices and measures of the normative order among inmates	108
Table 5.1	Perceived effect of incarceration by rejection of components of the institutional program	118
Table 5.2	Attitudinal conformity and behavioral conformity	123
Table 5.3	Private attitudinal conformity and perceived effect of incarceration	124
Table 5.4	Social background and response to incarceration	126
Table 5.5	The effect of age and social background on feelings of being harmed (% harmed)	134
Table 5.6	The effect of age and social background on attitudinal conformity (% harmed)	135

Table 5.7 Criminal background and response to incarceration 138
Table 5.8 The effect of age and criminal background on attitudinal conformity (% conform) 140
Table 5.9 The effect of age and criminal background on feelings of being harmed (% harmed) 141
Table 5.10 The relation between social and criminal background 143
Table 5.11 The relationship of current age to sensitivity to authority 147
Table 5.12 Relationship of social and criminal background to sensitivity to authority 148
Table 5.13 The relationship of age at 1st arrest to self-images about crime and law-abiding behavior 150
Table 5.14 Relationship of social and criminal background to self-images regarding crime and law-abiding behavior 151
Table 5.15 The relationship of age and sensitivity to authority to attitudinal conformity (% attitudinal conformists) 152
Table 5.16 The relationship of age and sensitivity to authority to behavioral conformity (% behavioral conformists) 153
Table 6.1 Items reflecting the nature and degree of contact and involvement among inmates 163
Table 6.2 Items reflecting the nature and degree of contact and involvement between inmates and staff 166
Table 6.3 Items reflecting nature % degree of contact between inmates and persons outside the prison 168
Table 6.4 Relationship between number of letters and visits from persons outside the prison 169
Table 6.5 Relationship between quantity of contact and feelings of harm by incarceration 171
Table 6.6 The relationship between patterns of contact and attitudinal conformity 171
Table 6.7 Relationship between patterns of contact and response to incarceration by type of prison 173
Table 6.8 Relationship between types of contact and inmate response to incarceration 175
Table 6.9 Relationship between varying patterns of content and inmate response to incarceration 176
Table 6.10 Relationship of outside contacts and inmate responses to incarceration 178
Table 6.11 Relationship between forms of outside contact and inmate perceptions of support from the outside world 179

Table 6.12	Relationship of the balance between initiation and receipt of communication to various inmate responses	181
Table 6.13	Relationship between inmate contacts with staff and contact with other inmates	187
Table 6.14	Relationship between inmate contacts with other inmates and patterns of conformity	188
Table 6.15	Relationship between inmate contact with staff and feelings of benefit from staff help	190
Table 6.16	Relationship of age and marital status to patterns of inmate contact with staff, other inmates, and persons outside the institution	193
Table 6.17	Relationship of age and number of previous incarcerations to inmate contact	195
Table 6.18	Relationship of age and quantity of contact to feelings of being harmed by incarceration (% who feel harmed)	199
Table 6.19	Relationship of marital status and quantity of contact to feelings of being harmed by incarceration (% who feel harmed)	200
Table 6.20	Relationship of age and patterns of contact to attitudinal conformity (% attitudinal conformists)	202
Table 6.21	Relationship of criminal experience and patterns of contact to attitudinal conformity (% attitudinal conformists)	203
Table 7.1	National differences in aspects of prison climate (percentages)	209
Table 7.2	Institutional differences in aspects of prison climate	212
Table 7.3	National differences in inmate response to incarceration	214
Table 7.4	Institutional differences in inmate response to incarceration	214
Table 7.5	Multiple regression for national and institutional effects	215
Table 7.6	National differences in beneficial aspects of incarceration	219
Table 8.1	Items reflecting inmate perceptions of the justice of their sentencing and treatment	224
Table 8.2	The relationship between perceived justice of sentence and perceived justice of treatment	225
Table 8.3	The relationship between perceived justice of sentence and perceived justice of treatment by institution	227
Table 8.4	Inmate perceptions of the justice of their treatment by institution	229

Table 8.5 Relationship of institutional justice of treatment to aspects of prison structure and climate 233
Table 8.6 Perceptions of just treatment for varying conditions of incarceration (% justly treated) 246
Table 8.7 Relationship of the length of time served to justice of treatment 248
Table 8.8 Patterns of contact and feelings of just treatment 251
Table 8.9 Refined patterns of involvement and feelings concerning justice of treatment 252
Table 8.10 The relationship between attitudinal conformity and justice of treatment by justice of sentence 256
Table 8.11 Relationship between behavioral conformity and justice of treatment by justice of sentence 259
Table 8.12 The relationship between behavioral conformity and length of time served 260
Table 8.13 Relationship between behavioral conformity and justice of treatment by length of time served (percent unjustly treated) 261
Table 8.14 Relationship between effect of incarceration and justice of treatment by justice of sentence 262
Table 8.15 National differences in feelings of justice or injustice of treatment 267
Table 8.16 Homogeneous subgroup analysis for national differences in feelings about justice of treatment 268
Table 8.17 National differences in feelings of justice/injustice of treatment by justice of sentence 269

1

Scandinavian Prisons in Perspective

This volume reports the results of a study of fifteen prisons in the Scandinavian countries. The prisons range in age from old bastilles built in the mid-nineteenth century to new modern institutions built in the latter part of the twentieth century. They also range in purpose and design, in style, and in the way they are staffed and managed.

The prisons are inhabited by almost two thousand inmates. They, like the prisons they inhabit, are a varied lot. Some are young, some are old, some are married, and some are single. Some have never seen the inside of a prison before, and others have been behind bars for a decade or more.

A central purpose of our study is to learn more about the phenomenon of imprisonment by examining variations, both in the prison and in its inhabitants. In the first major substantive part of our study (Chapters 3 and 4) we shall examine closely the differences between the fifteen prisons, with our focus on the prison itself rather than on its inmate inhabitants. We shall endeavor to describe differences between the prisons in some detail, and hopefully to suggest what effects those differences have on the social climate of the prison. In a second major section of our study (Chapters 5 and 6) we focus attention not on the prison but on its individual inhabitants, the inmates. Here we try to

S. Wheeler and H. F. Cline, *The Scandinavian Prison Study*,
Palgrave Studies in Prisons and Penology,
https://doi.org/10.1007/978-3-030-26462-8_1

describe and explain differences in inmate response to the prison based both on qualities the inmate brings with him into the prison and on the nature of the life he comes to lead while inside.

In a third major section (Chapters 7 and 8) we put together these two levels of analysis, attempting to say what we can about the extent to which individual inmate responses to the prison are a function, not only of the inmate himself, but of the nature of the type of prison in which he is confined. Finally, in a fourth and final section, we take up a number of issues that have concerned penologists for some time: the effect of adopting a psychiatric approach within the confines of a custodial prison, cross-national differences in the nature of inmate life and culture, and the nature of socialization within the prison.[1]

A basic assumption underlying our inquiry is that much can be learned about the nature of prison life from a study of inmate responses to different types of prisons. Our aim is to produce generalizations about the prison and its inhabitants. We are not primarily concerned with an immediate input to social policy, either with reference to the particular institutions we studied or to others. Many of the institutions have changed since we originally studied them some fifteen years ago (in ways we describe in an epilogue) but our purpose even then was not to solve some immediate administrative problem. Our hope is to learn something basic about the nature and structure of prisons, about the effect of that structure on individual prisoners, and on the other factors that may influence the way they respond to confinement. We do feel some inferences about prison policy may be drawn from some of our findings, and we detail these considerations in a concluding chapter. But our primary aim is a more basic description of an explanation of prison phenomena, as they may be understood through the use of systematic social research.

In form, this study could have been carried out wherever inmates inhabit prisons. In fact, it was conducted in the distinctive territory of the world known as Scandinavia, including Norway, Denmark, Sweden, and Finland. And since both institution and inmate are likely to be shaped by their surrounding culture, we shall devote most of the

[1]Editors note: A draft existed only for a Chapter 10, which overlapped with Chapter 7 and so was combined with it.

remainder of this chapter to a description of the most salient features of the Scandinavian countries, and the differences between them. Before doing so, however, we pause briefly to locate our type of inquiry among the varied types of writings on the prison.

Perspectives on the Prison

The seemingly endless stream of writings on the prison in recent years gives evidence both of the symbolic importance of imprisonment as our most severe form of punishment short of death, of the dramatic qualities of prison life, and of the enormous range of practical questions facing those who would improve the functioning of prisons. Although there are innumerable ways of classifying the literature in the field, for our purposes this vast body of reports, studies, and accounts can be divided into four general types. We do not intend anything remotely approximating a full review of each of these types of writing, but we do want to describe what lies at the core of each, in order to make clear where our own work might be placed in reference to that of others.

Perhaps the most important writing in terms of sheer volume falls into what might be called policy-oriented studies. These studies will run the gamut from brief reports prepared for a given state correctional system concerning some aspect of prison administration to broad and synthetic studies bearing upon prison policy. Among the latter would be included, for example, the report of the President's Crime Commission, Jessica Mitford's review of the California prison system, The American Friends' Service Committee's report on prisons, and the report of the Special Committee formed by Senator Goodell.[2]

Also important in this category are technical studies designed to answer particular questions of prison policy. Such studies might include the most appropriate way to classify inmates, the nature and effects of the parole

---

[2]President's Commission on Law Enforcement and Administration of Justice, *The Challenge of Crime in a Free Society* (Washington, DC: US Government Printing Office, 1967); Jessica Mitford, _____; American Friends' Service Committee Report, _____; Report of Senator Goodell's Special Committee, _____.

system, the effects of treatment programs, the general relationship of imprisonment to recidivism, or the development of criteria for deciding when a person should be released from prison.[3] Another important type of policy-oriented study is that of the investigative commission, typified in fairly recent American experience by the Attica Commission Report.[4]

Some of these studies have been conducted by lawyers, some by sociologists, some by statisticians, some by humanists with a clear eye and a strong pen. They differ greatly, therefore, in method, in readability, and in range and scope. But they do have in common an explicit focus on prison policy.

Autobiographical writings comprise a second important category of literature on the prison. Most of these accounts are by prisoners. Some, like Aleksandr Solzhenitsyn and Albert Speer, are internationally famous.[5] Others are by well-known national figures, such as Caryl Chessman or Eldridge Cleaver.[6] Still others would be known to very few were it not for their prison writings.[7] Less frequently (perhaps because there are so many fewer keepers than kept) are the autobiographical accounts of prison officials, such as Kenyon J. Scudder's *Prisoners are People.*[8]

These autobiographical accounts are a crucial source of information about the prison experience, since they reveal that experience through the sensitivities of those who have lived life on the inside of the prison.

---

[3]M. Q. Warren and Staff, *Interpersonal Maturity Level Classification* (Sacramento: State of California Youth Authority, 1966); Paul Herman, *Community Treatment and Social Control* (Chicago: University of Chicago Press, 1975); Daniel Glaser, ______; David A. Ward and Gene G. Kassebaum, *Prison Treatment and Parole Survival* (New York: Wiley, 1971); and Thomas Mathiesen, *The Defenses of the Weak* (London: Tavistock Pubs., 1965); Donald Martinson, ______; Donald Gottfredson, et al., ____________.

[4]Attica Commission Report, ________.

[5]Aleksandr Solzhnitsyn, August 1914 (New York: Farrar, Straus & Giroux, 1972); *The Cancer Ward* (New York: The Dial Press, 1968); *The First Circle* (New York: Harper & Row, 1968); *The Gulag Archipelago* (New York: Harper & Row, 1974); *One Day in the Life of Ivan Densiovich* (New York: E. P. Dutton & Co., 1963). Albert Speer, *Spandau: The Secret Diaries* (New York: Macmillan, 1976).

[6]Caryl Chessman, *Trial by Ordeal* (Englewood Cliffs, NJ: Prentice-Hall, 1955); Eldridge Cleaver, *Soul on Ice* (New York: McGraw-Hill, 1964).

[7]Malcolm Braly and Alfred Hassler, *Diary of a Self-Made Convict*, __________.

[8]Kenyon J. Scudder, *Prisoners Are People* __________.

Indeed, short of imprisonment itself, these accounts may be the best way to get a phenomenological sense for the prison experience. One does not read them for an objective, dispassionate account of prison life or conditions, for their authors are typically too deeply immersed in prison life and culture to provide that sort of account.

A third body of literature on prisons consists of sociological case studies. These are reports of inmate life and culture within a single institution. The original classic of this type was Donald Clemmer's *The Prison Community*.[9] These studies attempt to present an objective portrait of the prison. They are typically done by social scientists who base their analyses on experience within the prison either as an observer, or as an active participant on the staff, or occasionally as an inmate. A number of such studies have appeared since Clemmer's original writings. They include the writings of Clarence C. Schrag, Gresham M. Sykes, and, most recently, James B. Jacobs' Stateville.[10] There are also studies of women's institutions.[11] Finally, there are a number of such accounts for English and European prisons.[12] And in addition to the published book-length works, there has been an enormous flow of articles in social science journals devoted to one or another facet of life in prison.

These works form the basis for most of what is "known" in social science terms about prison life. A number of themes recur throughout these studies: the nature of inmate culture within the prison, the variety of roles inmates come to play within the prison, the nature of the authority relationships between inmates and staff, the process of socialization into (and out of) the prison, and the like. In short, these case

[9]Donald Clemmer, *The Prison Community* (New York: Rinehart & Co., 1958).

[10]Clarence C. Schrag, ________; Gresham M. Sykes, *The Society of Captives: A Study of a Maximum Security Prison* (Princeton University Press, ______); James B. Jacobs, *Stateville: The Penitentiary in Mass Society* (The University of Chicago Press, 1977)

[11]Rose Giallombardo, *Society of Women: A Study of a Women's Prison* (New York: Wiley, 1966); David A. Ward and Gene G. Kassebaum, *Prison Treatment and Parole Survival* (New York: Wiley, 1971).

[12]Terence Morris and Pauline Morris, *Pentonville* ________; Thomas Mathiesen, *The Defenses of the Weak* (London: Tavistock Pubs., 1965).

studies have provided the principal development and testing ground for hypotheses about the organization of life within the prison.

The central limitation of such studies is their focus on a single institution. Some of the major structural features of the prison, such as the nature of its physical plant, its rules with regard to inmates, its style of recruitment of staff, and its relation to the central prison administration, will necessarily be "constant" for the single case in question; because of the absence of other institutions where these structural conditions are different, such studies are logically ill-suited to tell us about the importance of those variations. In some instances (the Jacobs study referred to above is one) variation over time in a single institution can be used as a substitute for structural variation across institutions. But for the most part, these single case studies are well designed to tell us about variation among inmates within a single setting, but little about the variation in the settings themselves.

This limitation has given rise to a felt need for the simultaneous examination of many prisons, where we can have variation in the prisons themselves, as well as variations in their inmate inhabitants. Over the last decade or so, at least three book-length studies of this type have appeared. In the oldest of the three, four juvenile institutions that differ in their goals with respect to custody and treatment are examined, to trace the corresponding differences in inmate organization.[13]

In a second study, a variety of federal prisons were examined in order to trace the relationship between inmate behavior inside and their later conduct on parole.[14] And in the most recent example, Ulla Bondeson examines thirteen Swedish prisons to note similarities and differences in the responses of their inmates.[15]

In overall design, our own study falls clearly within this tradition of research. At the time of its conception, however, the idea came not from other studies in prison settings, but from the growing interest

[13]David Street, Robert A. Vinter, and Charles Perrow, *Organization for Treatment: A Comparative Study of Institutions for Delinquents* (New York: The Free Press, 1966).

[14]Daniel Glaser, Prison Conditions and Parole Effectiveness ____________.

[15]Ulla Bondeson, *Scandinavian Studies in Criminology* (London: Tavistock Pubs., 1968)

on the part of students of social organization in the relationship of the individual to the organization. The hallmark of work in this tradition was Lipset, Trow and Coleman's Union Democracy, a classic work which prompted the development of a new body of writing that stressed the properties of organizations as well as individuals, and laid the conceptual groundwork for the development of a series of studies in which organizations rather than individuals were the primary units of analysis.[16]

The basic model through which we examine the relationship of organizations and individuals—in our case the fifteen Scandinavian prisons and the nearly two thousand inmates who inhabit them—is presented in Chapter 2, with the fruits of applying that model hopefully evident in the following chapters. But this brief review of the literature should give the reader an initial understanding of what we are trying to accomplish and what we are not. The study is in the tradition of basic rather than applied research, in that we are attempting to describe fundamental features of the prison and inmates' relationships to the prison, rather than to solve any particular practical problem. Our study lacks the personal sensitivity to the harsh fact of imprisonment that often flows from autobiographical accounts, and it necessarily lacks the richly detailed understanding that may come from the intensive study of a single institution over a long period of time. Its special claim to significance must rest on the understanding of the prison and its inmates that comes from the simultaneous and extensive examination of large numbers of inmates in divergent prison regimes.

A second basis for such a claim lies in the Scandinavian setting for the research. Prison developments in Scandinavia provide a very wide range of institutional designs and programs, including what are regarded as some of the most innovative developments in penology

[16]Seymour Martin Lipset, Martin Trow, and James S. Coleman, *Union Democracy*; James S. Coleman, *The Adolescent Society* (New York: Free Press, 1961); Wolf Heydebrand, *Hospital Bureaucracy* (New York: Dunnellen, 1973); Peter Blau, *The Dynamics of Bureaucracy* (Chicago: University of Chicago Press, 1963).

throughout the world.[17] In the remainder of this introductory chapter, we provide a brief overview of the Scandinavian countries, the chief differences between them, the nature of the crime problem in Scandinavia, and the basic features of the criminal justice systems in Scandinavia. Any such review runs the risk of grave oversimplification, for volumes could be (and have been) written on each of these subjects. Our intent, however, is to provide only that minimum of background that is needed to understand the societal context within which both the prisons and their inmates are functioning. Our apologies in advance, then, to our Scandinavian colleagues for what they would have to regard as a vastly oversimplified account.

The four countries included in this study are independent, sovereign states, but they share a number of common geographical, historical, and socioeconomic characteristics which distinguish them from other countries in Western Europe. Firstly and most obviously, they are geographically in close proximity. Sitting atop Northern Europe, this relatively isolated position placed the Scandinavians beyond the major trade routes which developed in Europe during the Middle Ages and the Renaissance; it also excluded them from most of the wars that ravaged the Continent during these periods. This common location has also produced a similarity in basic economy, with each country having important agricultural, fishing and lumber industries.

Secondly, the Scandinavian countries are recognized throughout the world as having developed exemplary social welfare states. No other nations in the world have developed as extensive programs in such areas as national health insurance, public education, pension, and the like. Historically, all these countries lacked sufficiently large and diverse domestic resources and markets, and this produced a continuous reliance on export markets, producing economic insecurity that is dependent upon fluctuations of the economy of other nations. In addition, both large-scale emigration in the late nineteenth century and internal

[17]John Conrad, *Crime and Its Correction: An International Survey of Attitudes and Practices* (Los Angeles: University of California Press, 1965); David A. Ward, "Sweden: The Middle Way to Prison Reform," in *Prisons: Present and Possible*, ed. M. E. Wolfgang (Lexington: Lexington Books, 1979).

migration to urban areas since the turn of the century effected the stability of the traditional, rural, extended family and thereby reduced individual involvement and initiatives in caring for fellow citizens. This responsibility was eventually taken up by the state. Since World War I, all four countries have had long periods of Labor Party rule, which resulted from a widespread and effective labor movement. These Labor governments promoted the legislation establishing the welfare states.

A third characteristic which distinguishes the Scandinavian countries are the extensive linguistic and historical ties which bind them together. Norway, Sweden, and Denmark share a language which has a common origin. Although the three spoken languages sound quite different—especially Danish—the written languages are for the most part understood by all. Finland stands out as linguistically quite different, for it is a Slavonic language rather than of Germanic root as are the other three. However, as Finland was ruled for many centuries by Sweden, the Swedish language is, or was until recently, the second official language. It is still true that one can converse in Swedish with most educated Finns. Despite the unique Finnish language, all four countries have been merged since the Middle Ages in various types of political and military alliances, and Norway, Sweden, and Denmark in particular are still bound together through the intermarriage of the royal families.

A fourth shared characteristic is the extensive economic agreements made in the post-World War II period concerning trade, tariffs, and travel under the auspices of the Nordic Council. The Council has representation from all four countries, and it also includes Iceland. The Council is primarily responsible for the various economic agreements, and there is frequent and continued discussion of further steps that might be taken toward standardization and consolidation. The Scandinavian Airlines System is probably one of the outstanding examples of international cooperation in the world. SAS is owned and operated jointly by the four countries. The emergence of the Common Market and the corresponding Outer Seven Nations, which includes the Scandinavian countries and England, have made the future of the Nordic Council somewhat unclear. Regardless of how these economic arrangements eventually come out, it seems quite certain that Norway,

Sweden, and Denmark, and to a somewhat lesser extent, Finland, are all committed to continuing further economic and political alliances.

Although these many factors differentiate the Nordic countries from the rest of Europe, there are indeed many important distinguishing features of each. Before turning to a description of the major social, economic, and political institutions of Scandinavia, we present a very brief profile of each of the four countries.

Norway is an independent parliamentary monarchy which gained its independence from Sweden in 1905. Fifty percent of the land in Norway consists of mountains and 25% of the land is dense forest area; only 3% of the total area of Norway is cultivatable. It is no surprise then that timber is the largest natural resource of Norway and accounts for 21% of her exports. Fishing and shipping are the other large industries. More recently, Norway has discovered substantial off-shore oil and gas reserves, and this natural resource will greatly enhance her economic position.

Norway has slightly over three million people and roughly one million live in urban areas. After World War I, Norway's Labor Party gained in strength and the elections of 1933 established it as the largest political party in the country. Since 1935 it has held the reins of the government, even though until 1945 it lacked a clear majority in the Norwegian Parliament, due to the continued existence of a relatively large conservative farm vote. Norway has experienced the longest continual labor rule of any country in the world and is the only one of the Scandinavian countries where socialism has enjoyed an absolute parliamentary majority. The Consumer Cooperative Movement started in Norway in the early part of the twentieth century, and it is still a very strong economic influence. Since 1900 the Norwegian gross national product has had an average yearly increase of 3%. During the post-World War II period it has continued to rise at an increasing rate.

Sweden is the third-largest country in Europe. Two-thirds of its 7.5 million people currently live in urban areas. Sweden enjoys the highest standard of living among the Scandinavian countries, and she also has the largest supply of natural resources including timber, water and electric power, fishing and iron ore. Just over one-half the total land area is forest. Sweden has traditionally strong ties with France and Germany.

Sweden is probably the best known social welfare state among the Scandinavian countries. Rapid industrialization in the late nineteenth and twentieth centuries had brought about widespread social change. A sharp rise in population and early improvements in public health produced widespread poverty in the late nineteenth century. Immigration to the United States also had its effect. Elderly people were left without children and the welfare state was officially declared an objective of politics in Sweden in the early twentieth century. Today Sweden has a compulsory health insurance plan, a national pension plan, and a children's allowance. More recently, an unemployment insurance program has been adopted. The Swedish economy has grown tremendously in the postwar period.

Denmark is also an independent monarchy with a population of one and a half million people. The proximity of Denmark to Germany involved her in the affairs of Europe more than the other countries. Denmark's position as "gate keeper of the Baltic" made it strategically important for the English, the Russians, and the Prussians. It was in their mutual interests that no one overrun the little kingdom and seize permanent control.

Modern social welfare in Denmark dates from 1933. The Danish system of social security is voluntary. The National Health Insurance Plan covers all persons in the country, but individuals in the highest income groups are not required to participate in the program. They may join privately run health insurance societies, but all individuals are eligible for old age pensions. Labor unions rather than the State handle unemployment insurance in Denmark. Unlike Norway or Sweden, the Labor Party in Denmark has never been able to win a majority in the Parliament. This is in part due to the relative overrepresentation of rural districts in the Danish Parliament and in part due to the failure of the Socialists to capture as large a slice of the middle-class and farm vote. The Socialists and Agrarian Liberal Conservatives in coalitions with the radical left have alternated in power since 1945. They have had to function as minority governments, each with the tolerance of the other.

Agriculture is the largest industry in Denmark, and the cooperative farming system, which began in 1882, is the largest in Europe. In Denmark, producers' cooperatives dominate; in Sweden and Norway, consumer cooperatives are more important. Danish business establishments are very small; half of the 100,000 registered enterprises are family operated, and only 19,000 firms employ more than five men. Compulsory public education has a long history in Denmark. In 1814 the Education Act was passed by the Danish Parliament and for the first time in the history of Western Europe peasants and farm workers were given the opportunity for a public education.

Finland is the northernmost of the Scandinavian countries. It is also the easternmost country and its history and present affairs are intricately interwoven with the Soviet Union. Its population is just under 4.5 million. Finland itself is 71% forest land, the highest percentage of any of the four countries. The Finns have gone furthest in the development of consumer cooperatives, with one-fourth of the people belonging. Their share in total retail trade is double that of Norway, Sweden, and Denmark. The Credit Societies constitute one of the nation's financial bulwarks. There is no national health insurance policy, but all hospitals are public. Unemployment insurance is voluntary. The largest item in the social welfare program is social security, and child and family allowances are second.

The political history of Finland is marked by many transitions between Eastern Europe and Western Europe. In 1152 Sweden conquered Finland and eventually it became a Swedish province. During the near five hundred years of Swedish rule, the Finns came into closer contact with Western Europe. Finland later became the battleground and source of the manpower for the endless wars between Sweden and Russia. In 1809, following the Napoleonic Wars, Finland became a Grand Duchy of Russia, and a strong policy of Russification began. The Russian Revolution in 1917 and the subsequent Civil War left deep scars in Finnish society for a generation, scars which are still visible in the ideological gulf between the middle classes and the workers. In 1920 the Finns signed a treaty of peace with Russia, but by 1929 a Fascist group emerged to compete with the Communists in controlling the government.

The Winter War of 1939 against Russia forced Finland into an alliance with Nazi Germany, and this led to the Finno-Germanic War on Russia in 1941. Then in 1944, the Finns fought against the

Table 1.1 Demographic inidicators for Scandinavia

	Sweden	Norway	Denmark	Finland
Area—sq. miles[a]	125,064	173,378	16,619	130,165
Population—millions[a]	3.6	7.5	4.5	4.5
Density—persons per sq. mile[a]	29	43	272	34
Life Expectancy—years[a]	73	72	71	67
Percent living in urban areas[b]	49%	73%	58%	56%

[a]Adapted from *Statistiska Arsbok for Sverige*, Statistiska Centralbyran, Stockholm, 1961
[b]*A Survey of Europe Today*, The Readers Digest Association, London, 1970

Nazis. The two wars were very costly for Finland. Her reparations bill was $500,000,000 and she had 5,000,000 refugees to be resettled. Following the war, Russia took one-tenth of the Finnish territory, including her only ice-free port. In the post-World War II period, Finland has again gained some political and economic freedom. But the proximity to Russia, the many recent wars, and the language difference all make the cultural barriers between Finland and the other three countries greater than in any other combination of the Scandinavian countries.

We now present a brief comparative description of the major social, economic, and political institutions of Scandinavia. Turning first to demographic information, Table 1.1 presents several sets of vital statistics on each country.

Norway, Sweden, and Finland are roughly equivalent in terms of landmass with Sweden being somewhat larger. One can readily see the appropriateness of the label of "tiny Denmark," which the Danes frequently use with some mixture of both pride and despair. Of course, all four Scandinavian countries are small by comparison with the United States. In terms of population, Sweden is also the largest with 7,500,000 inhabitants. The combination of small landmass and relatively large population gives Denmark the highest population density in Scandinavia, indeed one of the highest densities in the world. This difference in density, which is roughly six times greater than Sweden and nearly ten times greater than Norway and Finland, helps in understanding some of the economic problems which Denmark, primarily an agricultural and export nation, has faced over the centuries in maintaining a favorable balance of trade.

All four countries experienced rapid expansions in birth rates following World War II, but the overall growth rates have been relatively slow in recent years. This has produced a bulge of young people in each country's population pyramid. The structure of Finland's population reflects the long history of political and economic difficulties. The most rapid increases in population in all of Scandinavia in the future will be in the older age groups. By 1980 Sweden will have the highest proportion of old people in Europe.

One should keep in mind that most of the populations in Norway, Sweden, and Finland are concentrated in the central and southern portions of the countries, and there are large northern areas that are virtually uninhabited except for small groups of migrant Lapps and some mining communities near the Arctic Circle.

Sweden is the most urban of the Scandinavian countries with almost three-fourths of the population living in towns or suburbs. This process of urbanization occurred very rapidly in Sweden. At the turn of the century, roughly 75% of the Swedes lived in small farming communities and in seventy-five years, two-thirds of the rural population has migrated to the cities. The other three Scandinavian countries are also undergoing urbanization, but the rate is nowhere near as great as Sweden. Finland, the least industrialized of the countries, has the slowest rate of industrial growth.

Average life expectancy is usually interpreted as an indicator of both the quality and quantity of health care available in a nation. Life expectancy in Norway, Sweden, and Denmark, as well as the United States, are all quite comparable, indicating roughly equivalent health care systems; but here again, Finland stands out as the exception with a rate of four to six years lower, indicating a less well-developed health system. As mentioned above, in all the countries, the birth rate has leveled off following the post-World War II baby boom. This coupled with the increasing life expectancy rate is producing a gradual shift upward in median age of the population—a trend which Scandinavia is experiencing along with other industrialized nations of the world.

Table 1.2 Economic indicators for Scandinavia

	Sweden	Norway	Denmark	Finland
Per Capita GNP (U.S. $)[a]	$1167	$1512	$1213	$892
Average Annual GNP Growth, 1957–1967[b]	3.50%	4.20%	4.50%	2.60%
Average Hourly Earnings (U.S. $)[b]	$1.09	$1.36	$1.06	$0.87
Percent of Labor Force in:[b]				
Agriculture	18%	10%	17%	21% (1)
Manufacturing	36%	42%	41%	–
Service	46%	48%	42%	–

[a]Adapted from *Statistiska Arsbok for Sverige*, Statistiska Centralbyran, Stockholm, 1961
[b]*A Survey of Europe Today*, The Readers Digest Association, London, 1970

Table 1.2 presents selected comparisons on economic indicators. Per capita Gross National Product is a standard measure of the relative economic wealth of a nation. It represents the value of all goods and services produced by a country's residents in a year on a per capita basis to cancel out differences in population size from country to country. The data show a clear ranking of the Scandinavian countries: Sweden, Denmark, Norway, and Finland—with all four countries significantly behind the United States. This is a pattern we shall see repeatedly. Sweden is the economic leader in Scandinavia and Finland is the economic trailer. The relative positions of Denmark and Norway in the middle often reverse on different indicators and on the same indicators over time. Norway's recently discovered off-shore oil reserves will affect this pattern.

The average annual growth of Gross National Product for the decade 1957–1967 gives an indication of economic expansion during this period. Usually it is easier for less developed countries to increase their growth rate or GNP because their productivity levels are lower to begin with. For example, during this same period Greece and Spain had growth rates of 5.7 and 5.4%, respectively; but their per capita Gross National Product rates are far below any of the Scandinavian countries. All four countries experienced substantial economic growth during this decade, but Finland clearly lagged behind the others.

Average hourly earnings is a good indicator of how workers are paid and can be used to give a rough comparison of standards of living. Here again we see that Sweden is the leader and Finland's average earnings are substantially lower than the other countries. We notice again that earnings in the United States are more than twice as high as in Sweden (approximately $2.00 per hour).

The percent of the labor force employed in various sectors of the economy are widely used indicators of the degree of industrialization. Here again, we note the same pattern, with Sweden having the highest proportion engaged in manufacturing industries and the lowest proportion in agriculture, forestry, fishing, and mining, although the differences are not great. Finland has the highest proportion in agriculture, 21%. Unfortunately, comparable Finnish data on the other two sectors were not available. Both Norway and Denmark have large proportions of the 1.23 labor force employed in agriculture, reflecting Denmark's continued reliance on agriculture as the mainstay of its economy, and the large lumber and fishing industries in Norway.[18]

A further explication of economic conditions can be gained from examining indicators of individual consumer patterns in the Scandinavian countries. Table 1.3 presents data from several different sources on characteristics of dwelling units and consumer products. On all seven indicators presented, the pattern of Sweden, Denmark, Norway and Finland is consistent. There are some ties or very close comparisons between Norway, Sweden, and Denmark on characteristics of dwelling units, reflecting the acute shortage of housing throughout Scandinavia. But for the most part, the patterns are remarkably consistent with those noted earlier.

Political party affiliations for the Scandinavian countries are presented in Table 1.4. In each country, political majorities are attained

[18]We should point out that the position of the United States relative to the Scandinavian countries on these measures indicates what many social scientists have called "the post-industrial state." In such a nation, the percent of the labor force engaged in agriculture is very small, i.e., 5% in the United States, reflecting a highly mechanized agricultural sector. The percent employed in industry also decreases as a result of automation, and the service sector which includes service industries, trade, and transport, expands picking up displaced industrial workers. See Daniel Bell, *The Coming of the Post-Industrial Nation* (New York: Basic Books, 1973).

Table 1.3 Consumer indicators for Scandinavia

	Norway	Sweden	Denmark	Finland
Average no. of occupants per room[c]	0.8	0.8	0.7	1.3
% of dwelling units with running hot water[b]	84%	90%	84%	44%
% of dwelling units with shower/bath[b]	69%	83%	71%	32%
No. of radios per 1000 inhabitants[a]	282	360	327	267
No. of telephones per 1000 inhabitants[a]	194	340	224	128
No. of TV sets per 1000 inhabitants[a]	22	81	74	7
No. of private cars per 1000 inhabitants[a]	54	143	78	36

[a]Adapted from *Statistiska Arsbok for Sverige*, Statistiska Centralbyran, Stockholm, 1961

[b]*A Survey of Europe Today*, The Readers Digest Association, London, 1970

[c]"Compilation of Development Indicators," United Nations Research Institute for Social Development, Geneva, 1969

Table 1.4 Political and social welfare indicators of Scandinavia

	Norway	Sweden	Denmark	Finland
Political party affiliation[d]				
Socialist	50	50	44	43
Center	31	40	35	38
Conservative	19	10	20	19
Social security spending in 1961 as % of GNP[e]	10.6%	12.9%	11.0%	10.3%

[a]Adapted from *Statistiska Arsbok for Sverige*, Statistiska Centralbyran, Stockholm, 1961

[b]*A Survey of Europe Today*, The Readers Digest Association, London, 1970

[c]"Compilation of Development Indicators," United Nations Research Institute for Social Development, Geneva, 1969

[d]Adopted from "Class Structure and Party Choice" by H. Vusitalo, Res. Report #10, U. of Helsinki, 1975

[e]Adopted from *The Welfare State and Equality*, H. L. Wilensky, UC Press, Berkeley, 1975

through coalitions of the left and center parties, producing the dominance of Social Democratic and Labor Party governments. However stable this may have been since World War II, each election is intensely battled; outcomes are never clear until the coalitions are delicately rearranged. All major government programs require the support of various political factions, for no party has claim to a majority.

Of course the conservatives are weakest in Scandinavia, and especially in Sweden where they account for only 10% of the electorate. It will probably come as a surprise to many that the conservatives are so strong in Finland, accounting for almost one-fifth of the electorate. However, the conservatives are sufficiently strong in each country, that when aligned with the center parties they frequently determine the outcome of political issues. This is especially true in Sweden where, despite the fact the conservatives are most weak, the center parties are largest. Scandinavian governments are frequently referred to as governments by compromise" and these data on party affiliation give a clear indication of why this is so.

Table 1.4 also presents some particularly interesting data on social security/expenditures in each country. Again the same pattern emerges among the four countries: Sweden has the largest proportion of GNP expended for social security, 12.9%, and Finland the lowest, 10.3%, with Denmark in between. But the most notable comparison is really between the Scandinavian countries and other nations. United States expenditures, for example, are substantially lower at 7.7%. Although these figures use social security expenditures as a surrogate for all social welfare expenditures, it seems likely that a similar pattern would emerge if we had comparable data on one particular welfare component, expenditures on persons.

2

Research Design and Methods

In this chapter we take up a number of issues concerning the design and research methods used in our study. First, we introduce the conceptual scheme or "model" employed in the overall design of the study. We then present in some detail the sampling and data collection procedures used in gathering information about prisons and their inmates. Finally, we discuss a number of questions concerning data analysis techniques.

A Generalized Model for Analyses

Social science research offers a variety of ways of defining problems, gathering relevant data, and analyzing the results. When a particular field of inquiry is well developed, there will be an explicit body of theory and hypotheses that can serve as a rigorous guide to the selection of measures to be employed and analyses to be made. Much of the experimental research in social psychology comes close to fitting this idealized description as do some applications in economics.

S. Wheeler and H. F. Cline, *The Scandinavian Prison Study*,
Palgrave Studies in Prisons and Penology,
https://doi.org/10.1007/978-3-030-26462-8_2

There are many areas of inquiry, however, where this degree of theoretical development and enclosure is simply not met. That is why so many studies are described by their authors as "exploratory." The very concept suggests a lack of assurance as to the most important things to be examined and a lack of clear theoretical guidance in the search for relevant evidence. Under these circumstances, the researcher may develop data using whatever guesses and hunches he or she has, but typically will cast a wide net in the search for interesting themes and materials.

Our study of the prisons of Scandinavia falls somewhere between these two extremes, though closer to the exploratory study than to the clean test of theoretically derived hypotheses. We begin with an orienting framework that grows out of a great deal of past research on individual and organizational behavior in a variety of settings other than prisons and that provides a general orientation and direction for analysis. But within this very general orientation, there is a great room for variation in the way in which particular problems are attacked.

The generalized model is based on the distinction between organizational and individual levels of analysis. Imprisonment may be examined both as an organizational and an individual phenomenon. There is a parallelism in the analysis of these two different levels, but the problems involved are analytically distinct. They correspond crudely to the distinction between a sociological level of analysis and a social psychological level.

At the sociological level we wish to learn about differences in how prisons are organized, why the differences exist, and what effect those differences have on the modal patterns of responses made to each prison by its inmates. In short, we want to describe and explain variation in prisons. At the social psychological level, we are concerned with the differing experiences of individual inmates. What are the major individual differences in inmate experience while in prison, what are the sources of those differences, and how do they affect the inmate's personal response to the prison?

This difference between the organization and the individual, in our case between the prison and the individual inmate, serves as a major organizing theme in our approach to the prisons we studied. Part II of our book is devoted largely to the institutional level of analysis, and Part

III to the individual level, with a combination of the two levels appearing in the analysis of special topics taken up thereafter. In analyzing our material this way, we are following a tradition by now reasonably well established in sociological work, but one that was just being formed when our research was initially conceived. For although such a distinction has been implicit for generations in much of social science, and explicit in some theoretical writings, there has been very little research until relatively recently that treated organizations, as well as individuals, as major units of analysis. There are of course individual case studies of organizations, and sometimes comparative studies of two or three. But until recently, it was rare to find an empirical study that contained data on enough different organizations, as well as on their individual participants, to permit examination of both organizational and individual differences.[1]

The basic scheme for our approach is suggested by Diagrams 2.1 and 2.2, representing the organizational and individual level analyses, respectively. Box A of 2.1 includes basic attributes of the organizational structure of the prison. This includes any features of the prison that we can examine directly, without having to gather the judgments of individual inmates or staff members. We shall not try to fill in the box completely at this time since we will be dealing with it in more detail later. But we have in mind such characteristics as the size of the institution, its age, the ratio of inmates to staff, the types of programs available for inmate participation, the amount of time inmates are free to interact with other inmates, the restrictions that are placed by prison regulations on outside visits and contacts, and the like. Also included would be the formal type of institutions represented by the prison in question: whether it is a normal prison, a preventive detention institution, a youth institution, or one that falls in a different category. All of

[1]See Seymour Martin Lipset, Martin A. Trow, and James S. Coleman, *Union Democracy: The Internal Politics of the International Typographical Union* (Glencoe, IL: Free Press, 1956); James S. Coleman, *The Adolescent Society: The Social Life of the Teenager and Its Impact on Education* (New York: The Free Press, 1961); and James A. Davis, *Great Books and Small Groups* (New York: The Free Press, 1961). For prison studies, see David Street, Robert D. Vinter, and Charles Perrow, *Organization for Treatment: A Comparative Study of Institutions for Delinquents* (New York: The Free Press, 1966); and Daniel Glaser, *The Effectiveness of a Prison and Parole System* (Indianapolis: Bobbs-Merrill, 1964).

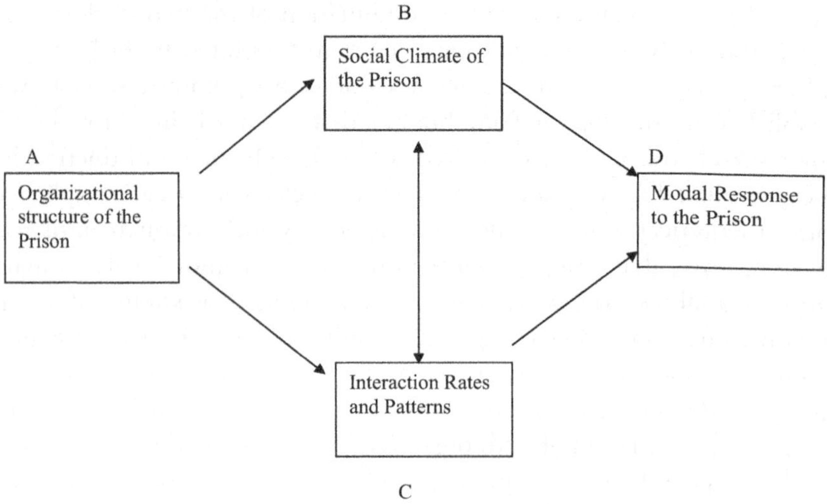

Diagram 2.1 The organizational level of analysis

these are primarily attributes of the prison itself, rather than its individual members or participants.

As our diagram shows, we assume that these basic structural features of the prison directly influence two of the other components in our scheme. Box B includes various indicators of social climate. The concept of social climate is vague, but is meant to connote the general "feeling tone" of the institution as perceived by its inmate members. We can count on the fact that most inmates, most of the time don't like being in prison. But beyond that it seems highly likely that prisons may differ widely in their general feeling tone or climate. And this climate, we hypothesize, is a major part of what an inmate refers to when he tells what it is like in a particular prison

Further, it seems likely that the social climate of the institution is not a unidimensional phenomenon. Prisons are complex social entities, and there may be many different dimensions of this social climate. One dimension may center on feelings regarding the coerciveness of the prison environment: institutions may vary in the extent to which their inmates feel under the thumb of the staff, under tight or loose control, under rigid or relatively flexible rules. Another dimension concerns the authority relationships between staff, especially whether the custodial functions of the prison are seen to predominate over the treatment functions or the other way around.

The above features of social climate refer primarily to inmate feelings about the staff and the administration of the prison. Other dimensions of the social climate relate importantly to inmate feelings about relationships with other inmates. In some institutions, the inmates may be perceived as being strongly opposed to the administration and its agents, while in others the degree of opposition may be much less. Also, inmates in some institutions may experience efforts on the part of other inmates to coerce them into holding particular attitudes or engaging in particular lines of conduct. This is an element of coerciveness from the inmates' side somewhat parallel to that discussed above which may come from the staff. And finally, there is the general balance of power between the inmates and the staff. Is the institution perceived as a place where the staff rule supreme and inmate power is at a minimum, or do the inmates "really run the place?"

These are examples of what we mean by the social climate of a prison. It is assumed that the prison is more than a congeries of buildings, personnel, inmates, and programs—that these components become organized in different ways, in different institutions, with a result that each institution may develop its own feeling tone. We will have more to say about the social climate and its determinants later, but for now the important thing is to establish the social climate of the prison as one of the major features of the prison that we want to explore.

Box C in the diagram refers to the modal patterns of interaction that characterize particular prisons. Do inmates have many friends, or only a few? Do they have frequent interaction with guards? With treatment staff? Are they isolated from contacts with relatives and friends outside the prison, or are there frequent communications with them? All of these are aspects of the interactional life of inmates in the institutions, and we assume they are an important influence on inmate response to the prison.

The arrow between Boxes B and C is meant to suggest the mutual interplay between interaction rates on the one hand and the social climate of the prison on the other. We assume that the structural features of the prison influence both, but the influence may not necessarily work directly. At the moment it is not important for us to argue whether social climate or interaction rates have temporal priority in most instances, and in practice it will be impossible for us to tell.

Box D in our diagram reflects the modal responses to the prison on the part of its inmates. A variety of different indicators of response might be developed, but three very general ones seem most relevant; they will be briefly introduced here, and described in more detail later. One has to do with the degree of attitudinal conformity inmates show toward the goals and norms of prison staff. The dimension of conformity and deviance from official goals and purposes is one that flows throughout all organizations, and it has been a central one in the description and discussion of prisons. We want to examine differences in the average degree of conformity across different prisons, and to trace out the sources of those differences.

The second has to do with whether inmates subjectively feel that their stay in prison is helpful or harmful to them in terms of their ability to adjust successfully when they leave the institution. Some prisons produce many inmates who may feel that their stay in prison is helpful to them, while other prisons produce many who feel harmed by the experience.

Third, we are concerned with the dimension of justice within the prison. Prisons are institutions within the criminal justice system and it is natural to inquire whether inmates feel that they are being justly treated, and to examine the structural features, as well as those of social climate and interaction, that may produce such a feeling. One reason for examining such feelings is the belief that those who feel justly treated are likely to be more amenable to change from programs within the institution, and are more likely to accept whatever rehabilitative efforts the staff attempt.

The full scheme, then, reflects our basic conception of the way in which the prison influences its inmates: basic structural characteristics of the prison influence the social interaction patterns of its inmates, and they also influence the kind of social climate that develops within the prison. These two categories interact with one another, and each also influences the modal response to the prison among its inmates. Throughout this level of analysis we are concerned primarily with differences produced across the prisons, and not with the individual differences produced within each institution, through the impact of an inmate's own personal background and experience on his response.

Diagram 2.2 reflects our basic conception of the way in which the social psychology of imprisonment works. Box A reflects the differences in personal background that individual inmates bring to the prison. We will elaborate these characteristics later, but they will include primarily social background characteristics such as age and marital status, criminal background characteristics such as type of offense and previous experience in crime, and some measures of inmate self-conception. We presume that these personal background characteristics lead to differing predispositions to perceive the prison experience in particular ways (Box B), and to interact in differing ways with inmates, staff, and persons outside the institution (Box C). And like the organizational level, we assume that the inmates' patterns of interaction and their perceptions are interrelated, and mutually influence one another.

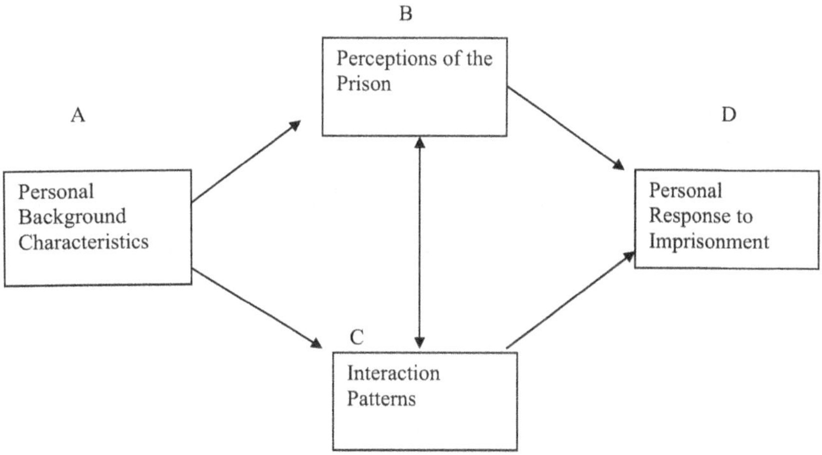

Diagram 2.2 The individual level

Finally, Box D refers to the dimensions of personal response to imprisonment: conformity, the sense of being helped, and the sense of being justly treated. At the individual level, we presume that these feelings may be a direct result of the personal background characteristics the man brings to prison, but that in the usual case these characteristics have their impact through the perceptions and interactions an inmate has while in prison.

Just as the model at the organizational level introduces nothing about the individual backgrounds of inmates, so the model at the individual level introduces nothing about the characteristics of the prison itself, save indirectly through the perceptions inmates may have. At the individual level, we will be attempting to say something about the social psychology of imprisonment as a general phenomenon. We will do this either by treating our total sample of roughly 2000 inmates without regard to the nature of the prisons they are in, or by treating each prison as a separate locale within which to test the relationship at the individual level, thereby giving us, in effect, fifteen replications of the same relationship.

In Parts II and III of our volume, respectively, we will treat these two levels of analysis as analytically distinct. But in Part IV we will be concerned primarily with the way in which they fit together. Having attempted to describe the nature and determinants of response to the prison at both an organizational and an individual level of analysis, we will try to show their interrelationship by asking, in effect, what difference the organizational context makes in producing differing individual responses.

A number of observations about the general scheme are called for. First, there is a direct parallelism between the two levels of analysis. In fact, Boxes B, C, and D of both models will be filled empirically with the same data, the only difference being whether the data are used in aggregated form, such as a mean or variance, to characterize the institution, or whether they are used as individual measures to differentiate among inmates. For example, we can use inmate reports on the number of friends they have made in prison to contrast the loners or isolates and the gregarious ones in a particular prison, or we can sum their responses in order to characterize an institution as a whole. The only area lacking this strict parallelism is in the "A" Boxes, where there is no direct individual counterpart for the inmate–staff ratio, or the amount of time inmates are free to interact with others, etc. It is the near parallel structure of the two levels of analysis that enables easy movement from one level of analysis to the other.

Second, we assume that preceding both the basic structure of the prison on the one hand, the personal characteristics of inmates on the other, is the nature of the broader culture and social environment within which both prison and inmates exist. That is to say, there will be features of Scandinavian countries in general, and of each one in particular, that we may anticipate will influence both organizational and individual phenomena. We have already described some of the principal differences between the countries and the prison systems, and will have occasion to refer back to these differences in our efforts to further understand inmate response to imprisonment.

Third, we do not propose to be exhaustive in our description of all of the interrelationships within our materials. We include a variety of different measures within each of the component categories of our conceptual scheme. We will look at the interrelationships between those measures whenever they would appear to shed light on our understanding of the prison experience. But our basic concern is for tracing the relationships between the various categories rather than within them. In this sense, the scheme is useful primarily as a way of organizing our variables into broad, categories, rather than as generative of particular testable hypotheses.

Finally, while we propose to give roughly equal attention to both the organizational and the individual levels of analysis, our concerns within each level are different. Our concerns at the organizational level fall heavily within the sphere of social climate. On theoretical grounds we feel it is a most important area for exploration, and as a result of that belief, our indicators of social climate are richer and more varied than our indicators of some of the other phenomena at the organizational level. At the individual level, on the other hand, we find the inmates' perceptions of the prison less interesting in many ways than their patterns of involvement with other inmates, staff, and the outside world, and it is these patterns that we relate systematically to their responses to the prison. Thus, although the relationships charted within our conceptual scheme give the appearance of a formal symmetry between the two levels of analysis, our substantive concerns at the different levels will lead us to give much greater weight to the analysis of social climate in Part II where we focus on the organization level, and greater weight to patterns of interaction and involvement in Part III, where we focus on the individual and his response to imprisonment.

Sampling and Data Collection

The Sample of Institutions

When the senior author of this study ventured to Norway as a Fulbright Research Fellow, his plan was to conduct a modest comparison of a Norwegian prison setting with one he had studied in the United States. His plans for this modest comparison were expanded far beyond the original scheme when, through excellent cooperation and help from Norwegian social scientists, soon followed by similar aid from those in Sweden, Finland and Denmark, it became possible to envision a study on a much larger scale. At the same time, there were severe budgetary constraints, such that the final sample of fifteen prisons represents a compromise between a theoretically satisfactory sample of institutions, and a pragmatic dealing with real possibilities.

In each country, we sought to have one institution that could be thought of as a relatively normal or typical prison, one that was inhabited by the general run of adult prison inmates, rather than those who had been singled out for some special purpose. We also wished to have a youth institution in each country, and finally, a "preventive detention" institution of the type described earlier as typical of the Scandinavian countries. But beyond this simple sampling requirement our choice of particular settings was a compromise worked out with social scientists and institutional officials in the various countries. A discussion of the selection country by country, in the order in which the study developed, will clarify the basis for a choice of particular institutions and will suggest both the strengths and weaknesses of the ultimate sample.

In Norway, the country in which the study originated, our problems were minimal because there were only three institutions that fitted our primary study design: Botsfongslet, then the main state prison in downtown Oslo; Ila, a preventive detention institution some miles outside Oslo; and Berg, the working school for youthful offenders whose main section was located down the peninsula from Oslo, with another closed section in Oslo itself. Aside from these institutions there were local jails for short-term offenders, and a major (and controversial) institution for alcoholics.[2] But our interest at the time was in the three aforementioned institutions, and those are the three we examined in Norway. They represent, in effect, the three principal institutions for Norwegian offenders aside from those whose primary problems stem from alcohol, and they could be thought of as a population, rather than a sample, of Norwegian prison inmates.

In Sweden the situation was very different. Sweden has developed a very large number of institutions, mostly small facilities, and to have a population of prisons for Sweden comparable to that for Norway, we would have studied thirty to forty institutions. In fact we studied only three, again trying to fill our design for the three major types of institutions. For preventive detention institutions the choice was simplified by the presence of Hall, the chief preventive detention institution in Sweden, which was located reasonably close to Stockholm. But our choice of a normal prison and a youth institution for Sweden was constrained by a desire to keep costs down by remaining close to Stockholm, and also to gather data in what were then examples of Sweden's new type of prison design and architecture. As mentioned earlier, Sweden was the forerunner in a number of developments in modern prison architecture, and we did not wish to miss the opportunity to learn how inmates were responding to those institutions. Thus our choice of a normal prison was Norrtalje, located north of Stockholm, although we undoubtedly would have gotten a different picture of inmate life in Sweden if we had studied Langholmen, an old bastille in central Stockholm, and the rough equivalent of Botsfongslet in Norway

[2]Nils Christie, ______.

in terms of prison design and architecture. As our youth institution we studied Mariefred, again within striking distance of Stockholm, and again representing what was then the best of modern prison design in Sweden.

A detailed description of these and the other prisons in our sample may be found early in Chapter 3. Here our intent is simply to provide a broad overview of the sample itself. In the case of Sweden, all three of the institutions are drawn from the Stockholm region, and even there we have only a portion of the total number of institutions available. We therefore have much less basis for a belief in the representativeness of our Swedish inmates than we have for their Norwegian counterparts. We do have represented, however, each of our primary institutional types.

In Finland, there was a total of some dozen institutions that might have been selected for our sample. After discussion with Finnish authorities, we settled on four, three of which exemplify our primary institutional types. These include Konnunsuo, a prison for normal inmates located in the easternmost section of Finland; a preventive detention institution in Turku, like Hall and Ila the primary preventive detention institution in its country; and Kerava, a youth prison not far from Helsinki. There was also interest on both our part and our social science colleagues in Finland in studying Seutula, an open labor colony meant for short-term offenders, many of whom were convicted of drunken driving. The addition of Seutula was of interest to us primarily because it had the promise of earmarking the "non-criminal" end of the spectrum with regard to prison inmates, for most of the inmates had not been in prison before and were unlikely to return again. The other three Finnish institutions in our sample give us a more reasonable basis for making inferences about the Finnish prison experience than is the case for Sweden, though clearly not as strong a basis as for Norway.

Denmark had fifteen major institutions at the time of our study. We sampled five of them. The choice of a preventive detention institution was again made easy by the presence of Herstedvester, the most internationally known of the institutions in our sample, where special forms of psychiatric treatment were being provided to inmates. If there was an "ideal-type" preventive detention institution in Scandinavia,

Herstedvester was it, and it was a natural for our study. Across the street from Herstedvester is Vridsloselille, one of the oldest institutions in Scandinavia, and a normal prison housing adult prison inmates. It became a natural to add to our sample by virtue of its location, and because it housed the normal adult prison population we were seeking.

The choice of a youth institution in Denmark was more complicated. There were three institutions fitting our description, and the one finally chosen for inclusion in our study, Sobysgard, was regarded as the most benign of the three, and the one that received young Danish inmates who were likely to have the best chances for rehabilitation. Thus while it fits our requirement of a youth institution, it is not a good basis for generalization to all youthful inmates in Denmark.

Two additional Danish institutions were included in our study. One was Nyborg, a prison of the normal type, though housing inmates somewhat younger and perhaps less tractable than the inmates housed in Vridsloselille. The fifth institution is Kragskovhede, on the northern tip of Jutland, a special open colony for recidivists. This institution was especially attractive for study, for the theory underlying its operation had been drawn largely from correctional development in the United States, and it was a serious effort to develop a treatment institution of a rather special kind. So just as Seutula in Finland might mark the non-criminal end of the prison spectrum, and Herstedvester the ideal typical preventive detention institution, so Kragskovhede might serve as a model of an effort to put a relatively fully rationalized and developed correctional treatment program into practice.

In summary, we think it can fairly be said that we have a reasonably representative sample of institutions of the three major types we were seeking in Norway, Finland, and Denmark, with the exception of the Danish youth institution which has a population of less troublesome youthful offenders. With regard to Sweden, we simply do not know, since we did not study the other institutions, whether our own sampling is representative or not. But we should note that representativeness is less important in many respects than our belief we have something roughly approximating the range in types of correctional institutions. From that point of view, with the addition of special institutions in our study, we think the sample is reasonably successful, although there are no formal criteria that we can apply to it. An assessment of the strength of our sample may best await a discussion of the particular characteristics of the individual institutions that follows in Chapter 3.

Data Collection on Institutions

Each of the institutions in our study was visited at least twice; once when the survey data were gathered for inmates, and again when each institution was revisited as we fed back information from the survey. On each occasion we did whatever we could do to learn as much as possible about the operation of the institutions. A typical routine was to observe a full day's operation, starting before the inmates began their activity in the morning, and continuing throughout the day, during which there would be occasions for conversation with the inmates and staff (always and unfortunately constrained by a need to talk in English, thereby limiting informal contacts to that small proportion of inmates and somewhat larger proportion of staff who could handle the English language). These occasions provided a modicum of information on the operation of each of the institutions in question, and on occasion provided the basis for important though idiosyncratic bits of evidence.

For example, on two occasions we encountered inmates who had spent time in other institutions in our sample in countries other than their own, and these provided an opportunity for direct comparison, from the inmate's own experience, on many of the attributes we were examining. And much was learned on occasion through late-night conversations, dinner engagements with major institutional officials present, and all the various other means of learning informally and indirectly about the institutions in a society.

But our chief means of gathering systematic information about the institutions came from interviews with a chief informant, usually the warden, unless he was unavailable for some reason. Those interviews followed the format suggested in Appendix I, which lists the general questions asked of the chief informant, as well as the schedule of information used to record institutional characteristics. Those interviews were typically conducted by a social scientist from the country being studied, sometimes in company with the senior author. As is evident from those instruments, our primary interest was in gathering systematic information about the nature of the staff, the institution, and the program. Those interviews with the directors of the institutions provided the basic data on institutional characteristics that are analyzed in Chapter 3 and in part of Chapter 4.

The Inmate Sample

The primary data for our study come from the inmates themselves, in the form of responses to a questionnaire administered to inmates in the fifteen prisons. Here a concern for representativeness was crucial, for any comparison of the fifteen institutions on the basis of the responses of their inmates would depend heavily on a relative constancy in the quality of the data achieved from each setting. We therefore worked carefully to define the inmate population we sought to reach, to reach as many of them as possible, and to gather data from them under conditions that would be similar across the fifteen institutions.

Our degree of success in that endeavor is suggested in Table 2.1, which indicates the target population for each institution, the sample that we attempted to reach, and the percentage that supplied us with usable questionnaires. Table 2.1 also introduces the system that will be used throughout the volume to identify the institutions. The numbers refer to each individual institution, and the symbols surrounding the numbers identify the type of institution.

The target population consisted of all inmates in the institution save for those few in the infirmary or hospital, an even smaller number subject to special discipline, or away on furloughs, and those whose mental functioning was deemed by institution officials to be too unreliable to allow for the orderly administration of a questionnaire. Save for these rules of exclusion, we sought participation from all members of the inmate population of the institution in question.

That we reached such a high average rate of response—85% overall—is undoubtedly due in no small part to two or three crucial features

Table 2.1 Institutions and number of inmate respondents (see Key for prison type)

	Name of Institution	Target Population	Sample	Usable Questionnaires	% Usable of Target
NORWAY					
1	Ila	71	57	53	75
2	Botsfengslet	189	167	150	79
3	Berg	52	50	50	96
	Totals	312	274	253	81
SWEDEN					
4	Hall	184	145	139	76
5	Mariefred	77	72	67	87
6	Norrtalje	97	90	89	92
	Totals	358	307	295	82
FINLAND					
7	Konnunsuo	291	285	274	94
8	Karava	84	84	84	100
9	Turku	157	118	113	72
10	Seutula	182	172	161	88
	Totals	714	659	632	89
DENMARK					
11	Herstedvester	182	155	141	77
12	Vridsloselille	224	190	177	79
13	Nyborg	216	208	194	90
14	Sobysagard	91	89	89	98
15	Kragskovhede	186	158	156	84
	Totals	899	800	757	84
	Grand totals	2283	2040	1937	85

(continued)

Table 2.1 (continued)

Key: normal prison □ preventive detention △

youth institution ○ special institution. ⯃

of the administration of the questionnaire. We have no idea how these considerations ranked in the minds of the typical inmate, but we are convinced that all three were important. First, inmate participation was "rewarded" by the gift of a pack of twenty cigarettes for each inmate who showed up at the appropriate time and place. Cigarettes are both a staple in the life of many inmates, and a medium of exchange in most inmate economies. The fact that such a large proportion of the inmate population agreed to participate in our study may conceivably be due in no small part to this very direct means of reward.

Second, the inmates were fully briefed on the fact that the study was designed and being executed cooperatively by both American and Scandinavian sociologists. Institution officials were not the sponsors, though they allowed the administration of the questionnaire. As sociologists, the investigators occupied a status recognized by many Scandinavian inmates as one that would not be hostile to their views.

Third, the inmates were specifically told that we were not interested in the response of any particular individual, that the questionnaire was anonymous, and that they should not reveal their name or number. Whatever data we have about the inmate comes from the inmate himself. We did not examine a single inmate's file nor did we make any surreptitious attempt to learn about any inmate, save what he revealed about himself through his questionnaire responses. Of the 2040 persons who participated, only 1937 usable questionnaires resulted. We examined all questionnaires for the general seriousness with which they appeared to have been taken, and threw out those with obviously inconsistent, extreme, or silly answers. Another basis for exclusion were those who simply had not completed enough items in the questionnaire to make the total worth using. Any questionnaire that had more than 15% of the items unanswered was excluded from all analyses.

We feel that the resulting inmate sample is extraordinarily strong. We have a usable response rate of 85%, high by any standards, from an inmate population in four different countries with four different languages, and among persons who by and large had not been known for their compliance in the past. We feel that an important ingredient in the successful administration of the questionnaire goes to the conditions of its administration, as we discuss below.

The Questionnaire

The questionnaire that provided the basic data for this study is reproduced in Appendix II, along with the marginal response frequencies for all inmates. As is evident from the questionnaire, our interests ranged across a wide variety of aspects of imprisonment. Many of the items were designed to tell us about how the prison was organized, as seen from the inmate's perspective. This is true, for example, of those items that ask about guard and treatment staff power, about how the rules are enforced, about who really runs the place, and so forth. Other items are designed to tell us more about the inmate's own particular experience, for example, the frequency of his interaction with guards, treatment staff, other inmates, or persons in the outside world. Drawing upon research previously conducted in the United States, we also asked inmates to respond to a number of hypothetical situations that might arise within the prison. Finally, we had a brief inventory of feelings about the self for which we sought inmate response. The final form of the questionnaire emerged after several drafts, and after pretesting in a Norwegian honor camp.[3]

It is one thing to develop what appears to be a decent research instrument, quite another to have the instrument taken seriously by respondents. As noted above, we worked hard to get a high response

[3]The various versions, the pretest, and the final version were worked out during the course of weekly meetings with Nils Christie and Thomas Mathieson of The Institute of Criminology and Criminal Law, University of Oslo. We remain enormously indebted to them for their help during this crucial phase of the study.

rate and we were successful in that. We were also most concerned that our inmate respondents take the questionnaire seriously. Part of the pretesting involved getting rid of questions that were subject to ambiguous interpretations, or that might have been thought of as foolish or ill-conceived by inmate respondents. Another important part of the administration was to assure as close as possible the constancy of conditions of administration of the questionnaire from one prison to another. This is no easy task given the different architectural design of institutions, differences in scheduling, and differences in attitudes of their superintendents with regard to the disruption of regular activities for the purpose of questionnaire administration. At the time of our survey, this was the first large-scale piece of social research conducted within most of the institutions we studied, and some prison directors were understandably apprehensive about the way in which the project would be received by inmates.

The questionnaires were administered to groups of inmates, usually in a classroom although sometimes in a dining hall. The groups varied in size from ten to ninety, with a median size of twenty-five. The groups were typically formed from living units: the tier of a cell block, the wing of a pavilion, a dormitory room, etc., depending on the structure of the particular institution in question. And in one or two instances it seemed easier for institution officials to use work assignment groups rather than living units for the administration.

When the groups were assembled, there was a brief introduction to the study, including reference to the conditions of anonymity. The administration was in the hands of social scientists from the country in question. The pace of the questionnaire administration was controlled by having each question read aloud and asking respondents to answer the questions as they were read, rather than moving through at their own pace. This was done in an effort to ensure correct reading of the items, and as an aid to those inmates who may have had reading problems. Inmates were seated far enough apart so that their answers could not be easily read by fellow inmates. At the end of the questionnaire administration we responded to the questions inmates had about particular items, the purpose of the study, or whatever.

We go into this amount of detail, rather than merely noting that "a questionnaire was administered…" both because a reader has a right to know the details of administration, and because in our view it is attention to these details that often makes the difference between a successful and an unsuccessful study. We are convinced that many social science studies that report weak or inconsistent results do so only in part because the underlying theory is wrong or because the real world is so complex. The results are often weak because of sloppy or haphazard circumstances of interviewing or of questionnaire administration. These problems would seem even more acute in working with populations in confinement. In any event, we took this step of our work most seriously, and feel that the relatively small rate of non-usable questionnaires is evidence that most of the inmates took it seriously as well.

The questionnaire as it appears in Appendix II is of course the English version. We developed four questionnaires, one for each country. We worked hard to standardize items so that they would have the same meaning when expressed in different languages, using the traditional device of having the items translated into the foreign language and then back into English in two separate steps, and noting any difference in meaning that might result. We feel that for the most part this process was very successful. The close similarity between Norwegian, Danish, and Swedish of course made problems less severe there than with the translation into Finnish, but with the exception of a very small number of items we feel that the final form of the questionnaire in all four countries was quite comparable. The major exception is in the case of three or four background items, where the criminal justice system itself is different enough to require wording that cannot be drawn parallel for all four countries. In those cases we used a freer translation.

Some months after the initial administration of the questionnaire, and after we had had an opportunity to prepare the data for computer analysis and to examine the responses across the institutions, we sent a preliminary report of findings to each of the institutions, and then revisited each of them to discuss the report. This made it possible for the cooperating staff at the institutions to get some feedback on the study, to comment on particular findings that might appear anomalous concerning their institutions, and in general to provide interpretative comments that would help us in understanding the results. This stage in the research process proved most valuable, and what we learned from those contacts supplements the more formal descriptive material on each institution discussed above.

Data Analysis

Our data are complex. The complexity is reflected both in the institutional and individual level and their potentials for analysis, and in varieties of levels of measurement, from nominal and ordinal scales to ratio scales. Consequently, we use a variety of methods of data presentation and analysis. We have used scatter diagrams, contingency tables, Kendall's rank-order correlation coefficients corrected for ties, rank-order Pearsonian product–moment-correlation coefficients, and multiple regression analyses.[4] Our guiding principle in choosing among the various possibilities has been to select the techniques that would give both a full and yet parsimonious presentation of evidence. In reporting correlations, if there is some ambiguity concerning the level of measurement, or if we feel it would aid the reader's interpretation, we have reported both product-moment and rank-order coefficients, and readers may choose whichever summary measure of the relationship they prefer.

With some exceptions, we have not used tests of significance in reporting our results. Given our sample design, we do not feel that it is appropriate or necessary to report statistical significance levels. This study includes data from the universe of available inmates in the fifteen institutions, and a test of significance to determine the generality of results to the entire inmate population would be meaningless. Furthermore, since the institutions are not a random but a purposive sample of the population of institutions in each country, there is no basis on statistical grounds for generalizing to any larger group of institutions. In the few instances where we do report tests of statistical

[4]See Sidney Siegel, *Non-parametric Statistics for the Behavioral Sciences* (New York: McGraw Hill Book, 1956), pp. 213–223.

significance, the purpose is not to generalize to any population, but rather to test the probability of obtaining certain patterns of differences in replications or dummy-variable analyses.

Finally, we wish to acknowledge the problems that have confronted us in producing a book using quantitative data that might be readable and understandable to several different audiences. We hope the volume will be read by many of our quantitatively sophisticated colleagues in the social sciences, some of whom might have preferred a more elaborate quantitative analysis. But we also want to reach those who care about prisons and their inmates, including professionals in the field of corrections. This "two-culture" problem is in one sense unsolvable, but we hope that our method of presentation will at least make the problem less painful for many readers.

3

Social Change and the Prison

The oldest prison in our study was built in 1851, the newest in 1959. The institutions thus cover over a century of correctional history. In this chapter, we wish to use the date at which our prisons emerged onto the correctional scene to help us learn about processes of social change.

We assume that the date of origin of a prison is a most significant fact. That date anchors the prison at a particular point in the development of correctional philosophy. The prevailing ideology will be given physical expression in the design and construction of the institution. That design and construction, in turn, will limit and constrain what can be done with the institution even at a later time. We should be able to find, then, systematic relationships between a prison's date of appearance on the correctional landscape, and other features of its structure and organization. Finally, the structural and organizational features should have discernible consequences for the actual, ongoing life of inmates in the institutions.

In short we suggest a series of causal links: from the underlying ideology of imprisonment to the prison's physical design and construction; from the physical design and construction to rules and other organizational features that reflect both the design and the ideology;

S. Wheeler and H. F. Cline, *The Scandinavian Prison Study*,
Palgrave Studies in Prisons and Penology,
https://doi.org/10.1007/978-3-030-26462-8_3

and lastly, from the organizational and structural features to the organization of daily life among the inmates. We shall try to trace this line of development in this chapter.

The logic of the argument is not unique to the field of penology. A social history of any institution will undoubtedly suggest some sort of tie between the physical layout of the institution, its major organizational features, and the social life of its inhabitants. But of all the possible forces that give rise to the particular form of social life obtaining among people in a particular setting, there is reason to believe that the prison setting should be distinctively sensitive to such relationships. First, as institutions of confinement there is a natural concern for walls, fences, and other mechanisms for controlling the freedom of movement. Equally important is the fact that prisons are twenty-four hour living establishments, with a consequent need for designing not merely a work or study place, as in the case of a factory or a school, but the total set of living arrangements including sleeping quarters, dining and recreational facilities, places of religious worship—all those places necessary to establishing even the minimal conditions for community life. And perhaps because there has usually been concern with a moral dimension to imprisonment, often with respect to potential contamination of one inmate by another, none of these physical features of imprisonment were allowed to escape the attention of the prison architect.

This concern appeared early in the correctional experience of the United States, and since prison design was a uniquely American contribution to the field of penology, it is relevant to note the great debates about prison design that have occurred in this history of that penology. Much of that history centers on the choice between the Pennsylvania system of prison architecture, with emphasis literally on penitence and isolation, in contrast to the congregate but silent Auburn system, a rival form of prison philosophy and architecture that emerged in New York State in the 1820s, and that allowed inmates to work together during the day in prison workshops.[1] The controversy over these rival systems

[1]David J. Rothman, *The Discovery of the Asylum: Social Order and Disorder in the New Republic* (New York: Little Brown, 1971).

was regarded as extremely important by penologists in Europe as well as America, and de Tocqueville was only one of the many European observers.[2]

This debate was perhaps the most visible of the concerns for the relationship between correctional ideology and physical design. Many years later the State of Illinois brought back the Penopticon Design made famous by Bentham in the eighteenth century.[3] The Norfolk prison colony in Massachusetts was designed to give a feeling of openness and freedom of movement not unlike that to be found on a college campus, made possible by virtue of a double wall around the perimeter of the institution that made real escape virtually impossible.[4] These are only illustrative examples of the long-standing interest in the relationship of physical design to correctional purposes.[5]

We thus propose to capitalize on the fact that our institutions cover over a century of correctional practice to give us a chance to look more closely at the date of origin of the institutions, their current structural features, and the resultant effects upon the daily life of inmates. But before turning to those relationships, we must introduce the reader to the concrete settings in which the prisoners were located. We shall describe them, not in the order in which we studied them, but in the order in which they emerge in the correctional systems of the Scandinavian countries. In this way, we hope to convey a sense both for the uniqueness of each of the institutions, and simultaneously for the historical development of correctional philosophy and ideology as it becomes reflected in the physical features of the institutions themselves.

---

[2]Alexis de Tocqueville, *Democracy in America.*

[3]James B. Jacobs, *Stateville: The Penitentiary in Mass Society* (Chicago: The University of Chicago Press, 1977).

[4]Edwin H. Powers, *The Norfolk Prison Experiment.*

[5]A.C.A. Handbook.

The Prisons

Mid-Nineteenth Century: Botsfengslet and Vridsloselille

The oldest institution in our study is the central prison for offenders in Norway. Built in Oslo in 1851, Botsfengslet (2) was modeled after the early prisons that developed as part of the Pennsylvania system in the United States during the late eighteenth century, the prison system being, apparently, one of the first cultural exports from the United States to the European countries. In fact the importation was not direct, since Norwegian officials copied their institution directly from Pentonville in England, which in turn had been modeled after the Pennsylvania system.

Whatever the details of its origin, Botsfengslet, by the time it was built, represented in its very physical structure the prevailing correctional ideology of the times. Each inmate had his own cell, and they were rather large by contemporary standards. Cells were organized into radial-winged cellblocks in the manner of the typical Pennsylvania system. At the end of some of these cellblocks were individual recreation yards, thus enabling the inmate to receive his exercise free from the contamination of other prisoners. These separate recreation yards were only one of a number of features designed to keep contact among inmates at an absolute minimum. Among the others were a policy that inmates eat in their own cells rather than in the congregate or cafeteria-style that later became more common, and that inmates work in their cells rather than in the mass production style now familiar to modern industry. In more recent years, of course, Botsfengslet has added a workshop area and some inmates are out of their cells at work during much of the daytime. But there are still visible reminders of the older regime, one of the most distinctive being the chapel, where each inmate had his own booth which he entered through his own separate door, and where there were curtains on each side so, like a horse with blinders, the inmate could look only at the minister, and not take sidelong glances at his fellow convicts. The chapel was still in use in the 1960s, though attendance was not compulsory and the procedures for minimizing contact among inmates were less rigidly policed than in earlier times.

The Danish prison, Vridsloselille (12), like Botsfengslet, was modeled after the Pennsylvania system and contains most of the features described for Botsfengslet, though it was some eight years later in date of construction. Just as Botsfengslet was built on what then must have been the outskirts of Norway's largest city, so Vridslfiselille was built about ten miles from Copenhagen, and at the time we gathered our data, both institutions housed a fairly typical group of inmates for their respective countries, a group bearing no special mark of distinction by type of crime, mental incapacity, or prior record. A majority of the offenders in both institutions (71% in Botsfengslet, 61% at Vridslyfselille) were serving time for property offenses, with much smaller proportions serving for offenses against persons and sex offenses. Finally, these two institutions were the largest in terms of their inmate population in their respective countries, the total inmate population at the time of our study being somewhat under 200 at Botsfengslet and somewhat over 200 at Vridsloselille.[6]

These two institutions, then, exemplified a distinctive era in the history of penology, an era whose main features have been outlined elsewhere. The institutions tended toward a massive "fortress" style in their architecture, and in their philosophy they left little doubt that the confinement of criminals was a serious business, and that isolation, both from the outside world and from the contaminating effects of other convicts inside, was a principal ingredient of the system. There were other institutions in the Scandinavian countries that emerged during this period but were not included in our study, notably Langholmen, a notorious old custodial prison in Stockholm. But it was not until the early twentieth century that we add to our own sample of institutions.

[6] This contrasts, of course, with their much larger United States counterparts whose inmate populations reach ten-fold this size. The Attica Correctional Facility, for example, at the time of its uprising (1971) housed well over 2000 inmates.

The Early Twentieth Century: Turku, Nyborg, and Konnunsuo

The most famous prison in Finland, apparently, is the institution known informally as Kakola, located in the western port city of Turku (9) some three hours by train from Helsinki. It is a huge gray and Bastille-like maximum security institution, surrounded by a high wall. There is a red brick building outside the wall which houses inmates in a preventive detention unit. The institution itself dates from 1908. It was not until 1954 that provisions were made in Finland for the preventive detention of mentally abnormal prisoners, and a separate section of Kakola was set apart for this purpose. Our study is concerned only with the preventive detention section, and all descriptions and figures pertain to that section alone unless otherwise specified.

Facilities are provided for 172 men, though there were 215 being detained at the time of our study, some of whom are considered the most dangerous in the Finnish correctional system. The men are housed in one large cell block containing three tiers of cell units along a long corridor. Most of the inmates live in single cells; only 22 are in double rooms. All eat in their own cells. On the fourth floor, there are hobby shops which evidence a reasonably active program although only about 12% of the eligible men participate.

The rigid military atmosphere so pronounced at other Finnish institutions is noticeably more relaxed here as far as inmates are concerned, though it is strictly upheld in staff-to-staff relations as a model for prisoners to observe. Because of the greater incidence of mentally unbalanced detainees, the prison population, it is held, is better handled by a somewhat less authoritarian philosophy than at other Finnish prisons.

The Danish state prison at Nyborg (13) was opened in 1913 and is used primarily for "tough" first offenders, many of them younger adults who committed relatively serious crimes, and recidivists who demand maximum custody. The institution is located on the eastern coast of the island of Fyn. The imposing main building is an extremely long, red brick, three-tiered cell-block patterned after the Auburn system.[7] It is separated by administrative offices into a closed block for inmates who work in their cells and do not get out at all, and a main or "open" block for those inmates who go to the workshops. Beyond the open block are the library, school, and gymnasium. At the far end is the colonnade leading into the youth prison with its own administrative offices and personnel. The youth prison is not included in our study.

Custodial control at Nyborg appears more strict than at Vridsloselille, the older Danish prison in our sample, with the threat of isolation apparently being the primary sanction. The institution has single cells for all of the slightly over 200 prisoners, and most eat individually in their cells. Those in the closed section have made trouble or choose to do piece-work alone in their cells.

Konnunsuo Central Prison (7), the state institution for normal offenders in Finland, is located in Joutseno, a desolate area some 130 miles northeast of Helsinki and only 6 or 7 miles from the USSR border. Here in the agricultural marshland of Karelia, facilities designed to hold 403 inmates, actually housed 434 inmates at the time of our study. Of these, only 75 were classified as serving "ordinary imprisonment." Two hundred and thirty-eight were serving terms of "hard labor," and another 121 were doing up to 4 1/2 years for their inability or refusal to pay fines.

As early as 1844 there was talk of draining the swampland in Joutseno, but it was not until 1918 that a group of 150 prisoners was sent there to do the job, and the institution became informally established. Two years later, in 1920, the Prison Administration took over the operation of Konnunsuo with the aim of running it as an agricultural prison. When the necessary funds were allocated by Parliament in 1921, the serious work of constructing permanent buildings began, continuing until 1934. Industrial facilities were slowly added to round out the

---

[7]The Auburn system, a rival form of prison philosophy and architecture, emerged with the construction of New York's Auburn State Prison in the 1820s. It stressed a congregate system of organization in which inmates were housed alone in single cells, but worked together during the day in workshops. This contrasted to the Pennsylvania system, described earlier, where prisoners ate, worked, and slept in their own cells. See David Rothman, *The Discovery of the Asylum*.

vocational program and to supply the needs of the prison community: carpentry, tailoring, shoemaking, mechanical work, and a peat industry. As at other Finnish institutions, the main emphasis is on hard work.

The institution has no single rooms. Two-thirds of the men eat in their rooms; the other third in a dark, corridor-like dining area. Inmates are locked in their cells during free periods except for special program evenings. No pictures are allowed on the walls—"they would disturb the image of order." Furnishings are meager: a metal bed, small table and stool, and a slop bucket.

The Period Between the Great Wars: Kerava, Sobysogard, Herstedvester, Hall and Ila

The institutions built during this period in the Scandinavian countries begin to show a differentiation in types of penal institutions, each designed to handle special types of inmate populations. Kerava (8) in Finland and Sobysogard (14) in Denmark, the first two institutions constructed during this period, were both for young inmate populations. The average age of inmates at Kerava at the time of our study was 19, and at Sobysogard, 18. Indeed, both represent the response of the correctional system to the problems of youthful inmates. All the Scandinavian countries previously had means of dealing with young offenders in their early teens, but they tended not to differentiate the special problems associated with older adolescent populations. Both Kerava and Sobysogard are aimed at precisely that population.

But at that point their similarity ends. Kerava is a youth prison designed very much like an institution for adult offenders. It was regarded as a "tough" institution, even judged against other correctional institutions in Finland. It was an institution marked by a military type of custodial control with armed guards and little of the special character that is associated in Western ideology with the image of an institution for young offenders.

The prison, located about twenty miles from Helsinki, was opened in 1927. Formerly a foster home, buildings were added on as was a twelve-foot high wire security fence. The physical plant consists of two large buildings which contain the main cell housing units. One building dates from the opening of the prison; the other is about thirty-five years older.

The 90 odd inmates at Kerava are grouped in one of three categories of the classification system: learner, trial, and trusty class. Those who have reached the level of trusty are accommodated in single rooms where they eat; the others are housed dormitory style in units of 4, 6, and 8 and eat in larger dining areas. The rooms are meagerly furnished with a small table, an accompanying stool, a metal bed with a two-inch mattress and blankets, earphones and a slop bucket. Pictures are allowed only if they have a frame around them, but there are no frames available. The rooms are more or less identical, completely lacking any show of individuality—spartan but clean. Huge brown doors, with only peepholes to provide contact with the corridor outside, clamp shut with a swinging rod and seal the inmates in. Except for the trusties, who are allowed free interaction in the corridors until 8 p.m., all inmates are locked in their cells during the free time period.

Sobysogard, by contrast, was one of three Danish institutions designed for this particular age group, and the one of the three that received the "best" risks among this group of offenders. It was an institution run according to what are generally conceived to be benign and humanitarian standards. From 1921 to 1933, when it became a youth institution, Sobysogard was a residential finishing school for upper-class young women. Even by the time of our study, the director occasionally received applications from mothers trying to enroll their daughters in the school. Prior to that, it was a stately old manor home.

The institution includes over 400 acres of natural surroundings—tall trees, rich farmland, and a lake for fishing. Inmates are housed in rooms and dormitories, and they have a great deal of time under minimal custodial control, working in the fields and gardens of the pretty area in the island of Fyn where the institution is located. The director of the institution at the time of our study, Mr. Audi-Hansen, was the prototype of a stern but kindly figure who could combine warmth and discipline. He had been director for over a score of years. Almost all of the 91 inmates had single rooms, but there are a few triples available when needed, no doubles. The inmates dine together in common dining facilities.

The rooms in one of three buildings are lively looking and very individualistic with numerous pictures and pin-ups on the walls. The boys are locked in their rooms for the night at 8:30.

Like Kerava, much of the vocational emphasis at Sobysogard is on agriculture. But there is a much heavier emphasis also on school and athletic programs. The teachers play an important role both in the formal education process and also as non-resident directors in the housing units in late afternoons and early evenings. And just as the director at Sobysogard had been there many years, so had several of the teachers. Perhaps this is one of the traits that lends a sense of calm and continuity to Sobysogard that is infrequently observed in correctional settings.

These two institutions, then, though constructed only a few years apart and intended for roughly the same aged inmate population, are radically different in their guiding philosophy and spirit, with Kerava reflecting a relatively harsh and punishment-centered prison philosophy and regime; and Sobysogard, the more benign and welfare-oriented institution often written about in the rhetoric of juvenile court philosophy in the Western world, reflecting something of the pastoral quality of the Danish countryside.

Herstedvester (11) is perhaps the most widely known of the institutions included in our study. It is a preventive detention institution in Denmark, and the first of the institutions in our study to be primarily under the control of a psychiatrist rather than the more traditional correctional administrator. About a fourth of its somewhat fewer than 200 inmates had committed sex offenses, this fact reflecting the special treatment program for sex offenders introduced by its well-known director, the psychiatrist Georg K. Sturup. Although the reputation of Herstedvester stresses its special mode of dealing with sex offenders, it shares with other preventive detention institutions in Scandinavia a general effort to apply a "treatment" orientation to offenders, all of whom are judged to be less than fully responsible for their own actions. As institutionalized by Sturup and his staff at Herstedvester, the preventive detention approach includes conceiving of the inmates as more sick than criminal, as needing a very general kind of social psychological and social psychiatric help, with individual or group therapy sessions for some inmates, and with a system of staff conferences similar to those common in mental hospitals for the evaluation of patients.

The prison, located about nine miles from Copenhagen, was opened in 1935. An open farm unit located outside the walls and housing around forty inmates was added on in 1944. The prison complex, surrounded by high walls, contains eight rectangular, yellow brick buildings. Three of the buildings house prison workshops and one serves a combination of administration and hospital functions. The others are cellblocks, each two stories high and divided into sections of cells with a common room. Almost all of the inmates are housed in single cells, in which they may choose to eat rather than in the small common dining rooms.

The idea of special preventive detention institutions took its first full form at Herstedvester, but shortly thereafter was copied in some form in both Norway and Sweden. Ila (1), located about eight miles from Oslo, is Norway's preventive detention institution based very largely on the Herstedvester model, intended for a similar population, and also headed by a psychiatrist. It was a good deal smaller than Herstedvester, and at the time of our study had not, at least in the eyes of most observers, gone as far in implementing a full treatment ideology. Indeed, shortly before its formal opening in 1940 as a Women's Institution, it was taken over by the German occupation forces and used as a concentration camp in which to house members of the Norwegian underground and others detected in the fight against the Nazis. Upon defeat of the Germans, prisoners and guards changed places, and for the first years after the war, Ila was used primarily as an institution for German prisoners and Quislings. It was not until 1951 that Ila opened as a preventive detention institution. Thus Ila had had somewhat less time to institutionalize its pattern of preventive detention than had its parallel institution in Denmark.

Like Herstedvester, the average age of inmates at Ila is in the early thirties, and a sizeable proportion of the inmates, though less than at Herstedvester, have been sentenced for sex offenses. Its population covers the range of abnormal, but not insane prisoners: neurotic, psychopathic, epileptic, feeble-minded. The 75 inmates were incarcerated within a four-story main building, which contained six living units and a solitary confinement section. Each inmate lived in a private room; half ate in their cells, and half in small common mess halls.

Hall (4), in Sweden, was also opened in 1940, and provides the Swedish version of preventive detention. Although the legal terms of commitment to Hall are similar to those for Herstedvester and Ila, the organization of the institution is quite different. The Swedish system has made less explicit use of a clearly medical model of institutions than has either Norway or Denmark, and this is reflected in its preventive detention institution. The then director, Gunnar Marnell, brought a benign attitude to Hall, and helped encourage a number of the innovations that have developed in the Swedish system, including conjugal visits for selected inmates, furloughs prior to parole, and the like. Indeed, his philosophy depended much more on such programs and on establishment of a general "feeling tone" in the institution, than on the specific use of clinically oriented staff. Thus inmates may decorate their rooms pretty much as they wish; they control their own lighting and may lock their room from inside when they want privacy. And unlike many of our institutions, inmates may decide for themselves whether they want to work. The absence of any sizeable treatment staff is in part a function of the shortage of such personnel in the Swedish prison system, but it is not inconsistent with Mr. Marnell's style of operation. His own background and college training had been in English and the humanities rather than in medicine, thus distinguishing him from the directors of the two preventive detention institutions in Norway and Denmark.

Hall is a walled institution located about 25 miles southwest of Stockholm, containing two pavilions, each housing about 70–75 inmates and a small barracks outside the walls for 40 inmates. Most inmates are in single cells; all dine in a common mess hall. The institutions opened in the Scandinavian countries between the two World Wars, whatever the differences alluded to above, exhibit the beginnings of a very stable process of differentiation in the correctional system. All five of these institutions are meant for special inmate populations, two of them for the young and three for those whom the courts have found to be operating under reduced levels of responsibility. In comparison with the institutions described for earlier periods in Scandinavia, these five offer more diversity both in their physical plant and in their programs than do the others. But with the exception of Sobysogard and some sections of Hall and Ila, they are still institutions of close custody. The process of differentiation became clearly established between the wars, and as we shall see, it has continued since.

The Immediate Post-World War II Period: Kragskovhede, Seutula and Berg

Shortly after the end of World War II, the Danish prison system opened a new institution near the northern tip of Jutland. From its beginning this institution had a very special cast for it was designed as a completely open institution, without walls, yet one that was meant exclusively for recidivists. Although at an earlier point in correctional philosophy this might have seemed a contradiction in terms, the developing ideology both in Denmark and elsewhere stressed the need for smaller institutions and those that were differentiated as to purpose; hence, an open colony for recidivists. Inmates at Kragskovhede (15) were primarily property offenders, with a careful screening out of those who were thought likely to attempt to run away and of those who had records of violence. Save for these characteristics, the offenders were much like those in the other institutions we have described as normal prisons.

Kragskovhede, in its administrative operation, made an explicit attempt to follow the most modern correctional ideology. Many of its program components were based on the Handbook of American Correctional Standards, as these were interpreted by its director, Mr. Rafael, who had spent a period of time examining the United States system. Each inmate, for example, was assigned to one or another of two treatment teams, and these teams were responsible for him during the course of his stay at Kragskovhede. Strong efforts were made to provide individualized treatment and counseling along with work assignments based upon a diagnosis and assessment of the inmate's capacities and interests. Inmates were housed in three-man rooms in barracks-like buildings, and unlike their fellow inmates in Vridsloselille or Nyborg, they were not surrounded by imposing walls, but rather by the rugged country near the northern shoreline of Jutland. Freedom from the walls, however, did not mean freedom from surveillance for the possibility of running away was still present. The result was that guards, in effect, replaced the walls, and the inmates in this open colony were under rather close supervision as they walked in assigned groups from barracks, to work place, or to the dining hall.

Another distinguishing feature of Kragskovhede is the revolving division of the work week into a different schedule for each pavilion. The week is divided into five working days, one free day, and one "home-day," but arranged so that each day a different housing unit has "home day." On this day, inmates are expected to get their haircuts, bathe, clean their rooms, visit doctors, social workers, psychiatrists, and take care of any other obligations that would otherwise interrupt a working day. In this way, too, the pressures on the treatment staff as well as on the physical facilities (adequate hot water for baths, etc.) are evenly distributed throughout the week, and in the eyes of the staff the entire institution runs more smoothly.

Finland's very different version of an open colony began in 1950 at Seutula (10), some twenty. miles from Helsinki. Seutula housed primarily minor offenders, including a substantial number of drunken drivers, some of them professionals and businessmen, who must serve a mandatory four months' confinement under the Finnish system, and others incarcerated for non-payment of fines. Inmates at Seutula were therefore less likely to have long records in crime, were more likely to be of middle-class background, and to be serving short sentences. The result is that, unlike Kragskovhede, the risks of escape and runaway were lessened, and the institution could literally be run with minimum security. There were no walls or fences and very few guards. Another important feature of the program at Seutula was the stress upon labor, with the inmates assigned to work on either roads or on airport runways. Indeed, the program at Seutula was the work program, with no emphasis whatever upon therapy, psychological diagnosis, and the like. Such programs, of course, were atypical against the background of the Finnish prison system, and in this particular instance specialists in corrections could argue that they were not needed because of the character of the inmate population. Thus Seutula has been hailed for the combination of an effective work program, in which inmates are paid a normal wage scale, similar to what they would be earning for such work in the outside world, along with a minimum custody program. Thus Seutula is very inexpensive to operate.

It may be difficult to convey in the space of a brief outline of the institutions how different Seutula was from the other institutions in our sample, and especially from the other institutions in Finland. A total of some 12 staff, including 10 work supervisors, were employed to operate an institution with some 380 men. This extremely low ratio of staff to inmates was all that was needed, for apart from the work program the inmates had a great deal of freedom. They were quartered in dormitories, with anywhere from 10 to 22 per room. They had the option of buying their meals in the cafeteria or purchasing food and preparing it themselves in their dormitories. They wore their own clothes and could bring whatever they wished from home to furnish their living quarters. The result was that some of the dormitories were elaborately equipped with hi-fi's, flowers, pictures, and even wallpaper—altogether a far cry from the conditions prevailing in the other Finnish institutions—Kerava, Konnunsuo, or Turku.

The last institution to be described during this postwar period is Berg Arbeidskole (3) in Norway dating from 1951. Like the youth institutions in the other countries, Berg was meant to fill the need for an institution specifically designed for inmates in their late teens. During the short period of its operation prior to our study, it had changed from a "youth prison" where stress was on the routine of confinement similar to that found in normal prisons, to a "working school," with emphasis upon education and vocational training. But with a smaller inmate population than neighboring Denmark or Sweden, Norway faced the problem of trying to combine these elements with a single population of inmates, not being able to classify them into categories as did the Danes, with three institutions to handle this same population. The result is that there have been strains within the Norwegian youth system: the more it is run as an educational and training program with attention taken away from custody, the greater the number of escapes and complaints from the local community. On the other hand, to reinstall secure levels of custody seems to make it more difficult to operate along benign lines. This conflict was partially resolved at Berg by building a separate unit in downtown Oslo that had secure custody, while leaving the more pastoral countryside institution on the outskirts of Oslo under reduced degrees of security. In the latter unit, inmates were housed in one of three sections containing single rooms and communal dining facilities. In any event, Berg, like Seutula and Kragskovhede, illustrates the continuing tendency toward diversification in the Scandinavian systems, and a continuing effort to grope for new institutional forms to solve prison problems.

The Modern Era: Norrtalje and Mariefred

The newest institutions in our study had been occupied less than three years prior to our period of data collection. It is not surprising that they are both in Sweden, for Sweden, as indicated earlier, has invested much more in the building of new institutions for the handling of offenders than have any of the other Scandinavian countries. These two institutions may be taken as prototypes of the modern Swedish prison philosophy developed under the well-known director of the Swedish prison system, Thorsten Erikson. Each institution lays stress upon confining inmates in small groups of ten to twenty per unit, rather than in large dormitory or cell-like facilities. Indeed, the basic design for both institutions is a one-story pavilion, with single rooms for each inmate, a large day room, and a dining room. An even more crucial ingredient of the Swedish system under Erikson's direction was the factory, and each of these institutions, especially Norrtalje (6) had a special modern factory for the making of furniture and related objects.

Each of the institutions gave evidence of that special "1984- ish" quality sometimes associated with modern means of communication. Norrtalje and Mariefred are both walled institutions, relatively secure from escape save by climbing the walls. However, replacing guards on the walls are television cameras, which are monitored by an official in the central office. The cameras click on and off in a routine cycling of the perimeter of the institution, though the guard monitoring the cameras can switch to any station at will.

Equally important to the communication and surveillance system is the walky-talky and the two-way radio. Each inmate has a radio in his room, one channel of which is connected to the central office. This makes it possible to lock each inmate in his room at night with no official in his pavilion. If for any reason he is ill or needs help, he simply signals the central office. They in turn contact a pair of guards who are on patrol in the institution and who carry a walky-talky. These guards can then go to the pavilion in order to find out more about the inmate's problem, and assist him in getting medical help, in going to the hospital, or whatever.

Although these institutions have in common the modern factory, the low pavilion-style housing, and the stress upon rapid communication using the most modern equipment, they are designed for rather different inmate populations. Norrtalje, located about 45 miles northeast of Stockholm, is for normal adult prison inmates, though because of its stress on the work program an effort is made to screen out those who cannot, for medical or other reasons, spend a regular day at factory work. A modern factory, providing work for 105 inmates, manufactures furniture and other wood products. The same building also houses a garment factory employing 20 men. Inmates, who may number up to 140, are housed in three single-story, red-brick pavilions, 40 to a building. Each building, in accordance with the small group principle, is divided into two separate groups of 20 each. There is also a semi-open pavilion with 20 beds. Each pavilion is equipped with hobby rooms and two dayrooms where the two groups dine separately. The men are housed in single rooms, comfortably furnished with rugs, draperies, foam-rubber mattresses, radios, desks, and latticed windows which conceal the steel bars.

Mariefred (5) is for youthful inmates, most of whom are serving time for property offenses. They are a somewhat more sophisticated group of offenders than those in the youth institution in Norway and Denmark, being some two years older and having somewhat longer criminal records. Most of the youths have been transferred from Langholmen prison in Stockholm, but some have been referred directly by the courts. The minimum term there is six months, the average one year. Total capacity of the institution, which covers almost fifteen acres, is ninety. Eighty places are provided in the main, closed section, ten in an open section for pre-releases. The boys are housed in single rooms within four buildings within the walled area and feed ten together in their sitting-rooms. Employment is provided in the shops for carpentry, plastics, electricity (radio and TV repair), mechanics, and in outdoor work. There is no real organized educational program, though limited classroom instruction is available three or four hours a week for those who want it.

This brief description of our fifteen institutions should serve to give a sense of the range and variety of prisons in Scandinavia, and hopefully some sense of the changes in prison ideology over the century spanned by our institutions. The major trends are fairly clear: from uniformity to diversity, from a single-minded concern with isolation and custody to multiple concerns for both custody and treatment, from large institutions holding a heterogeneous group of inmates to smaller institutions with a more homogeneous population. It is within the context of these general changes that we begin to examine the structural features of imprisonment and their effects on life inside the prison.

The fifteen institutions we have just described are each unique and only part of the uniqueness is suggested in our brief account. Each institution has its own special quality and "feeling tone" and each will have a distinctive culture that has emerged from past situations, from the particular types of men—both captors and captives—who have inhabited the institution over time. Yet as we noted in Chapter 2, a primary aim of our work is to establish generalizations about imprisonment based upon our findings in these fifteen institutions. Indeed, precisely because of their diversity, they can be used to establish generalizations about the field of corrections as a whole, at least as it is found in Scandinavia and, we feel, probably throughout much of the Western world. For the most part, these generalizations will cut across the four countries and the different types of prisons, though later we will devote a separate chapter to these differences.

The Effect of Date of Origin on Prison Structural Features

We begin our analysis by taking advantage of the fact that our institutions cover over one hundred years of correctional history in the Scandinavian countries, thus enabling us to examine the relationships between the date of emergence of the institution on the correctional scene (in fact the construction date for the institutions) and the structural characteristics that they exhibit at the time of our study. This gives us an opportunity to examine social change in the field of corrections—to note the correlates of modernity in prison regimes.

Our measures of the structural features of the prisons fall into three main categories. First, there are measures that reflect in gross terms some of the main physical and material features of the prisons. Four of our measures fall in this category. The sheer size of the institutional population is one such measure. The Scandinavian countries have rarely built the huge institutions with inmate populations in the thousands that are still found in the United States, but there is still a range in size, with our smallest institutions less than one-fourth the size of our largest. And there is reason to believe from studies of other types of organization that size alone may be a determinant of other organizational characteristics.

Another indicator is the degree of custodial control exercised over inmates. Some of our institutions are open, unwalled, and with little attention to matters of custody. Others maintain close control through the use of high walls, constant visual supervision of work crews, and in some Swedish institutions electronic surveillance devices. Although many institutions have several degrees of custody, and shift inmates from one to another depending on their presumed adjustment in the institution and on the length of sentence remaining, it is not difficult to rank the institutions according to the degree to which close custodial control is a matter of policy.

Our third and fourth measures relate more to the material conditions of prison life. The average wages inmates are paid for their work reflects both the potential work incentive and also the amount of money inmates may have available to purchase items of food, clothing, magazines, cigarettes and other materials that may ease the rigors of imprisonment. And our fourth measure reflects the extent to which a wide variety of such objects are available for purchase. These four measures, of course, do not begin to exhaust the possible indirect indicators of the quality of life within the prison, but they do give us a beginning and were among the more accessible of variables on which we could obtain reliable information.[8]

A second category of structural features has to do with the staffing of the institutions, specifically the ratio of inmates to custody staff, inmates to treatment staff, and custody to treatment staff. These measures are based on the actual number of persons occupying each of these positions at the time of our study. The concept of "treatment staff," it should be noted, is broader than that conveyed by the notion of a professional treatment staff engaged primarily in psychotherapy or related therapeutic efforts of whom there are very few in any institution. It includes persons who are working in education, religion, vocational training, medical and psychiatric care, social work, classification, and parole. The common element is that all of these personnel are there because of their presumed benefit to the inmate and not primarily as custodians. A close examination of the actual work done by such personnel reveals much that is more custodial than initially conceived; and one of the themes of the modern critique of corrections centers on the use of classification and treatment efforts, for example, as a means of obtaining docility and conformity while inmates are inside, thus easing the problems of custodial control. Nonetheless, there is a perceptible difference recognized by inmates between the custodial and non-custodial personnel, often reflected in their dress, speech, and manner within the institutions. And it is these ratios that are often changed by design when an institution wishes to become more "treatment-oriented." So it makes sense to treat them as potentially important structural features of the prison.

[8]Details on the construction of an index of custodial control as well as all other indices used in this study are presented in Appendix III.

The third and final category of structural features are measures that directly reflect official efforts to control the social life of inmates—both within the institution and in contacts between those inside and the outside world. We regard these as structural measures of social deprivation, as they directly affect the inmates' possibilities for contacts with two important groups of people in his current condition—his family and friends outside the institution, and the inmates with whom he must work, eat, sleep, and live inside the institution. From a review of the rules regarding letter-writing and the frequency and length of visit, we developed an index of restrictions on outside contacts. Like our other structural measures, this is an index based on the rules or operating procedures of the institutions and does not necessarily reflect the actual behavior or feelings of the inmates in question. It is a measure of the possibilities for interpersonal contact with the outside world given in the structure of institutional life, and not of the actual practices engaged in by a particular inmate.

Similarly, we developed an index of limits on interaction between inmates in the institution—an index that reflects the freedom of movement of inmates within the institutions by calculating the time available for free interaction with other inmates in a typical week. Clearly, inmates who are locked in their individual cells at 4:00 or 5:00 p.m., as was true at Botsfengslet in Norway and Vridsoselille in Denmark, do not have the opportunity to interact with other inmates that is available in institutions with later hours set for retirement in the evening and dormitory style housing. And finally, by combining these and other measures of the possibilities for social contact within the institutions, we developed a number of alternative indices of social deprivation, each of which expresses a slightly different picture of social deprivation, but in all cases reflecting the rules regulating contacts inside and outside the institution rather than actual amount of contact.

We give great attention to social deprivation because of all the features of imprisonment that are embedded in both correctional ideology and inmate life experience, the possibilities for human contact appears as absolutely central. One of the earliest establishments in history to take on the characteristics of prison were the leprosaria of thirteenth century Europe. And leprosaria, of course, existed precisely because of their capacity to keep a tainted few out of contact with the untainted masses. When the early prison system developed in the United States under Quaker influence, the interest in protecting against contamination was as great as in the leprosaria, only now it was moral contamination that was an issue. The inmate should be deprived of any contacts with those who might be evil influences and only the Bible could be allowed to work its influence—hence, separate cells, isolation, and social starvation. This theme has continued in correctional philosophy, and is reflected in its non-philosophical, pragmatic version by the "do-your-own-time" doctrine, a principle admonishing inmates to stay out of their fellows' business and mind their own. In any event, the idea of controlling the inmate's life by controlling his patterns of human interaction is perhaps the most ancient and critical of ideas behind the prison, one which retains its importance across centuries of prison experience, and therefore one worthy of detailed study in any broadly comparative examination of prison regimes.

Table 3.1 presents the relationships between the construction date of the institutions and these various measures of institutional structure and policy. The data are presented in two separate columns. First, we show the correlation coefficients between the date of construction and the various measures for all fifteen of our institutions. This represents the most general statement of the relationships for the institutions we studied. In addition, we show the results separately for the eleven adult institutions in the sample. We do this because, as our later analysis will show, the age of inmates is one of the most powerful variables in our study, and we want to make sure that our main findings are not primarily a function of the average age of offenders housed in particular institutions. As a quick examination of the table shows, removal of the four youth institutions tends on the whole to strengthen other relationships rather than to weaken them, and in no instance does it require a radically different interpretation. Thus we will confine our interpretive remarks primarily to the results for the fifteen institutions taken together.

As Table 3.1 shows, the physical and material features of the prisons bear definite though relatively mild relationships to the date of the institution's origin. The newer institutions are more likely to have a smaller

Table 3.1 Structural correlates of modernity in prison regimes[a]

	Structural features	All 15 Prisons	11 Adult Prisons
I. Physical and material features			
A.	Number of inmates	−0.41	−0.40
B.	Degree of custody	−0.40	−0.40
C.	Wages	0.16	0.22
D.	Store items	0.35	0.32
II. Staffing policies			
A.	Ratio of inmates to custody staff	0.25	0.31
B.	Ratio of inmates to treatment staff	0.07	0.22
C.	Ratio of inmates to total staff	0.20	0.27
D.	Ratio of custody to treatment staff	0.13	0.22
III. Constraints *on interaction patterns*			
A.	Restrictions on outside contact	−0.43	−0.43
B.	Limits on interaction time	−0.75	−0.82
C.	Social deprivation index	−0.77	−0.84

[a]Entries are Pearson r's between feature and age of prison

number of inmates, a lower degree of custody, to pay higher wages and to offer a wider variety of items for purchase by inmates. These trends appear clearly in the eleven adult institutions as well. The differences suggest that inmates in the newer institutions are a bit better off than their mates in the older prisons in terms of the sheer material and physical conditions of imprisonment. But these relationships are by no means striking in their magnitude and leave much room for the operation of other forces.

The second block of variables, namely those that reflect staffing policies, have perhaps the least clear-cut results. The ratio of inmates to custody staff appears to be higher in the new institutions than in the old, perhaps reflecting in part the use of new forms of prison design and technology to replace guards as a means of custodial control, as well as the general tendency toward a lower degree of custodial security in the new institutions. Neither the ratio of inmates to the treatment staff or to the total staff (save in the eleven adult institutions) bears any consistent relationship to the newness of the institution. The one figure that does seem clearly interpretable among our ratios is that reflecting the decline in the ratio of custody staff to treatment staff in the newer institutions. And that decline, it seems clear from the other results, is a function of the relative shrinking of custodial personnel rather than the relative increase in personnel devoted to treatment. In any event, it is apparent that for these institutions, knowledge of their date of origin enables us to predict relatively little about the composition of their personnel.

The problems of interpretation with these sorts of materials are great and are illustrated by our findings regarding staffing of the institutions. With a number as small as fifteen, it only takes one or two striking departures from a general pattern to obscure what would otherwise seem to be a clear and clean relationship. But the reality of correctional regimes is that, despite a fairly general trend in ideology from pure custodial control to something called a treatment orientation, there are often grave difficulties in implementing a changed ideology in the life of the institutions in question, and the ideology itself is subject to debate and different interpretation leading to special cases that are seemingly inconsistent. Both of these types of "exceptions" are indicated in our materials. One reason the correlation between the ratio of custody staff to treatment staff and the construction date is not more strongly negative is because the Swedish institutions have been unable to attract trained manpower for the treatment positions. Therefore, despite an ideology stressing the importance of small groups and reflected in the building of small institutions, the ratio of inmates to treatment staff is higher in Sweden than either Norway or Denmark.

A contrasting case is presented by Seutula (10), the Finnish institution primarily for drunken drivers. This is a relatively new institution meant to house offenders for short terms, often serving for an offense that many do not see as terribly criminal. As a result, it is not deemed necessary to rehabilitate the offenders through a heavy program of treatment, and there are no persons on the Seutula staff who could be classified primarily as treatment personnel. Inmates are working in the open, building airstrips. In the evenings they return to dormitory-like facilities where they may read, play cards, or watch television. There is no perception of a special need for treatment, either among Finnish authorities or among the inmates themselves. So here is an institution that looks modern in terms of its low degree of custodial control and its relatively open housing arrangements, and indeed has been regarded as innovative by correctional experts, yet lacks concern for counseling and more orthodox treatment devices. Such institutions provide the interesting deviant cases in the analysis of general trends in correctional systems.

When we turn to our measures reflecting constraints on interaction, a strikingly clear pattern is found. For the fifteen institutions taken together, even the weakest of the three relationships is stronger than any of those relating to physical and material features or staffing policies. The weakest of the three relates solely to outside contact: the newer the institution, the fewer the restrictions on outside contacts, and thus the greater the possibility for inmates to have significant interaction with friends, relatives, and others outside the institutions.

Restrictions on contacts within the institution are even more strongly related to the date of the prison's origin. Our measure of limits on interaction time reflects the fact that the new institutions, in contrast to the old, enable inmates to eat together and to be housed in rooms or dormitories rather than cells, where a greater amount of interaction can take place. And importantly, the new institutions are likely to be more liberal with regard to freedom of movement and activity during the time between the end of the working day and final lockup. The total effect of these forces is that the social deprivation of the inmate is much greater if he is housed in one of the older institutions than if he is in one of the newer ones.

This result is shown graphically in Fig. 3.1, displaying the relationship between the date of construction of the institution and the ranking of each institution on our general measure of social deprivation. These differences are particularly apparent if one contrasts the two oldest institutions in our study, Botsfengslet (2) and Vridslyiselille (12), with the two newest, Norrtalje (6) and Mariefred (5). In the former, inmates are housed in single cells and they are fed alone in their cells because of the absence of any central dining facility. Both institutions, we recall, are a product of early American prison design, specifically the Pennsylvania system. Symbols of the prevailing ideology requiring that inmates be kept in solitary confinement are still reflected in the daily routines of the institutions, though they are no longer a well-developed part of a correctional ideology.

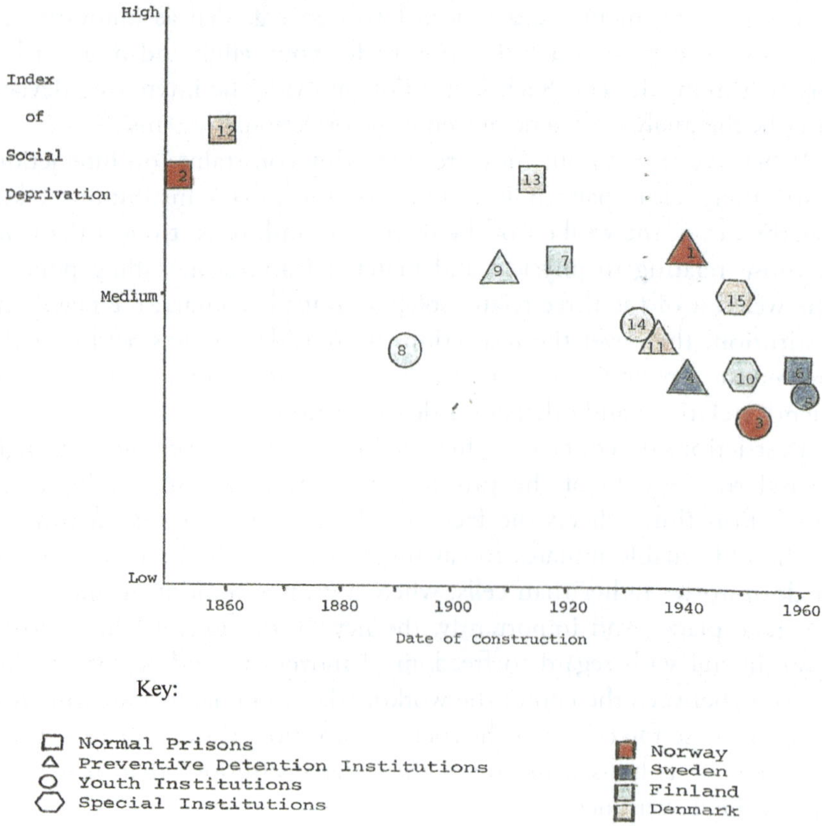

Fig. 3.1 The relationship of prison age to social deprivation ($r=-.77$)

In contrast, at Norrtalje and Mariefred, the inmates are housed in rooms within low, ranch-style buildings. They are fed in a common dining hall and they are allowed relatively open interaction with their fellows in the day rooms that are a part of each housing unit. There are no such rooms in Botsfengslet and Vridslofselille, with the result that unless inmates are on some special mission, they are locked in their cells at around five in the afternoon, there to remain until the next morning. It is no wonder, then, that we find a strong relationship between the date of construction of the prison and the interaction possibilities available to inmates within it.

Interrelations Among the Structural Features

The structural features of the prison regimes bear interesting relationships to each other. As we might anticipate from the commonly high relationships between construction date and measures of social interaction, our various interaction and deprivation measures are relatively highly related to each other. Our general measure of social deprivation is related ($r=.79$) to our measure of limits on interaction inside the institution, and ($r=.78$) to our measure of restrictions on outside contacts. The relationship between the restrictions on inside and on outside contacts is somewhat weaker, but is still clear ($r=.39$). This relationship documents the tendency of prison regimes to be relatively consistent in their policies with regard to contracts both inside and outside: when they adopt more permissive policies for interaction between inmates inside the institution, they also tend to make it easier for inmates to have contacts with the outside world. It is not the case that the officials open one avenue while closing another. The result is that the prospects for a relatively full set of social experiences while inside the prison are very much greater for inmates in some prisons than for those in others.

There is also a slight tendency for the degree of custody and size of the institution to be related ($r=.22$), with the larger institutions devoted more to maximum custody. And in part because the preventive detention institutions tend to be both maximum custody and staffed with more treatment personnel, there is only a weak relationship between degree of custody and the custody-treatment staff ratio ($r=-.38$). But that same ratio, one of the better indirect indicators of correctional philosophy once one discounts the special cases created by preventive detention, bears important relationships to our various isolation and social deprivation measures. Where the custody-treatment staff ratio is high, of course, that means predominance of custodial over treatment staff personnel and reflects the relative dominance of custodial over treatment concerns in the institution—at least as reflected in staffing policies. That measure is correlated with restrictions on outside contact ($r=-.01$), restrictions on inside contact ($r=-.07$), and with our overall social deprivation measure ($r=-.13$). Thus the institutions that are more treatment-oriented, at least as reflected in their staffing policies, are also those that permit wider amounts of interaction both within the inmate community and between inmates and the outer world. Both the reasons for and the effects of this relationship will form an important part of our later analysis.

The relations among the items reflecting the balance between inmates, custody staff and treatment staff are interesting and straightforward. The ratio of inmates to custody staff and of inmates to treatment staff are positively related ($r = .90$), indicating that there is a general "staffing" effect irrespective of type of staff. But the ratio of inmates to total staff is related hardly at all to the ratio of custody to treatment staff. We might then say the institutions face two staffing decisions, one concerning the general ratio of inmates to staff, another concerning the type of staff, and that these two decisions are apparently independent.

Alternative Interpretations

Our principal finding at this point is the clear and discernible effect of the date of origin of the institutions on certain of their structural features, particularly the possibilities for interaction between inmates within the institutions. Before examining what effect these possibilities may have on the actual patterns of interaction, we pause to consider alternative explanations of the link between construction date and structure. Why is it that approximately two-thirds of the way through the twentieth century one can seemingly find differences among the set of institutions that appear traceable, at least in part, to the date of origin of the institution? We think it is unlikely that the sheer age of the institutions offers much of the explanation, for institutions, even more so than individuals, can be modernized with new construction, new paint, new furniture, and the like. Indeed, a number of the features we have examined are matters of social policy established by the prison administration and bear no necessary tie to the sheer age of the institutions in question.

The important thing about the date of origin of the institutions is that it anchors the institution at a particular point in correctional philosophy. This anchoring has two important effects quite apart from age itself. First, it anchors the architecture of the institution or the intended use of the physical and social space at a particular point in time, and the architecture will be a response to the correctional ideology of that time. The physical plant itself sets important constraints on the kinds of things that can be done in institutions. This is perhaps particularly the case in the field of penology as physical structure has always been one of the chief expressions of penal philosophy. That the potential for interaction between inmates is much less in the older institutions than in the newer ones is in part an expression of this effect, for the older institutions were constructed in a way that makes interaction between inmates more difficult. Thus we get a sense for the sustained effect of the past correctional ideology through its effect on the physical structure of the institutions and on the patterning of life in those institutions long after the older ideology has fallen into disuse.

But there is another effect of the ideological history of the institutions that tends to reinforce these relationships—one to which we have not yet given attention. As correctional philosophy changes, and as new categories of "deviants" are recognized and categorized in the system, new institutions are developed to house them. In all the countries we studied there have emerged new categories of deviants since the mid-nineteenth century. The concept of differentiating young from older offenders emerged around the turn of the century. Similarly, the whole concept of differentiating inmates who are half sick and half criminal, and therefore requiring preventive detention, reached full flower since that time. Finally, the special categories of deviants reflected in the development of an open colony for recidivists in Denmark and a special institution for drunken drivers in Finland are more recent arrivals on the correctional scenery.

Thus, in addition to the staying power of the institutional structure itself, we have the additional fact that inmates reflecting a newer ideology are housed in the newer institutions, and that the remnants of earlier perspectives tend to remain in the older institutions. Most of our "normal prisons" are older than the other institutions, and in them are housed the offenders for whom classical penology was designed: the mature, adult, rational, calculating criminal unmarred by youth or psychological complexities.

Perhaps the most interesting indirect indicator of this relationship of time and history to ideology is that the age of the institutions is related to the age of their directors—the newer institutions tend to be headed by younger men. We would argue that newer and younger directors might have difficulty embodying a new ideology in some of the old physical structures because of the constraints physical structure places on programs; but it is significant that by and large the new directors are not faced with that problem, since they are given the newer institutions in which to work.

The Effect of Institutional History and Structure on Interaction Patterns

It is one thing to show that some of the important structural features of the prisons are related to the dates of the prison's origin and hence to the kind of philosophy that came to characterize it. It is quite another to show that the same structural features have a real effect on the daily life of the institution and its inhabitants. We proceed to examine those relationships now and begin by introducing several alternative measures of interaction that were employed in our study. The measures are relatively highly interrelated, as one might expect, but each gives a somewhat different expression of the interaction patterns, and we will report the results separately for each measure.

Perhaps the weakest of our measures of interaction is a simple index of the amount of talking inmates do with other inmates during the course of a day, a week, a month. Inmates were asked, "How often do you have an informal talk with other inmates in this institution?" The ranking of each institution is based upon the proportion of inmates who responded "several times a day." Our two indices of friendship formation are based on a single item: "Have you made any good friends among other inmates in the institution?" In one index, the ranking of an institution is based on the percentage of inmates that report having made one or more friends, in the second index, on the number of inmates who report having made five or more friends. We used two indicators for the simple reason that they seemed to reflect somewhat divergent aspects of interaction, and while the two indicators are highly correlated, the correlation ($r=.89$, $r=.69$) is by no means perfect.

We also asked inmates how they spend their free time and ordered the institutions according to the proportion who spent their free time with other inmates, rather than mostly by themselves. As one might expect, most inmates most of the time spend their free time with other inmates, but the proportions vary from a low of 57% at Vridsloselille (12) to a high of 91% at Sobysogard (14). Our interest in the question derives from the joint issues of protecting privacy on one hand, and avoiding isolation on the other.

Finally, we employed an index that might not be thought of as a measure of interaction at all, but rather a measure of attitude toward interaction. We asked the inmates whether they would prefer to have more contact with other inmates than they now have, less contact, or about the same. We may view this measure as an indirect index of an important feature relating to interaction in the institution. Just as the actual amount of contact is likely to be important to both inmates and officials, inmate feelings about contact are a critical feature of prison life. The old, isolating bastilles must have generated an enormous need for human association, and some of the newer institutions with their group living arrangements raise just the opposite need—for privacy, time to be alone and to one's self. The capacity of this single item to reveal major institutional differences is suggested by the enormous range of response across our fifteen institutions. In Norway's Botsfengslet (2), over 80% of the inmates desired more contact, while in Sweden's Hall (4) preventive detention institution, with its more liberal policies of association, only 16% desired more contact. Within the same country, differences are almost as extreme. In Denmark, 80% of the Nyborg (13) inmates want more contact with other inmates; at Kragskovhede (15), 21% want more. So to a degree even greater than for items reflecting behavioral patterns of association and friendship, this single item regarding desires seems to bring out important institutional differences.

If the logic of our argument is correct, we would expect to find that the newer institutions, because they are more open and less socially depriving, should produce higher rates of contact and friendship formation, and correspondingly less need or desire for contact. But that

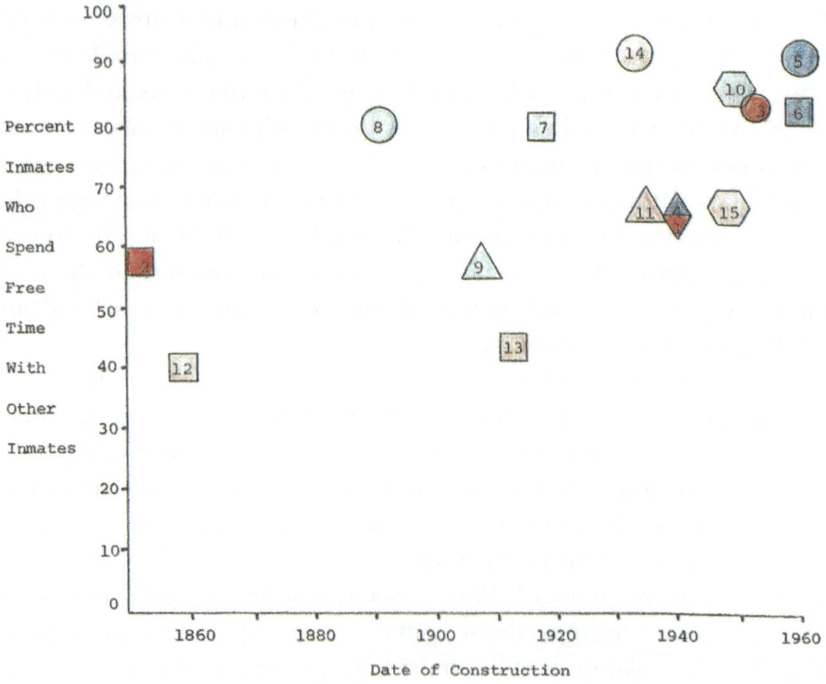

Fig. 3.2 The relationship of prison age to inmate association with other inmates ($r=.63$)

relationship should be due in large part to social deprivation rather than age itself. We thus anticipate that the relationships between the institution's date of origin and the actual amount of contact will be positive, but lower than the direct relationship between those structural features that reflect contact policy and actual patterns of contact.

That the first of these claims is true is suggested by Fig. 3.2, which shows the relationship between the age of the institution and the percentage of inmates who spend their free time in association with other inmates rather than by themselves. This relationship is the strongest of those relating institutional age to patterns of contact ($r=.63$). The newer the institution, the more likely inmates are to spend their free time with other inmates. The pattern holds even when we examine each country separately, with the single exception of the Danish youth

Table 3.2 Relationship between structural features and interaction patterns[a]

Indicators of contact and association	Construction Date	Social Deprivation	Interaction Potential
All fifteen prisons			
Number of informal contacts with other inmates	0.29	−0.51	−0.30
% of Inmates with one or more friends	0.45	−0.67	−0.52
% of Inmates with five or more friends	0.22	−0.61	−0.36
% of Inmates spending free time w/ other inmates	0.63	−0.83	−0.80
% of Inmates wanting more contact w/other Inmates	−0.49	0.52	0.62
Eleven adult prisons			
Number of informal contacts with other inmates	0.42	−0.54	−0.27
% of Inmates with one or more friends	0.64	−0.66	−0.43
% of Inmates with five or more friends	0.34	−0.55	−0.18
% of Inmates spending free time w/ other inmates	0.69	−0.82	−0.81
% of Inmates wanting more contact w/other Inmates	−0.59	0.64	0.69

[a]Entries are Pearson's r's

institution Sobysogard (14), where there is more association than might be expected on grounds of its age. But with that minor exception, each country illustrates what holds overall, with the oldest institution having the lowest rates of contact, the newest the highest, though in each country the rate and pattern of growth over time is somewhat different.

But the more general test is given in Table 3.2. This table shows, separately for all fifteen institutions and for the eleven adult institutions, the relative strength of the relationship between our measures of human association and the date of origin of the institution on one hand, and our measure of social deprivation on the other. And because these measures of contact relate to contacts between inmates rather than in association with the outside world, we also report the relationships between them and an index of limits on interaction, based solely on a calculation of the amount of time during a week in which an inmate is free to interact with other inmates if he so wishes.

Since Table 3.2 provides the evidence for the fullest and most general test of the relationship between structural possibilities and actual interaction processes, we will examine it in some detail. Perhaps the most important thing to note is the general consistency of the relationships presented there. No matter which of the five indicators of patterns of association (or attitudes toward it), no matter which structural feature we examine, no matter whether we test against all fifteen institutions or only the eleven adult institutions, the general result is the same: the more of it occurs, and the less it is felt to be needed. The relationships vary considerably in magnitude, from a low of +.22 (the newer the institution, the more inmates who have made five or more close friends) to a high of −.83 (the greater the social deprivation, the less the inmate spends his free time with other inmates). But it is the consistency that seems most crucial, and that so clearly documents a concern of prison reformers since de Tocqueville's time.

The relative strength of the relationships is also much as would be anticipated by the argument that the effect of age is largely through the structural features. Both the general measure of social deprivation and the more restricted one of limits on interaction bear substantially higher relationships to the various indicators of interaction patterns than does the sheer age of the institution alone. The general pattern holds in every possible comparison for the fifteen institutions, where the average correlation with date of origin is +.42, and with social deprivation it is −.63. And it is true in seven out of ten possible comparisons for the eleven adult institutions, though the patterns are less clear partly because the date of origin itself is much more strongly related to the patterns of interaction when the four youth institutions are removed from the analysis. (The average correlation with age is +.53, with social deprivation +.64, and limits on interaction +.48.) None of the three reversals or exceptions to the common pattern are of great magnitude: indeed they are smaller in the "reverse" direction than all but one of the seven comparisons that are in the expected direction.

It thus seems reasonable to conclude, to the extent that any causal inferences can be made from correlational data of this kind, that while the date of origin of the institutions bears a systematic relationship to the rates of interaction among its inhabitants, it does so mainly as a function of the relationship of institutional age to the structural possibilities for interaction that the physical plant and, to some degree, the operating rules of the institution allow.

Although we would emphasize the patterning and consistency of results rather than any particular relationship, one comment about particular relationships may be warranted. Note that the strongest relationships by far are those relating to how inmates spend their time when they are not locked in their rooms or cells. The fact of spending free time with others, more so than the actual making of close friends on the one hand, or the mere having of a conversation on the other, seems to be the most critical aspect of association or interaction as it relates both to age of the institution and to structural constraints on contact. Thus we suggest that a basic and primitive need for human association seems most powerfully related to institutional structure, rather than the more developed or intensive expression of human association caught up in the concept of close friendship—a result that is not surprising, but which we would not have been brave enough to predict.

Conclusion

Three main topics have occupied us in this chapter. First, we introduced the fifteen prisons in order from oldest to newest, in an effort to give some sense for the development of institutions over time. In that discussion, we were able to suggest some of the main themes of correctional development in the Scandinavian countries, themes which probably have their parallel in other areas of the western world—the declining emphasis on large custodial bastilles housing every type of offender to institutions with a more open, less custodial-oriented outlook, typically housing smaller groups of more homogeneous inmates.

Second, we examined the relationship between the institution's past history and ideology, as roughly indexed by its date of construction, and certain of its current structural features—features that characterize the institution as a whole rather than the backgrounds of its inmate inhabitants. The main results of that examination were to show the very strong relationship of the institution's date of arrival in society, and the extent to which it provides open avenues of interaction for its inmates, this relationship being much stronger than those reflecting the institution's staffing policies or features of its physical and material environment. We showed the interrelationships among the structural features, and then presented very briefly the alternative arguments that might explain the strong linkage between the institution's date of origin and the constraints it places on interaction among the inmates, stressing both the importance of physical structure as an expression of correctional ideology, and the related notion that institutions at a given point in time tend to get the inhabitants for which they were designed even though the ideology may have become somewhat outdated.

Our third and final task was to show the effects of those structural features that relate to inmate interaction on the actual patterns of interaction themselves. We moved, in effect, from the study of structural or ecological possibilities to the realm of behavioral actualities. We introduced several related indicators of the rate and intensity of interaction within the institutions, and then showed how that rate was a function of the possibilities for interaction built into the design, structure and rules under which the institutions were administered. As a part of this analysis, we showed the strength and consistency with which the actual patterns appear to be related to the potential for interaction and the strong relationship of the structural features, themselves dependent upon age of the institution. Finally, we noted that the single most powerful of the interaction measures, in relation both to age and to social deprivation measures, was the rate of group affiliation and association.

In sum, we think we have shown the interlinking sequence from ideology to ecology to behavior. Correctional ideology is built into the structure of an institution at its date of origin, thus constraining, through the powerful effects of physical design on behavior, the possibilities for open interaction and communication among inmates. These ecological constraints are reinforced by policies, themselves partly a result of the ecology, that govern the potential for interaction. The result is a powerful effect on the actual patterning of social life in the institutions we have studied, with wide variations across the institutions in the rate of group association and friendship formation.

In the next chapter we examine the social climate of the institutions, after which we shall return to examine the extent to which variations in that climate appear traceable to patterns of interaction. In the meantime, we conclude by noting that our findings would seem to give further credence and reinforcement to the crucial role assigned to constraints on interaction and association by penologists, historians, and sociologists of the prison, and, it goes almost without saying, by the prisoners themselves.

4

The Social Climate of the Prisons

The idea of the "climate" of an institution, an organization, or indeed any social system with a modicum of complexity is common to all of us from our daily lives. We speak of some systems as warm and inviting, others as cold; some as harsh, others as pleasant. These are ways of describing the "feeling tone" of the institution or agency in question in the eyes of its members. When we say that one organization is better than another as a place in which to work, we often have this sort of feeling tone in mind, in addition to more direct and mundane matters such as pay scales, job tenure and security, and retirement benefits.

Although a common phenomenon in daily experience, serious efforts to study the social climate of institutions or organizations do not have a long history. Perhaps the first attempts at such study were the investigations of the group climates produced by different styles of leadership—work spawned by the group dynamics movement under the influence of Kurt Lewin, and later associated with Ronald Lippitt and others at the University of Michigan.[1] They focused on the differences

[1]Kurt Lewin, Ronald Lippitt, and Robert K. White, "Patterns of Aggressive Behavior in Experimentally Created 'Social Climates'," *Journal of Social Psychology*, 1939, 10: 271–299.

S. Wheeler and H. F. Cline, *The Scandinavian Prison Study*,
Palgrave Studies in Prisons and Penology,
https://doi.org/10.1007/978-3-030-26462-8_4

between "authoritarian" and "democratic" leadership styles as creating group feeling tones that might encourage or discourage creativity and high levels of productivity. A principal achievement of their work was to establish the idea of social climate as a legitimate object of research.[2]

There are a variety of ways of approaching the study of the social climate of the prison. As in any institution that processes people, it is likely that the feeling tone will be reflected largely in the kinds of relationships that obtain between those doing the processing and those being processed—in this case between the staff and the inmates. We begin our analysis of the social climate of the prisons by focusing on three different aspects of inmate perceptions of the staff: (1) perceptions reflecting the amount of power and influence staff members have in the daily life of the institution; (2) the amount of understanding they show toward inmates; and (3) perceptions of the coerciveness of the prison regime as judged from items reflecting feelings about rules and regulations. We begin with the staff because they, after all, have more official authority in setting the tone for the institution. We then take up the relations between staff and inmates, particularly perceptions of competing pressures—from the staff to behave one way, and from inmates to behave another. Finally, we turn to the normative system of the inmates themselves, and to an effort to assess the extent to which the normative climate among the inmates is defined in opposition to staff norms.

Throughout, our assessment of social climate is based upon systematic questionnaire data in which inmates report their perceptions of the roles and views of others in the institution. We use these perceptions as a basis for making inferences regarding the social climate of the prison.

[2]For other work on-social climate, see G. Stern, "The Measurement of Psychological Characteristics of Students and Learning Environments," in *Measurement in Personality and Cognition*, eds. S. Messick and J. Ross (New York: Wiley, 1962); and Renato Tagiuri and George H. Litwin (Eds.), *Organizational Climate: Explorations of a Concept* (Boston: Harvard University Graduate School of Business Administration, 1968).

Before proceeding with our analysis, we should explain why we adopted the approach we did, rather than alternatives that might have been used.

The two most natural alternatives are contrasting ones. On the one hand, we could have used a much less formal instrument in order to ascertain the feeling tone of the institutions. We might simply have spent several days in observation of the daily rounds, and from that tried to make inferences regarding the relative amounts of power held by either the custody or the treatment staff, the relative coerciveness of the environment of the prison, the strength of the inmate normative system, and the like. As rich as observations based upon such informal experience in the institution may be, and important as they are in analyses of single institutions, they do not provide a realistic basis for assessment of the institutions relative to one another. First, the investigator can necessarily spend only a limited amount of time in each of the institutions in question, and he is therefore subject to limitations as to the number of inmates, staff, or institutional situations he can investigate. Unless he has done his "sampling" of situations very carefully, he may well draw conclusions about differences in the institutions that are based on differences in the particular constellation of events he witnessed, and these may not be valid indicators of the life of the institution. Secondly, he may have great difficulty in ordering this complex set of observations as between institutions. Which factors should be given the most weight? Is a dramatic observation in one institution worth three or four more mundane observations in another?

Questions of judgment must always be faced, of course, but these are complex judgments to make when one is trying to organize a massive body of information on a large number of institutions into a single comparative analysis. One necessarily surrenders the rich and variegated sense of institutional life that comes from ethnographic accounts of the institution, and that is typical of the best case studies of single institutions. We feel that it is a cost worth suffering if one can begin to develop general statements in which the institutions themselves are the principal units of observation, a task requiring measurement or assessment using some <u>standardized</u> instrument such as the questionnaire we employed.

But in turning away from the more informal means of assessing social climates, we could have turned to what might seem to be a more "objective" basis. We might have gone to great lengths to get objective measures of institutional functioning from which inferences could be made about the climate of the place. The numbers of items inmates have in their cells might be an index, for example, of the degree of the "spartan" quality of institutional life; the number and variety of foods served in the dining hall another index of an important part of the daily routine for inmates, and so on. Our measures of institutional functioning reported in Chapter 3 provide indirect evidence along these lines, but we could have gone much further and did not. The reason is simply that we feel these objective items of institutional functioning are at best a problematic basis for making inferences to the social climate of the institution. We feel that the best and most direct way of operationalizing that social climate is through the attributes and qualities that the institution's inmates and personnel are believed to have—that it is the aggregate perceptual world of the institution in the eyes of its members that provides the most direct evidence on the climate of the place. We therefore chose to measure those perceptions directly, rather than to devote our primary efforts to the development of objective checklists of institutional features.

The question still remains, of course, whether the dimensions of social climate we have chosen are the most crucial ones. We can give no precise answer to that question. The dimensions have grown out of our understanding of prison life and of the studies others have conducted into that life. We aimed for indicators of social climate that could be reliably responded to by inmates, and that would be general enough so that, hopefully, they would not be overly sensitive to particular conditions of administration, which necessarily varied somewhat from prison to prison.

In retrospect, if there is a bias in the indicators, it is a bias that may well have grown out of our much greater familiarity with the American prison scene, where conflict between inmates and staff is assumed to be endemic, and where it is therefore natural to emphasize the degree of that conflict in getting any sense for the climate of the institution in question. Other investigators will go about the operationalization in differing ways, and hopefully this will be treated as only one of the first of a series of efforts to assess on a broad scale the differing climates of prison regimes. It is enough for our purposes if the dimensions we have examined are relatively important in the daily life of the institutions in question, though surely their importance would not be articulated by either inmates or staff in the precise way in which we go about it.

Inmate Perceptions of Officials

Power, Understanding, and Their Interrelations

The two principal categories of staff in penal institutions are the custodial and the non-custodial staff. We begin our examination with an effort to assess the relative degree of influence over the daily life of the institution that these two categories of staff are perceived to have. In Fig. 4.1 we present the perceptions of the inmates for each of the fifteen institutions in our study. We will discuss this figure in some detail since a large portion of the analysis that follows is based on similar figures and modes of presentation. The figure reports inmate responses to two questions, one regarding the guards or custodial staff, and the other regarding treatment staff members. The numbers, symbols, and colors referring to the fifteen different institutions follow the conventions introduced in Chapters 2 and 3. In this figure the plot of each number represents, on the horizontal axis, the percentage of inmates who feel that guards in that institution have a significant influence over the daily life of inmates, and on the vertical axis, the same percentage for treatment staff members.[3] In this figure, as with all figures and tables in this chapter, all variables are percentages or transformations of percentages and are therefore ratio scales. Consequently, product-moment correlation coefficients will be reported throughout this chapter.

[3]We remind the reader that the term "treatment staff" broadly includes, in addition to persons engaged in therapeutic efforts, of whom there are very few in the prisons we studied, other non-custodial personnel working in education, vocational training, medical and psychiatric care, social work, classification, parole, and religion.

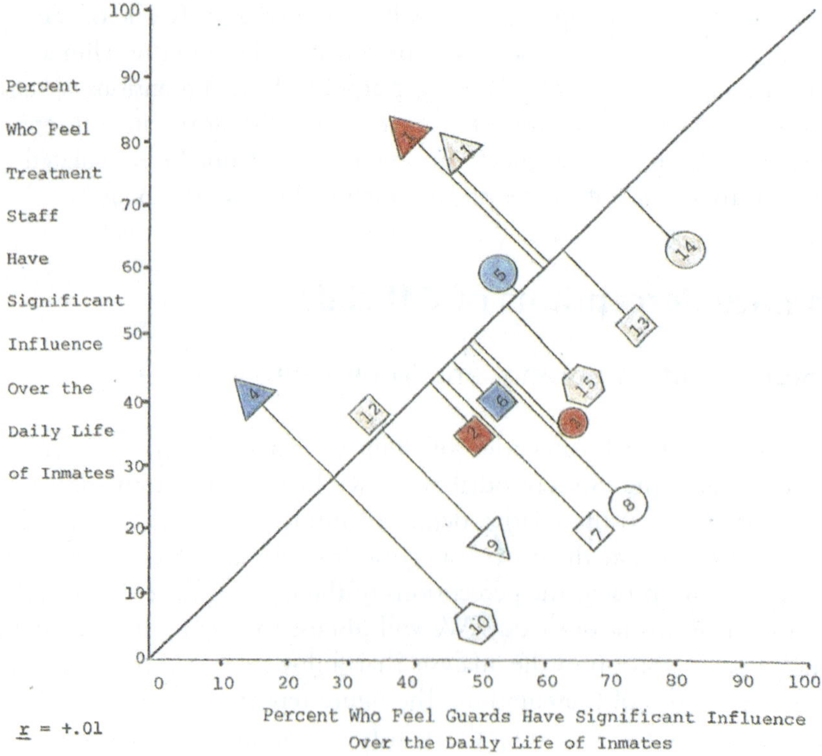

Fig. 4.1 The balance of power between guards and treatment staff

The diagonal line in the middle of the figure represents the point on which an institution would fall if the relative power of these two categories of staff were the same. Lines to the right and below the diagonal indicate that in the institution in question the guards are perceived to have more power than the treatment staff, while the reverse is true for lines above and to the left of the diagonal. The length of the lines gives an indication of the degree to which the balance of power is skewed in one direction or the other. It can be noted, for example, that in all the Finnish institutions (numbers 7, 8, 9 and 10) the balance is very strongly on the custodial side—indeed more so than for any other of the institutions in the other three countries. In all the Finnish institutions, then, the treatment staff are not influential in comparison to the guards. Later we will use this relative positioning on either side of the diagonal as a measure in its own right, reflecting the balance of power between the custodial and treatment staff.

A different dimension of power can be seen by different points of location on the diagonal. Institutions (4) and (10), though they differ in where the balance of power lies, are both institutions in which the two categories of staff taken together are perceived as having a relatively low degree of influence over the daily lives of inmates in the institution. Institutions (4) and (14), in contrast, show a marked difference. At Hall in Sweden (4), fewer than 40% of the inmates feel that the treatment staff has a significant influence over the daily life of inmates, and only 16% feel that the custodial staff has a significant influence. These figures contrast strongly with Sobysogard (14), the Danish youth institution, where 80% of the inmates feel that the custodial staff has a significant influence over the daily lives of the inmates, and 65% of the inmates feel similarly about the treatment staff. So here is an institution where the staff as a whole is considered to have a large degree of influence.

Several other observations may be made from Fig. 4.1. First, with the exception of the Finnish pattern already noted, there are no other striking differences that pattern out primarily by country. All the other countries have at least one institution on the "treatment" side of the custody-treatment balance, and they are split fairly widely along the diagonal. Thus even though the top three institutions along the diagonal are all Danish, one of the bottom four is also Danish.

A further observation concerns the relationship between the custody staff and the treatment staff. The product-moment correlation between these two dimensions is +.01, suggesting strongly that power neither accrues to one category of staff by virtue of its presence in the other, nor does one lose the power that the other gains. In other words, it would be inappropriate to conceive of custody staff and treatment staff as locked in a struggle for power which has the form of a zero-sum game. For at least as the inmates see it, it is quite possible for both groups to be powerful or for neither to be powerful, and for the balance to vary a good deal between them.

Let us concentrate on the three institutions where the balance of power is substantially on the side of the treatment staff. All three are "preventive detention" institutions, where inmates are judged to be only partially responsible for their actions, by dint of an emotional or pathological disorder. Institution (11), Herstedvester, served as a model throughout the world under the regime of its psychiatrist-director, Dr. Georg Sturup. It is a treatment-oriented penal institution specializing in a kind of social psychological therapy and run according to a medical model. The goals and organization of institution (1), Ila in Norway, were derived quite directly from Herstedvester. These are the two institutions in our study with the most explicit commitment to a medical-psychiatric model, and it is suggestive both of the power of those models and of the capacity of our instruments to differentiate meaningfully between institutions that these two institutions are located where they are in the figure.

It should be noted that institution (4), Hall, while being similar to Herstedvester and Ila in terms of the legal mandates for the institution and the type of inmates it receives, is different in the very important matter that the director is not a psychiatrist, and that the institution is not committed to a medical treatment model. Rather, there was a distinct effort made on the part of its then director, Gunnar Marnell, to play down the visibility and control of the staff—a fact undoubtedly responsible for the relatively low degree of staff influence perceived by its inmates.

Finally, note the dominance of custodial power over treatment staff power across the institutions as a whole. While it is extreme in the case of the Finnish institutions, it seems clear in the case of most of the others, save for the preventive detention institutions. In some cases, Norrtalje (6) and Mariefred (5) in Sweden, Vridsloselille (12) in Denmark, the power balance is perceived as being relatively equal between the two sides. But in no case, save those operating under the preventive detention mandate, is the power substantially on the side of the non-custodial personnel. From one point of view this merely documents "what everybody knows"—that prisons are for the holding of inmates and that custodial authority must be dominant. But it should surely serve as a guard against those who too quickly assume, because

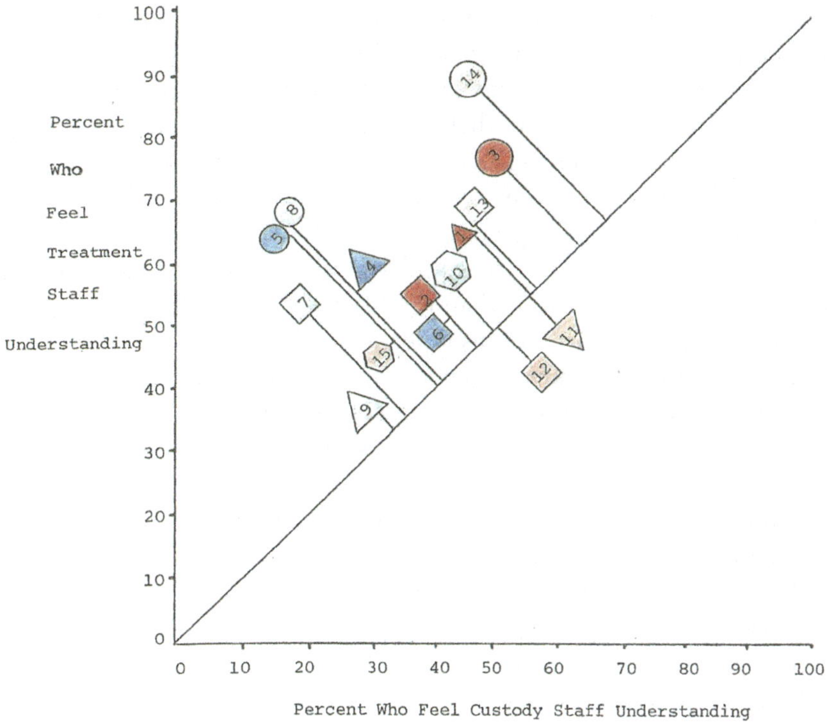

Fig. 4.2 The balance of understanding between custody and treatment staff ($r = -.10$)

many institutions speak and talk through a language of rehabilitation and therapy, that the daily life of the inmate is necessarily strongly affected thereby relative to the power lying within the guard staff.

We turn now to inmate perceptions of the degree of understanding staff members show for inmates' problems. Figure 4.2 shows the "balance of understanding" between custody staff and treatment staff as perceived by the inmates. Two observations are apparent from even a cursory inspection of the figure. First and most clearly, just as the balance of power was typically on the side of the custody staff, so the balance of understanding is on the side of the treatment staff. Only two of the fifteen institutions show this balance to be reversed. From one point of view, this finding simply documents cultural expectations regarding the role of custody versus treatment staff. Although in the modern prison all staff members are supposed to be understanding and empathic toward the problems raised by inmates, it is the special role of the treatment staff to take these interests into view in their own conduct with regard to inmates. Indeed the very definition of the staff as "treatment" may induce inmates to perceive them that way, such that the inmates are merely repeating a cultural stereotype when they say that the treatment staff is more understanding than the custody staff. We think there is more to it than that, but it is difficult to separate the two empirically with data of this type.

The second observation is that the items with regard to the understanding of the staff toward the inmates in comparison with the power and influence items do not produce as clear a separation of institutions, either in terms of the balance between custody and treatment or in terms of their location along the diagonal. We think that of the two dimensions, the dimension of influence and power is much more salient in the daily lives of inmates than is the dimension of understanding, and that the former is probably a more important indicator of the climate of the institution than is the latter.

This feeling is based in part upon our knowledge of the relatively low rates of interaction between the inmates and the staff, such that even if staff are generally helpful and understanding when they meet individually with inmates, the occurrences themselves are seldom frequent enough to make for a meaningful influence in the life of the institution. At the same time, real differences are suggested by the relative positions of the two youth institutions, Berg (3) and Sobysotgard (14), at the top of the "understanding" scale; and of the Finnish institutions, Turku (9) and Konnunsuo Central Prison (7), at the bottom.

It may also be significant that the two institutions with the balance most strongly in favor of the treatment staff (though at very different levels) are youth institutions, and that one of the two institutions where the balance is greatest on the custodial side is the internationally known treatment center, Herstedvester (11). At a later point we will examine in more detail the differential effects of our two primarily psychiatrically oriented treatment institutions (Herstedvester and Ila) relative to normal prisons. Here it may simply be noted that the balance on the

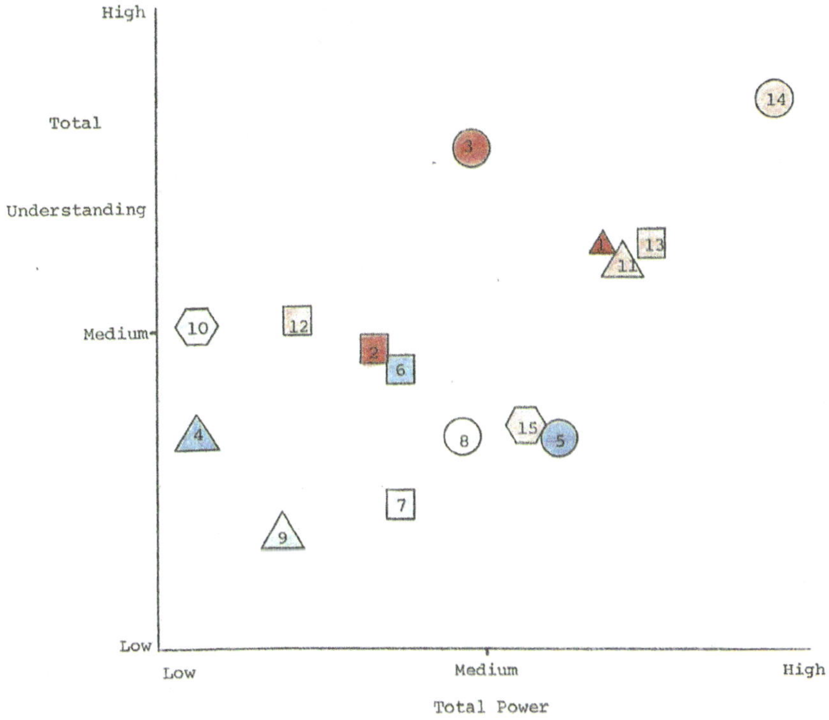

Fig. 4.3 The relationship of total power to total understanding ($r = .58$)

custodial side and the relatively low ranking of the treatment staff at a treatment institution may represent a form of inmate reaction to what is publicly defined as a treatment center, or perhaps a shifting of the balance of understanding toward the custody staff where the treatment staff has the balance of power. This is clearly not the universal rule since Ila, the other primary treatment institution, shows a balance that remains on the treatment side.

We would like to explore more closely the relationships between the total amount of power and understanding reflected in our figures, and the balance of power and understanding as between the custody and treatment staffs. Figure 4.3 shows the relationship between total power and total understanding. The total measures are formed by adding the percentages of inmate who perceive treatment staff and custody staff as

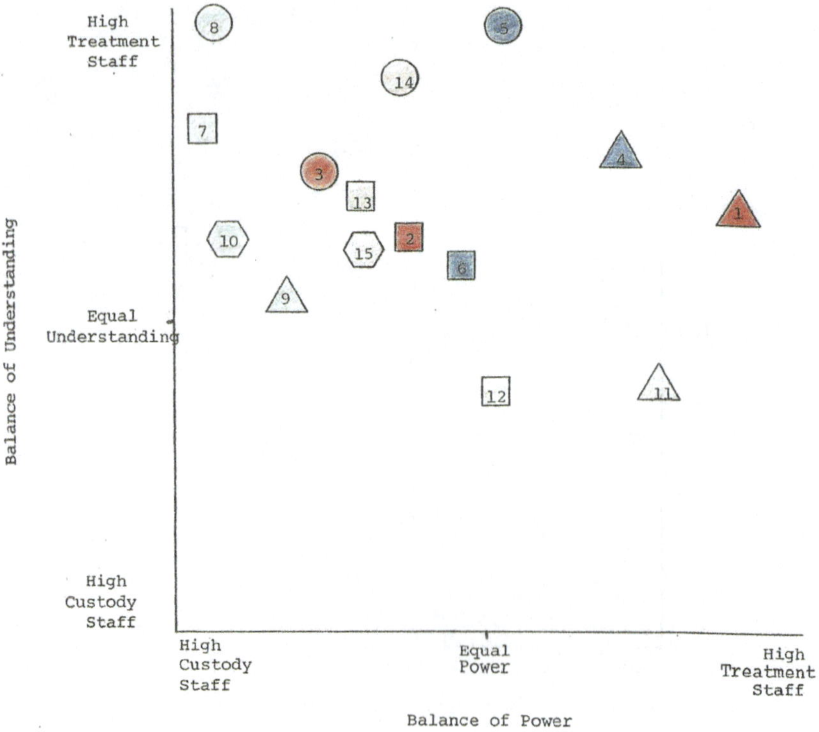

Fig. 4.4 The relationship of the balance of power to the balance of understanding ($r=-.25$)

having power and understanding. It is clear from that figure that as total power increases, so does total understanding. Indeed, the product-moment correlation between the two is +.58. There are virtually no institutions where power is non-existent and understanding very high, though perhaps our institution for drunken drivers in Finland (10) comes closest to that point. Similarly, there are no institutions where power is everywhere and understanding non-existent.

It is interesting that as the total power increases, the balance of power moves slightly toward the treatment staff ($r=-.23$). But where the balance of power moves toward the treatment staff, the balance of understanding shifts toward custody. This is shown in Fig. 4.4. Again, the correlation is not high ($r=-.25$), but it is suggestive of the general

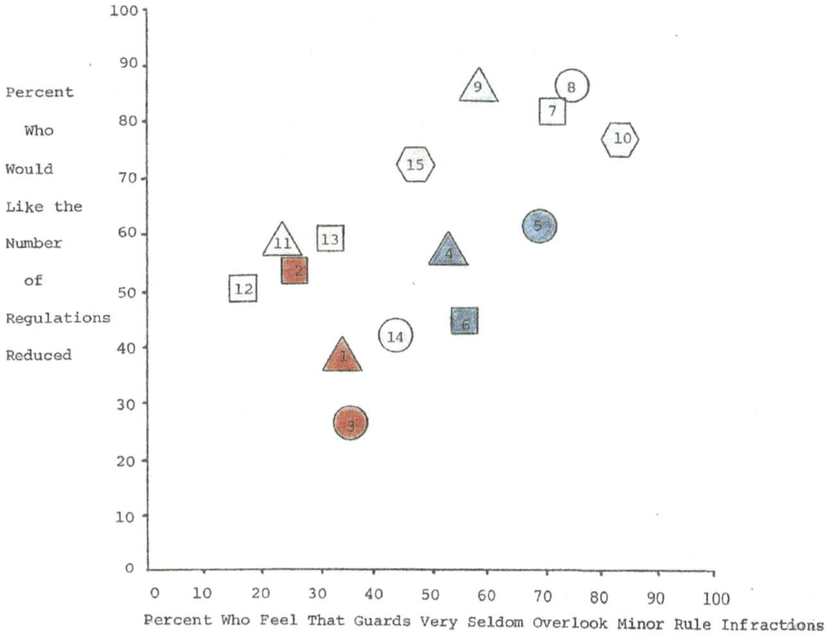

Fig. 4.5 The relationship between two items reflecting coerciveness of the prison regime

relationship between the two for our institutions as a whole. It suggests a kind of "you can't have your cake and eat it too" principle: the group that is weaker in power is the one perceived to be more sympathetic or understanding and vice versa (Fig. 4.5).

Coerciveness as an Element of Social Climate

The position of Kragskovhede on these aspects of coerciveness is interesting and could be viewed as anomalous, given the fact that Kragskovhede has been described as having the best treatment program in the Western world. Our field observations give us a clear indication of why this may be the case. On the one hand, Kragskovhede is an open colony with no walls, and extraordinarily easy opportunities to escape if an inmate is so minded. At the same time it is a colony for recidivists, and the staff are clearly mindful of the risks of escape. Lacking the physical constraints against escape, the staff themselves must engage in the control of men in the institution, serving through their own behavior as the replacement for walls and fences that constrain men in closed environments. The result is that the inmates at Kragskovhede have the sense of being guarded and watched more closely than those in institutions that are walled. One is reminded of the experiment at the Norfolk prison in Massachusetts, where some fifty years ago a prison reformer designed an institution with double walls and with absolutely no opportunity to escape, so that the inside could be run relatively freely like a college community.[4] In any event, our impression is that the total power of the institution lies in some combination of its rules and physical constraints on the one hand, the constraints imposed by its personnel on the other, and it may well be that these two maintain a kind of functional balance.

Again, it is clear from this figure that our institutions vary widely in the extent to which they give a sense of coerciveness both within and between countries, with percentages ranging from 15 to 81% with regard to enforcement of rules, and 25–85% with regard to desires to have the number of rules reduced. These two items appear to be relatively sensitive barometers of this aspect of the climate of institutions.

Let us now examine how the coerciveness of the institutions is related to the other aspects of climate we have already introduced. First, coerciveness bears a stronger relationship to the balance of power than it does to the total power of the staff: its correlation with custody staff balance of power is +.66, though it is only +.24 with custody staff power itself. So in one sense, coerciveness is a characteristic in systems dominated by custodial concerns. The relationship is shown in Fig. 4.6.

Another element of the prison climate which is highly correlated with coerciveness concerns the total understanding of the custodial and treatment staff. We find that the greater the coerciveness of the environment, the less the sense that the staff understands the inmate point

[4]The Norfolk Prison Experiment. See, for example, M. S. Serrill, "Norfolk—A Retrospective—New Debate Over a Famous Prison Experiment," *Corrections Magazine*, August 1982, 8(4): 25–32.

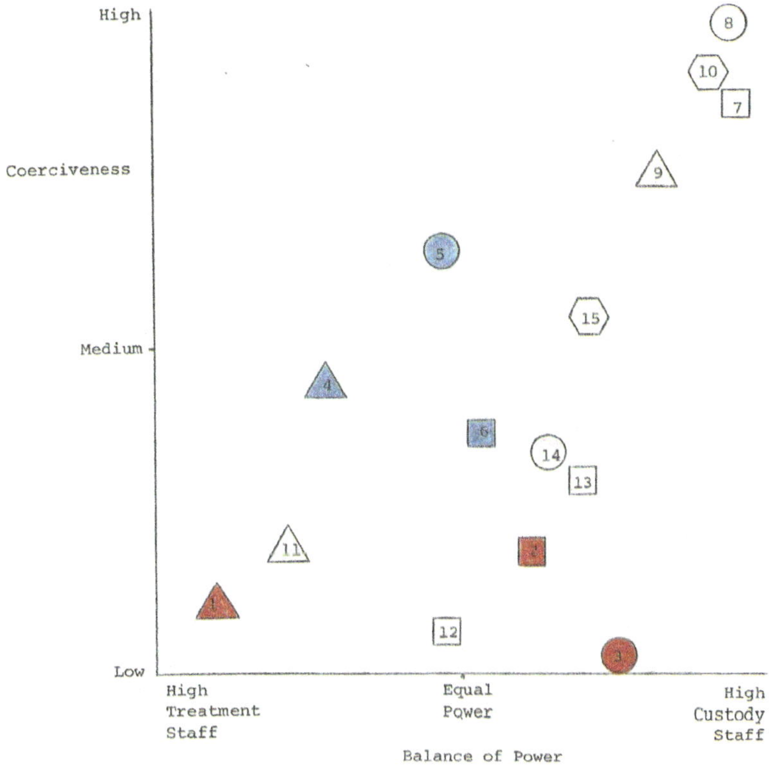

Fig. 4.6 The relationship of coerciveness to balance of power ($r = .66$)

of view ($r = -.68$). This relationship between coerciveness and understanding is portrayed in Fig. 4.7.

Again, it is not surprising to find that those institutions perceived by inmates as most coercive tend also to be institutions where the staff is believed to lack understanding of inmate perspectives. But it provides further evidence of the general consistency of the findings relating to inmate perceptions of the staff, findings we might provisionally summarize as follows: there is wide variation across these institutions in the extent to which the staff are perceived as powerful, and as to which category of staff are so perceived, though custodial staff are generally perceived as more powerful than treatment staff. There is a similarly wide

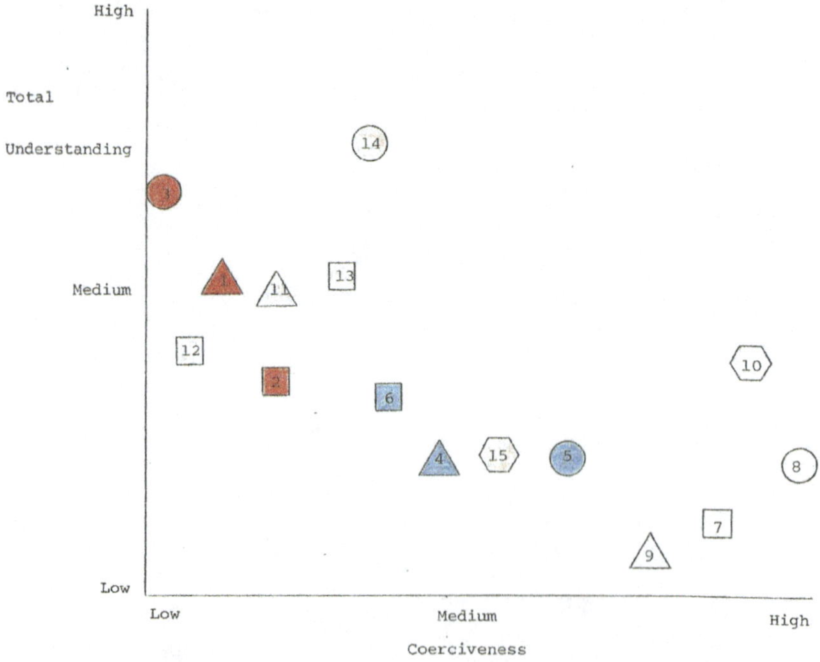

Fig. 4.7 Relationship between coerciveness and total understanding of prison staff ($r = -.68$)

variation in the extent to which the institutions are felt to be coercive as judged from inmate responses to items about rules and their enforcement. There is less variation in inmate responses to the felt capacity of the staff to understand the inmates' point of view, though the balance here, unlike the balance of power, lies clearly on the side of the treatment staff. And when we examine the interrelationships of the indices, we begin to see the importance of the power dimension, and particularly the balance of power. As total power increases and as the balance of power moves toward the treatment staff, the staff are generally perceived to be more understanding and the environment less coercive. We move, in effect, from environments where emphasis is on custody, with high rates of coerciveness and low rates of understanding, to institutions that are more in the hands of treatment personnel, and that are seemingly more permissive and understanding environments.

Relations Between Staff and Inmates: The Development of Competing Pressures

We have begun by tracing inmate perceptions of the staff, but we could hardly proceed very far before getting into the relations between staff and inmates. One of the most persistent themes in the literature of the prison and of other institutions that process people is the propensity for a strained relationship between those being held, treated, trained, and those doing the holding, treating, and training. Many of the case studies of prison environments give testimony to the importance of the quality of the relationship between keepers and kept as the key to understanding the prison.

Staff in every total institution have a preferred way of thinking about the relationship between staff and inmates. In the history of American prisons, staff, it seems, have generally been suspicious of any tendency on the part of inmates to group together and develop their own norms and belief systems. They have therefore encouraged inmates to look out for themselves, stay out of involvements with other inmates, "keep your nose clean," and obey staff rules and orders. In more recent years, with the development of various forms of group counseling and in some cases forms of inmate self-government, new modes of relation between staff and inmate have been called for, but often resisted for fear they will undermine the ultimate authority of the staff. In any event, the extent to which these two castes in the prison—the staff and the inmates—manage to create a conflict situation for each other is a crucial and oft-noted aspect of the social climate of the prison, and we want to examine it in some detail.

But it is not the easiest concept to operationalize. Our own approach to assessment of this concept was to speak directly of competing pressures, of pressure applied by inmates concerning an inmate's relation with staff, and of pressure applied by staff concerning that same relationship. Although we initially attempted to assess this concept by examining three different aspects of the relationship between inmates and staff, one item proved to be highly correlated with the other two, somewhat more ubiquitous as a dimension across all settings, and

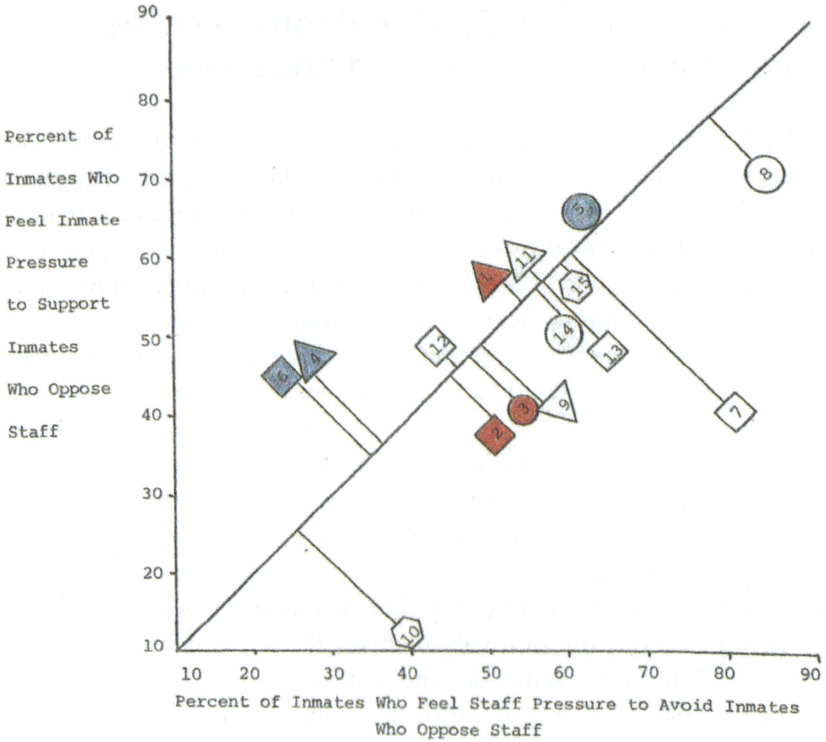

Fig. 4.8 Balance of pressure between inmates and staff ($r = .53$)

perhaps most reflective of the "basic" quality of relationship between inmates and staff. It is the one we report on in detail here. Each inmate was asked how often staff members in his institution try to get inmates "to keep away from inmates who oppose the staff?" He was also asked how often inmates in his institution tried "to get other inmates to support those inmates who oppose the staff?" As in Fig. 4.1 on power relations between custody and treatment staff, we show the results in Fig. 4.8 simultaneously for both felt pressure from staff and from inmates so that the relation of the two can be more easily examined.

We begin by noting one major difference between the figure reporting power relationships and this one. In the former the two aspects of power were unrelated. The relationship between them was non-existent, and we had to think of power neither as an attribute lost by one category of staff as it was gained by another, nor as something gained by one component because of its presence in the other. But here the situation is different: the more inmates tend to feel pressure from one side of the equation, the more they come to feel it from the other. The pattern is by no means uniform, nor is the correlation of +.53 anywhere near perfect, and the pattern is unclear in the middle. But especially at relatively low and high ends of the pressure indices, the two tend to go together. We cannot tell whether one side initiates the pressure and is then responded to by the other, or whether each makes incremental shifts in response to the other. But the result makes for a very clear difference in the feeling tone in different institutions.

Consider the difference between two institutions both in Finland. Seutula (10), the open colony for relatively short term offenders of the less serious type, finds virtually no pressure being exerted by inmates against other inmates. It is hardly the kind of a place one would think of in connection with the usual stereotypes of a hostile inmate society in revolt against a brutal regime. Kerava (8), however, presents the opposite picture: over 80% of its young inhabitants feel pressure from staff, and over 70% encounter pressure from other inmates. This sort of tension between the two could be clearly felt during field visits. Although the balance of pressure in both institutions, as in others in Finland, is clearly on the staff side, the enormous difference in degree of felt tension and pressure was evident in walking the grounds of the two institutions, one a walled and well protected prison for young offenders, and the other a relatively pastoral working colony for adults. The latter had been characterized, as we learned, by relatively easy relations between staff and prisoners, and the former by a history of difficult and inharmonious relationships.

A second point concerns the relative range of responses concerning staff and inmates. The institutions are less differentiated by the inmate pressures than by the staff. With the exception of Seutula, the effective range of response for felt pressure from other inmates is about 35%, from 40 to 75%. For feelings about staff pressure, however, it is close to 60%. We don't know whether this is a stable trait of correctional systems, but it is clear enough in our material to be worthy of comment. Staff, of course, as the formal authorities in the institution, can do more to control the feeling tone than can inmates and it may be that real differences in staff policies are perceived and reacted to by the inmates and reflected in their responses.

A final point about Fig. 4.8 concerns the balance of pressure. Save for the aforementioned Finnish pattern, there are few sizeable departures from the diagonal line representing "equal" pressure from the two sides. The longer departures on the inmate side tend to be at low ends of the staff pressure scale; indeed there is a negative correlation between the total pressure (a summation of the two separate measures) and having the balance of pressure on the inmate side. In other words, there is a slight tendency for inmate pressure to occupy the vacuum left when staff pressure is low. But perhaps the most important point to note about the pressure flowing from either inmates or staff is that, save for the Finnish institutions, the number of prisons where inmates feel more pressure from inmates than from staff is the same as the reverse pattern where staff pressures dominate. In five institutions the balance is on the inmate side, in five on the staff side, and in one, Mariefred (5) in Sweden, the pressures are equally balanced between inmates and staff. In other words, despite the obvious fact that the authorities are in command and inmates are expected to subjugate themselves to official authority, the pressures from inmates to oppose the staff appear to be about equal to the pressure from staff to pay no attention to such opposition. At Norrtalje (6) and Hall (4) in Sweden, at Vridslosselille (12) and Herstedvester (11) in Denmark, and Ila (1) in Norway, more inmates report feeling pressure from other inmates than report feeling pressure from the officials. So the two sides are stuck in what is evidently felt by inmates as a relatively balanced system of pulls and pushes, with the inmate side of the ledger at least holding its own and in some institutions being more insistent in the pressures it exerts than are the officials of the institution.

We turn now to the question: what is it that explains why the balance of pressure is on the staff or the inmate side? Our attention is immediately drawn to those dimensions of social climate we have just examined, because the single variable in our study that relates most strongly

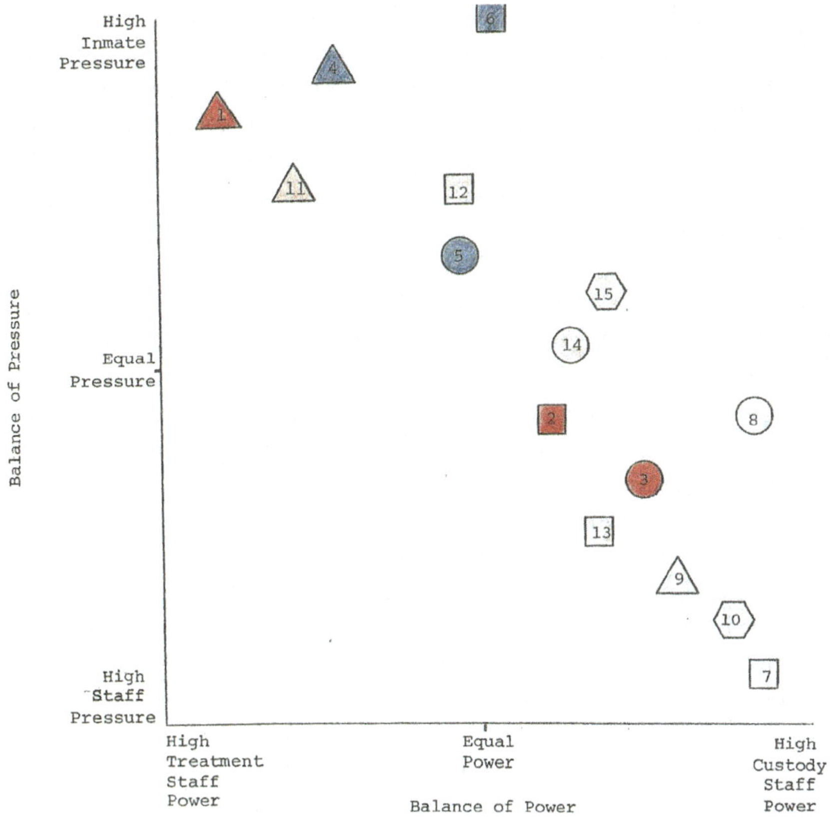

Fig. 4.9 The relationship between balance of power and balance of pressure ($r = .84$)

to the balance of pressure is the balance of power. The relationship is portrayed in Fig. 4.9. As the balance of power shifts from the custodial to the non-custodial staff, the balance of pressure shifts from staff to inmates. This relationship is one of the strongest in our study ($r = .84$) and is equally strong when only the adult institutions are examined ($r = .87$). Similarly, though less powerfully, our measure of coerciveness is negatively related to the balance of pressure being on the inmate side. It is the less coercive environments where inmate pressure tends to be greater than that of the staff.

We find this an intriguing result for several reasons. First, it suggests the sensitivity of the inmate population to the changing balance of authority and power relations in the prison, a phenomenon often noted in case study accounts but seldom documented across a range of institutions. Second, it seems entirely consistent with, indeed tends to reinforce, commonsense interpretations of the role of strict rules and regulations and the running of a "tight ship," namely, that when these procedures are relaxed and a more permissive regime is introduced, the sources of influence and pressure on the inmate become other inmates rather than the staff. And third, it seems to go beyond many of the accounts of such phenomena in the prison by systematically linking, or at least strongly suggesting the link between the changing balance of power among officials, and its relation to power among inmates. For most accounts of the battles between custody and treatment for control of institutions give little explicit attention to the effect of the outcome of that struggle on the normative pressures coming from the inmate side. Our results suggest that, at least as it has been working in the Scandinavian institutions, the transfer of authority from custodial to non-custodial personnel is accompanied both by a slight lessening of the general sense of pressure in the institution (the correlation between custody staff balance of power and total pressure is +.16) but much more significantly by a shift in the balance of that pressure from staff to inmates. And that leads us quite naturally into a closer look at the normative world generated among the inmates themselves.

The Normative Order Among Inmates

Our measure of the competing pressures on inmates emanating from staff and other inmates begins to get us into the inmate normative system itself, but only partially. A fuller and more intensive assessment of that order is essential to any full understanding of the social climate of the prison. For the idea of an inmate normative system defined in opposition to that of the staff has been a mainstay of both correctional ideology and of sociological analysis. And while this concern has dominated the American correctional scene more so than that of the Scandinavian countries, it has by no means been absent there. We therefore made an effort to develop a valid index of the extent to which the inmate culture in each prison stressed opposition to the staff and to conventional, conforming conduct. Our approach to measurement of this dimension of inmate life was derived from earlier work in the United States and will be reviewed briefly here.

We make the assumption that what is important in assessing the normative system of the inmates is not what each inmate privately believes or values. Although such beliefs or values may be crucial in determining at least in part his own response to the prison, they can have little effect on inmate culture as a whole unless they are communicated to other inmates and thus enter the perceptual world of the other inmates. The important element, then, is what values, opinions, and attitudes other inmates are perceived to hold. Of course, if each inmate simply assumed that his own views were those of his fellows, there would be no difference between his private expression of beliefs and his sense of what others believe. But there is good reason both in the literature of social psychology and in studies of the prison to assume that more than this simple process of projection is going on—specifically, that there is often a systematic bias in the perception of social norms, such that the norms are perceived to be rather different than the aggregate of the private belief systems of each inmate. The reasons are many, but chief among them is the common idea that some people are much more visible and expressive than others, and that some, therefore, have a larger voice in establishing the normative climate of the institution than do others. The remainder may not express their views openly, especially if they sense their own views are not shared. One name given to this pattern is that of "pluralistic ignorance."[5]

Since we had a strong interest in both the privately expressed beliefs of inmates which we will examine more closely in later chapters, and in their perceptions of the beliefs held by others, we gathered data with

[5]Floyd H. Alport, *Social Psychology* (Boston: Houghton Mifflin, 1924). See also Stanton Wheeler, "Role Conflict in Correctional Communities," in *The Prison Studies in Institutional Organization and Change*, ed. Donald R. Cressey (New York: Holt-Rinehart-Winston, 1961), pp. 229–259.

regard to both interests through use of a common set of questions with two sets of answers, one expressing the inmate's own personal response, and the other expressing his estimate of other inmates' responses to the same question. Our questions were based on hypothetical situations drawn from the life of the prison, questions which we had used in an earlier American investigation but which, after pretesting, seemed applicable with minor modifications to the Scandinavian setting.

For example, one question reads:

Inmates Jansen and Lund are very good friends. Jansen has some money that was smuggled into the institution by a visitor. Jansen tells Lund he thinks the officers are suspicious, and asks Lund to hide the money for him for a few days. Lund takes the money and carefully hides it.

How do you personally feel about Lund hiding the money?

Strongly approve
Approve
Disapprove
Strongly disapprove

How many inmates in this institution do you think would approve of what Lund did?

Almost all would approve
About three-fourths would approve
About half would approve
About one-fourth would approve
Almost none would approve

The other items used in our index stress similar conflict situations between inmates and staff, and ask both for the inmate's personal response, and for the response he assumes others would give. The other items are as follows:

An inmate, without thinking, commits a minor rule infraction. He is given a "write-up" by a correctional officer who saw the violation. Later two other inmates are talking to each other about it. One of them criticizes the officer. The other inmate, Hansen, defends the officer, saying the officer was only doing his duty.

How do you personally feel about Hansen defending the guard?
How many inmates in this institution do you think would approve of Hansen defending the guard?

Inmate Olsen goes before a committee that makes job assignments. He is given a choice between two jobs. One job would call for hard work, but it would give Olsen training that might be useful to him on the outside. The other job would allow Olsen to do easier time in the institution, but it provides no training for a job on the outside. Olsen decides to take the easier job.

What do you personally think about Olsen taking the easier job?
How many inmates in this institution do you think would approve of what Olsen did?

From the inmates' answers to these questions, we can compute a composite score for each institution reflecting the average beliefs of men in that institution, both as privately expressed and as perceived.[6] The results of this scoring are shown in Fig. 4.10. The figure tells us something in its own right, and it is useful in providing an explanation for two of the measures we will report on in more detail below.

Figure 4.10 shows that the two measures are quite strongly related, as we would expect: institutions where many inmates have private beliefs conforming to staff norms are also likely to have higher estimates of the number of other inmates who conform ($r=.69$). This surely should be the case. For if many inmates really do hold attitudes and values that are out of conformity with those of the staff, it should come to be known and perceived, at least to some degree, by other inmates. Thus Seutula (10), to use it yet again as an example, is an institution where most inmates hold conventional values and where they presume other inmates do also—and by and large they are right.

[6] For details on the construction of all indices, see Appendix (Editors note: This Appendix was not completed).

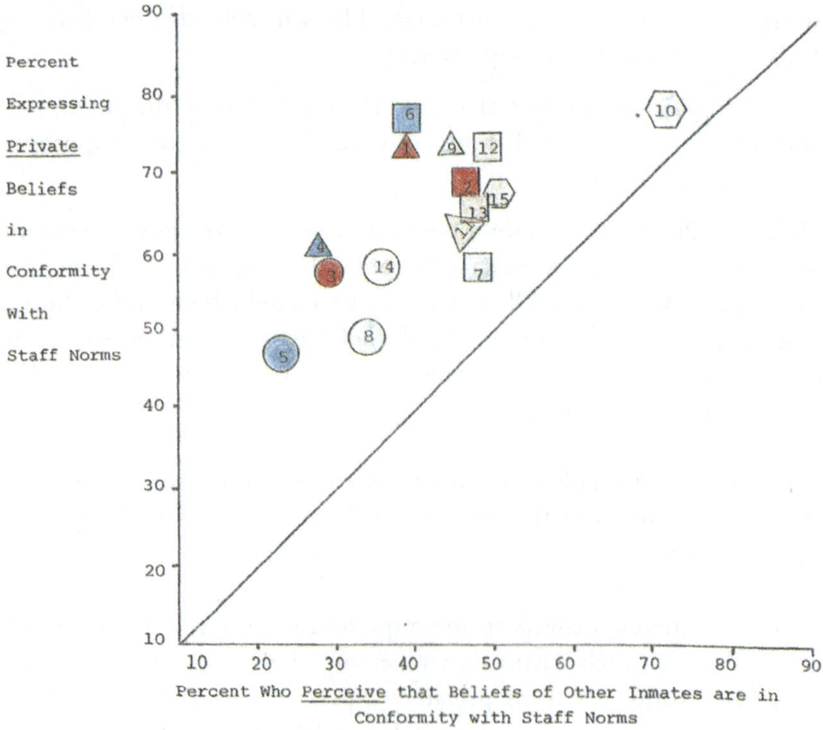

Fig. 4.10 The relationship between private and perceived conformity ($r = .69$)

But what is even clearer is that the "pull" of the normative system is toward the anti-staff position. There is not a single institution (though there are a few individual inmates in each institution) where the average inmate thinks he holds views that are more at odds with the staff than other inmates. For every prison in our study, including Seutula (10), the average inmate thinks that others are at least slightly more at odds with conventional norms than he is. In other words, in each institution, the average inmate is more of a conformist to staff norms than he thinks others are! The normative pull is away from the staff and from conventional societal norms.

Now we should ponder that for a moment for it is likely that the same general tendency might be found in a study of nursing homes, insurance companies, manufacturing plants, and banks, shipping companies, department stores—wherever a group of people, be they workers, prisoners, students, trainees or whatever, are being judged and formally controlled by faculty, administrators, employers, or bosses.[7]

But whatever might be true elsewhere, we think this is probably a basic fact of life in confinement and of life as an officially defined deviant. The conflict between keepers and kept is indeed a basic one. Rarely can a day go by without the inmate being aware of his status as a captive and a deviant. Most of us don't want to see ourselves as deviants. There are strong norms against it. We would like to believe that eventually, ultimately, we will be accepted and valued and therefore we reject deviant labels. What this means in the prison setting is that most inmates privately see themselves as basically more conforming to broad societal mandates. There are few true revolutionaries in prison, and many more persons whose prison stay is experienced as a stay in a kind of moral limbo. They may have done something wrong but they are not basically wrong, or sick, or weak, or at odds with society. Most inmates still feel a basic tie to the society that confines them, experience the confinement as rejection, and tend by and large to want reinstatement in that society. Most inmates covertly believe they are not as negative in attitude as their cellmates, their work partners, or their teammates in sporting events. Hence, a basic perception that others are more deviant than they. So it is not surprising to find that the basic tendency in all these institutions is for inmates to feel that others hold more hostile oppositionist attitudes than they do.

We shall return to questions of private conformity in later chapters but want here to concentrate on two main ways of assessing the normative order of the institution as a whole. One way is simply to use the institutions' ranking on perceived norms as an index itself. It tells us, in effect, in which institutions the normative pull is most strongly against the staff. Note from Fig. 4.10 that four of the five institutions with norms perceived to be most opposed to staff are youth institutions,

[7]Indeed, for a similar tendency in a very different setting see Raymond C. Baumhart, "How Ethical Are Businessmen?" *Harvard Business Review*, 1961, 39: 6–19,156–176.

and of course the most extreme institution at the other end of the scale is Seutula (10). This suggests among other things the importance of personal background variables such as age and prior criminality in contributing to the normative climate. Young men, as we shall see in detail later, are more likely to hold anti-staff values and in part, this is the reason institutions holding young men are high in anti-staff orientations. We will look at such factors in a moment but here want simply to note their potential influence, and to introduce the idea of perceived normative climate as a relevant measure.

A second measure is based on the assumption that stress for inmates will be greater in institutions where there is a wide gap between privately held views and the views perceived to be held by others. We have already noted that the two are interrelated, but as Fig. 4.10 shows, there is great variation in the degree to which the two are the same for any institution. Compare, for example, Konnunsuo (7) with Turku (9). The two fall at nearly the same point on our index of perceived normative climate, the climate being perceived as slightly more conforming at Konnunsuo. But there is a major difference in the level of private conformity, with Turku's inmates being much more conformist than those at Konnunsuo. The gap, therefore, between private and perceived norms is much greater at Turku and, hence, we would argue the normative climate is more stressful. Employing this general idea systematically, we constructed an index of normative stress by subtracting the mean private response score for an institution from the mean of the perceived response. The greater the difference, the greater the normative stress. And we employ both the actual level of perceived conformity or nonconformity, and the gap between perceived and privately expressed norms, as two main indicators of the normative climate in the institutions.

The two indices are themselves related in a revealing way. As Fig. 4.11 shows, the greater the perceived nonconformity, the greater the difference between perceived and private nonconformity ($r = .62$). Thus as the normative order becomes more strongly opposed to the staff, there is a greater gap between the perceived and the private world and hence a greater sense of felt stress. The tendency then is for institutions with high rates of anti-staff feeling, as indexed by our measure

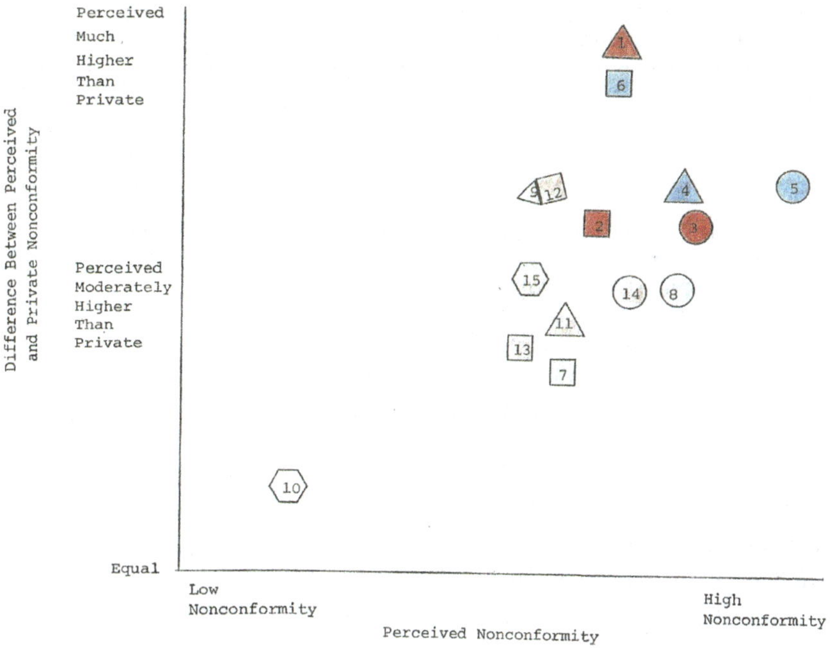

Fig. 4.11 The relationship of perceived norms to the gap between perceived and privately expressed norms ($r = .62$)

of perceived nonconformity, to also be places where there is a relatively larger gap between what an inmate himself believes and what he thinks others believe. One might say that the anti-staff normative order presents the problem for staff of having inmates in a posture of opposition, and that it simultaneously presents a problem for inmates in the greater gap between private beliefs and public perceptions. We would guess that the mechanism generating this relationship is something like the following: where an institution contains only a relatively mild degree of opposition among its inmates, relatively few visible acts of challenge to the staff occur; nor is there great talk about hostility of inmates toward staff and related subjects. But as the culture of the inmates turns somewhat more negative, more acts occur, even though perhaps by only a small number of inmates, that generate the perception that others are greatly opposed to the staff. In this manner,

Table 4.1 The relationship between staff social climate indices and measures of the normative order among inmates[a]

		Perception of anti-staff climate	Normative stress (perceived) minus private beliefs
	All fifteen prisons		
A.	Custody staff balance of power	0.22	0.44
B.	Coerciveness	0.11	0.25
C.	Inmate balance of pressure	−0.29	−0.51
	Eleven adult institutions		
A.	Custody staff balance of power	0.51	0.49
B.	Coerciveness	0.29	0.45
C.	Inmate balance of pressure	−0.57	−0.59

[a]Entrees are tau_b correlations

the perceived social world of the prison may take on a climate that is increasingly at odds with the values of its individual members.

We now turn to the relationship of the measures we have already introduced to these indicators of the normative order. Table 4.1 shows the relationships of these two measures to the three measures we have already introduced in connection with inmate–staff relationships, namely the balance of power between custody and treatment staff, coerciveness, and the balance of pressure between inmates and staff. What the pattern clearly shows is that the anti-staff normative climate apparently thrives in settings where the power of the staff is relatively greater on the treatment side, where coerciveness is low, and where the balance of pressure between inmates and staff tends to be on the inmate side. The pattern is stronger for the measure of balance of pressure, and is also consistently stronger for the measure of normative stress (perceived minus privately expressed norms).

A closer sense for the patterning of these relationships can be gleaned from Figs. 4.12 and 4.13 which present diagrammatically the relationships between our index of the balance of pressure, and our two measures of the normative climate. They suggest again, though more clearly for our measure of normative stress than for perceived nonconformity, the degree to which the anti-staff climate and its associated stress tend to be found in those institutions where the balance of pressure between inmates and staff has already tipped toward the inmates.

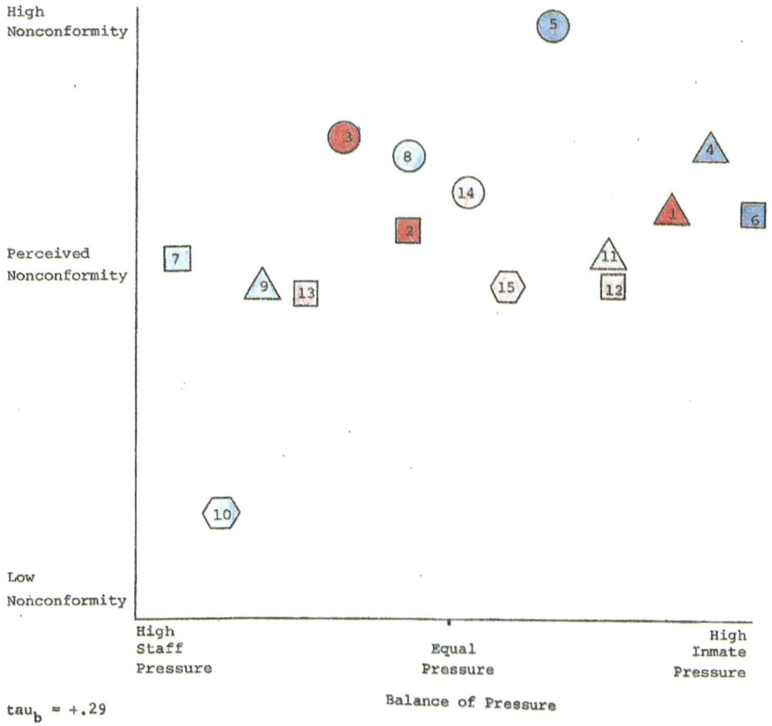

Fig. 4.12 The relationship between perceived nonconformity and the balance of pressure between staff and inmates

And they take us full circle in our examination of social climate in the prison—from inmates' perceptions of staff, to their perceptions of the relationships between staff and inmates, to their perceptions of the normative standards held by their fellows. To make the clearest and most direct interpretation: inmate culture, as represented by an anti-staff normative climate, tends to flourish where staff power has been shifted, relatively at least, from custodial to non-custodial personnel, with a consequent increase in the amount of pressure emanating from the inmate side of prison relative to the staff, and where the constraints represented by a close administration through rules and their enforcement have been reduced.

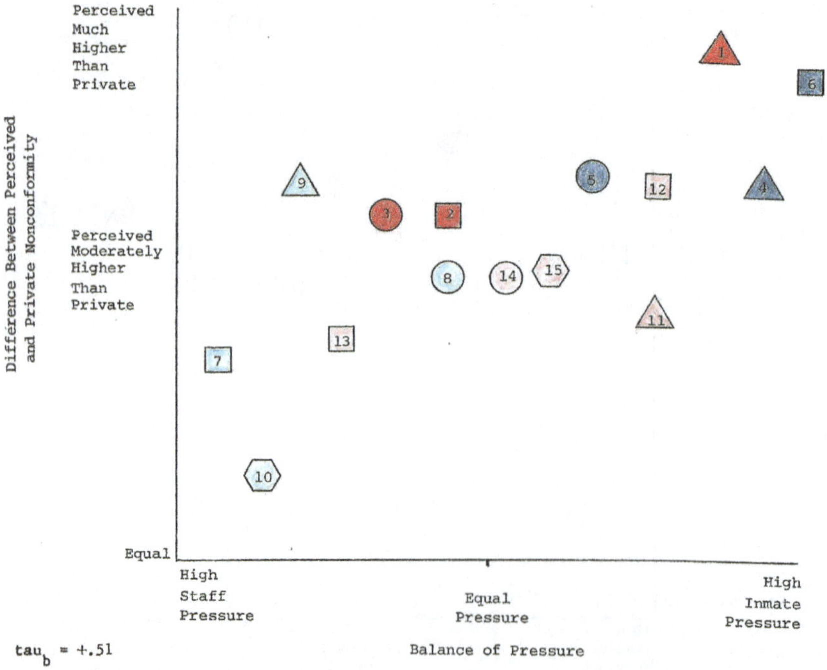

Fig. 4.13 The relationship of the gap between perceived and privately expressed norms to the balance of pressure between staff and inmates

A Cautionary Note

What we have presented in this chapter is essentially an interpretation of a set of relationships, largely an after the fact, post hoc interpretation. We feel that the indicators we have used for the various social climate variables are sound ones, and that the interpretation is consistent not only with our data but with what is generally known about prison environments. The strength of the interpretation is suggested by the consistency of the patterns and the interlocking character of the data. But it is still an interpretive theme, rather than the direct empirical test of a series of propositions derived prior to the data collection, and as such it is subject to a number of limitations, all well known in dealing with materials of this sort, but worthy of comment nonetheless.

First, there just aren't enough institutions to enable us to hold one variable constant while examining variation on others. The classic kind of approach to this problem, through use of partial correlation coefficients, is impractical with only fifteen institutions. We say "only" advisedly, for it is more than any other study has ever used, to our knowledge, when a single standardized instrument is going to be applied to all of them. But the risks are still great, and it is quite possible that someone else, examining the same data, would come up with a different ordering of the relationships and a different interpretation. In a sense these materials allow interpretation more akin to a diagnostician's interpretation of projective tests than, say, the interpretation of the MMPI or an intelligence test.

A related limitation has to do with the cultural variation across the Scandinavian countries. In a number of instances, for example, Finnish institutions occupy a distinctive place in our figures. Our interpretation is based on the assumption that other institutions would be similarly located were they operated under similar rules and policies, and with generally similar physical design. But it is conceivable that there is something uniquely "Finnish" about them that our analysis loses or fails to detect. It is a bit similar to the kind of problem Durkheim had in interpreting suicide statistics for the European countries, and our own approach to the study of national differences is derived in part from the logic of his analysis. We prefer to think of the countries as exemplifying locations on theoretically derived variables, rather than as unique cultural entities, which of course from a different analytic perspective they are. But this is simply to note that had we included, say, Italy instead of Finland, or West Germany instead of Norway, we might have found rather different patterns. And had we included institutions from even more distant cultures than those in Europe, still more distinctive patterns might have been found.

The dimensions we selected for study were derived primarily from our understanding of the prison, an understanding based almost entirely on experience and literature in western nations, and undoubtedly dominated by experience in the United States itself. They seem to provide us with a rich and substantively interesting line of reasoning and argument consistent with our findings for these institutions. But they are undoubtedly different than the set of dimensions we might have arrived at had we begun the study from a different experiential or analytical perspective.

Another reason for caution is that we have implicitly, perhaps explicitly, assumed a temporal ordering among variables which we have no necessary right to assume. At least in Chapter 3 we could argue that an institution's date of construction is necessarily prior to the rules, staffing policies and related features that the institutions now have. We cannot make a similar argument from the ordering assumed in this chapter—from power relations among staff, to relations between staff and inmates, to the inmate culture itself. Conceivably one could argue that the temporal ordering is reversed. And in any case we would argue that there is obviously an interplay between the various elements with a flow of influence back and forth that detailed data gathered at several points in time would undoubtedly reveal, rather than the simple temporal sequence suggested by our analysis.

Finally, the more we move through the analysis, the more the aggregate personal background characteristics of the inmates come into view. Although we examine them at the individual level later, we should note now that they become increasingly relevant as we get closer to variables that reflect the inmate's own immediate orientation. They have little to do with perceptions of power and authority on the staff, or with assessments of coercion. They have somewhat more to do with items relating to the balance of pressure. And they have a great deal to do with the measures of perceived norms. These are chiefly items relating to age, age at first arrest, and marital status, with young single men more likely both to be nonconformists at the private attitudinal level, and also having more conflicted perceptions of the inmate normative order. It is for this reason that we often report both the results for all fifteen institutions and the results from the eleven institutions where the more immediate effects of youth are removed. This is simply to note that the backgrounds inmates bring into the institutions, along with the conditions they find there, determine their response to the prison and its members. By focusing here on the institutional level of analysis, we do not mean to imply that the personal backgrounds of the inmates are unimportant. Indeed, we shall examine the interaction between these two sets of variables in Chapter 7.

5

Personal Background and Response to Incarceration

We now turn our attention away from the fifteen institutions and the aggregate responses of their inmate and focus on the close to 2000 individual inmates who comprise our sample. We move, in effect, from the social organization of institutions to the social psychology of individuals. Since individual inmates rather than the institutions they inhabit will remain in the center of our attention throughout the next two chapters, we begin this chapter with comments about the logic of our analysis at the individual level.

In this chapter, we begin by introducing two primary measures of response to the prison. Next, we examine the extent to which we can explain variation in those responses by virtue of variation in the social and criminal backgrounds of the inmates prior to the time they began their current incarceration. We then turn to some indicators of the conceptions inmates have about themselves, conceptions which we assume to an important degree preceded their incarceration and examine how these conceptions are related both to their backgrounds and to their response to the prison. Throughout this analysis we assume that, despite our treatment of each institution as a single entity in Chapters 3 and 4, the individuals that make up each institution come from a variety

S. Wheeler and H. F. Cline, *The Scandinavian Prison Study*,
Palgrave Studies in Prisons and Penology,
https://doi.org/10.1007/978-3-030-26462-8_5

of backgrounds and respond to the prison in ways that reflect this variety. This is the same general assumption we might use in examining the experience of almost any group of individuals, where we would assume that differences in their social and personal backgrounds would lead them to respond differently in whatever setting we examine them.

For these purposes, we wish again to ignore differences between the Scandinavian countries, and to concentrate on the varying experiences of the 2000 inmates as though, in effect, they were from a common cultural heritage. The important differences between men from different countries will be examined in the context of our assessment of national differences in Chapter 7. But in treating our inmate respondents in this way, we should recognize that our total picture of the social psychology of inmate experience is not contributed to equally by each of the four countries. Specifically, since more inmates in our study came from Denmark and Finland, the Danish and Finnish experience contributes more heavily to our overall picture than does the experience of Norway and Sweden. But our own examination of the cross-national differences leads us to think that at this level, even more so than at the institutional level, the differences are minimal. That is, basically, the same relationships between personal background and response to the prison tend to hold whether we are examining inmates from Norway, Sweden, Finland, or Denmark. We therefore ignore the relatively minor modifications we would have to make in our statement of the general relationships were we to treat each country separately, in favor of the virtues of parsimony and simplicity this procedure allows.

Two Basic Response Measures: The Perceived Effect of Imprisonment and Attitudinal Conformity

What is it one wants to assess in examining inmate response to imprisonment? Perhaps the most frequently asked question concerns the effect of a man's stay in prison on his conduct after he leaves it. We ask "what impact did the prison have on his behavior?" and often we mean something more specific, namely, does it lead him away from or further into crime? At least in the hands of social policymakers, the typical question has to do with recidivism: does incarceration teach a man to behave himself, or does it further induce him into criminal activity? In this study, we do not have good direct measures of the "impact" of incarceration on the offender after he leaves the prison. The Scandinavian record systems did not yield such information, and even if they had we would have been hard-pressed to match general information about institutions with the specific information about each offender, for we promised the offenders anonymity and we meant it. This means that our sense of the inmates' response to imprisonment had to come from their answers to our questionnaire.

We feel that there were two important forms of response which our questionnaire enables us to tap, and which will provide the basis for most of the analysis in this and the following chapter. A third measure, having to do with the inmates' sense of justice, will be treated separately. One of the measures derives primarily from both therapeutic and common sense understandings that the prison may be either a helpful or a harmful place, and we make an effort to assess which of these it has been for the inmate in question. A second measure derives more from sociological study of institutions, and focuses not on whether an inmate feels helped or harmed by his stay, but on whether he adopts the conventional, conforming attitudes the staff would like him to have, or attitudes resistant of the staff and supportive of many inmates. Since these two measures occupy a prominent place in our analysis, we will describe them in some detail.

The Measurement of the Perceived Effect of Imprisonment

The first of the two measures, which we variously refer to as "the subjective effect of incarceration" or the "help-harm" dimension, is taken directly from the following questionnaire item: "What effect do you think your stay in the institution will have on your ability to get along successfully when you are on the outside?"

The response categories, frequency distribution, and percentages of inmates responding in each category are listed below:

Response categories	N	%
It will help me a lot	183	10
It will help me a little	151	8
It will neither help nor harm me	461	24
It will harm me a little	446	23
It will harm me a lot	674	35
No response	22	1
Total	1937	100

Clearly, the distribution of responses to this item is skewed to the direction of "feelings of being harmed." The majority of inmates feel that their stay will be harmful to them, and although a large number feel that the stay will neither help nor harm them, fewer than 20% respond in categories indicating a net balance of help over harm.

Now we cannot tell from responses to this question what it is about their stay that gives most inmates a feeling of being harmed. In part it has to do with disruptions their prison stay causes in their life on the outside, and in part it has to do with the boredom, isolation, and essential irrelevance they feel about the life within. Nor can we tell why those few who feel helped think their stay will help them. Questions of that sort are difficult to put and to answer in the format of a structured questionnaire, and in any event, although we would be interested in the answers, they are not crucial to our analysis, for our main point is to note which inmates feel their stay will be harmful and which helpful, and this single item seems to produce considerable variation on that score.

Yet it may be questioned whether a single item can serve as an effective basis for making inferences about offenders' subjective feelings of help or harm. Supportive evidence on this score is yielded by examining the relationship of this single item to a more complicated series of responses located elsewhere in our questionnaire. We were interested in whether anyone or another of six different components of the institutional program might have had a positive effect on the inmates. So we asked the following question:

"Have you benefitted from your stay here in any of the following ways?"

Response categories	Yes		Don't know		No	
	N	%	N	%	N	%
Vocational training	433	24	148	8	1208	68
Classroom education	420	25	102	6	1187	69
Understanding of myself by having had time to think problems through	457	52	206	11	690	37
Understanding of myself as a result of help from someone on the staff	271	15	162	9	1336	76
Better physical condition	408	23	165	9	1197	68
Better relationship with my family	396	22	235	13	1197	65

Again, lest there be any doubt about inmates' general feelings of how helpful institutions are, it's clear that the modal response in every category save one is that the inmate has not been helped. And the one exception has to do with what some would argue is an unintended consequence of incarceration, namely the abundance of time the inmate is left by himself to "think problems through." For each inmate, we computed a score based simply upon the number of "no" responses to each of these six possible ways of being helped. His score could therefore vary from zero, which would mean that he either has been helped or wasn't sure whether he had been helped in all the various ways, up to six, which meant that he perceived having benefitted in none of these ways from his stay.

Now if our single item measure of perceived help or harm has some validity as a generalized measure of the inmate's response to the institution, we would expect it to be related to the inmate's general tendency to feel that he was being helped or not being helped in these specific ways. Table 5.1 shows the relationship between the single item eliciting his subjective response, and the frequency with which he denied receiving help in the various ways indicated in the questionnaire. As is very clear from the table, the more an inmate tended to reject the specific program or areas of concern, the more likely he was to feel generally

Table 5.1 Perceived effect of incarceration by rejection of components of the institutional program

	Number of components rejected							
	0	1	2	3	4	5	6	Total
Help (%)	72	67	53	45	37	31	29	42
Harm (%)	28	33	47	55	63	69	71	58
	100%	100%	100%	100%	100%	100%	100%	100%
N	(123)	(136)	(196)	(248)	(329)	(365)	(383)	(1780)

harmed by his stay. This suggests to us that there is indeed validity to the use of this single item as a measure of subjective harm or help, and we continue to use it in this way during the discussion that follows.

The reason for stressing the subjective experience of being helped or harmed as a critical component of response to the prison may be obvious, but perhaps it needs some elaboration. From a cold, hard, detached "scientific" analysis, one would probably argue that the prison has a number of functions, and that assessments of response to imprisonment should be geared to those separate functions. We might, for example, have stressed custodial control as an important function of the prison, and measured our response in terms of the rate of escape from imprisonment. Indeed, on that criterion, most of our prisons would be judged successful. But if that had been our primary interest we could have done the study without ever contacting the inmates directly.

To the extent that questionnaire responses can tap an important dimension of response, we think that the concentration on feelings of help or harm is one easily justified both by official goals of a system, and by its importance in the eyes of inmates, staff, and the larger society. Whatever else the prison is supposed to do, at least in recent years it has become common to recognize that the prison is not itself designed to be harmful, even though it may have harmful effects. We have come to hope that inmates will be helped by their stay, and that such help is one of the reasons for their confinement. And this feeling is evident in the rhetoric of all the prison systems we studied, though substantially more important in some prisons than in others. But the general feeling of being helped or harmed by one's stay is precisely the sort of thing we have come to want to know about the effect of incarceration on a man's feelings.

The Measurement of Conformity and Nonconformity

One of the most familiar ideas in the world of the prison is that a basic gulf separates the keepers from the kept. The prison institution, as an agent of a broader and more conventional society, wants inmates to adopt the rules, norms and goals that are typically held to, at least in their verbal form, by conventional members of society. These norms include strictures to work hard, to spend one's time usefully and productively, to obey the rules and norms of the institutions in which one is functioning, to support conventional members of society as against deviants and the like. On the other hand, the inmate world, it is argued, may pull a man in just the opposite direction. For the inmate world is composed at least in part of men who have already fallen afoul of the rules, norms, and standards of conventional society, whose conduct may suggest that they don't take such rules seriously or regard them highly, and who have no particular affection or respect for official agents.

The incoming inmate may be faced with a conflict between these views, with the most active vocal inmates on one side and the officials on the other. And quite apart from whatever strongly held moral beliefs he might have about the right or wisdom of one side of this debate versus the other, as a practical matter of daily living, he may be forced to choose between which side to give his allegiance, with one side offering more in the way of official rewards through reduced custody, reduced restrictions on movement, and eventually the release, and the other side offering perhaps unofficial rewards of being accepted by fellow inmates.

In the daily life of most prisons this conflict rarely appears quite as stark as the above description may make it sound, but at least it points to an important undertone of life in the prison. At one extreme one can make up his mind to conform to the conventional world of the guards, and get along as best he can with his fellows under the circumstances, or at the other extreme he may choose to resist the official system, engage in rule-breaking and other forms of making trouble. In any event, it is a common idea that inmates will vary in their orientation toward this dimension of conformity or nonconformity to the official world, and that a very important part of their life within, and potentially their life on the outside, may depend on how they respond.

We indicated how we proposed to assess an inmate's position on this dimension in our discussion of the perceived normative order among inmates. Very briefly, we pose hypothetical situations for inmates—situations that typically pit a "conventional" against an "unconventional" response, and asked the inmate what he personally thinks a person in the hypothetical situation should do. We take his response to be an indication of where he falls along this continuum.

The three items we used to tap his response are as follows:

> Inmate Olsen goes before a committee that makes job assignments. He is given a choice between two jobs. One job would call for hard work, but it would give Olsen training that might be useful to him on the outside. The other job would allow Olsen to do easier time in the institution, but it provides no training for a job on the outside. Olsen decides to take the easier job.

What do you personally think about Olsen taking the easier job?

> An inmate, without thinking, commits a minor rule infraction. He is given a "write-up" by a correctional officer who saw the violation. Later two other inmates are talking to each other about it. One of them criticizes the officer. The other inmate, Hansen, defends the officer, saying the officer was only doing his duty.

How do you personally feel about Hansen defending the guard?

> Inmates Jansen and Lund are very good friends. Jansen has some money that was smuggled into the institution by a visitor. Jansen tells Lund he thinks the officers are suspicious, and asks Lund to hide the money for him for a few days. Lund takes the money and carefully hides it.

How do you personally feel about Lund hiding the money?

We argue that an inmate who approves of Olsen's taking the easier job, disapproves of Hansen's defending the guard, and approves Lund's hiding the money is an inmate who holds beliefs that are at odds with those of most of his keepers, and hence he is a nonconformist from the official point of view. We shall refer to his opposite as "attitudinal conformist," again judging conformity from the official point of view and not meaning to take a stand in favor of conformity or nonconformity.

Responses to the three items are positively related one to the other, and we thus formed an index of attitudinal conformity by simply assessing whether an inmate answered all three, two, one, or none of the items in the "conforming" direction. The number and percentage of inmates responding in each combination is as follows:

Attitudinal conformity	N	%
Three conforming responses	540	28.6
Two conforming responses	689	36.5
One conforming response	478	25.3
No conforming response	182	9.6
No response	48	2.5

The distribution of responses is plainly in the direction of attitudinal conformity, though a much larger proportion of the inmates are in the "nonconforming" categories than was true for those in the "helping" categories on our other principal measure. In what follows, when we speak of conformity we mean those who had two or three of their responses in the conforming direction.

As in the case of our measure of help or harm, one might ask whether we are really measuring conformity or not. Indeed, we did not do a separate study of the staff to determine whether they uniformly would have wished for an inmate to give what we are calling the "conforming" response. (We did in our much earlier study of an American reformatory, and the staff so responded, but it could easily be argued that that evidence is not relevant in this cultural context.) In our informal communications with staff in the various institutions, we learned of nothing that would lead us to think they would disagree with this mode of classification, but we did not make it a matter of serious and sustained inquiry. And we think there are a number who would have felt that the inmates in question might well have been advised to give a "nonconforming" response, if only to get along better with their fellows. They might particularly feel this way with regards to an inmate refusing to hide money for a friend, or defending an officer in front of his mates.

But from whatever we know about the prison setting, we imagine we might have chosen other items and would still have gotten basically the same general direction of response, and that even a broader sampling of items would have tended to place inmates in roughly the same postures of conformity or nonconformity relative to staff norms.

Our only independent evidence for this, however, comes from another item in the questionnaire, and concerns not their feelings but their behavior. In fact, to be more precise, it concerns the behavior of prison officers toward them. The question reads as follows:

"Have any disciplinary actions been taken against you since you have been here?"

Responses	N	%
Never	1463	77
1 or 2 times	306	16
3 or 4 times	69	4
5 or more	78	4
Total	1916	100

We note from this distribution that disciplinary sanctioning is a rather infrequent occurrence, with less than a quarter of the sample indicating ever having been disciplined.

Now we would hardly expect a perfect association between the conforming attitudes reflected in our index drawn from the hypothetical situations, and conforming behavior reflected in the absence of disciplinary actions. On the one hand, only some of those who engage in rule violations are caught and therefore some nonconformists will be among those who have never had disciplinary actions. And on the other hand, a large number of persons may conduct themselves in ways that are not a direct reflection of their attitude—they may be attitudinal conformists but behavioral nonconformists or what is perhaps more likely, given the power of the officials, attitudinal nonconformists and behavioral conformists. In any event, we would not expect the same degree of consistency in comparing attitudes with behavior that we might expect in comparing one attitude with another. But we would still anticipate that there ought at least to be some relationship between attitude and action,

Table 5.2 Attitudinal conformity and behavioral conformity

Behavioral conformity	High conformity	Moderate conformity	Moderate nonconformity	High nonconformity	Total
Conformity (0 discipline actions	85%	79%	68%	63%	(1424)
Moderate (1–2 discipline actions)	12%	16%	19%	24%	(300)
Nonconformity (3+discipline actions)	3%	6%	14%	14%	(144)
Total	(536)	(685)	(470)	(177)	(1868)

and that our measure of attitudinal conformity might be a dubious one if it bore no relation whatever to the inmate's behavior while he was in the prison, or the behavior of the officials toward him.

The relationship is presented in Table 5.2. The results show that the measure does indeed reflect some consistency of attitude and behavior: those who are attitudinal conformists are also more likely to have had no disciplinary actions taken against them. We thus feel reasonably safe in interpreting our measure as indicative of attitudinal conformity or opposition to the staff, and in what follows we treat our measure of attitudinal conformity in just this way.

But one might ask why we don't use the measure of behavioral conformity as well, since it also tells us something important about the prison and its inmates. Our reason is simply that since it reflects the action of the officials, even though ostensibly in reaction to an offending inmate, the measure is likely to reflect institutional variations in policies of surveillance and detection, while it is the purpose of this chapter to concentrate on explaining inmate reaction. In any event, the two bear similar directions of relationship to virtually every other variable we examine, and one will not go far wrong by assuming that the measure of behavioral conformity will relate much like the measure of attitudinal conformity to whatever we are examining.

Table 5.3 Private attitudinal conformity and perceived effect of incarceration

Private attitudinal conformity	Perceived effect		
	Harm	Help	Totals
Conform	65%	66%	(1215)
Nonconform	35%	34%	(654)
Totals	(1095)	(774)	(1869)

The Relationship Between Attitudinal Conformity and Feelings of Help or Harm

We have argued that two basic modes of response to the prison on the part of inmates are contained in the concepts of perceived help or harm and attitudinal conformity. And in what follows in this chapter we shall be showing the relationships of background items to conformity on the one hand, and to feelings of being helped or harmed, on the other. The simple relationship between them, as they will be divided in much of what follows, is indicated in Table 5.3. As this table shows, there is virtually no relationship between our two main response measures. The largest single category contains those who both feel harmed and conform, and the smallest category contains those who are nonconformists and who do not feel harmed, but there is virtually no relationship between the two items. So we are dealing with two measures of response to the institution that are essentially unrelated one to the other. Having observed their basic independence, we can now turn to examine the way in which each response is related to the backgrounds men bring to prison.

Social Background and Response to Incarceration

A person's attitudes toward the world are a function of his experience in it, and that experience, in turn, is a function of one's position in the social structure. This is the common theme underlying a wide variety of studies of the relationship of social background to attitudes and beliefs. It is in part for this reason that major polling agencies report public opinion poll data separately for males and females, for the rich relative to the poor, for the more educated relative to the less educated, and, where there are ethnic cleavages, separately for different ethnic groups. Indeed, there are some general findings from such studies that appear to cut across national boundaries and to be found in most of the societies of the western world. For example, more educated people tend to be more tolerant, older people more conservative in political outlook, poorer people generally less happy with their lot, and so on.

We anticipate that this same general linkage between attitude, experience and social position should hold for that special subset of the population convicted and imprisoned for crimes, but with two major modifications. First, persons convicted of crimes in most western societies tend to be relatively homogeneous with regard to some of the attributes that are more widely dispersed in the general population. Officially registered and convicted criminals tend in all western societies to be drawn primarily from the lower stratum of the population. They are less educated, less well-to-do, less likely to have stable employment, and such employment as they have is likely to be at relatively menial jobs. We need not here decide whether this is a true reflection of the relationship of social status to criminality, or largely the result of systematic bias in the operation of the criminal justice system. That subject is an important one both for theoretical criminology and for public policy, but for our purposes the important fact is that those drawn into the prisons come with rare exceptions from a relatively narrow segment of the total society, thereby reducing the role that social class-related variables may play in individual differences between inmates. In part for this reason, our measures of social background are restricted to age, marital status, educational level and type of residence prior to commitment, the latter being assessed along an urban–rural dimension. We do not attempt to get precise information on social status as might be indicated, for example, by items reflecting family income or father's occupation, in part because such information is difficult to get in a reliable way, but also in part because of the lack of great variability on such matters within the prison population.

The second modification involves the choice of the most relevant items of prior background. It is probably a maxim of attitude research, or if not perhaps it should be, that the most important dimensions of social position with regards to any attitude are those that are closest in experience to the attitude in question. Thus, we expect that attitudes toward religion will reflect one's religious experience; attitudes toward rural or urban living, one's rural or urban background and the like. Now the most relevant set of prior experiences for prison inmates would seem to be those related to their backgrounds in crime. For this reason, although we have a rather limited array of items with regards to social background, we have an extended array of items relating to the criminal experience of our inmates, and those will form an important part of a general analysis relating the inmate's background to his response to the prison.

But we turn first to the social background items. Table 5.4 shows the relationship of our four social background variables to our two main measures of response to the prison, attitudinal conformity and perceptions of help or harm. We shall first examine the background variables

Table 5.4 Social background and response to incarceration

		Percent who are attitudinal conformists		Percent feeling that stay will harm them	
		%	(*N*)	%	(*N*)
Current age	Under 18	47	(70)	45	(69)
	18–20	51	(191)	48	(191)
	21–24	60	(271)	58	(273)
	25–29	62	(328)	54	(331)
	30–39	68	(587)	61	(596)
	40–49	74	(285)	66	(295)
	50+	80	(137)	62	(139)
Marital status	Single	58	(956)	56	(957)
	Married	75	(438)	61	(445)
	Div/widow	70	(470)	62	(486)
Education	Primary	63	(1116)	55	(1130)
	1–2 post-prim.	66	(361)	61	(368)
	3+post-prim.	71	(365)	66	(368)
Residence	Capital	64	(852)	56	(864)
Prior to commitment	Urban	62	(639)	58	(646)
	Town	72	(115)	62	(118)
	Rural	72	(247)	64	(252)

in relation to the response measures taken separately, and then make some observations about the patterning of the results and the relative strength of the background variables.

With regards to conformity, it is clear that an inmate's age has a powerful effect on the extent to which he is a conformist to staff norms, with inmates becoming progressively conformist with each advance in years. The pattern is striking in its consistency and strength. It suggests the gradual burning out of flames of resistance to the prison regime as inmates get older and gives us a strong hint as to why prison authorities often find older inmates "easier to deal with" than their younger associates.

An inmate's marital status also shows a substantial though less powerful relationship to attitudinal conformity, with married inmates clearly more "conformist" in attitude than those who are single. Since part of its relationship may be due to age, with younger inmates of course more likely to be single, we will later examine the relationship of marital status to our response measures, taking out the effect of age. But for the time being it is clear that single men are much more likely to be nonconformist in attitude than are their married comrades.

Educational level and residence are only modestly related to attitudinal conformity. The great majority of inmates had attained an educational level at or below the completion of primary school, which in the Scandinavian countries is approximately equivalent to the eighth grade in the United States. And it is those inmates with the least schooling who are least likely to be "conformists" as measured by our attitude items. But the relationship is indeed small, there being only an 8% difference between those with three or more years of schooling and those who at least completed primary school.

A similar result is evident when we examine residence. Since each of our countries has a single dominant "capital" city that was relatively close to the location of many of our institutions, we recorded residence in the capital as perhaps the most extreme form of "urban" residence in our study, these being the capital cities of Oslo, Stockholm, Helsinki, and Copenhagen. But at least as the results with regard to conformity work out, the only real difference is between the capital or urban cities on the one hand, and towns or rural districts on the other.

(It should be noted that, aside from residents in the capital city, there is a large subjective component in the other three categories, since inmates themselves chose between the designation of city, smaller town, and country.) In a moment we will ask why this particular pattern of results is obtained, but for now we rest with the following generalization: it is the young, single, city dweller with low educational attainment who is most likely to hold attitudes in opposition to those of the prison regime.

When we turn to inmate perceptions of the effect of incarceration on them the results are a bit less clear. Age, again, bears a substantial relationship to attitudes, with older inmates more likely to feel harmed by their stay than younger ones. But feelings of help or harm are little influenced by marital status. To a small degree, men who have ever been married are more likely to feel harmed, less likely to feel helped, then are single men, but again, the differences are small. And our other two background variables, educational level and residence, bear about the same magnitude of relationship to feelings of help or harm that they did to attitudinal conformity, with the more educated inmates and those from small-town or rural backgrounds more likely to feel harmed by their stay in the institution. And if a single generalization was to be formed describing the results for all four variables it would be identical in form to the generalization above: it is the young, single city dweller with low educational attainment who is least likely to feel that his stay in prison will be harmful to him after release.

The relationship of social background to response measures was also examined in a multiple regression equation. This analysis provides an opportunity to determine two additional aspects of the relationship. First, the squared multiple correlation coefficient is an estimate of the total amount of variation in the response measures explained by the social background variables. And second, the standardized regression coefficients are indicators of the relative contribution of each social background variable in predicting the response. Listed below are summaries of the multiple regression equations for social background and response:

	Conformity	Harm
Multiple correlation	0.24	0.16
Multiple correlation^2	0.06	0.03
Standardized coefficients		
Age	0.12	0.12
Marital status	0.13	0.00
Education	0.06	0.09
Residence	0.08	0.04

These results generally confirm the findings reported in Table 5.4. The social background measures are better predictors of conformity, multiple correlation coefficient = .24, than of harm, multiple correlation coefficient = .16. As is usually the case with large-scale survey research data, these coefficients are quite small; and the squared coefficients indicate that only a small proportion of variance in either conformity, 6%, or harm, 3%, are attributable to social background characteristics. In addition, the standardized coefficients indicate the relative strength of each social background variable as a predictor of the response measures; and the pattern is similar to the percent differences noted in Table 5.4, i.e., current age and marital status are the better predictors of conformity and current age is the best predictor of harm.

When we introduced our two basic response measures, we showed that the relationships were entirely independent, that is, that there was no relationship between an inmate's status as a conformist or a nonconformist and his feeling of being helped or harmed by his stay. But when we examine their relationship to social background items, we find that they relate in what might be thought of as opposite ways to the various measures. Whatever predicts conformity predicts harm. An attribute that leads to attitudinal conformity on the one hand apparently leads to feelings of being harmed by one's stay on the other. The pattern seems quite clear and consistent, and appears to belie any simple notion that there is a set of benign qualities that will lead an inmate both to conform to conventional expectations with regard to work and attitude within the prison, and at the same time will lead him to feel that his stay in the prison is helpful and useful for him. Instead, the same characteristics that lead the inmate to "accept" conventional and conformist

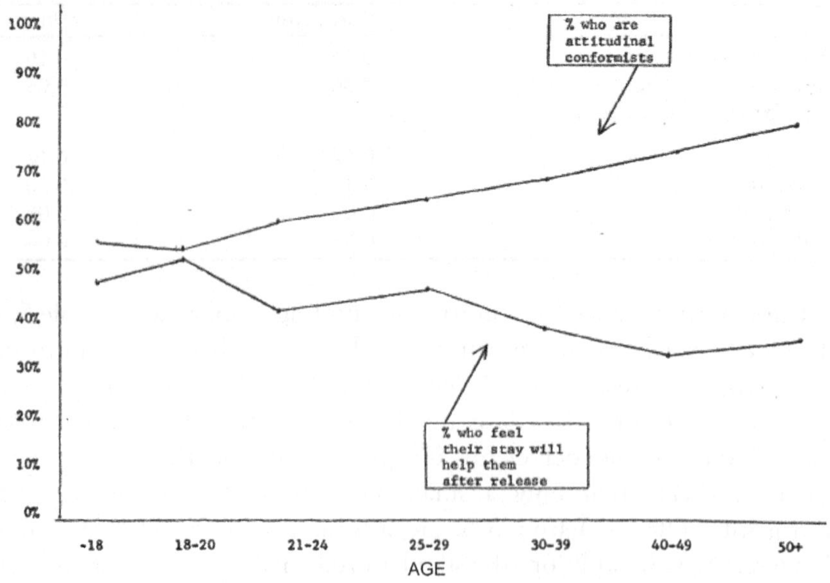

Fig. 5.1 Relation between age, attitudinal conformity, and feelings that prison will help them

orientations in attitude apparently lead him to reject the notion that anything about his stay is going to be helpful to him after release.

Since this pattern is clearest with respect to age, and since age is clearly the most powerful of our four social background variables, we would like to explore it further. Figure 5.1 portrays graphically the relationship of an inmate's age to the two response measures. The older the inmate gets, the more likely he is to conform in attitude, but the less likely he is to feel that his stay will have either no effect or a positive effect on him after he leaves. In other words, he is simultaneously less likely to openly resist official norms, and more likely to feel harmed by being incarcerated. We think these two results are by no means inconsistent, and that there is a fair amount of support for such a finding from other social science research. The studies of the youth culture, for example, would seem to suggest that the period of greatest rebellion against authority is in the middle and late teens; advancing years bring advancing propensities to accept the existing regime.[1] Similarly, the crime rate itself falls rapidly with advances in age.[2] At the same time, a number of studies suggest that older people are more likely to be pessimistic about the future, more likely to have negative feelings about the way the social order is working, and the like.[3]

One way of thinking about our measure of feelings of help or harm is as an indirect measure of more general feelings of optimism or pessimism, and we have learned to expect pessimism to grow with age. In this way, we can perhaps see the general dynamics of prison life as not so terribly unlike what one might find in the outer world, with advancing age bringing on both a sort of passivity and quiescence in attitude—less feistiness, less aggression and open hostility, while at the same time producing a more negative and pessimistic or a more subdued orientation to surrounding events. At least, this is the way in which we would interpret our main findings.

A similar interpretation would seem to be appropriate for the weaker but still clear patterning of results with regards to our other variables. Both being married and more educated would seem to connote a greater stake in the social order than being single and uneducated, and hence the constraints against nonconformity. At the same time, more may be lost by one's stay in prison, for the married man with higher educational attainment may indeed have literally more to lose—wife and family on the one hand, a higher paying job and generally higher social status on the other. Residence prior to commitment we would interpret as an indirect index of immersion in delinquent and criminal subcultures, given what is known about the relative weakness of such subcultures in small towns and rural areas relative to large cities. And we would expect the smaller town or rural offender both to be somewhat more "conforming" in attitude than the offender from the big city, and

[1]See Matilda White Riley and Anne Foner, *Aging and Society, Volume 1: An Inventory of Research Findings* (New York: Russell Sage Foundation, 1968), p. 400.

[2]Ibid., p. 400.

[3]Ibid., pp. 328–329.

in part for this reason less likely to have built-in protections against feeling harmed by his stay in prison.

But the most important variable by far is the offender's age, and we think it worth raising the question why age, among all the attributes a man may bring to prison, seems to be so importantly involved in his response to the prison regime. We have already suggested that part of the reason is through the relationship of age to other more general social psychological states. But we don't know of other studies showing such a sizeable influence of a single background factor like age, and we are therefore moved to ask: what is it about the prison experience that makes one's age while going through that experience such an important determinant of response?

Four factors seem most relevant. First, the whole ideology of imprisonment and the use of the threat of imprisonment as a deterrent suggest that it ought to have fateful consequences for one's future. Young men may be able to ward off these negative consequences psychologically, with thoughts about a new start, a second chance, and a new life after release. But these kinds of rationalizations must be increasingly difficult to sustain as more of one's life lies behind and less of it lies ahead. The whole rhetoric of "ending up" in prison suggests the importance of incarceration for the self. And as the ultimate negative sanction these societies have to offer, imprisonment seems almost to demand reflection on one's life and one's place in the broader scheme of things—even among men not often given to abstract philosophizing.

Second, the boredom, loneliness and isolation of imprisonment—the amount of time on one's hands with only endless routine days lying ahead, leave an enormous amount of room for self-reflection. The importance of this dimension was suggested earlier by our finding that the only way in which the majority of these inmates felt they might have been helped by imprisonment was through self-understanding—"by having time to think problems through." We imagine that many of those problems have to do with basic life choices, the kinds of choices that are most likely to be affected by age and experience.

Third, these men are not only of widely differing ages themselves, but they are confined with men often very different from themselves in age. Indeed, prisons and mental hospitals are two of the few institutions where young and old are often brought together in very close interaction. With the exception of family and extended kinship ties, modern societies tend to an important degree to be age-segregated, with interpersonal ties drawn largely from persons similar in age. Our prisons are a major exception to this pattern. In all but the youth institutions, men aged 20 may be intermingled with men 50 or 60 years old. And although they may choose their friends from among those closer to them in age, the living example of both decaying old men and rebellious youth are visible in the daily rounds of life within the institution.

A final point is that even when age-differentiated groupings appear in settings other than total institutions, they are typically age-graded, with older persons occupying higher status and younger ones lower status. Whether the status is marked simply by seniority, as in many factories, or by badges of differential status and prestige as in the distinctions of a senior and junior partner in a law firm, the doctor and the intern in the hospital, a senior professor and his junior colleague, it is rarely sheer age itself that is at issue, but rather age-graded differentials in experience, prestige, reward. But not in the prison. Indeed, the prison reverses the normal assumption of age grading. Many of the older men have literally spent the best years of their lives in prison, while young inmates, especially given the short sentences obtained in most Scandinavian countries, can see that they will soon be out and may sustain the belief that they will not follow in the footsteps of the fated older men around them.

For all these reasons, then, and undoubtedly others we haven't thought of, age looms as a critical variable in relation to prison life. We cannot do a great deal more to further explore the relevance of age within the context of our study, though later we will examine the joint affect of age and criminal career variables on response. But the last two of the four reasons given above suggest that age is important not only in the absolute sense, but that it ought to be important within the confines of each of our institutions. That is, whether a man is older or younger relative to others in confinement with him ought to be related to both conformity and feelings of help or harm, just as we now know it is related for the inmates taken as a whole.

Table 5.5 The effect of age and social background on feelings of being harmed (% harmed)

Social experience favorable to crime	Age				
	Under 21	21–29	30–39	40+	Total
High	45% (101)	51% (170)	53% (106)	71% (44)	52% (421)
Medium	50% (108)	58% (246)	59% (255)	59% (155)	57% (764)
Low	56% (18)	61% (119)	68% (180)	70% (171)	66% (488)
Total	48% (227)	56% (535)	61% (541)	65% (370)	59% (1673)

To examine that hypothesis, we computed the correlation between age and the two response measures within each separate institution. The results lend further confirmation: in 14 of the 15 institutions, older inmates are more conforming in attitude, and in 12 of the 15 they are likely to feel more harmed. Thus in 26 out of 30 possible "tests" the results confirm our expectations.

Since our various social background measures seem to be related in similar ways, though in differing degrees, to both of our response measures, we can get a sense for the total effect of social background on response to imprisonment by combining an inmate's responses to the four items so as to form a more general index of social background. We do this by retaining age as a single item, and by combining an inmate's responses to the other three items into a social background index that locates single men of low education and urban background at one pole, those who are married, of higher educational background and more rural residence at the other. (In fact, because of the very small number of cases that are at this less "crime conducive" pole, we have combined the latter two categories so that our scale makes three distinctions.)

The results of this analysis for feelings of being harmed by one's stay appear in Table 5.5. As that table shows, even when we control for social background, age retains a strong predictive power. And within all age groups save for those over 40, social background makes a systematic difference. Well under half of the young single urban dwellers of low

Table 5.6 The effect of age and social background on attitudinal conformity (% harmed)

Social experience favorable to crime	Age				
	Under 21	21–29	30–39	40+	Total
High	45% (102)	57% (172)	56% (110)	67% (42)	55% (426)
Medium	51% (107)	61% (243)	66% (248)	71% (151)	63% (749)
Low	63% (19)	68% (119)	76% (177)	86% (168)	77% (483)
Total	49% (228)	61% (534)	67% (535)	78% (361)	65% (1658)

education feel that their stay in prison will harm them when they get out, while over two-thirds of the older men at the other end of the spectrum feel that their stay will be harmful to them.

A similar result, even stronger in overall effect, is apparent in the relationship of background to conformity. Table 5.6 displays the relationship. Both age and social background work their influence so that there are almost twice as many conformists at one end of the spectrum as at the other.

Criminal Background and Response to Incarceration

In the common sense judgment of prison administrators throughout the western world, an inmate's prior criminal experience has an extremely important effect upon his reactions to imprisonment. Countries with large numbers of institutions are likely to segregate first termers from recidivists, and even within the confines of a single institution, there is often concern for separating those new to the prison from what are thought of as hardened repeaters in crime. Indeed, this commonsense experience is built into the penal code, with harsher sentences for repeaters, especially habitual criminals. The role of prior criminal experience is suggested as well in the large number of parole prediction studies carried out in the United States and elsewhere. The best predictors of future recidivism tend to be items reflecting one's prior criminal activity.[4]

Finally, within the life of the prison community itself, important social distinctions made by one group of inmates vis-a-vis another often concern the prior experience with crime and imprisonment. At least in the language of American prison inmates, the "Square John," a situational offender not usually caught up in the criminal or delinquent subculture, will be carefully distinguished from "right guys," "outlaws," "thieves," "gorillas," and other social types reflecting differing varieties of prior criminal and prison experience and behavior. Although such vocabularies are less developed in the Scandinavian institutions we studied, even in these prisons, with their somewhat less developed inmate culture, there is always a word that is a rough approximation of the English concept of "jailbird," to refer to those persons who spend most of their lives behind bars, and who when released quickly find their way back to the prison.[5]

It comes as no surprise, then, to find that serious students of the prison and theorists about crime and imprisonment have placed great emphasis on prior experience in crime, especially that connected with incarceration, as influential in accounting for differentials in response to imprisonment. One of the most important theorists in criminology, Edwin H. Sutherland, developed a theory of criminality precisely out of such experiences. His "differential association" theory, although developed to explain criminality, may be applied with very little change in meaning to the experience of imprisonment. The theory has two central assertions: first, that crime is a function of differential association with ideas favorable to criminality; and second, that those associations will vary in priority (the age at which they are first experienced by an individual), frequency, duration, and what Sutherland called intensity. Persons whose experience with "definitions favorable to crime" are early, frequent, of long duration, and of great intensity, would be expected

---

[4]Edwin H. Sutherland, *Principles of Criminology*, 4th ed. (Philadelphia: Lippincott, 1947).

[5]See Chapter 9 for a detailed discussion of this point. But see also U. Bondeson, *Socialization Processes in Training Schools, Youth Prisons, Prisons, and Internment Centers—Summary* NCJRS Abstracts Database (1974)

to continue in patterns of criminality to a far greater extent than those whose experience occurs later, less frequently, with shorter duration and less intensity.[6]

The differential association theory has been the subject of much development and critical scrutiny which need not directly concern us here. In any event, three of our background items can be conceived as at least partial indicators of the dimensions Sutherland noted. First, we asked each inmate how old he was when he was arrested for the first time. This item has surface plausibility as a measure of priority of criminal experience. Second, we know which inmates have been in a youth institution and which have not. This item reflects both priority and perhaps intensity of experience with offenders. Finally, we have the number of previous sentences served by each inmate—a measure of frequency and duration of contact with the criminal world. The relationship of each of these items to our two primary response measures are shown in Table 5.7.

It is immediately apparent that age at first arrest bears a very strong relationship to attitudinal conformity, while the other two items thought of as indicators of differential association bear weaker and less consistent relationships. But a moment's reflection suggests that the actual chronological age of the inmate may serve to confound the relationships presented in Table 5.7. For both age at first arrest and number of sentences are highly correlated with the inmate's actual age: one cannot have served many sentences and be young, nor can one have been arrested for the first time at, say, age 40 or beyond and be young. And since we know that age is related to conformity, it may serve to enhance the relationship between age at first arrest and conformity, and to suppress the relationship between the number of previous sentences and conformity.

For these reasons, which also influence the relationship of criminal background characteristics to feelings of being harmed, we move to an index of criminal background that is similar in format to our index

[6]Sutherland, op. cit.

Table 5.7 Criminal background and response to incarceration

Background characteristics		% who are attitudinal conformists		% saying their stay will harm them	
		%	(*N*)	%	(*N*)
Age at first arrest	Under 14	43	(171)	57	(172)
	14–17	59	(408)	51	(408)
	18–20	64	(405)	56	(416)
	21–24	65	(320)	64	(320)
	25–29	72	(213)	61	(215)
	30–39	76	(195)	62	(200)
	40–49	89	(74)	66	(74)
	50+	92	(37)	56	(39)
Commitment to a youth institution	Never	66	(1608)	59	(1631)
	1 or more	58	(267)	56	(270)
Number of previous sentences	0	67	(696)	58	(703)
	1	66	(301)	55	(301)
	2	58	(231)	53	(232)
	3–4	68	(236)	65	(242)
	5–9	66	(284)	64	(289)
	10+	59	(99)	66	(103)
Type of committing offense	Property	63	(1101)	58	(1115)
	Person	65	(237)	57	(235)
	Sex	69	(143)	61	(148)
	Other	70	(323)	61	(331)

of social background presented earlier, and examine the relationships within the various age categories introduced earlier.

But before we turn to that analysis we pause briefly to note the effect of type of offenses on our response measures. Unfortunately, but necessarily given the format of our study, we make only the crudest of divisions of offenders into property offenders, offenders against the person, sex offenders, and others (the latter category including drunken driving, offenses against public order, and the like).[7] As is evident in Table 5.7 from the marginal distributions, the bulk of offenders are serving

[7]Because our instrument was administered in groups of varying size, sometimes small, we were concerned that with a more refined breakdown by type of offense an inmate might feel that he could be uniquely identified by listing his particular offense. For this reason, in addition to the problematic relation between what an inmate actually did and the offense with which he is formally charged, we did not use a more refined classification of offenses.

time for property offenses, many fewer for offenses against the person (assault, homicide, robbery) and even fewer for sex offenses. And the differences in their response to imprisonment are minimal, though in a direction that most criminologists would probably anticipate: the property offenders are least likely to be attitudinal conformists, but also least likely (along with offenders against the person) to feel harmed, and the sex offenders and others are most likely to be conformists and also to feel harmed.

It is also of interest to note that different types of offenders come from different backgrounds. The sex offenders are a good deal older, on the average, than are offenders against the person or property. Furthermore, they are much less likely to have a rich background of experience in crime, as reflected by our various indicators. Property offenders are at the other extreme, being much more likely to have been arrested early and to have served many sentences, with offenders against the person somewhere in between.

Finally, before turning to the effect of age on the relationship of criminal background to response, we present the multiple regression of criminal background characteristics on response.

	Conformity	Harm
Multiple correlation coefficient	.24	.16
Multiple correlation squared	.06	.03
Standardized coefficients		
Age at first Arrest	.16	.06
Youth institution	−.10	−.07
Previous Sentences	.00	.14
Offense	−.03	−.05

Again, the regression analysis confirms the tabular presentations in Table 5.7. Age at first arrest is the best predictor of conformity and number of previous sentences is the best predictor of harm. We turn now to a more detailed analysis of the effect of current age on these relationships. Age remains a powerful predictor of attitude within each type of offense, just as it does elsewhere in our data. But despite its general relevance, it is particularly strong in relation to offenders against the person. The men in our sample who are under 20 years of age and have

Table 5.8 The effect of age and criminal background on attitudinal conformity (% conform)

Criminal experience favorable to crime	Age				
	Under 21	21–29	30–39	40+	Total
High	28% (18)	55% (94)	59% (110)	68% (37)	57% (259)
Medium high	33% (40)	58% (113)	63% (138)	72% (105)	61% (396)
Medium low	52% (85)	61% (173)	70% (196)	74% (129)	66% (583)
Low	59% (85)	67% (154)	76% (91)	92% (90)	73% (420)
Total	49% (228)	61% (534)	67% (535)	78% (361)	65% (1658)

committed offenses against a person have the lowest rate of attitudinal conformity of any combination of age and type of offense, namely 30%. On the other hand, offenders against the person who are over 40 years of age had the highest rate of conformity, some 81%. We suspect that what is concealed in that finding is a great diversity in the kinds of offenses committed by the youngest and oldest segment of our population. From what is generally known about offenders, we might anticipate that youthful offenders against the person have committed crimes of robbery and assault, perhaps as an outgrowth of participation in delinquent groups. Those over 40 are more likely to be serving time for more "situational" crimes such as negligent homicide. Thus, we anticipate that these offenders against the person differ in many ways in addition to the differences in age, and probably in more ways than is true for offenders against property.

We return to our index of criminal background. As with our social background index, three items comprise the index of criminal background: number of previous sentences (dichotomized between those with none and those with one or more), prior reform school experience, and age at first arrest. Because of the strong correlation between age at first arrest and current age, however, our "cutting points" for age

Table 5.9 The effect of age and criminal background on feelings of being harmed (% harmed)

Criminal experience favorable to crime	Age				
	Under 21	21–29	30–39	40+	Total
High	65% (17)	42% (93)	54% (113)	55% (38)	51% (261)
Medium high	60% (41)	51% (113)	62% (141)	69% (108)	61% (403)
Medium low	53% (85)	63% (175)	61% (196)	64% (131)	61% (587)
Low	35% (84)	62% (154)	66% (91)	67% (93)	58% (422)
Total	48% (227)	56% (535)	61% (541)	65% (370)	59% (1673)

at first arrest are different for each of the four age groups.[8] And unlike our social background index, our index of criminal background is not so skewed as to require "collapsing" of the extreme categories.

Table 5.8 shows the relationship of criminal background and age to conformity. As that table makes abundantly clear, both age and criminal background have a powerful effect on rates of conformity. Indeed, each cell in the table moves in the expected direction: within any category of age, the greater the criminal experience, the less the conformity, and within any given level of criminal experience, the older the inmate the more conforming he is.

The effect of criminal experience on conformity appears to be particularly strong at the youngest age levels. Fewer than 30% of those with great exposure to crime and youth institutions are conformists on our measure of attitudinal conformity, while almost 60% of the least experienced are conformists. A large difference is also apparent among the older men. And the combined effect of the two variables explains a large part of the variation of conformity: there is a 64 percentage point difference between our older men with little criminal background and

[8]For those under 20, we distinguish between those who are arrested before 14 versus those arrested at 14 or later; for those in their 20s, between persons arrested prior to 17 and those arrested later; for those in their 30s, between those arrested by age 20 or before versus those arrested later, and for those in their 40s between the ones who are 24 or younger at first arrest, and the remainder.

our youngest offenders who have been exposed to the criminal justice system early and often.

Far less striking differences are apparent when we examine, in Table 5.9, feelings of being harmed as they are distributed among inmates of different ages and criminal experience. Overall, the same relationship between age and feelings of harm appears here, of course, as appeared when we introduced age earlier. A weaker and less uniform relationship shows for the effect of criminal background. Indeed, it appears that the effect of criminal background operates very differently for young offenders than it does for older ones. For the age groups from 21 and older, the less experienced one is in crime, the more likely one is to feel harmed by his stay in prison. It is the first offender, so to speak, who is least immune to the prison's damaging influence. That result is shown clearly for the 21–40 age categories, somewhat less clearly for men over 40.

But the striking thing is the reversal among the youngest offenders. There, the less exposure to the institutions of crime, the less likely one is to feel harmed by incarceration. And it should also be noted that it is among those most heavily exposed to what Sutherland called "definitions favorable to crime" where the effect of age is, if anything, reversed. Among those least exposed to criminal definitions, there is a 32% difference between the youngest and the oldest age category. Among those with the next higher degree of exposure, there is an 11% difference, and a 9% difference among those with one further degree of exposure. But among those with the greatest exposure, the relationship is irregular and if anything reversed, with the oldest men feeling less harmed by their stay than the youngest. In part this may be due to the small number of cases on which our results for the youngest and most criminally exposed offenders rest.

We do not have a good explanation for this anomaly. Perhaps the best is that it may well be an artifact of our procedure for sampling institutions. Among our youngest offenders, clearly the most "benign" institution, and the one in which offenders were most likely to feel helped, was Sobysagard in Denmark. That institution also tends to have the inmates with the least prior exposure to crime. Sobysagard is underrepresented in the high criminal background categories, and

Table 5.10 The relation between social and criminal background

Criminal experience favorable to crime	Social experience favorable to crime High	Medium low	Low	Total
High	25%	11%	3%	(265)
Medium high	26%	19%	15%	(408)
Medium low	33%	38%	29%	(591)
Low	16%	33%	53%	(427)
Total percent	100%	100%	100%	
Total	(430)	(416)	(73)	(1691)

over-represented in the low which may help account for this apparent reversal of the relationship.

Combining Social and Criminal Background

We have shown that both our indices of social and of criminal background are related to our primary response measures, though in differing degrees. We now ask, first, about the interrelationship between our indices of criminal and social experience, and second, whether we gain any additional explanatory power by examining their joint effect on our response measures.

The interrelationship itself is interesting. Table 5.10 shows the relationship between an inmate's social background and his criminal background, using the two indices we have already introduced. Of those who are high in social background on our index (single, city dwellers, with low education) and therefore having social experience favorable to crime, 25% are in the highest crime categories, compared to only 3% among the low social experience category—married men who live in small towns in rural areas and who have a higher level of education. This interrelationship is hardly surprising, for no one would have thought that criminal experience would be randomly distributed across social categories. But the nature of the connection between the two is not entirely clear from our data, largely because we cannot establish the temporal ordering between our two indices.[9]

We now consider the joint effect of criminal and social background on response to imprisonment. We might not expect a great deal of improvement in explanatory power, in part because the use of either measure alone, in combination with age, produces very large percentage differences thereby reducing the room for improvement, and in part because as we have just shown, the two are highly interrelated. And, in fact, we find very little we didn't already know by examining the two dimensions separately. When we compare those whose combined social and criminal experience is most conducive to crime with those where the combined effect is least conducive, the effect on conformity is some 63% (from 31 to 94% conformity) as against 61% (from 31 to 92%) using criminal background alone. Nevertheless, the relationships are extremely consistent: within any age and social background category conformity increases as experience in crime declines; and within any age and criminal experience category, conformity increases as social experience conducive to crime declines. But regarding feelings of help and harm, we gain little or nothing by combining the two background measures, nor do we find consistent patterns of movement within the various categories. It thus appears with our combined data, as with each index taken separately, that an inmate's social and criminal background relates more strongly to conformity than to his feelings of being helped or harmed by his stay in prison.

Finally, we present the multiple regression analysis relating both the social and criminal background indices to the response measures.[10]

---

[9]It seems likely, for example, that some of our social background indicators occur prior to indicators of criminality, and others after. At least for many men, their city of residence and their education may precede involvement in crime, which might well precede marriage. And one person's education may be cut off because of incarceration, and others may move to the city because it has more criminal opportunities. The fundamental fact is that the two sets of indicators are closely intertwined, but the nature of their interconnection remains unclear.

[10]The multiple correlation of social and criminal background to conformity is .23 and to harm is .10. The unique variances are .034 for social and .008 for criminal backgrounds when regressed on conformity and .010 and .001, respectively, when regressed on harm. In addition, regression equations using institution, type institution, and country as dummy variables were constructed. The multiple correlations were slightly higher in these regressions, but the overall patterns

	Conformity	Harm
Multiple correlation coefficient	.23	.10
Multiple correlation squared	.05	.01
Standardized coefficients		
Social background	.19	.11
Criminal background	.09	.04

Here, again, we can see that our background measures are better predictors of conformity, $r=.23$, than of harm, $r=.10$; the social background index contributes more variation to both response measures than does the criminal background index.

The Impact of Self-Conceptions on Response to Incarceration

To this point our analysis rests solely on "objective" indicators of social and criminal background. We now want to introduce a more subjective component of background, namely the inmates' own feelings about themselves. The importance of one's self-image as a determinant of other feelings and attitudes is by now well documented in many spheres of human conduct. And it has a long history of relevance specifically to studies of the prison and prison inmates. In the first book length sociological study of the prison, Donald Clemmer, who had been influenced by sociologists Robert E. Park and Ernest W. Burgess at the University of Chicago, wrote about the extent to which the individual's self-conception was a function of the social groups of which he had been a member.[11] He did not proceed to investigate systematically the actual views about themselves held by inmates in the prison he studied, however. Since that time, the self-defining character of the experiences

remained constant. Furthermore, the unique variances did not reveal any strong effect of institution or country on these relationships.

[11]Donald K. Clemmer, *The Prison Community* (New York: Holt, Rinehart and Winston, 1958), Chapter 5, especially pp. 111–112.

persons undergo while being processed through the criminal justice system has received continued attention.[12]

But which aspects of the self should be examined? The possibilities are nearly endless, and especially in a limited investigation such as this one, it is necessary to make crucial choices as to what to investigate. One set of choices in particular seems crucial, and that has to do with the extent to which one conceives of self-conceptions as being deeply rooted phenomena relatively unrelated to the immediate social situation, or whether one assumes that an inmate's self-concept is highly situational. Under the former view, one would assume that there are a number of basic personality traits that are important in individuals irrespective of their recent past background in crime or their present experience in prison. If one takes the latter view, then it is those aspects of self more immediately relevant to the situation of criminals and inmates that would seem most worthy of study.

We adopted the latter view. The aspects or dimensions of self that we tapped through questionnaire items were those we believed particularly relevant to the situations in which inmates find themselves. Two of those aspects of self, those closest to the social life of inmates in the prison, are examined in Chapter 6. Two others are examined here.

Sensitivity to Authority

The importance of the first, which we call sensitivity to authority, lies in the awareness that prisons, at least most of them, provide a very heavy structure of authority, with a dominant group of rulers and a mass of men subject to their rule. This means that the whole idea of finding it easy or difficult to take orders from people seems especially relevant to the way in which the inmate spends his time in prison. We therefore

[12]Lloyd E. Ohlin, *Sociology and the Field of Corrections* (New York: Russell Sage Foundation, 1956).

Table 5.11 The relationship of current age to sensitivity to authority

Sensitivity to authority	Age				
	Under 21	21–29	31–39	40+	Total
Low	17%	25%.	36%	41%	(532)
Medium	48%	47%	47%	48%	(817)
High	35%	28%	17%	11%	(381)
Total percent	100%	100%	100%	100%	
Total	(247)	(566)	(550)	(367)	(1730)

asked inmates whether they felt the following statements were true of them or false[13]:

"I'm the kind of person who doesn't like to be told what to do."
"I don't mind taking orders from people."
"It irritates me when people tell me what to do."

A "true" response to the first and third of these items and a "false" response to the second is the pattern for an inmate who is highly sensitive to authority. We have grouped our inmates into three categories in order to distinguish those who are low, medium, and high in sensitivity to authority.

We might anticipate that men of differing ages and differing backgrounds will differ as well in their generalized sensitivity to authority. This anticipation is strongly confirmed with respect to age, as shown in Table 5.11. Over a third of those inmates who are under 21 years of age are high in sensitivity to authority, compared to only 11% among men over 40. And at the other end of the scale, over twice as many men in the oldest age category are low in sensitivity to authority relative to youths under age 21.

This pattern is clear and consistent, and undoubtedly would come as no surprise to those who inhabit the prison, either inmates or staff. For it is well understood that it is the "hot-headed youngsters" who are often defiant and resistive of authority, while the older men are much

[13]Item 58 of the questionnaire (see Appendix II) gives the full set of instructions and all of the items we used to measure inmate self-conceptions.

Table 5.12 Relationship of social and criminal background to sensitivity to authority

Sensitivity to authority	High	Medium high	Medium low	Low	Total
Social experience favorable to crime					
Low	26%	29%	35%	42%	(529)
Medium	47%	48%	49%	49%	(839)
High	27%	23%	16%	8%	(379)
Total percent	100%	100%	100%	99%	
Total	(453)	(787)	(434)	(73)	(1747)
Criminal experience favorable to crime					
Low	33%	26%	31%	32%	(521)
Medium	42%	47%	50%	50%	(823)
High	25%	27%	20%	18%	(377)
Total percent	100%	100%	101%	100%	
Total	(268)	(416)	(603)	(434)	(1721)

less so. This is so even though many of the older men have spent most of their lives in prison. In other words, there appears to be a "burning out" phenomenon related to the aging process within the prison that is similar in structure to that phenomenon as it has been used to describe offenders generally.

The relationship of our social and criminal background indices (Table 5.12) to sensitivity to authority is less straightforward. The inmates most sensitive to authority are those who come from the least favorable social background, e.g., single urban dwellers of low education. It is interesting to note that our self-conception measures produce real differences among persons who come from broadly differing social strata. The more one moves toward educated, rural and married backgrounds, the less sensitivity to authority.

The relationship to our index of criminal background, however, shows no such neat linear trend. There appears to be no systematic relationship to sensitivity to authority. Persons with wide exposure to the criminal justice system are not more sensitive to authority than those with the least exposure. This contravenes our intuition, and we are at a loss to explain why the result occurs. Perhaps systematic exposure, through arrest and incarceration, to authorities in criminal justice produces over time an increasing acquiescence on the part of some and hostility on the part of others, leading to little net effect. There is a modicum of evidence in support of this argument in the declining percentage of cases in the "middle" category of the table, but hardly enough to be conclusive.

The Self as Criminal or Deviant

We turn now to our second set of measures relating to self-conception, namely those reflecting a sense of self as criminal and/or as having little in common with law-abiding society. The two items we asked were:

> "I don't have much in common with law-abiding people."
> "I'm not really a criminal."

On a face validity basis, each of these questions relates to some aspect of sense of self as deviant or as criminal. But we chose not to form an index of the two, for they were sufficiently uncorrelated to suggest that they were tapping separate constructs.

The relevance of these two items seems plain. Whatever a person's actual experience with crime, if he thinks of himself as a criminal, or as not having much in common with law-abiding society, we might anticipate that reform and rehabilitative efforts will fail. Further, persons who think of themselves in these ways might be more likely to be nonconforming to the staff in their attitudes. We see these as straightforward implications of "labeling theory" in sociology.

But before testing these propositions, we would like to raise the question: What kind of an inmate is most likely to develop these feelings of alienation from the law-abiding world? Clearly, one would think that the most important characteristics are likely to be those relating to their actual criminal experience. Simply put, the more one's experienced in crime, the more likely one will come to think of himself as a criminal and as having little in common with law-abiding people. We might also anticipate, though less strongly, that our social background index will be related to these items in the same way as criminal background, namely, that the more the social background prepared one for crime in the first place, the more it will prepare one for a conception of self as a criminal.

Table 5.13 The relationship of age at 1st arrest to self-images about crime and law-abiding behavior

	Age at first arrest							
	Under 14	14–17	18–20	21–24	25–29	30–39	40+	Total
% without much in common with law abiders	32% (169)	22% (402)	18% (401)	20% (308)	12% (202)	13% (188)	17% (106)	(1776)
% do not see selves as really criminals	56% (169)	57% (400)	60% (407)	66% (307)	65% (206)	78% (192)	75% (111)	(1792)

Our clearest and most direct test is to refer back to Sutherland's concept of differential association, and to one of the inferences we drew from that concept. So we examine the relationship of priority in experience with crime (through our item "age at first arrest") to these two indicators of self-conception. The results are portrayed in Table 5.13. Clearly, the earlier one is formally involved with the criminal justice system, the more likely he is to feel that he "doesn't have much in common with law-abiding people," and the less likely he is to say that he is "not really a criminal." This would seem to be convincing evidence that one's background (or more accurately, one's background in the criminal justice system) produces a conception of self as different from conventional society. The trend in both cases is rather consistent, save in the oldest age category, where there is some increase in feelings of alienation.

Given this consistent relationship to one of our criminal background measures, one might anticipate that these self-concept items would relate' even more strongly to our criminal background index. As Table 5.14 shows, that is not consistently the case. Although our criminal background index relates consistently to the item "I am not really a criminal," it is weak and inconsistent in its relationship to "law-abiding people." On the other hand, the relationship we might not have anticipated shows up consistently: Just as one's social background apparently

Table 5.14 Relationship of social and criminal background to self-images regarding crime and law-abiding behavior

	High	Medium high	Medium low	Low	Total
	Social experience favorable to crime				
% without much in common with	23%	20%	16%	12%	
With law-abiders	(102)	(152)	(70)	(8)	(1725)
% do not see selves	60%	63%	67%	70%	
as really criminals	(267)	(497)	(296)	(51)	(1745)
	Criminal experience favorable to crime				
% without much in common with	25%	20%	15%	19%	
With law-abiders	(260)	(414)	(603)	(425)	(1702)
% do not see selves	52%	59%	63%	74%	
as really criminals	(267)	(404)	(609)	(434)	(1714)

produces different feelings with regard to sensitivity to authority, so does it with respect to these two measures of self-conception—the less one's social background has prepared him for crime, the less it prepares one to think of himself as a criminal, or as having little in common with law-abiding people. The differences are quite small, but they are consistent, and give us at least a hint as to the way in which prior background helps to shape feelings about the self with respect to crime.

In summary, it seems apparent that men of different ages, and of differing social and criminal backgrounds, bring different sets of attitudes toward themselves into the prison. It remains to be seen whether these features of self-conception bear their own independent relationship to our most important response measures. The measures most closely related conceptually to sensitivity to authority would seem to be those of attitudinal and behavioral conformity, which we might also expect to be related to feelings about being different from law-abiding people. We now examine the evidence on behalf of these expectations.[14]

[14]There is no reason in principle why feelings of sensitivity to authority or of alienation from conventional ways of life should not also be related to our other major response measure, namely feelings of being helped or harmed by imprisonment. But the connection is intuitively less clear than with the measure of conformity (either attitudinal or behavioral) to staff norms and authority patterns, which is what our indices of conformity would seem to measure. And empirically, it turns out that feelings of help or harm are relatively independent of these self-conception measures.

Attitude Toward the Self in Relation to Attitudinal and Behavioral Conformity

We reintroduce our measure of behavioral conformity at this point, though conscious of the shortcomings we described earlier, particularly that the measure is by definition at least partially a measure of staff behavior rather than inmate conduct. But as we argued earlier, behavior and attitude in this instance are not that sharply divergent, and we are concerned to note that our measures of self-conception have implications for conduct as well as for other attitudes.

The most important background correlate of sensitivity to authority is age: the older the inmate, the less sensitive is he to authority. Age is thus the most critical variable to control in order to learn whether feelings of sensitivity to authority have an independent contribution to attitudinal or behavioral conformity. Tables 5.15 and 5.16 we present, separately, the relationship of sensitivity to authority to attitudinal conformity on the one hand, behavioral conformity on the other, with the relationship portrayed separately for our four major age categories. With regard to attitudinal conformity, the differences are large and consistent in virtually every case. Even within groups that are homogeneous by age, feelings of sensitivity to authority predict attitudinal nonconformity: the men most sensitive to authority are those most willing to support conduct opposed by the officials.

Table 5.15 The relationship of age and sensitivity to authority to attitudinal conformity (% attitudinal conformists)

Sensitivity to authority	Current age				
	Under 21	21–29	30–39	40+	Total
High	67%	75%	79%	86%	
	(42)	(142)	(191)	(146)	(521)
Medium	50%	60%	67%	68%	
	(117)	(261)	(254)	(168)	(800)
Low	41%	51%	54%	78%	
	(86)	(156)	(91)	(40)	(373)
Total	(245)	(559)	(536)	(354)	(1694)

Table 5.16 The relationship of age and sensitivity to authority to behavioral conformity (% behavioral conformists)

Sensitivity to authority	Current age				
	Under 21	21–29	30–39	40+	Total
High	77%	83%	83%	86%	
	(47)	(151)	(200)	(160)	(558)
Medium	57%	73%	77%	83%	
	(122)	(274)	(278)	(196)	(870)
Low	62%	74%	76%	72%	
	(89)	(164)	(97)	(47)	(397)
Total	(258)	(589)	(575)	(403)	(1825)

Of course, we cannot be certain of the temporal relationship between these two measures; undoubtedly there is a good deal of mutual interplay between them. But we would argue that the generalized sensitivity to authority reflected in our self-conception index becomes translated into a specific willingness to violate the mandates of authority within the prison context. And it is of course precisely those who are willing to support the "counter culture" within the prison who are most likely to feel the strong constraints of authority in the form of pressure from guards and other staff.

When we turn to behavior as distinct from attitude, the pattern remains consistent, though with smaller overall differences. But it is surely enough to suggest that it is the combination of generalized self-conceptions with which a man enters prison, attached to specific attitudes of nonconformity, that prepare persons for overt acts of nonconformity, or if not for such acts, at least for the perception of them as deviant that will bring about official sanctions.

But what of social and criminal background? We showed that they too bore a relationship to sensitivity to authority, and it is possible that such sensitivity bears no independent relationship to conformity once we control for background just as we have controlled for age. Unfortunately, applying simultaneous controls for age, social background, criminal background, and sensitivity to authority, produces tables with alarmingly small numbers of cases. But with a few unsystematic exceptions, wherever there are enough cases to make a stable judgment, sensitivity to authority continues to show a relationship to both attitudinal and behavioral conformity even after applying all of the controls.

We therefore make two major points with regard to sensitivity to authority. First, persons who feel highly sensitive to authority are not randomly distributed in the prison population. They are more likely to be the younger inmates, with the most severe prior exposure to criminality, and with the least favorable social backgrounds. But second, these differences are not enough to explain away the effect of feelings about authority on actual attitudes and conduct within the prison. There remains a substantial effect of sensitivity to authority on both attitudes and conduct.

Similarly, though to a much lesser degree, those inmates who think of themselves as criminals, or as not having much in common with law-abiding people, are more likely to be found among the attitudinal and behavioral nonconformists. But the differences are not large enough to excite much interest in finding whether they disappear completely when the appropriate controls are applied. They do not appear to, but that only means that their relatively lesser explanatory power is not completely vitiated by controlling for background characteristics.

A fair summary would seem to be that generalized feelings of alienation from conventional society, though springing in part from past criminal conduct, are not the sort of feelings that get translated immediately and importantly into the daily round of life within the prison, or at least not nearly so immediately and importantly as do feelings about authority figures. But that is perhaps to be expected. If we had data on the lives men lead after they leave the institution, we might well find that feelings of sensitivity to authority recede once authority, in the highly visible form of guards and officials, itself has receded. And perhaps at that point more generalized attitudes of alienation may come into play in relationship to decisions about future careers in crime. Unfortunately, we have no data linking an inmate's attitudes at one time to his conduct at a future time, and there are enough situational contingencies that will intervene to make us extremely cautious in predicting any such associations.

Summary and Conclusion

In this chapter we have shifted our focus from the institutional to the individual level. We are directing our attention to the social psychology of inmate life, as distinct from the social organization of the prison. We have done this by introducing two primary indices of inmate response to the prison, a measure of conformity to staff norms and goals on the one hand, and an indicator of feelings of being either helped or harmed by imprisonment on the other. These two indicators, we have argued, are basic to much of the thinking about imprisonment, and we have tried to show that each one has some validity as a measure of inmate response.

We then turned to the effect of an inmate's social and criminal background on his response to the prison. Perhaps our central and most provocative finding is the enormous importance of age as a predictor of response. The older a man is, the more likely he is to conform to the norms of the prison (as against the informal norms of inmate society), while simultaneously the more likely he is to feel that his stay in prison will be harmful to him after he leaves. Although we are also able to show consistent effects of one's social and criminal experience, and although they add to the effect of age, age remains the most important of our predictors of inmate response.

We then turned from "objective" background factors to inmates' feelings about themselves and their effect on response to the prison. We showed the considerable effect of sensitivity to authority on response, and the effect as well of feelings of being a criminal, or of being alienated from conventional society. These effects, although related to age and other background variables, do not disappear when such variables are controlled: there is an independent effect of self-conception on response to the prison.

Throughout this chapter we have tried to take note of the frailties as well as the strengths of our findings and of the indicators on which they are based. We want to remind the reader once again of the relatively limited amount of information we have on the social background of the inmates, and the richer though still limited information available with regard to their prior criminal experience. In addition, we would be happier if we could locate more precisely the temporal order of our variables, particularly the relationship of self-conception items to both our background and our response measures. Finally, we note again the extent to which, of necessity for this type of study, we must rest upon an inmate's paper and pencil response, rather than on observations of his conduct.

But with due consideration for such limitations, we want to stress the positive features of what we have found. Many pieces of survey research are forced to make much of relatively small percentage differences in responses among various categories of respondents. Many of our differences, fortunately, are extremely large by survey research standards. By combining social and criminal background characteristics with self-conception indices, for example, we can really go a long way toward explaining why some inmates conform to staff norms and others are nonconformists. Similarly, by having a very heterogeneous group of inmates with regard to age, we are in a position to note the extremely important effect of one's age on one's response to the prison, a finding not easy to document in studies based upon single institutions.

Throughout all this analysis, however, we have been treating the inmate implicitly as though his response was determined solely by what he brought with him to the prison, in the form of attitudes and self-conceptions shaped by his prior social and criminal background. Yet the single most important thing about imprisonment, in the eyes both of those who live in the prison and those who study it, is the nature of the social life that forms within the confines of incarceration, including the relationships with those inside to those out. And it is this crucial feature of the social psychology of inmate life to which we now turn.

6

Patterns of Social Involvement and Inmate Response to Incarceration

Patterns of social involvement are commonly believed to be among the most important determinants of human behavior. Whenever we become concerned with explaining why persons in a given setting act as they do, we are likely to argue that it is because of the amount and type of interaction they have with other people. People learn to behave the way they do because of the company they keep. And if they behave in ways we don't understand, it is often because they seem to keep no company at all. These themes are found throughout the literature of social psychology. Indeed, for social psychological analyses, patterns of social involvement are as central as personal motivations are for psychological analyses: a basic and pervasive feature of the human scene which accounts for a large portion of the variation in human behavior.

What is true of social life generally has proven to be distinctly important in the world of the prison. As we have already seen (in Chapters 3 and 4) both correctional philosophy and actual practice have led to major changes in the rates of social contact and involvement for inmates in different prison environments. And as we shall see shortly, studies of individual prisons frequently focus heavily, indeed crucially, on the patterns of social contact among inmates as an explanation for

S. Wheeler and H. F. Cline, *The Scandinavian Prison Study*,
Palgrave Studies in Prisons and Penology,
https://doi.org/10.1007/978-3-030-26462-8_6

their response to imprisonment. The importance of this theme leads us to devote this entire chapter to an assessment of the effects of differentials in patterns of involvement and contact among inmates. The responses that concern us most are by now familiar, for they include the same responses we have just examined in connection with personal background, namely, feelings of being helped or harmed by imprisonment, and attitudinal conformity or nonconformity to the prison staff. Throughout the chapter our guiding question is: what difference does it make if an inmate is in close contact with his fellow captives, with the guards, or with friends and relatives who are outside while he is in?

Fortunately, we need neither to speculate on the effects that might occur, nor do we need to search the data for the existence of possible relationships. We need not because important parts of general theory in sociology and social psychology provide us with two distinct but related sets of hypotheses about the differential effects of patterns of involvement on inmate response. We begin this chapter by reviewing these two bundles of hypotheses.

Emile Durkheim and the Theory of Social Integration

The importance of group ties for social functioning has been known to sociologists at least since Durkheim's classic book, *Suicide*.[1] In a powerful argument drawing on integration in religious systems, family systems, and political systems, Durkheim proposed that it was the fate of the least integrated, those who are free of the constraints social integration imposes, to lose a sense of meaningfulness and hence to be most disposed to suicide when stressful situations were encountered.[2]

[1]Emile Durkheim, *Suicide: A Study in Sociology*, trans. John A. Spaulding and George Simpson (New York: The Free Press, 1951).

[2]It goes almost without saying that Durkheim's total argument with regard to suicide is much richer and complex than that portion devoted to egoistic suicide, the one of Durkheim's types of suicide most germane to our analysis.

This theme, of course, has been felt to have consequences far beyond suicide itself. Or to put it differently, suicide is only one of the dependent variables that might be predicted from the degree of social integration. The same theme of the importance of integration, particularly through primary groups, has been echoed in major studies of the work environment,[3] the resettlement of immigrants,[4] and the fate of soldiers during wartime.[5] Although a rereading of Durkheim reminds one that he placed emphasis on social integration in a wide variety of contexts, much of the work that has derived from his initial insights has come to stress informal involvement with others of the type captured best in his own analysis by the strength of family ties. One's sense of identity, of mental or emotional health, of general wellbeing, seems to be intimately tied up with the density of group involvement.

We can apply this theme to the prison by a reformulation of Durkheim as follows[6]:

1. Social involvement provides psychic support to persons facing threatening and difficult social situations;
2. Confinement in prison is a potentially threatening and difficult social situation;
3. Therefore, the stronger the inmate's social ties, the less he will feel psychologically harmed or damaged by imprisonment.

As stated, the argument pertains to the sheer quantity of social contact during the time a person is imprisoned and says nothing about the source of that contact. Hence, we shall provide the most direct test of the argument by developing an index of the total amount of contact a

---

[3]Elton Mayo, *Human Problems of an Industrial Civilization* (New York: Macmillan, 1933); F. J. Roethlisberger and W. J. Dickson, *Management and the Worker* (Cambridge, MA: Harvard University Press, 1939).

[4]William I. Thomas and Florian Znanieki, *The Polish Peasant in Europe and America*, 2 vols. (New York: Octagon Books, 1971).

[5]Samuel A. Stouffer, et al., *The American Soldier: Studies in Social Psychology During World War Two*, 4 vols. (Princeton, NJ: Princeton University Press, 1949).

[6]Robert K. Merton, *Social Theory and Social Structure*, revised and enlarged edition (Glencoe, IL: The Free Press, 1957), p. 97.

person has while in prison and relating this index to feelings of being harmed by prison life.

Edwin H. Sutherland and the Theory of Differential Association

As we saw in the previous chapter, the theory of differential association directs our attention to the content of the value systems to which one is exposed as a result of his social ties. It places emphasis on content rather than sheer density—on who one's involvements are with, rather than on the total amount of involvement. Men differ widely in the degree of their exposure to conservatives or liberals, atheists or true believers, athletes or artists, and each combination of these differences is likely to yield a different pattern of attitudes and values.

Sutherland's theory of differential association has provided a formal statement of this doctrine, particularly as it applies to the process of becoming a criminal.[7] Without repeating our presentation of Sutherland's theory from Chapter 5, let it simply be noted that the same argument has been applied to the prison setting at least since Donald Clemmer's first in-depth sociological study of incarceration.[8] Here the argument is simply that whatever benefits may accrue to mental health from social contact with others, such contacts also expose the individual to values and attitudes which may or may not be conducive to social reformation. Indeed, Clemmer developed the theme of prisonization to refer at least in part to what happens to inmates as they spend an increasing amount of time with other inmates in the prison, the general theme being that they will develop a set of attitudes that are hostile to conventional society, to the legal system which has imprisoned them, and to institutional staff who are the executors of the judgment and sentence rendered by that system. From the perspective of Sutherland's

[7]Albert K. Cohen, Alfred Lindesmith, and Karl Schuessler, eds., *The Sutherland Papers* (Bloomington: Indiana University Press, 1956). See also Edwin H. Sutherland and Donald R. Cressey, *Criminology* (Philidelphia: Lippencott, 1974)

[8]Donald Clemmer, *The Prison Community* (New York: Holt, Rinehart and Winston, 1958).

differential association theory, as inmates interact more with other inmates, and have less contact with the staff or outside world, they have far greater opportunities to learn and adopt the prevailing beliefs and values of inmate society as opposed to those of the conventional society. To formulate the hypothesis in propositional terms:

1. The values and attitudes one holds are a function of the values and attitudes to which one is exposed in interactions with others.
2. The values and attitudes held by prison staff and persons outside the prison tend to be more conventional and conformist in character than are the attitudes and values obtaining within the inmate social system.
3. Therefore, the more a given inmate has contact with prison staff or persons outside the institution, and the less he has contact with other inmates inside, the more conventional his attitudes will be.

Two qualifications need to be stressed immediately. First, this argument rests on a very large assumption, untested within the body of this research, with regards to the values held by our three major sources of contact; namely inmates, staff, and persons in the external world. By now there is a fair body of independent evidence on some of the major themes in the inmate value system, at least in the United States.[9] One of us has presented elsewhere some data regarding the divergent orientations of inmates and staff in an American institution.[10] The contrasting value systems of inmates and staff are of course not unknown within the Scandinavian systems as well.[11] But little is directly known about the values and attitudes of those persons outside the prison with whom

[9]Gresham M. Sykes, *The Society of Captives: A Study of a Maximum Security Prison* (Princeton University Press, 1958); Gresham M. Sykes and Sheldon L. Messinger, "The Inmate Social System", in *Theoretical Studies in Social Organization of the Prison*, Social Science Research Council Pamphlet No. 15, eds. Richard A. Cloward et al. (New York: Social Science Research Council, 1960), pp. 5–19.

[10]Stanton Wheeler, "Role Conflict in Correctional Communities," in *The Prison: Studies in Institutional Organization and Change*, ed. Donald R. Cressey (New York: Holt, Rinehart and Winston, 1961), Chapter 6.

[11]Ulla Bondeson, *Fangen i Fangsamhallet* (Malmo: P. A. Norstedt and Soners Forlag, 1974).

an inmate is in contact while he is inside. Furthermore, even the aforementioned studies in the United States are rooted in an earlier period in corrections and may be subject to modification in the rapidly changing relationships between inmates, staff, and the broader community.

A second and related qualification goes to the crude and oversimplified nature of the argument. For by stating the argument so that it applies generally to inmates, staff, and the community outside, we overlook the important differences within each of these social worlds. Studies of the inmate world alone testify to the rich variety of orientations inmates may bring to the prison and to each other.[12] We should undoubtedly anticipate similar variation among staff and perhaps particularly among people outside the institution. Thus it is quite easy to imagine particular instances in which inmates support one another in a relatively pro-social or conventional orientation, only to be tempted toward deviancy by a particular staff member or relative. Again, survey research is probably at its best in establishing the general direction of relationships for large categories of people, and at its weakest in enabling one to disentangle the subtle influences that may obtain among special sub-groups. But recognizing these shortcomings, the main argument still stands, and indeed is supported by an abundance of evidence from other studies.

Measuring Patterns of Involvement

We asked a number of questions regarding contacts between inmates, one of which receives our primary attention in this analysis. That question is simply: "Have you made any good friends among the other inmates in this institution?" It may say something about the general character of prison environments to note that almost a quarter of all the inmates report having made no good friends in the institution, and a total of 60% of the inmates had made at most one or two good friends. In any event,

[12]Esther Heffernan, *Making It in Prison: The Square, the Cool, and the Life* (New York: Wiley, 1972).

we use as our most direct indicator of involvement with other inmates the number of friends an inmate has made while in the institution.

Our other questions reflected efforts to assess an inmate's ties to and feelings about other inmates in the institution, short of detailed sociometric data about who were friends (or enemies) of whom. Each question tells us something slightly different about inmate life, and although we feel that the question regarding friendship is our single best indicator of inmate involvement, the others give us a fuller sense of the quality of that life. One item asked how often inmates talk informally with other inmates, with categories ranging from "several times a day" to "never." As the responses in Table 6.1 indicate, responses to this item

Table 6.1 Items reflecting the nature and degree of contact and involvement among inmates

Number of inmate friends	%	(*N*)
None	23	(449)
One or two	37	(708)
Three to five	18	(339)
More than five	22	(422)
Total	100	(1918)
Informal conversation, other inmates		
Never	3	(67)
Less than once a month	2	(38)
At least once a month	2	(34)
At least once a week	5	(104)
At least once a day	16	(316)
Several times a day	71	(1362)
Total	99	(1921)
Use of free time		
Mostly by oneself	33	(615)
With one or two inmates	21	(394)
Several inmates, not any one group	31	(582)
Mostly in group who are together a lot	16	(296)
Total	101	(1887)
Preferences for more or less contact		
Want more opportunity to be alone	18	(356)
It is all right as it is now	35	(672)
Want more opportunity to be together with others	47	(900)
Total	100	(1928)

give a rather different sense of inmate contact than do responses concerning the development of "good friends." Whereas almost a fourth of the inmates report not making any good friends, fewer than 15% of the inmates report having informal talks with inmates less often than once a day. One might characterize inmate response as suggesting fairly extensive informal contacts on a casual basis, but without the development of really deep ties.

That interpretation is further reinforced when we examine another question, this one having to do with the use of free time. Again as portrayed in Table 6.1, almost two-thirds of the inmates report spending their free time either by themselves, or with several different inmates, but not in any one group. This again suggests the lack of development of really deep ties and commitments on the part of most inmates. And when we examine the joint responses to questions about friendships made on the one hand, use of free time on the other, even further confirmation of this picture emerges. Although it is certainly true that inmates who have made no friends are likely to spend their free time alone (54% so report), it is also true even among those inmates who have made the most friends, some 16% report spending most of their free time alone. And among all the inmates who have made more than three close friends, the modal use of free time is not "with a group of inmates who are together quite a lot" but rather "with several different inmates but not in any one group."

Now this lack of intensive involvement with other inmates is certainly a variable, not a constant. It varies across types of inmates, with older inmates being much more isolated than younger ones, and across types of institutions, with youth institutions predominating in the development of friendships, preventive detention institutions next, and the normal prisons last. But it might still be asked whether the basic tendency of inmates to spend time alone and not to develop deep involvements with other inmates is a matter of personal choice, or a matter of the structure of the prison environment.

In part with that consideration in mind, and in part because the prison environment as a twenty-four hour living arrangement, gives little opportunity for privacy, we asked one further question of our inmates: "If you yourself could decide, would you prefer to have more opportunity to be alone, or would you prefer to have more opportunity to be together with other inmates?" The responses (as indicated in Table 6.1) suggest that Scandinavian prison inmates suffer more from isolation than from over-involvement with other inmates. At least when given a choice, about two and one-half times as many opt for more contact with other inmates as opt for less. Perhaps a different way of putting it is that if inmates were free to choose their own living arrangements, they might very likely choose both for more opportunities for privacy, and for more opportunities for contact; but when forced to choose between one or the other, the clear choice is for contact over privacy.

Although our interest in this chapter is in the general form of relationships between inmates, and not in the effects of particular institutional environments, it should be noted that the relationship between responses on our various indices of inmate contact tend clearly to show up within the separate institutions, as well as across our population of inmates. For example, in all fifteen institutions the relationship between having many inmate friends and spending free time with other inmates is positive, while in thirteen out of fifteen institutions the more inmate friends one has, the less likely one is to want more contact with other inmates. Similarly, the more contact one has with other inmates, as measured by our "weak" item of informal talk, the more likely one is to have inmate friends, to spend free time with other inmates, and the less likely one is to want even more contact. So there is a consistency in both their responses and in their interrelationships that gives us a sense of confidence about the quality of inmate reports on their own behavior and feelings with regard to other inmates.

We have less extensive data about contacts between inmates and staff. Our basic information (apart from observations on staff power and influence as reported earlier) comes from items asked separately about the custody staff and the "treatment" staff with regards to amount of contact, and desired contact. The responses, as reported in Table 6.2, would seem to tell a very clear and consistent story. The story reinforces what we learned at the institutional level, namely, that surely in terms of quantity and quite likely in terms of quality of relationships, guards are the dominant official force within these institutions. Inmates have

Table 6.2 Items reflecting the nature and degree of contact and involvement between inmates and staff

Frequency of informal talk with:	Guards		Treatment staff	
	%	(*N*)	%	(*N*)
Never	22	(423)	27	(510)
Less than once a month	12	(228)	35	(667)
At least once a month	9	(165)	19	(366)
At least once a week	16	(313)	15	(287)
At least once a day	23	(436)	3	(50)
Several times a day	19	(358)	1	(16)
Total	101	(1923)	100	(1896)
Desire for more or less informal contact with:				
Desire for more	46	(879)	66	(1257)
It is all right as it is	33	(638)	23	(455)
Desire for less	21	(406)	11	(202)
Total	100	(1923)	100	(1914)

far more contact with guards than they do with treatment staff personnel. Indeed, four-fifths of the inmates report having contact with social workers, psychologists, or psychiatrists less than once a week in contrast to about half as many who report that little contact with guards. And when we look at desired contact, six times as many inmates want more contact with treatment staff rather than less contact, compared to a little over twice as many who feel that way about guards. These figures should serve forcefully to remind us about the basic functions of the institutions we are studying. Whatever rhetoric or professional gloss is put on the nature of such institutions, most of them remain basically, and primarily, institutions for the punishment of convicted offenders, rather than institutions for the treatment of the ill or the irresponsible. And similar to the relations with inmates, the desire clearly is for more rather than less contact with the staff.

One apparent effect of the structure of relationships among inmates on the one hand, and between inmates and staff on the other, is what would appear to be a fairly even balance, overall, in the extent to which one or the other of these two dominant social forces in the prison gives direction to inmate life. We asked two further questions of the inmates: first, whether an inmate would take a personal problem to another inmate or to one of the staff, and second, whether he usually finds out about rules and regulations in the institution from other inmates or from staff. Slightly over half of the inmates (54%) report that they would take a personal problem to a staff member, while slightly under half (48%) report that they learn about rules and regulations from the staff.

Now it is not at all clear what to make of these figures. On the one hand, given the fact that staff have all the formal authority, much of the power, and in the conventional wisdom are there to "correct" those who have gone wrong, it could be seen as a massive failure where over half of the inmates get their basic orientations from other inmates, and almost half would reject staff in favor of other inmates in search for a solution to a personal problem. On the other hand, considering all that is known about life in total institutions, it is perhaps remarkable that as many as half of the inmates would turn to the staff rather than their fellows for information or guidance. In any event it seems fairly clear that inmate contacts with staff, as with other inmates, are marked more by frequency than by intensity, and that the frequency is virtually entirely in relationship to custodial personnel. This latter fact, coupled with the extremely skewed distribution of contacts with treatment staff, leads us to rely on an index of contacts with guards as an indicator of contact with the staff. It is somewhat reassuring to know that inmates who report contact with one category of staff are also more likely to report contact with another, so that we do little violence to the data by allowing contact with guards to stand for contact with officials more generally.

We turn now to indices of involvement with persons outside the institutions. As in the case with inmates and staff, the best we can do is to get some rough indicators of the amount of contact and involvement with relatives and friends outside, without being able to inquire in detail as to the nature and extent of the involvement, precisely whom the involvement is with, and other questions one would surely want to know for a detailed examination of the effect of life outside on life within. But even the crude indicators reported in Table 6.3 tell us something about the nature of ties to the outside world.

Table 6.3 Items reflecting nature % degree of contact between inmates and persons outside the prison

	During past month, letters that inmate:			
	Wrote		Received	
Frequency	%	(*N*)	%	(*N*)
None	24	(441)	28	(505)
One or two	26	(474)	23	(424)
Three or four	25	(469)	22	(392)
Five to seven	13	(243)	13	(238)
Eight to ten	7	(122)	8	(154)
Eleven or more	5	(83)	6	(110)
Total	100	(1832)	100	(1823)
	Number of visits during past month:			
None	64	(1196)		
One	18	(332)		
Two	8	(157)		
Three or four	7	(131)		
Five or more	3	(62)		
Total	100	(1878)		

Roughly a fourth of the inmates report no mail contact with relatives and friends outside the institution during the past month, with another fourth having at most two contacts during the month. Responses then trail off, whether we examine letters written or letters received, to a very small percentage who have fairly dense involvement as indicated by the sheer quantity of mail written and received. But the important data would seem to be that as many as a fourth of the inmates have virtually no contact outside by way of letters or postcards, which are the only widely available means of contact with relatives and friends. Furloughs were a possible means of contact for a relatively small number of inmates in some institutions. Telephones in most institutions are available only for emergencies. As the remainder of Table 6.3 shows, visits are none too frequent. Almost two-thirds of the inmates have done without a visit during the previous month, and over 80% of the inmates have had at most one visit. Again, it is a tiny fraction for whom visits are frequent occurrences. And this despite the fact that a number of our institutions were located near major population centers or capital cities.

Table 6.4 Relationship between number of letters and visits from persons outside the prison

	% of inmates with one or more visits among those who have:			
	Written letters		Received letters	
Number of letters	%	(*N*)	%	(*N*)
None	16	(433)	12	(498)
One	22	(184)	24	(181)
Two	34	(281)	29	(234)
Three	35	(175)	46	(155)
Four	51	(286)	52	(233)
Five to seven	52	(240)	52	(234)
Eight to ten	58	(120)	63	(152)
Eleven or more	64	(83)	66	(110)
Total		(1802)		(1797)

Given this relatively low rate of contacts to the outside world, one might ask whether the various types of contact are in effect compensating for one another, or whether they are mutually reinforcing. The answer with regard to letters written and received is plain and simple: those who write letters receive them in return (or those who receive write). The relationship is so strong that we could locate only a small proportion of inmates whose writing and receipt of letters is "out of balance," that is, who write many more letters than they receive, or who receive many more than they write.

Is the same thing true of the relationship between letters and visits? Table 6.4 shows convincingly that it is: the percentage of inmates who have received one or more visitors during the past month increases steadily as the number of letters written or received increases. Thus, mail and visits reinforce one another rather than compensate for one another—the inmate with contacts from one source tends to have it from the others as well. We are left, then, with an image of a quarter of the institutional population having very little contact with the outside world, and a small percentage who have anything that could be regarded as a high amount of contact.

A Direct Test of the Durkheim and Sutherland Hypotheses

In order to provide a direct test of the hypotheses suggested by our reading of Durkheim and Sutherland, we scored each inmate according to whether he was above or below the median for the entire population of inmates on (a) number of close friends, (b) frequency of informal contact with guards, and (c) frequency of contact with the outside world as judged by a combination of letters received and written. The logical possibilities lead to an eight-fold typology defined by the patterning of responses to the three items. The most simple and direct test of the two hypotheses, however, can be made by collapsing the eight categories in differing ways depending on the hypothesis in question. The Durkheim hypothesis suggests that it is the total quantity of involvement, regardless of source, that is crucial, and for that purpose we classify inmates according to whether they are above the median in contact with all three possible sources of involvement. To test the hypothesis inferred from the work of Sutherland, we classify inmates according to whether they are high on inmate contact and low on the other two categories (the most complete form of exposure to criminal or deviant conceptions of reality) or, at the opposite pole, whether they are high in contact with staff and the outside world and low in contact with inmates; that is, whether two of their three patterns favor the "criminal" side of the equation, or two out of three favor the "conventional" side. And we are now prepared for the first main test of the theories.

Clearly, at least at this simple and most direct level, both ideas receive confirmation. The first evidence appears in Table 6.5. The less contact one has with others, the more likely he is to feel harmed by his stay in prison. Fewer than half of the inmates who were above the median on all types of contact feel harmed by their stay, compared to over three-fifths of those who were below the median on all three types of contact. The relationship is not overwhelming, but clearly consistent with the Durkheim hypothesis.

When we turn to the relationship of the pattern of contact to attitudinal conformity (Table 6.6), a much stronger relationship is observed,

Table 6.5 Relationship between quantity of contact and feelings of harm by incarceration

	% who feel harmed	
Quantity of contact	%	(*N*)
Low	63	(228)
Medium low	62	(643)
Medium high	57	(661)
High	48	(224)
Total		(1756)

Table 6.6 The relationship between patterns of contact and attitudinal conformity

	% attitudinal conformists	
Pattern of contact	%	(*N*)
Low inmate contact	76	(328)
Medium low inmate contact	67	(720)
Medium high inmate contact	62	(553)
High inmate contact	40	(133)
Total		(1734)

and in the direction consistent with Sutherland's thought. Over three quarters of the inmates who are low in inmate contact and high in contact with staff and the outside world are conformists on our measure of attitudinal conformity to staff norms, while that is true of only two-fifths of those who are high in contact with inmates, and low with the other two groups.

Thus at the simplest level, both hypotheses receive support, though the one derived from Sutherland more strongly than that derived from Durkheim. These findings are reinforced when we look at the related measures of conformity and help that we introduced in Chapter 5. Behavioral conformity, like attitudinal conformity, is strongly influenced by an inmate's patterns of involvement: 82% of the inmates who have high contact with the staff and the outside world but low contact with other inmates are free of any conduct infraction reports, compared to 65% who are high in contacts with other inmates but low in contacts with the outside world and staff. The relationship is not as strong as attitudinal conformity, perhaps in part because, as we noted before, the measure is a report of the behavior of guards as well as of inmates. But it does lend further confirmation to the general relationship between patterns of involvement on the one hand, attitudes (and actions) on the other.

The validity measure we introduced in Chapter 5 for help and harm was a measure of the extent to which inmates felt they benefitted, or failed to benefit, from one or another of some six institutional programs. This measure relates even more strongly than our general measure of help and harm to the quantity of inmate involvement with others in the prison. Some 57% of those inmates who are low in interaction with other inmates, staff, and the outside world deny receiving benefit from all or all but one of the various possible sources. This contrasts with less than half of that number (26%) whose rate of denial is that high among inmates with a high quantity of involvement with others. Again, then, those who are most extensively involved in social life are least likely to reject the institution's programs.

If these results are truly general we should find that they hold up across our three major types of institutions, though perhaps with some modifications of the relationships.[13] The results of such analysis appear in Table 6.7, which shows the variation in percentage of inmates who feel harmed by their stay in relation to the quantity of their social involvement, and variations in attitudinal conformity in relationship to the content of that involvement. The results lend further confirmation: for each major type of institution, and for both of our measures, the

[13]For purposes of this analysis, we excluded the two special institutions, Seutula and Kragskovehde, because of their special characteristics that make them atypical of our three major types of institution. The analysis is based upon five normal prisons (two in Denmark and one in each of the other three countries), a preventive detention institution in each country, and a youth institution in each country. For further discussion of the different types of prisons, see Chapters 2 and 3 Supra. Probably because of age differences correlated with type of institution, the patterns of involvement are not spread equally across the different types of prison. Youth institutions in particular tend to have many persons who are high on all forms of involvement, few who are low. This is in contrast to the normal prisons and preventive detention institutions. Specifically, 15% of the inmates in preventive detention and normal prisons are in the lowest category on our quantity of involvement index, in contrast to only 4% of inmates in youth institutions. At the other extreme, 31% of the inmates in youth prisons are in our highest quantity of involvement category, in contrast to 9% in the other two types of institutions.

Table 6.7 Relationship between patterns of contact and response to incarceration by type of prison

	Normal prisons		Preventive detention institutions		Youth institutions	
	%	(*N*)	%	(*N*)	%	(*N*)
Quantity of contact	% who feel harmed					
Low	64	(116)	67	(64)	75	(12)
Medium low	64	(317)	64	(163)	61	(64)
Medium high	61	(282)	61	(144)	42	(113)
High	53	(85)	59	(29)	34	(83)
Total		(800)		(400)		(272)
Pattern of contact	% attitudinal conformists					
Low inmate	73	(174)	87	(68)	67	(42)
Medium low inmate	70	(352)	67	(143)	59	(123)
Medium high inmate	61	(224)	59	(135)	50	(82)
High inmate	41	(49)	44	(39)	26	(23)
Total		(799)		(385)		(270)

pattern shown overall is reconfirmed. Inmates with high quantities of involvement are least likely to feel harmed by their stay, and those who are low in inmate contact but high in contact with staff and the outside are most likely to hold attitudes in conformity with those we presume are held by the staff.

Despite the general consistency in the patterning of the responses, there is an important difference in the strength of the relationships as we move from one type of institution to another. Specifically, in the normal prisons, the relationship of patterns of involvement to attitudes appears generally to be somewhat weaker than is the case overall, while in the youth institutions it tends to be much stronger: there is a 41% differential in the youth institutions between those who are at one end of the involvement pattern versus those at the other, and that is true for both conformity and for feelings of harm. In the normal prison there is a 32% differential in conformity, only an 11% differential in feelings of harm. The differences with regards to feelings of being harmed are particularly impressive: three-fourths of those youths who are low in involvement with other inmates, staff, and the outside world (though the total number is very small) feel that their incarceration will harm them, compared to only one-third of those who are heavily involved with others. But among normal prison inmates, the percent who feel harmed is very restricted, and not nearly as clearly determined by patterns of contact. Just why this patterning occurs remains unclear. Perhaps the combined effect of young age and somewhat more open institutions make it easier for differential patterns of contact to eventuate in very different attitudes in the youth institutions, while older inmates under somewhat more constrained conditions do not sort themselves out so clearly with respect to contact and attitude. Or it may be a simple effect of the somewhat greater variation on response measures for youth institutions.

In any event, one can predict an inmate's attitudes from knowledge of his patterns of involvement much better in the youth institutions than in the normal adult prisons. The preventive detention institutions tend to fall in between, with even higher predictability than the youth institutions for conformity, much lower for feelings of help and harm.

Decomposing and Elaborating the Relationship

The above general findings hold for our indices of quantity and quality of involvement. These indices, we argued, are justifiable on theoretical grounds as giving a crude but fair mode of operationalizing both Durkheim's and Sutherland's ideas. But what of the individual items that make up the patterns of contact? Does each contribute the same amount to the overall index? Are the patterns of involvement themselves interrelated or are they independent? Does the effect of one source of involvement depend on the inmate's patterns with regard to the other two? It is these questions we would now like to explore.

Table 6.8 Relationship between types of contact and inmate response to incarceration

	% attitudinal conformists		% who feel harmed	
	%	(*N*)	%	(*N*)
Inmate contact				
Low	67	(1050)	61	(1068)
High	61	(684)	55	(688)
Outside Contact				
Low	60	(808)	61	(816)
High	69	(926)	56	(940)
Staff contact				
Low	58	(733)	62	(747)
High	71	(1001)	56	(1009)

Table 6.8 presents the relationship between response to incarceration and the three types of contact separately, each dichotomized as they were in the construction of the overall involvement typology. As can be seen from the table, the differences for each item taken singly are quite modest, ranging from 5 or 6% at the smallest to 13% at the largest—hardly the kinds of findings that excite the analyst. Yet when these modest differences are combined into indices of the quantity and the type of contact as shown above, they produce much sharper and more substantial differences. This apparently happens in part because each of the items tends to be independent of the other: the various forms of contact are simply not highly related to each other, and their additive impact appears to be considerable.

The combined effects of the various patterns of involvement can be seen in Table 6.9, which shows the rates of conformity and the feelings of being harmed separately for each combination of involvement. A number of observations flow from the results in this table. First, when we examine the overall effects of any source of contact when the other two are held constant, it is apparent that the effects of all three are about the same, though the average percentage difference is slightly greater for staff contact than for the other two sources.

Second, on both measures the differential effects of different patterns of contact with staff and the outside world appear to be much greater for those who are high in their contacts with inmates than for

Table 6.9 Relationship between varying patterns of content and inmate response to incarceration

Staff/ outside Contact	% attitudinal conformists: High inmate contact %	(N)	Low inmate contact %	(N)	% who feel harmed: High inmate contact %	(N)	Low Inmate contact %	(N)
High/ high	68	(221)	76	(328)	48	(224)	59	(331)
High/ low	66	(186)	70	(266)	53	(184)	60	(270)
Low/ high	65	(144)	64	(233)	58	(146)	61	(239)
Low/ low	40	(133)	57	(223)	59	(134)	63	(228)
Total		(684)		(1050)		(688)		(1068)

those who are low. This is especially true for feelings of being harmed, where the various patterns produce no more than a 4% difference on inmates who are low in their contacts with other inmates, and a 21% difference among those who are high. The same thing is true though to a lesser extent for attitudinal conformity. Why this occurs is not readily apparent. Perhaps low inmate contact signifies a kind of psychological withdrawal from the system that limits the effects of any other kind of contact, while being highly involved with inmates heightens the other effects.

Third, much of the difference observed in attitudinal conformity is traceable to one particular pattern of contact, namely those who are high in involvement with inmates, but low in involvement with staff and the outside world. That is the category that has by far the lowest rate of attitudinal conformity, 40%. Indeed, the rate of conformity shoots up at least 24% for inmates who have a high amount of contact with either staff or with the outside world or both.

Finally, with regards to feelings of being harmed, it is apparent that the effect of inmate contact reverses itself when we contrast inmates who are high in both outside and staff involvement with those who are low. Among those who are high in both, being high in contact with inmates as well reduces feelings of being harmed by some 11% (from 59 to 48%). But among those who are low in contacts with the staff and the outside world being heavily involved with inmates increases feelings of being harmed by 4%. Another way of saying it is that a high amount of contact with inmates is positively helpful provided one is also high in contacts with the outside world and with staff, but it is harmful if one is low in those contacts. The effect of inmate contacts thus depends on the pattern of contacts elsewhere, a finding not predicted by a straightforward application of the Durkheimian idea.

In sum, we find generalized support for our major hypotheses although important qualifications must be made when we look at particular combinations of types of involvement. The principal limitation, of course, is that a questionnaire study like this one simply is not well suited to detect nuances and subtleties of interaction in the prison setting, as might be done in an observational study or through detailed in-depth interviews with members of the prison community. However, we can take the analysis one step further than we have done so far by examining more closely the nature of contacts both outside and inside the prison using additional items and measures, other than those that have formed the primary bases of our inquiry. We now turn to that more detailed analysis.

A Closer Look at Outside Contacts

Our primary measure of contacts with the outside world is an index based on the number of letters written and received during the past month. In Table 6.10 we show the relationship between an inmate's location on that index[14] and some of our primary response measures. Inmates in the lowest category on the index are those who have received and written no letters during the past month. Inmates in the highest category are those who have written or received (usually about an equal number of both) a total of at least ten letters over that same period. The main contrast, then, is between those with no contacts, and those who

[14]It was this index, dichotomized at the median, which was employed in the previous analyses which examined contacts with the outside world.

Table 6.10 Relationship of outside contacts and inmate responses to incarceration

Outside contact	% attitudinal conformists		% behavioral conformists		% who feel harmed		% denying better family relationships	
	%	(*N*)	%	(*N*)	%	(*N*)	%	(*N*)
Low	60	(368)	75	(376)	64	(376)	83	(359)
Medium low	60	(533)	69	(537)	59	(536)	69	(517)
Medium high	69	(459)	80	(468)	56	(464)	59	(447)
High	72	(396)	85	(401)	55	(402)	55	(381)
Total		(1756)		(1782)		(1778)		(1704)

either write or receive a communication with the outside world on the average of once every three days.

As Table 6.10 shows, those inmates who are heavily involved in contacts with the outside world are more likely to be conformists in both attitude and behavior. They are also less likely to feel harmed by their stay in prison. Though the magnitude of the differences is not great, there is a reasonable level of consistency in the patterning. There is a strong difference, however, on the single item that might be thought of as most closely reflecting the virtues of contacts through writing and receiving letters. One of the items that made up our six-item index of whether inmates have benefitted from particular features of their stay in prison was an item that inquired about "improved family relationships." On that index, over four-fifths of those who have written or received no letters deny that they have benefitted from their stay through better relationships with their family, a figure that drops to 55% among those who are highest in contacts with the outside. Thus contacts have their most immediate and important effects on family relationships themselves, with lesser effects on the inmates' generalized response to imprisonment.

Feelings of Support from the Outside World

We now examine whether this effect can be generalized to other features of an inmate's feelings about the outside world. One of our

Table 6.11 Relationship between forms of outside contact and inmate perceptions of support from the outside world

	% high on outside support						
	Letters written		Letters received			Visits	
	%	(*N*)	%	(*N*)		%	(*N*)
None	38	(417)	41	(481)	None	39	(1141)
One or two	35	(458)	35	(406)	One	47	(316)
Three or four	44	(448)	47	(378)	Two	49	(152)
Five to seven	49	(232)	50	(228)	Three+	52	(180)
Eight+	55	(197)	55	(252)			
Total		(1752)		(1745)			(1789)

self-conception indices was designed to tap feelings about the self in relation to persons outside the institution. Three items comprise the index:

1. "My family and friends outside the institution have confidence in me."
2. "People outside the institution do not respect me."
3. "People outside the institution think that I am a bad person."

Since two of the items refer to people outside the institution and a third to friends as well as to family, we assume that inmates who are high on perceptions of receiving support from the outside may well be including more than support received from a wife or parent, even though the letters written and received are primarily letters involving relatives.

Table 6.11 shows the relationships between various outside contacts, including visits as well as letters written and received, and perceptions of receiving support from the outside world.[15] Clearly, the results show a positive effect of contact on one's self-conception with respect to such

[15]Inmates classified as being high on outside support (comprising about 42% of all cases) indicated that they received "support" on all three items or felt "supported" in regard to two of the items and didn't know with regard to a third.

relationships. But there is one consistent deviation from the overall pattern. Inmates who write or receive one or two letters a month, in comparison with those who write or receive more, actually report lower feelings of outside support than those who write and receive none at all. It seems to us quite likely that, especially in the prison setting with its enforced separation from the outside world, those inmates who have a weak level of contact outside may well want much more, and suffer more from limited contact than those who have, for whatever reasons, cut themselves off entirely from the outside world. But this is a post hoc interpretation of a small percentage difference, and probably does not warrant more than a passing speculation.

Discrepancies Between Sending and Receiving Communications

So far we have looked at generalized levels of contact with the outside world. But what about that small group of inmates who write many letters but receive few in return, or that equally small group who receive many and write few? Prison lore (if not actual research) suggests that inmates who write more than they receive are seeking after a conventional way of life, while those who receive more than they write are rejecting it; hence conformity in attitude, and conceivably in behavior after release, might be found more often among the seekers than the receivers. We do not know of published evidence in behalf of this proposition, although an old unpublished parole prediction study in the state of Washington did suggest that inmates who write more letters than they receive are more likely to succeed on parole than those for whom the reverse pattern holds.

We query then whether major discrepancies in the balance between the initiation and the receipt of communication produce different results than those concerning the generalized levels of contact. In Table 6.12, we report the results on a number of our criterion measures for the 7 or 8% of the inmates who during the prior months, wrote at least two or more letters more than they received, and for the equally small number who receive two or more than they wrote. As Table 6.12

Table 6.12 Relationship of the balance between initiation and receipt of communication to various inmate responses

Letters during the past month	% attitudinal conformists		% behavioral conformists		% who feel harmed		% who indicate better family relationships		% high on outside support	
	%	(*N*)	%	(*N*)	%	(*N*)	%	(*N*)	%	(*N*)
None written and received	60	(368)	75	(376)	64	(376)	9	(359)	38	(359)
Two or more written than received	68	(140)	80	(141)	64	(140)	22	(130)	36	(135)
Balance of letters written and received	67	(1115)	77	(1130)	55	(1129)	25	(1087)	44	(1100)
Two or more received than written	65	(133)	79	(135)	67	(133)	29	(129)	48	(127)

indicates (with one exception noted below) virtually no effect is traceable to the discrepancy for our more generalized measures of attitudinal and behavioral conformity, and feelings of help or harm.

An effect does begin to show, however, for the measures that relate much more directly to family ties and a sense of support from people outside. Those who receive more letters than they write are more likely to feel that their family relationships have improved than are those who write more then they receive, though either are much more likely to report improved relationships than are inmates who have no contact at all. And with respect to outside support, 48% of those who receive more letters than they write are high on our index of outside support, in comparison with 36% of those who write more than they receive. One might say then that an imbalance in contacts itself produces some immediate effect on measures reflecting ties to family and persons outside, but that imbalance does not lead over into an influence on an inmate's more generalized response to prison. The one exception to this latter conclusion is the possibility, suggested in the data with regard to feelings of help and harm, that an imbalance itself is harmful relative to the balance, as persons at either extreme have higher feelings of being harmed by their stay in prison than do those who receive and write about an equal number of letters.

We should remind the reader as we conclude our section on outside contacts that the influences of the outer world on the inmate while he is inside are by no means restricted to influences reflected through letters and visits. Although we would expect that these would be perhaps the most important influences because they are typically with inmates' friends and relatives, there are many other sources of ties to the outside world that we were unable to examine directly in this study. These would include contacts through the mass media, including newspapers, magazines, radio, and television. They would also include contacts with the outer world through the staff, who come and go each day, and through the continual arrival of new inmates, many of whom will know of crucial people and events in that outside world that have relevance to inmates already in. At least according to one study in an American setting, a large portion of an inmate's thoughts while he is on the inside are still focused on the outer world.[16] We imagine that letters and visits make it a good deal easier for the inmate to conjure up realistic images of the outer world, but it would be nice if we had more detailed information regarding such mental processes, as well as the amount of contact through the other sources suggested above.

A Closer Look at Inside Contacts

A Refined Measure of Inside Contact

In order to explore as fully as possible the nature and effects of patterns of contact and involvement within the prison, we developed refined indices of contact with inmates and with staff. These refined indices accomplish three things which our cruder dichotomies could not accomplish. First, by using a larger number of items to characterize patterns of actual contact, we can look in a more refined way at contacts, particularly of those who are extremely high or extremely low in their contacts with either inmates or with staff. Second, by using items that reflect an inmate's orientation toward other inmates or to staff, as well as his actual rate of contact with them, we get an attitudinal dimension. This enables us, for example, to speak of inmates who have a low amount of contact with other inmates and who are also lacking a positive orientation toward inmates, versus those who have a high amount of contact and a positive orientation, and so on. Third, because we are using both items of behavior and reflections of an inmate's orientation, we can examine the effect of discrepancies or strains in the inmate's relationship to his environment. For example, we can locate those inmates who are extremely high on contact with other inmates, but who appear to be oriented away from their fellows. Taken together, these three additional features enable a more sustained and detailed examination of patterns of contact and involvement among those who inhabit the prison.

---

[16]Martha Baum and Stanton Wheeler, "Becoming an Inmate," in *Controlling Delinquents*, ed. Stanton Wheeler (New York: Wiley, 1968), pp. 153–185.

Our index of inmate contacts is based upon three items that measure the actual amount of such contact: number of friends, frequency of informal talk with inmates, and whether one spends free time with other inmates or alone. All three have been introduced earlier and will not be further discussed here. In addition, we employed five items reflective of what we call an inmate's orientation. These are a mixed bag conceptually, including whether an inmate has a preference for more or less contact with other inmates, whether he reports that he is a leader among inmates, whether he would take a personal problem to an inmate or to a staff member, and whether he generally learns about rules and regulations in the institution from other inmates or from staff. An inmate who answers three of these five questions in the "inmate" direction is presumed by us to show a strong orientation toward inmate life inside. When combined with the actual amount of contact, we have a refined index in which the lowest categories reflect both an absence of actual contact with inmates and an absence of a positive orientation toward such contact; the highest represents the presence of a very high degree of actual contact with a strong positive orientation, and various combinations are reported in the middle.

We developed a similar index, though one based on somewhat fewer items with regard to staff contact. The actual amount of staff contact is based upon our two items reporting informal contacts with guards and with treatment staff. Although these two items are positively related, such that those high in contact with one type of staff tend to be high in contact with the other, the two are skewed in very different directions because of the nature of prison life and the excess of guards over treatment staff in the institutions. To be in the highest category on guard contact, an inmate must report talking with guards several times a day, whereas to be high on treatment staff contact, the inmate must report talking with treatment staff at least once a week. We then developed a four-item index of orientation toward staff based upon two questions having to do with desire for more or less contact (one with guards, one with treatment staff) and the two questions described above relating to where inmates would take a personal problem and how they learn the rules. The highest "staff orientation" is found on behalf of an inmate who says he wishes he could have more contact with guards, more contact with treatment staff, who reports that he learns the rules from the staff rather than from inmates, and that he would take a personal problem to a staff member rather than an inmate. Inmates who answer three out of four of those questions in the "staff" direction are conceived of as having a strong orientation toward the staff.[17]

Because of the nature of prison life, our refined indices of inmate and staff contact are skewed but in different directions. Only 11% of the inmates are in the two lowest categories with regard to inmate contact, while 36% are in the top two categories. In contrast, 28% are in the lowest two categories on the staff contact index in comparison with only 16% in the top two categories. When this is coupled with the fact that the items assessing inmate contact concern friendships and group formation, as well as informal conversation, while those relating to staff contact are restricted only to having "informal talks," one gets a sense for the strong degree to which involvement with inmates dominates the quality of interaction within the prison.

One final note is in order regarding our refined indices. Since each of them contains both a behavioral and attitudinal component, it is important to examine the relationship between these two aspects of involvement within the prison. In the case of both inmate and staff involvement, the two dimensions are positively related, more strongly for staff than for inmates. About three-fifths of those inmates in the highest staff contact grouping are also high on our "orientation" index, in contrast to less than a quarter who are in the lowest category of staff contact. Similarly, two-fifths of the inmates in the highest category on actual contact with other inmates are also in the highest category in orientation toward inmates, compared to only a fifth of those in the lowest inmate contact category. We should of course expect such a relationship, as inmates are to some extent free to choose the amount of contact

[17]When we look at combined patterns of contact and orientation toward staff and inmates, we drop the two "forced choice" items relating to rules and to personal problems, because they force an inmate to choose between staff and other inmates, and thus may obfuscate relationships where an inmate feels rather equally about both categories, either by virtue of wanting less contact with either of them or by wanting more.

they may have with their fellows or with staff, and we would anticipate that those with a positive orientation would be higher on actual rates of contact.

Inside and Outside Contact

We begin our analysis by examining the relationship between patterns of contact inside, and the ties to the outside world which we have just been studying. Very briefly, and without providing the tabular detail, there is a consistent but modest relationship between contacts with the staff and contacts with the outside world: those who have more of one tend to have more of the other. Thirty percent of the inmates in our most extreme "low contact" group sent and received no letters during the entire month, in contrast to ten percent of those inmates in our highest contact group. So a relationship between the staff and outside contacts does emerge when we use a more refined measure than the dichotomies reported earlier, although the relationship is not a terribly powerful one. Interestingly, the single category of inmates who are in highest contact with the outside world through letters are those who have a lot of contact with the staff but who are not "oriented" toward staff on our items that more closely reflect attitudes than actual behavior. In other words, those who have a lot and who apparently want less contact with staff are the ones most deeply involved in the outside world.

This relationship between the inside and the outside world disappears when we examine inmate contact rather than staff contact. There is virtually no relationship between the amount of inmate contact and the amount of outside contact. Indeed, the single most interesting thing to be learned from a combined look at the joint relationship between inmate and outside contacts concerns one of our "discrepant" categories. Those inmates who are extremely low on actual contact with other inmates but who are "oriented" toward other inmates are the most deprived of all when it comes to contact with the outside world. Fewer than 8% of them receive or write as many as ten letters a month, in contrast to an average of 22% for all other inmates in the sample. And almost a third of this category has written or received no letters in the prior month, in contrast to about a fifth of the whole population.

Contacts with Staff and with Inmates

We turn now to relationships within the prison itself. Do inmates choose between the two major groupings that comprise the prison such that the more contact they have with one group, the less they have with another? Or does one reinforce the other, such that interaction with one segment increases the likelihood of interaction with the other? After examining the distribution of contacts and orientations, we will be in a better position to look once again at the effect of patterns of involvement on response.

The basic data are presented in Table 6.13. The two types of involvement do tend to be related: inmates who are relatively low in involvement with other inmates tend also to be low with regards to staff, whereas those who are high in involvement with inmates tend to be high in their involvement with staff. But perhaps the most important point is that the relationship is weak. Contact with either inmates or staff neither eliminates contact with the other, nor does it require such contact.

Contact and Conformity

The effect of inmate involvement with other inmates on patterns of conformity, both attitudinal and behavioral, is portrayed in Table 6.14. We are particularly interested, of course, in the relationship of inmate involvement to conformity, since that dimension of inmate life occupies a good deal of attention in the prison. As Table 6.14 reveals, an inmate's

Table 6.13 Relationship between inmate contacts with staff and contact with other inmates

	Inmate contact			
Staff contact	Low	Medium	High	Total
Low	45% (132)	37% (278)	35% (225)	(635)
Medium	34% (102)	33% (252)	30% (196)	(550)
High	21% (62)	29% (220)	35% (228)	(510)
Total	(296)	(750)	(649)	(1695)

Table 6.14 Relationship between inmate contacts with other inmates and patterns of conformity

	Attitudinal conformity		Behavioral conformity	
Inmate involvement	%	(*N*)	%	(*N*)
Very low	78	(127)	83	(129)
Medium low	75	(342)	79	(350)
Medium	65	(407)	77	(412)
Medium high	53	(277)	71	(281)
Very high	49	(241)	71	(243)
Involvement & orientation				
Low contact-High orientation	51	(41)	60	(43)
High contact-Low orientation	72	(379)	81	(386)

involvement with other inmates shows a marked relationship to our measure of attitudinal conformity: from 78% conformity among those inmates least involved with the inmate system, to 49% among those most heavily involved. The same general pattern appears, though with not as large a range, when we examine behavioral conformity. Eighty-three percent of those who are removed by contact from other inmates have had no conduct infractions during their stay in prison, in contrast to 71% of those who are heavily involved. This reinforces our finding using dichotomies, and adds about ten percentage points to the differences found using our cruder form of measurement.

This form of analysis also enables us to examine the effect of discrepancies or imbalances in contact and orientation. As Table 6.14 clearly indicates, those discrepancies turn out to reveal something important about life within the prison. We contrast that group of inmates, about one-fifth of our total sample, who are high in actual contact with inmates but are low in what we have called inmate orientation (that is, they are unlikely to say that they would take a personal problem to an inmate, that they would prefer more contact with inmates, that they learn the rules from inmates, that they are leaders, or that inmates come to them for advice) with that tiny group of inmates, a little over 2% of the sample, who are low on inmate contacts though high on inmate orientation. Indeed, something is learned by the difference between the 2 and 20%: the prison with its enforced interaction and its overall relatively high rates of contact between inmates tends to produce a large number who have much contact and would just as soon have less, a very small number who have very little and want much more. Indeed almost three-fifths of all the inmates who are in our two highest categories of contact are oriented away from inmate life, while only around one-fifth of those in the lowest two categories of contact are oriented toward it.

When we examine the effects, both on attitudinal and behavioral conformity, of being in such discrepant categories, a very clear pattern emerges. Despite the fact that generally, involvement breeds nonconformity, those inmates who are very low in actual contact but who are "oriented" toward inmates are almost as low (51%) in attitudinal conformity as those who are at the highest end in involvement and who would prefer even more (49%). For behavioral conformity, the lowest single rate of conformity (60%) is for those inmates with a very little amount of contact with other inmates who have had a very strong orientation toward inmate life. The next to the highest rate of conformity (81%), on the other hand, is among those inmates with very heavy involvement with other inmates in actual contact, but who are oriented away from inmate society. This finding helps us understand the more modest level of relationship found when we do not take an inmate's orientation into effect. For by looking solely at the number of friends, the use of free time, the amount of informal contact with other inmates, we fail to locate those inmates who, despite heavy involvement, are really not oriented toward inmate society, as well as that tiny group who despite very low levels of involvement are clearly oriented toward it. They appear as deviant cases, when in reality those cases tend to be as extreme in response to the prison environment as the more "pure" involvement types.

The same pattern is found when we look at our more refined index of contacts with <u>staff</u> in relationship to attitudinal and behavioral conformity. Without presenting the numbers, we will simply note that virtually the same pattern as existed with inmate involvement (though in the opposite direction) appears with regard to attitudinal conformity, although there appears to be no effect of the overall level of involvement on behavioral conformity. To put it sharply: the levels and degrees of involvement an inmate has with other inmates are of use in predicting whether he will be cited for conduct infractions within the prison. The levels and degrees of his contact with the staff do not. The only exception to this assertion concerns our discrepant categories, where the findings parallel exactly those with regard to attitudinal conformity. Eighty-four percent of those inmates who have little contact with staff but have a positive orientation are behavioral conformists, in contrast to 69% of those who have a great deal of contact but are not oriented toward the staff.

Contact and Help from Staff

We have not paid close attention to our measure of help or harm, because, despite its relevance for testing the general theory of social integration, it is not as close theoretically to our concerns in this chapter as measures that more directly reflect inmate orientations toward inmates and toward staff. But one item drawn from the index of "benefits" from imprisonment concerns whether an inmate feels he has benefitted in self understanding as a result of help from the staff. Table 6.15 shows that inmate responses to that single item vary with differing levels of staff involvement. Indeed, they show a very direct and powerful effect. No more than 3% of the inmates who had the least amount of contact with the staff report being helped in any way by such contact. That percentage rises to a high of 33% among inmates who are most densely and heavily involved with staff, and who are most oriented toward the staff.

Table 6.15 Relationship between inmate contact with staff and feelings of benefit from staff help

	Inmate feelings about self-understanding as a result of staff help			
Staff involvement and orientation	Has benefitted (%)	Doesn't know (%)	Has not benefitted (%)	Total
Very low	3	7	89	(180)
Medium low	6	7	87	(389)
Medium	15	11	74	(547)
Medium high	26	11	63	(321)
High	33	10	58	(135)

Thus the depth and richness of contacts do indeed enable us to distinguish between inmates who feel they are benefitting from those who do not feel that way.

But before being carried away with that relationship, and before leaving the subject of inmate involvement at least for the time being, a sobering thought is also apparent in Table 6.15. Even when we get down to those 135 inmates, less than 8% of our sample, who are highest in their involvement with the staff, both in their actual amounts of contact and in what we have called their "orientation" toward the staff, well over half of them still report that they have not benefitted from their stay in the institution as a result of help from the staff. That is, among these almost two thousand inmates spread throughout a range of institutions in Scandinavia, some of which were considered among the best and most modern in the western world, and among those inmates who were at the absolute extreme in terms of the density of their involvement with staff, still the majority deny receiving any help in understanding themselves from their contacts with the staff. This finding should surely give one pause in thinking about the virtues of the prison as a rehabilitative setting.

Of course, it could be argued that inmates don't know what is good for them—that whether they perceive it or not they are really being helped by their stay. Or perhaps more reasonably, it could be argued that it is an empirical question whether their perceptions relate to their actual conduct after release. Or, it might be suggested that the purpose of rehabilitative programs of prison is not necessarily assessed by an item referring to better understanding of one's self, since most prisons do not attempt to do such psychological work on their charges. Nevertheless, it is at least suggestive of the extent to which the inmate world in these institutions, at the time studied, was unprepared to acknowledge a great deal of help from the various people who comprise the prison staff.[18]

[18]Ulla Bondeson's more recent study of Swedish prisons, which included three of the institutions in our study, finds what appears to be even less of a sense that institutional stays are beneficial (see footnote 10).

The Sources of Differential Involvement

We know more than we did before about the consequences of variations in involvement with inmates, with the staff, and with the outside world. But we have not yet inquired into the sources of variations in patterns of involvement. We are interested in those variations for two reasons. First, since we have shown that patterns of involvement are related to an inmate's response to incarceration we very naturally want to know why an inmate has the particular pattern of involvement that he does. To what extent, for example, is the extent of his ties to other inmates, staff, or the outside world a result of the background he brings with him into the prison?

The second reason for an interest in sources of involvement flows from our analysis of the relationship between an inmate's personal background and his response to the prison, as documented in Chapter 5. Since we know from that chapter that an inmate's background helps us understand his response to the prison, and since we know from this chapter that his ties to others also help us understand his response, we are concerned here with how the two fit together. Do patterns of involvement still show an effect on response, after we hold constant variations in the background inmates bring to prison? Do they have an additive effect, so that we get more explanatory power from knowing both about background and involvement than we get by knowing about either alone? Or do they have an interactive effect, with patterns of contact variously constraining or enhancing the effect of background on response?

The Effect of Age and Marital Status

We begin by examining the effect of age and marital status. The relevant data are portrayed in Table 6.16.[19] As that table indicates, there are

[19]Whereas less than one-fourth of all inmates in our sample were married, this was true of 71% of those inmates incarcerated at Seutula, the Finnish open labor colony. In fact, one-fourth of all married inmates in the sample are from Seutula. Because of this overrepresentation, we were

Table 6.16 Relationship of age and marital status to patterns of inmate contact with staff, other inmates, and persons outside the institution[a]

Marital status	Age Under 21	21–29	30–39	Over 39
	Percent high in staff contact			
Single	68	59	59	56
Married	67	53	60	62
Other	100	60	57	62
	Percent high in inmate contact			
Single	68	35	34	42
Married	67	33	24	29
Other	67	36	25	26
	Percent high in outside contact			
Single	58	51	38	22
Married	100	78	77	69
Other	33	62	51	33
	(N's)			
Single	(222)	(358)	(197)	(90)
Married	(6)	(88)	(121)	(89)
Other	(6)	(80)	(177)	(166)

[a]All respondents from Seutula, the open labor colony in Finland, have been eliminated from this table

no systematic differences between single and married men in patterns of contact with the staff. But with regard to inmate contact, all three groups show a sharp decline in contact as persons move into their twenties, although the only comparison worth giving weight is for single men. Above age thirty there is a general tendency for single men to have more contact with inmates than men who either are or have been married. It appears, then, that being or having been married leads for some decline in involvement with inmates, but that this effect does not begin to show until age thirty and beyond.

concerned that our findings might reflect a "Seutula effect" rather than one attributable to marital status. We have therefore excluded all cases from Seutula in Table 6.16 and base our analysis on data pertaining to the other fourteen institutions. Whether analysis is based on all fifteen institutions or excludes Seutula, the relation-ships between age, marital status and various forms of contact is approximately the same. However, the inclusion of inmates from Seutula inflates the proportion of married inmates with high staff contact and deflates the proportion with high inmate and high outside contacts.

The major effect of marital status is on contacts outside the prison. Within the three age categories for which the numbers are sufficiently large, there is evidence of the enormous effect of marital status on contacts with the outside world through letters. For each age category, single men are much less likely than married men to have a high volume of letters written and received, with those who are divorced, separated or widowed somewhere in between. Furthermore, although there is a general effect of age on contacts with the outside world, with older inmates having fewer such contacts than the younger inmates, the effect of age on contacts with the outside world is extremely strong for single men, and much weaker for married inmates. Confining ourselves to the three older age categories where there are enough cases for comparison, the percentage of single men who are high in outside contact declines from 51 to 22% as one moves from under thirty to forty and over, a 29% decline. The comparable figures for married men are from 78 to 69%, only a 9% decline.

Being married, then, creates a strong bond to the outside world. Being single creates no such bond, and, especially as one grows older, appears to remove chances for strong ties through written communication except for about a fifth of the inmate population.

The effect of these various patterns on the total quantity of involvement is to produce a relatively sharp decline in involvement by age, a decline that is mostly a function of the big decline in inmate involvement as one moves into adulthood, combined with a steady decline in outside involvements with increasing age. The latter effect, as we have shown, is very large for single men, much smaller for married men. Taken together, age and marital status account for a great deal of variation in involvement.

The Effect of Prior Incarcerations

One of the major concerns of penologists is the effect on persons of many periods of confinement. There is a general belief that those inmates who are frequently in prison will become literally "institutionalized" though it has never been precisely clear what that means. In the eyes of some it may mean becoming wise to the ways of prison, used to functioning within the prison milieu, or being increasingly dependent upon the institution as a source of support. To others it may mean a tendency to withdraw from contacts with the outside world and to throw oneself into life within. In any event, this concern leads us to inquire into the effects of prior experience in incarceration on patterns of involvement and contact in the prison. Specifically, we examined the effects on involvement patterns of having no prior incarcerations, having one or two, or having three or more incarcerations preceding the present one. And we examined this effect within age categories, because age is related to the potential for many incarcerations, and since, as we have just observed, age is a factor in determining the nature and extent of contacts an inmate has with others while in prison.

In Table 6.17 we display the effects of many incarcerations, separately for each age category, on our indices of contact. The results seem quite

Table 6.17 Relationship of age and number of previous incarcerations to inmate contact

No. of prior	Age			
Incarcerations	Under 21	21–29	30–39	Over 39
	Percent high in staff contact			
Low	72	54	45	49
Medium	66	57	58	61
High	57	61	62	46
	Percent high in inmate contact			
Low	71	45	45	42
Medium	57	31	28	30
High	86	43	31	41
	Percent high in outside contact			
Low	61	64	72	67
Medium	52	56	50	37
High	43	46	46	22
	(N's)			
Low	(145)	(212)	(119)	(106)
Medium	(86)	(315)	(370)	(231)
High	(7)	(28)	(52)	(41)

clear. Frequent periods of incarceration appear to have little systematic effect on the pattern of an inmate's contacts within the prison. Inmates with many prior incarcerations are not consistently more likely, nor are they consistently less likely, to have a high amount of involvement with other inmates or with the staff. These inconsistent findings mean that there is really no strong evidence that men become progressively withdrawn while in the institution, nor that they become progressively enmeshed within the social system of the prison.

There is a powerful effect of prior incarcerations, however, on men's ties to the outside world. Prior incarcerations lower the amount of contact an inmate has with the outside. For men under thirty, there is an 18% difference in the likelihood of being high in contacts with the outside world between those who have no prior incarcerations and those who are currently serving their fourth (or more) sentence. Furthermore, the gap between those with no prior incarcerations and those with several grows with increasing age, with a 26% difference for men in their thirties, and a 45% difference for those in their forties.

A caution in interpreting these figures is in order. We know that older men tend to have fewer contacts with the outside world than younger men, and we anticipate that within any given age category, the men with most incarcerations are somewhat older than those with fewer, so that the differences may be attributable in some degree to age differences within the broad age categories we used. But the differences by degrees of institutionalization are much greater than could possibly be accounted for by the age factor alone.

These data would seem to suggest rather dramatically the effect that frequent periods of incarceration may have on an inmate's ties to society outside the walls. It would seem only natural that ties to the external world will atrophy without real experience in that world, and men who are currently spending their fourth period in incarceration have had less chance to nurture such ties than those who have seldom or never have been in prison before. It may also be the case that relatives, friends, and family literally give up on inmates as the inmate shows his inability to remain out of prison. Whatever the cause, or combination of causes, it seems apparent that men with many prior incarcerations face a double handicap when they return to the outside world—a handicap produced by their own past failures, and the further handicap of having little social support from family and others outside the institution. It should be noted that no such dramatic effect is observed when we compare inmates on our criminal background index, the index based on age at first arrest, prior jail sentences, and commitment to a youth institution. The patterning of relationships is the same, but they are weaker than those based on prior incarceration in a reformatory or penitentiary type institution.

The above findings are based on our simple original indicators of contacts with inmates, staff, and the outside. One major additional finding emerges when we use our more refined and complex indicators of contacts with inmates, the index that includes both behavior and "orientation" items, and thus permits analysis of discrepant categories— those inmates with low actual contacts with other inmates but who appear positively oriented toward the inmate world, and the much larger group who have a high amount of contact but do not appear positively oriented toward inmate society. The backgrounds from which these two disparate categories of inmates come are instructive and quite predictable from whatever else we know about prisons and their inmates. Those who have low contact but a strong positive orientation toward inmates are seldom drawn from the oldest category of inmates, nor from married men. Furthermore, and importantly, they are rarely drawn from those with the least criminal experience. They tend to be younger, single men with a heavy background of experience in crime.

The reverse is true for that larger group of inmates who are heavily imbedded in actual contacts with other inmates, but whose orientation appears to be away from inmate society. This group is much over-represented by those who have the least criminal background and experience, and is over-represented by married inmates—just the categories one might expect to be least anxious to become thoroughly immersed in the inmate world.

We learn, then, that patterns of involvement with others are importantly a function of the inmate's age and marital status, his past record of incarcerations, and, especially as it applies to those inmates whose attitudes and behavior diverge, a function of criminal experience. We now turn, in the final section of this chapter, to an examination of the way in which these background factors join with patterns of involvement in shaping the inmates response to imprisonment.

From Background to Involvement to Response

In Chapter 5 we tried to account for differentials in response to the prison by appeal to the personal background characteristics the inmate brought with him when he entered. For most of this chapter we have tried to account for the same responses by appeal to the nature of the social involvements the inmate experiences after arriving at the prison. And now we try to fit these two lines together by observing the way in which both background and involvement combine to produce effects that might not be observed by examining either one alone. We do so by returning to our indices of the quantity of involvement and of its content—whether oriented primarily toward other inmates, or toward staff and the outside world. And we do so by examining each one in relation to the response measure seemingly most relevant—feelings of help or harm in relation to the quantity of involvement, and attitudinal conformity in relation to its content.

Background, Quantity of Contact, and Feelings of Harm

As noted in Chapter 5, one's feelings of being harmed by imprisonment tend to increase with age, and as we saw earlier in this chapter, feelings of harm tend to decline with a high quantity of contact. Table 6.18 shows the joint effect of these two factors. Three findings seem most important. First, it seems clear that the effect of quantity of contact is very largely among our youngest category of inmates, and secondly among the oldest, with little systematic variation among inmates between 20 and 40. Among youthful inmates, only 32% of those who are above the median in their contacts with inmates, staff, and persons outside the institution feel that their stay will harm them. Each decline in quantity brings a substantial increase in feelings of harm, with over four-fifths of the inmates who have the least amount of contact feeling

Table 6.18 Relationship of age and quantity of contact to feelings of being harmed by incarceration (% who feel harmed)

Quantity of contact	Age Under 21		21–29		30–39		40+		Total	
	%	(*N*)	%	(*N*)	%	(*N*)	%	(*N*)	%	(*N*)
Low	83	(12)	58	(69)	58	(74)	71	(66)	63	(221)
Medium low	66	(64)	59	(208)	62	(219)	66	(148)	62	(639)
Medium high	44	(93)	54	(216)	64	(199)	60	(146)	57	(654)
High	32	(73)	52	(71)	58	(50)	60	(30)	48	(224)
Total	48	(242)	56	(564)	62	(542)	64	(390)		(1738)

that their stay will be harmful to them. We might perhaps write off this latter finding because it is based upon such a small number of cases. Still, it seems significant that among those twelve young inmates who have very weak contacts with any social group, ten of them are convinced their stay will be harmful to them after they leave.

Second, if we set aside the youngest age category, especially those with low levels of contact, there is a consistent relationship between age and feelings of being harmed, with older men more likely to feel harmed than younger men. Thus the pattern we found in Chapter 5 tends to hold up when we control for the quantity of contact an inmate has with others.

Third, the joint effect of age and quantity of contact, because of the interaction effects just described, is much greater than the effect of either taken alone. Indeed, as the marginal percentage distributions indicate, the two variables considered alone produce less than 20% differences, while taken together the differences are almost 40% if we contrast the young inmates with high quantities of contact with the old inmates with low quantities.

A similar kind of interaction effect, more striking in some ways, appears when we examine the relationship between quantity of contact with others and feelings of harm separately for different marital statuses. The results are portrayed in Table 6.19. Here it seems clear that the overall effect of the quantity of contact is the result of two contrary trends: a very

Table 6.19 Relationship of marital status and quantity of contact to feelings of being harmed by incarceration[a] (% who feel harmed)

Quantity of contact	Marital status							
	Single		Married		Other		Total	
	%	(*N*)	%	(*N*)	%	(*N*)	%	(*N*)
Low	68	(126)	48	(29)	63	(70)	64	(225)
Medium low	62	(312)	64	(132)	63	(189)	63	(633)
Medium high	53	(319)	60	(181)	63	(153)	57	(653)
High	40	(125)	61	(61)	56	(34)	48	(220)
Total	56	(882)	60	(403)	62	(446)		(1731)

[a]All respondents from Seutula, the open labor colony in Finland, have been eliminated from this table

powerful negative relationship between quantity of contact and feelings of being harmed for single men (and a weak negative relationship for the separated, widowed, and divorced) and a relationship that moves in the other direction for those who are married. Again, this may be very much a function of the special rate among married inmates with few contacts, a category with only 29 inmates in it. But even if that figure were considerably higher, it would document the absence of an overall relationship between quantity of contacts and feelings of harm for married men in contrast to a very strong relationship for those who are single.

Findings from these two tables combined give rise to a further idea with respect to the theory of social integration discussed at the beginning of this chapter. Table 6.18 shows that the effect of quantity of involvement is very powerful on younger inmates, much less so among older ones. Table 6.19 shows that the effect of quantity is powerful among single inmates, but much less so among the married, separated, widowed, or divorced. One of the attributes that might join both the young and the single men relative to their counterparts among the older and the married, is an absence of that kind of experience that may tend to make persons more impervious to the effects of their immediate social settings. With increasing age may come increasing experience with life, and a kind of experiential ballast that serves to limit the effect of one's immediate environment. Similarly, marriage may signify an anchoring in social relationships that may limit the effect of one's surroundings.

In contrast, the young single inmate may be much more susceptible to environmental influences, and hence there is a stronger correlation between his patterns of involvement with others and his feelings about the effect of the institution on him. The physical analogy is to a ship at sea. Empty sea vessels—those without weight and cargo, are subject to the pushes and pulls of the winds and the tides. As the vessel fills with cargo or ballast, it is less susceptible to such influences. Our young single inmates are closer to the empty vessel. We wouldn't wish to push the analogy too far, but we would suggest that the "empty vessel" idea may be a useful one in searching for conditions under which persons are more or less affected by their immediate interpersonal environments.

Background, Type of Contact, and Conformity

We now return to our measure of attitudinal conformity and to how that measure is affected by the joint impact of background characteristics and patterns of involvement with inmate, staff, and those outside. Table 6.20 shows the joint effect of age and what we have called the content of an inmate's involvement patterns on attitudinal conformity. (See the discussion of Table 6.6 for how the variable, "patterns of inmate contact," is defined.) As the marginal percentage distributions show, each variable is taken separately has a considerable impact on conformity, with the effects somewhat greater for patterns of involvement alone than for age alone. But the joint effect of the two taken together is extremely powerful. Among the youngest group of inmates who are high in their contacts with other inmates and low in contacts with staff and the outside world, only 17% are at the "conforming" end of our measure of attitudinal conformity. In contrast, among the oldest inmates who are low in contacts with inmates and higher with staff and the outside world, 77% are conformists. In other words, we get a 60% difference in response, in contrast to a 36% difference using the most predictive single measure.

Table 6.20 Relationship of age and patterns of contact to attitudinal conformity (% attitudinal conformists)

	Age									
	Under 20		21–29		30–39		40+		Total	
Pattern of contact	%	(*N*)	%	(*N*)	%	(*N*)	%	(*N*)	%	(*N*)
Low inmate contact	69	(26)	72	(126)	81	(113)	77	(61)	76	(326)
Med/low inmate contact	56	(115)	62	(229)	72	(226)	77	(146)	67	(716)
Med/high inmate contact	48	(79)	57	(158)	60	(158)	77	(146)	62	(541)
High inmate contact	17	(23)	41	(46)	40	(38)	58	(26)	40	(133)
Total	51	(243)	61	(559)	68	(535)	76	(379)		(1716)

It should also be noted that although the effects are generally consistent in both directions, the effect of the pattern of involvement is particularly strong among the young, as was the effect of the quantity of involvement in relationship to feelings of help or harm. And the effect of age on conformity is extremely strong among those who are heavily involved with inmates and only weakly tied to staff and the outside world, whereas it is quite weak among those who are low in inmate involvement and high in involvement with staff and the outside world.

Finally, we turn to the combined effect on conformity of past criminal experience and the inmate's pattern of involvement with others. As we showed in Chapter 5, an inmates conformity bears a systematic relationship to his criminal experience, a finding which is restated in the marginal distribution of Table 6.21. Again, we see the powerful effect of the combination of variables, going far beyond the contribution of either one taken alone. Eighty-five percent of those inmates with little prior experience in crime and with a pattern of contact stressing staff and outside values rather than those of inmates are high conformists in contrast to only 26% of those with a great deal of prior experience in crime who also have strong ties to inmates, and weak ties to others. It

Table 6.21 Relationship of criminal experience and patterns of contact to attitudinal conformity (% attitudinal conformists)

	Criminal experience									
	Low		Medium low		Medium high		High		Total	
Pattern of contact	%	(*N*)	%	(*N*)	%	(*N*)	%	(*N*)	%	(*N*)
Low inmate contact	85	(72)	78	(120)	73	(71)	60	(40)	76	(303)
Med/low inmate contact	73	(179)	70	(233)	60	(154)	62	(108)	67	(674)
Med/high inmate contact	73	(130)	59	(171)	57	(116)	55	(84)	61	(501)
High inmate contact	44	(23)	41	(44)	42	(40)	26	(17)	40	(124)
Total	74	(404)	66	(568)	60	(381)	57	(249)		(1602)

might also be noted that, although an inmate's pattern of involvement with others is quite strongly related to conformity within each of the separate categories of criminal experience, its strongest relationship is for those who have had the least prior experience in crime, as our "empty vessel" theory would suggest.

Two generalizations emerge from the data presented in Tables 6.20 and 6.21. First, as was the case in examining feelings of being harmed, our analysis of conformity shows that again, a man's experiences with others while he is in the institution are more powerfully predictive of his attitudes and orientations than are the personal background characteristics with which he enters the institution. Patterns of social life during incarceration take precedence over experiences prior to incarceration in explaining responses to the prison milieu.

Second, in contrast to our analysis of feelings of help and harm, the combined effects of personal background and involvement patterns tend to markedly magnify the overall relationships of each to conformity, rather than to qualify or modify them as was the case with age and marital status in relation to feelings of being harmed. We should note that the same theoretical rationale underlies both the dimension of prior criminal experience and the dimension of involvement patterns. That theoretical justification is Sutherland's theory of differential association. What we see in the last table of this chapter is that two independent modes of operationalizing the concept, one drawing from criminal experience prior to imprisonment and the other from patterns of social contact during imprisonment, combine to produce a powerful relationship to conformity. If we know a mans criminal history before he enters the prison, and also know his contact patterns within it, we can go a long way indeed toward explaining whether or not he conforms to staff and pro-social norms within the prison.

7

Personal Response in Divergent Prison Environments

Introduction

In this chapter we shall present synthetic analyses of several topics introduced earlier. Up to this point, we have virtually ignored the fact that the 1937 inmates come from four different countries and four different types of institutions. With the exception of the introductory chapters and several comments pertinent to the institutional scatter diagrams in Chapters 3 and 4, we have devoted very little attention to either national or institutional differences. It is now time to turn to systematic analyses of these differences.

We shall start with social climate and examine the variability among the four different nations and the four different types of institutions. The second major portion of the chapter will shift to the response variables. Here we will examine national and type institution differences on the two major response variables, attitudinal conformity, and feelings of being harmed as a result of incarceration. Then we shall take up again our multivariate model and introduce both country and type institution as dummy variables in the regression equation. The final section of this

S. Wheeler and H. F. Cline, *The Scandinavian Prison Study*,
Palgrave Studies in Prisons and Penology,
https://doi.org/10.1007/978-3-030-26462-8_7

chapter examines national differences in inmate opinion on some of the potential benefits of incarceration.[1]

Social Climate

National Differences in Social Climate

The uses and abuses of comparative research have been discussed in the social science literature for a number of years. Concomitant with an emerging interest in cross-cultural, societal, or national analyses among many of the social science disciplines has been the emergence of a new sub-discipline explicitly attuned to the methodological and analytic complexities of such research and to the articulation of its unique contribution to the development of social science theory. Justifications for comparative research have ranged from affording the opportunity to test the generality of one's hypotheses and findings to the facilitation of conceptual clarification.[2] However, most important, engaging in cross-system research affords one the opportunity to expand the range of variation of critical analytic variables and the frequency with which such variation can be observed. It allows one to locate the empirical variability necessary to test one's theoretical propositions and the multiplicity of cases across which such research can be replicated.

---

[1]Editor's note: this material was found in a draft of Chapter 10, the rest of which duplicated much of the analysis and discussion found in Chapter 7. Since the discussion of potential benefits was not discussed in the Chapter 7 draft, it was decided to place it here.

[2]See, for example, Robert R. Sears, "Transcultural Variables and Conceptual Equivalence," in *Studying Personality Cross-Culturally*, ed. Bert Kaplan (Evanston, IL: Row Peterson and Co., 1961); Frederick W. Frey, "Cross-Cultural Survey Research in Political Science," in *The Methodology of Comparative Research*, eds. Robert Holt and John Turner (New York: The Free Press, 1970); or Donald P. Warwick and Samuel Osherson, "Comparative Analysis in the Social Sciences," in *Comparative Research Methods*, eds. Donald P. Warwick and Samuel Osherson (Englewood Cliffs, NJ: Prentice-Hall, 1973).

In the case of our research, these justifications, and particularly the desire to increase the variability and quantity of observations, propelled our cross-national scope.[3] Once we had assured the theoretical and empirical equivalence of data gathered cross-nationally, we generally ignored national distinctions, merged our data, and focused on distinctions between institutions and inmates found in all four Scandinavian countries. That is not to say that we were disinterested in national differences, but that our theoretical orientation directed our primary focus elsewhere.

We have now reached the point, however, that we feel it appropriate to return to a consideration of the impact of national distinctions on the characteristics of prisons. Whether one holds the view that "nationhood" is a shorthand way of identifying a large and perhaps unrelated set of independent variables not yet included in the analyses, such as per capita income, political philosophy, population density, etc., or that "nationhood" represents a more well-defined construct, such as the structure of a national criminal justice system or "national character," an appraisal of the magnitude and patterning of national differences is appropriate.[4]

The following discussion, then, is concerned with the measurement and description of differences in prison climate and later with inmate response across national boundaries. Our approach to the assessment of national differences is largely inductive. In general, we do not expect prison nationality to be an important predictor of the major variables of our study. However, apart from our generalized impressions gathered during the data collection period and our knowledge of the prison systems in these countries, we do not bring to the analysis a set of hypotheses or hunches about the differential salience of nationality to explanations of study variables or theoretical accounts that might

---

[3]See the discussion of study design in Chapter 2.

[4]See, for example A. Inkeles and D. J. Levinson, "National Character: The Study of Modal Personality and Sociocultural Systems," in *Handbook of Social Psychology*, vol. 2, ed. G. Lindzey (Reading, MA: Addison-Wesley, 1954); or Alex Inkeles, "National Character and Modern Political, Systems," in *Psychological Anthropology: Approaches to Culture and Personality*, ed. Francis Hsu (Homewood, IL: Dorsey, 1961), pp. 172–208.

predict such a finding. This portion of our book, then, follows a course of movement from empirical research to theoretical development, illuminated for us in Merton's classic discussion.[5] Whatever the findings of our assessment of national differences, they will help shape the course of future theoretical development and advise us of the profitability of searching for independent or contextual variables that vary along national lines.

Clearly a potentially relevant source of variation cross-nationally can be attributed to aspects of research methods or study design. Before we can make meaningful comparisons between attributes of units, it is necessary to insure that characterizing these attributes through conceptualization or research method are equivalent. The problem of "nonequivalence" (whether in instrumentation, measurement, interviewer—respondent interaction, sampling, coding, or conceptualization) is pertinent to all theoretical development; but its dangers are especially acute in cross-cultural or cross-national research. Where one is not reasonably certain about either the equivalence of the methods by which units have been characterized or about the differences in these methods where nonequivalence has been ascertained, one has no business making variability in these characterizations theoretically problematic. Without such insight one cannot sort out what portion of observed differences is "genuine" and what portion is an artifact of nonequivalent measurement, etc. We have seriously considered these questions, and our judgment—that cross-national data which we present here meet the standards of equivalence—has been justified elsewhere in this monograph (see especially Chapter 2 and the Appendices). Where such judgments may be questionable in a particular analysis, it will be explicitly stated in the text. We therefore will attribute cross-national differences in this chapter to genuine differences that vary by nation and feel reasonably comfortable in so doing.[6]

[5]Robert K. Merton, "The Bearing of Sociological Theory on Empirical Research," in *Social Theory and Social Structure* (New York: The Free Press, 1957).

[6]The issue of equivalence has been explored in great detail in the literature of comparative methodology, see for example, A. Prezworski and H. Teune, "Equivalence in Cross-National Research," *Public Opinion Quarterly*, 1966–1967, 30: 551–568; Frederick Frey, "Cross-Cultural Survey Research in Political Science," in *The Methodology of Comparative Research*, eds. R. Holt and

Table 7.1 National differences in aspects of prison climate (percentages)

	Norway	Sweden	Finland	Denmark
% believing guards have little authority	51	66	37	43
% indicating authority of guards exceeds that of treatment staff	37	19	64	31
% believing institutional rules reflects coercive prison regimes	14	35	60	15
% feeling guards have little understanding of inmates	56	70	77	47
Percent who describe both staff and inmate pressure as high	14	12	28	21
% indicating inmate pressure exceeds staff pressure	36	18	51	27
% perceiving fellow inmates as conformist	42	30	45	47
% whose perceptions of others' nonconformity significantly exceed their own nonconformity	13	20	11	13
Number responding (ranges)	(239–252)	(272–294)	(446–470)	(517–597)

Table 7.1 presents the national distribution of various aspects of prison climate that were found significant in Chapter 4.[7] These figures clearly suggest there are quite pronounced national differences in prison climate, particularly in those elements of climate that reflect the nature

J. Turner (New York: The Free Press, 1970), pp. 173–295; Dell Hymes, "Linguistic Aspects of Comparative Political Research," in Holt and Turner, pp. 295–343; and Gunnar Myrdal, *Asian Drama: An Inquiry into the Poverty of Nations* (New York: The Twentieth Century Fund, 1968), pp. 16–26.

[7]This table does not reflect the responses of inmates from two of the "special" institutions included in our sample: Seutula, the Finnish open labor colony for drunk drivers and others with very short sentences; and Kragskovhede, the Danish open colony for recidivists. It was felt that these two institutions were so specialized and idiosyncratic, that characterizations of their climate might misrepresent the aggregate response of all inmates in their respective countries. These figures reflect inmate responses in prisons which have "structural" counterparts in all four nations: normal prisons, preventive detention, and youth institutions.

of the prison regime and the pressures which it attempts to impose on inmate conduct. We note that 60% of inmates in the Finnish prisons reflect sentiments indicating highly coercive regimes; for example, 82% of Finnish inmates feel that the rules should be reduced and 73% of the Finnish inmates believe the guards rarely overlook minor rules infractions. The Finnish inmates also feel that the guards have a great deal of authority over the daily life of the institution. Fully 77% feel that guards have very little understanding of the inmates. The Finnish inmates also report much higher levels of inmate pressure and much lower levels of staff pressure. At the opposite pole we note that Norwegian and Danish inmates are much less likely to consider their institutions coercive, their guards powerful, or their guards lacking in understanding.

These observations are only suggestive however, lest they reflect differences in the background of the prison inmates which color their perceptions, or the differential allocation of inmates to various types of prisons. We have repeated our analyses for 27 subgroups of inmates similar in age, criminal background and type of institution in which they are incarcerated.[8] Rather than presenting the extensive analyses of the 27 subgroups of inmates, we have decided simply to summarize this material.[9]

Proceeding inductively as we have thus far in this chapter it is difficult to assess whether the findings presented in Table 7.1 are surprising or rather unimpressive. Certainly given the fact that our explorations have focused on a very circumscribed and relatively homogeneous area in the international world of prisons and the fact that these findings from the homogeneous subgroup analysis reflect prior controls for cross-national differences in inmate and prison background, the handful of differences discovered take on at least a modicum of importance.

[8]This analytic technique was termed "homogeneous subgroup analysis" by Hannan Selvin who employed it in his study of leadership, *The Effects of Leadership* (New York: The Free Press, 1960).

[9]Editor's note: The subgroup analysis appeared in a draft of Chapter 10, which overlapped considerably with Chapter 7. The subgroup analysis was not well-articulated and for that reason was not included here.

We have found, generally, national variability in some dimensions of prison climate. In particular, those aspects concerned with the extent and allocation of authority among prison officials are subject to some differentiation by nationality. In expanding our knowledge concerning the social organization of the prison and the variability in institutional climates, it might be instructive then to explore national characteristics and their input into the nation's penal institutions. Such variables as the scope and organization of a national correctional administration; its resources; its ideology (both philosophical and operational) concerning punishment, retribution, or rehabilitation; the allocation, background, and training of its institutional personnel, etc., might be worthy of further exploration in this context. However, our analysis of the responses of inmates during incarceration suggests that our major attention should focus on the background of particular inmates, their contacts and experience while in prison, and the structure and climate of these institutions rather than on national distinctions.

Institutional Differences in Social Climates

In addition to nationality, the second major design feature of this study is the variability in the types of prisons included. In Chapter 3, we made a distinction between four major types of institutions: normal prisons which house a wide variety of adult offenders in institutions which by Scandinavian standards are quite large, usually housing several hundred inmates; preventive detention institutions in which inmates serve indeterminate sentences and are exposed to rehabilitation programs from either a psychological or vocational perspective; youth institutions which typically house a smaller number of young adult offenders; and special institutions which in our case includes only two institutions, The Finnish labor colony and the open institution for recidivists in Denmark.

We know from our earlier analyses that the age of the inmates is a powerful predictor of patterns of interpersonal interaction and inmate response to incarceration. And we naturally expect that these differences will show up in aggregate measures as well.

Table 7.2 Institutional differences in aspects of prison climate

	Normal Prisons	Preventive Detentions	Youth Institutions	Special Institutions
% believing guards have little authority	44	62	32	44
% feeling rules should be reduced	62	62	56	75
% feeling guards overlook minor rule infractions	43	43	57	65
% feeling guards have little understanding of inmates	61	58	67	57
% describing inmate pressure as high	58	47	66	48
% describing staff pressure as high	44	49	59	36
% perceiving fellow inmates as conformists	47	40	31	61

As noted earlier in this volume, the literature on comparative organizational studies generally and more specifically comparative studies of prisons is indeed quite meager. We do not have a large body of research literature discussing either substantive or methodological findings from such research. Nevertheless, we will use our earlier strategy in looking for differences in social climate by type of institution. In Table 7.2, we present differences in selected aspects of prison climate by type of institution.[10] The interesting comparisons in this table are to be made between youth institutions and special institutions on the one hand, and normal prisons and preventive detention institutions on the other. Generally speaking, inmates in youth institutions and special institutions tend to feel that guards have more authority, that the rules in the institution should be reduced, that guards do overlook minor rule infractions, that guards have little understanding of the inmates, that

[10]Editor note: from Hugh Cline to Stan Wheeler in original draft chapter: "Stan, I will have to make this Table comparable to 7-1 in terms of the variables that will be included. The discussion will probably change slightly but I will put a draft in at this point based on the current version of 7-2." A revised table was not found.

both staff and inmate pressure is perceived as being high and, in the case of youth institutions, that few fellow inmates are conformists.

Special institutions are different from the youth institutions on the conformity issue with almost two-thirds of the inmates in special institutions seeing their mates as conformists. The only important difference between normal and preventive institutions is on perceptions of guard authority. A much higher proportion of inmates in preventive detention feel that guards have little authority. This is consistent with our earlier findings where inmates feel that the treatment staff has more authority than the custodial staff in preventive detention.

The pattern of these differences in social climate by nation and type of institution are indeed quite consistent with earlier findings and our expectations. But our interest in the topic does not end here, for we are ultimately concerned with using our knowledge of varying social climates in the institutions to examine their effect on individual level relationships between inmates' background characteristics and involvement patterns with our response measures. In the next section, we will examine differences in these response measures by nation and type institution.

Inmate Response

National Differences

Keeping in mind the same rationale for cross-cultural comparisons used in our analysis of social climate, we present in Table 7.3 the national differences in inmate response to incarceration. As we see clearly from the table, there are essentially no differences in rates of attitudinal conformity by country. With the exception of Denmark, we note that there are only minor differences in the other three countries concerning feelings of being harmed as a result of incarceration. Denmark stands out very clearly on feelings of harm due to incarceration. As noted above, we believe our measure of this variable is equivalent in the four countries, so the much smaller proportion of the Danish inmates (48%) who

Table 7.3 National differences in inmate response to incarceration

Response	Norway	Sweden	Finland	Denmark
% who are attitudinal conformists	67	62	65	66
% feeling their stay will harm them after release	63	67	65	48

Table 7.4 Institutional differences in inmate response to incarceration

Response	Normal prisons	Preventive detentions	Youth institutions	Special institutions
% who are attitudinal conformists	66	70	53	73
% feeling their stay will harm them after release	61	66	44	55

feel that their stay will be harmful after release a true difference compared to the other countries. The very small differences in response to incarceration by type country are not surprising and are quite consistent with our earlier findings. Despite the fact that there are important differences among the four countries in criminal justice systems, we find a great deal of uniformity in the inmate responses to these systems in the four Scandinavian countries.

Institutional Differences

In Table 7.4, we notice rather large differences in rates of response to incarceration by type of institution. With respect to attitudinal conformity, just slightly over half of the inmates in youth institutions are conformists but 70 and 73% of the inmates in preventive detention and special institutions are attitudinal conformists, respectively. We find a similar range of variation in rates of feeling harmed as a result of incarceration. Again, the youth institutions have the lowest rate, 44%. But on this variable we find that preventive detention institutions have the highest rate, i.e., 66%. Again, the findings are consistent and support our earlier analyses.

Combined Effect of Nation and Type Institution

We now turn to our final regression analysis in which we examine the effect of nation and type institution on the response variables. The reader will recall that at the end of the last chapter we presented a multiple regression analysis which examined the relative contribution of social and criminal background variables and our indices of quality and content of interpersonal interaction with the two response variables of attitudinal conformity and feelings of help or harm. In this section, we will expand those regression equations to include the relative contribution of both nation and type institution.

In Table 7.5, we present a summary of the multiple regression which includes all of these independent variables. The data presented in this table are a summary of an analysis which is quite different from any presented earlier. The first half of the table reports the results of the multiple regression analysis for attitudinal conformity. We use dummy variables for measuring the relative contribution of each country and type institution. The multiple correlation can be used to compare contribution of all countries or all types of institutions. We note that all

Table 7.5 Multiple regression for national and institutional effects

	Attitudinal Conformity		Perceived Harm	
Multiple correlation:				
Without dummies	0.364		0.215	
With dummy variables	0.372	($p < .05$)	0.298	($p < .01$)
Change in intercept due to:				
Country				
Norway	−.03		+.02	
Sweden	−.08		+.29	
Finland	+.04		+.04	
Denmark	+.07		−.35	
Type of institution				
Normal	−.01		+.17	
Preventive detention	−.02		+.17	
Youth	−.08		−.32	
Special	+.11		−.02	

of the dependent variables produce a multiple correlation of .364 with attitudinal conformity before the dummy variables are introduced. When the dummy variables are added, the multiple correlation is increased to .372. We present the results of an F Test of significance for the difference in magnitude of these two multiple correlation coefficients. The F statistic is statistically significant with $p < .05$, which means that addition of the dummy variables taken as a whole adds significantly more variance explained.

The reader should note that the meaning of this test of significance is not to generalize from the sample of inmates included in this study to all institutionalized inmates in Scandinavia. As discussed earlier in Chapter 2, we make no pretense for such generalization given the very special and purposeful sampling procedures used in this study. Here the test of significance is used to determine the probability of a "goodness of fit" for the F statistic obtained as a result of the comparison of the two multiple correlation coefficients with a theoretical distribution of all possible obtainable differences in magnitude between such coefficients.

Below the F statistic, we report the relative changes in the intercept which can be attributed to each of the four countries and each of the four types of institutions. Noting that the F statistic is significant, we can then determine that none of the changes in the intercept, contributable to the country are very large with respect to attitudinal conformity. Looking at the second set of figures in the lower part of the table pertaining to type institution, we again note that none of the changes are very large. There seems to be a tendency for inmates from the two special institutions to cause a slight increase the intercept, i.e., +.11. This means that inmates in these institutions are more likely to be attitudinal conformists. Referring back to Table 7.4, this confirms the differences noted with a comparison of percentages. However, the reader should note that the results of the multiple regression equations including dummy variables not only confirms the earlier findings, but suggests that the contribution of special institutions is still discernable in an analysis which in effect holds constant the contributions of all other independent variables in the equation, including not only nation, but the social and criminal background characteristics and interaction patterns as well.

Turning to the right half of Table 7.5, we note the summary report of the multiple regression analysis including dummy variables for our second response variable, feelings of help or harm. The reader will recall that at the end of Chapter 6 we reported a multiple correlation of .215 for background characteristics and interaction patterns. Adding the dummy variables of country and type institution, the multiple correlation is increased to .298. Using the same F statistic for testing of goodness of fit, we obtain an F value which is significant with $p<.01$. This means that the dummy variables of country and type institution increase the multiple correlation with help and harm even more strongly than for attitudinal conformity.

Examining the relative contribution of country and type institution we note much larger changes in the intercept than we observed for attitudinal conformity. For example, there seems to be a very clear affect of both Sweden and Denmark on feelings of being harmed. Swedish inmates are much more likely to feel harmed, +.29, and Danish inmates are much less likely to feel harmed, −.35. The nation seems to have very little effect on feelings of help or harm in both Norway and Finland.

Looking at the type institution and its effect on feelings of help or harm, we note our earlier finding that inmates in youth institutions are much less likely to feel harmed −.32. We notice also a consistent, but somewhat weaker tendency for adult inmates in both normal and preventive detention institutions to feel harmed, an effect of +.17, for each. Again, these findings are quite consistent with the patterns noted in our analyses using percent differences. However, we point out that the multiple regression analyses not only confirm those earlier findings, but add an important dimension to our interpretation. These analyses show relative contribution of both country and type institution in the context of holding constant the relative contribution of other independent variables.

Feelings About Perceived Benefits[11]

As Table 7.3 indicates, Danish inmates were appreciably less likely to consider their incarceration harmful than those from the other Scandinavian countries, though still only slightly less than half of the Danes expressed these sentiments. Indeed, even after controlling for inmate background, overall 17% fewer Danes than Norwegians, 21% fewer Danes than Swedes, and 16% fewer Danes than Finns felt harmed by incarceration (the first comparison was significant at the 0.05 level, the latter two comparisons at the 0.01 level). Differences between Norway, Sweden, and Finland in the Propensity to find imprisonment harmful were small and insignificant.

How can we account for this rather sharp differential between Danish and other Scandinavian inmates in the extent to which they consider their incarceration to be helpful for their success in getting along subsequent to release? Perhaps Danish inmates more than the others consider aspects of the prison experience, the rehabilitation program, the nature of involvements with other inmates or staff to be beneficial to them.

Inmates were asked to evaluate whether they had benefitted from their stay in the prison in a number of ways.[12] These potentially beneficial aspects of incarceration and their distribution cross-nationally are displayed in Table 7.6.[13]

---

[11]Editors note: This section and the Conclusion section below was taken from a draft Chapter 10, which also included this material.

[12]Of all the items that we consider in this chapter, these questions that inquire about beneficial aspects of incarceration are potentially the most dated. They clearly reflect elements of prison regime or prison policy that are subject to change since the time period of data collection. Although they validly can be employed to explore overall feelings of help or harm, it is difficult to make inferences about contemporary perceptions or cross- national differentials. We will not attempt to do so here and warn the reader to beware as well: Concern for change in these variables is the topic of the epilogue to this volume.

[13]The data in this table reflect overall responses without controls for inmate background. Homogeneous subgroups were contrasted for the most relevant dimensions—classroom education, vocational training, and the summary measure for all six items and the findings for these analyses are reported in the text.

Table 7.6 National differences in beneficial aspects of incarceration

Percent benefitting from	Norway	Sweden	Finland	Denmark
Vocational training	32	25	18	27
Classroom education	36	19	11	36
Self-understanding from time to think problems through	66	42	47	54
Self-understanding from staff help	16	7	13	21
Better physical condition	25	22	22	23
Better family relationships	21	16	19	27
All of the above	6	6	5	9
None of the above	13	28	24	19
Mean number of benefits	1.47	0.93	1.02	1.46
(*N*'s)	(221–241)	(254–280)	(568–610)	(666–722)

Cross-national differences in these aspects of prison life are apparent, though not especially great. The greatest differentiation is on expressed benefit from classroom education, in which more than a third of the inmates in Norway and Denmark indicated having benefitted, compared to approximately one-fifth and one-tenth of the Swedish and Finnish inmates, respectively. The differences between Norway and Denmark relative to Finland and between Denmark and Sweden were found significant, after controlling for inmate background.

The cross-national differences highlighted in this table must be taken with a grain of salt, however, when we note that the second largest percentage spread cross-nationally is found in that item probing self-understanding through having time to think, the item perhaps least likely to reflect national differentiation in prison conditions or structure.

In Chapter 5 we presented an index which summarized inmate sentiments on all six aspects of incarceration. Although Table 7.6 does suggest some national differentiation in this index, perhaps most noteworthy is the overall lack of expressions of help shared by all nationals. In none of the nations is the mean number of expressed benefits greater than one-and-a-half.

However, it is the case that nations do array themselves differently on this overall summary of beneficial aspects of prison life. Norwegian and Danish inmates tend to be more positive about these features of incarceration than their counterparts in Finland and Sweden. Results of homogeneous subgroups analysis and the sign test reveal that only those differences between Norway and the other three countries are significant. Indeed Norwegians are significantly more likely ($p < .01$) than Danes to indicate this overall benefit from incarceration.

Having explored some of the more specific aspects of a feeling of having been helped by the prison experience, are we able to now account for the rather sharp differential between Danish and other inmates in expressions of being so helped? It is the case, as we noted above, that Danes do tend to be more positive about features of prison life than Swedish or Finnish inmates. However, their responses are not especially different from their Norwegian counterparts. And certainly, these rather weak differentials overall do not appear to account for the larger differences in the general help/harm response.

It is the case that expressions of being helped are most highly correlated with responses of having benefitted from staff help in self-understanding, improved family relations, and classroom education, exactly those items for which Danish inmates tend to be more positive relative to the others. This observation helps to account for Danish differentials in expressions of incarceration as not harmful, but must be viewed as only a partial explanation, given the small and generally insignificant national differences on these items. Even so, we still haven't suggested why Danish inmates do find more benefits accruing to them from staff help in self-insight, improved family relations, and classroom education. Is this a consequence of national prison policy or some other unique characteristic of Danish prisons or their inmates?

Conclusion

Proceeding inductively as we have in this chapter, it is difficult to assess whether our findings are surprising or rather unimpressive. Certainly, given the fact that our explorations have focused on a very circumscribed and relatively homogeneous area in the international world of prisons and the fact that these findings reflect prior controls for cross-national differentials in inmate and prison background, the handful of differences discovered take on at least a modicum of importance. We have found generally that variability in some dimensions of prison climate, particularly those aspects concerned with the extent and allocation of authority among prison officials and the interaction between this staff and its inmate population, are subject to some national differentiation. Elements of the normative order of inmate life and the response of inmates to their incarceration are much less responsive to national distinctions, at least on our indices and within our sample of prisons.

In expanding our knowledge concerning the social organization of the prison and the variability in institutional climates it might be instructive, then, to explore national characteristics and their input into the nation's penal institutions. Such variables as the scope and organization of a national correctional administration; its resources; its ideology (both philosophical and operational) concerning punishment, retribution, or, rehabilitation; the allocation, background and training of its institutional personnel, etc., might be worthy of further exploration in this context. In further analysis of the responses of inmates to incarceration our experience would suggest that attention focuses on the background of particular inmates, their contact and experiences while in the prison, and the structure and climate of these institutions rather than on national distinctions.

8

Considerations of Justice in the Sentencing and Treatment of Scandinavian Prison Inmates

Assessing Perceptions of Justice

Concern for variation in inmate perceptions of the justice of their prison treatment was tapped by a questionnaire item which asked: "Do you think that you have been justly treated here in the institution?" As noted in Table 8.1, 42% of the inmates considered their treatment just; 37% expressed feelings of injustice, and slightly over one-fifth of the inmates indicated that they didn't know. Unfortunately, the questionnaire contained only this single item probing perceived justice of treatment. Had we been able to anticipate the growing interest in these issues in the contemporary correctional literature and discourse, we would have included additional indicators in the questionnaire. Nonetheless, the realities of our data set force us to rely on this single measure, despite the methodological reservations attached to such a procedure. Although we certainly cannot present our item as the

Editor's note: The original manuscript had a short paragraph describing an intended section that would be a "Discussion of the study of justice (distributive, retributive) in the social science literature" and the relative absence of empirical data about justice at the time of the study and "the consequent scanty attention to these issues in the instrument [used for the SPS]."

S. Wheeler and H. F. Cline, *The Scandinavian Prison Study*,
Palgrave Studies in Prisons and Penology,
https://doi.org/10.1007/978-3-030-26462-8_8

Table 8.1 Items reflecting inmate perceptions of the justice of their sentencing and treatment

Question	Yes	No	Don' t know	*N*
Have you been treated justly here?	42%	37%	21%	1914
Was your sentence just in relation to what you did?	21%	64%	15%	1919
	Lighter	Same	Heavier	
Compared to others who have been sentenced for same thing, was your sentence lighter or heavier than most?	9%	35%	56%	1896

sophisticated indicator which it is not, we are confident that it is as valid and reliable as a single survey item can be, based upon its strong, predictable, and consistent relationship to other phenomena across our sample and across each of our fifteen institutions.

Clearly it is the case that inmates have sentiments about the justice of the various phases of their encounter with the criminal justice system. It is possible, then, that sentiments about the justice of institutional treatment may reflect these prior experiences more than the inmates' sensitivity to incarceration. We have therefore examined the relationship of these perceptions of prior encounters with the criminal justice system to evaluations pertaining only to incarceration.

Inmates were asked to evaluate the justice of their sentence, both in relation to what they did and in relation to others sentenced for the same crime. The distribution of responses to these questions, noted in Table 8.1, indicates that inmates are much more likely to feel unjustly sentenced than they are to feel unjustly treated. Almost two-thirds of the inmates felt unjustly sentenced in relation to what they did, and well over half of them felt that their sentences were heavier than others committing the same crime.

Our expectations of a significant interrelationship between feelings about sentencing and those about treatment are confirmed, as noted in the data presented in Table 8.2. Whereas 60% of those inmates who consider their sentence just (relative to the crime) also feel justly treated, only 36% of those inmates who feel unjustly sentenced share these feelings. This relationship is a good deal weaker when inmates compare

Table 8.2 The relationship between perceived justice of sentence and perceived justice of treatment

	Justice of sentence (relative to the crime)			
	Just	Don't know	Unjust	Total
Justice of treatment				
Just	60%	43%	36%	790
Don't know	15%	29%	21%	392
Unjust	25%	28%	43%	685
Total	392	279	1196	1867
	Justice of Sentence			
Justice of treatment	(Relative to others sentenced for same crime)			
	Lighter	Same	Heavier	Total
Just	46%	49%	38%	790
Don't know	19%	25%	19%	392
Unjust	35%	27%	43%	685
Total	171	647	1049	1867

their sentence to others committing the same crime, though it is in the expected direction.

However, what is significant about the data in Table 8.2 is not the strong relationship between feelings of sentence and treatment, but rather that the variability in sentiments about justice of treatment is by no means removed after controlling for justice of sentence. A quarter of those inmates who considered their sentence just relative to their crime still complained about unjust treatment and over a third of those assessing their sentence as unjust, nonetheless considered their institutional treatment just.[1]

It is the case, then, that our measure of just treatment does provide information distinct from inmate sentiments about the justice of their sentence. Nonetheless, we sought to separate out the effect of feelings about sentencing in this measure concerning treatment. Given cross-institutional differentials in the proportion of inmates who feel justly sentenced, one strategy to sort out these phenomena would be to explore

[1]Similarly over a third of those who felt their sentences lighter than others sentenced for the same crime expressed feelings of unjust treatment, while about the same proportion who considered their sentence harsher expressed feelings of just treatment.

assessments of treatment within categories of sentencing by institution. Then by weighting responses about treatment according to intra-institutional relationships, we would remove at least one level of the confounding of these two phenomena.[2]

However, we found a rather interesting pattern when these data were assembled (Table 8.3; see Table 2.1 for prison names). For any of the four constellations of justice or injustice of sentence and treatment, institutional characterizations about treatment arrayed themselves very similarly to their ranking prior to controlling for justice of sentence. We look, for example, at Institution #12, that institution which overall contains the highest proportion of inmates feeling justly treated (and therefore ranked 15). After controlling for feelings about sentencing, it still has the highest proportion of inmates feeling justly treated among those justly sentenced and the second highest proportion among those unjustly sentenced.

Similarly, Institution #8, which has the highest proportion of inmates overall who feel unjustly treated, contains the highest proportion feeling unjustly treated among those unjustly sentenced and the second highest among those justly sentenced. Indeed, if we explore the cross-institutional rankings in these categories, there is a rather strong consistency in ranks for each institution (particularly when we note the near similarity of many institutions and the fact that a 1 or 2% difference can have major implications for the assigned rank).

The data presented in Table 8.3, of course, do not diminish the argument that sentencing and treatment are related. It is consistently the case that within each institution, feeling justice in sentencing inflates the proportion of inmates who feel justly treated and feeling injustice in sentencing deflates this proportion and inflates that proportion of inmates who feel unjustly treated. However, rather than finding that

[2]For example, in institutions in which all inmates justly sentenced feel unjustly treated, each inmate could be assigned a score of +1 for the unjust treatment response. Where 75% of the responses in this category express unjust treatment, each inmate in this institution expressing un-just treatment could be scored +0.75, and so on. Similarly, responses of just treatment could be weighted by the proportion of inmates who express these sentiments among those who feel unjustly sentenced.

Table 8.3 The relationship between perceived justice of sentence and perceived justice of treatment by institution

	Overall		Justly sentenced		Unjustly sentenced	
Institution	%	Rank	%	Rank	%	Rank
		% Justly treated				
1	26	(2.5)	25	(1)	26	(5)
2	45	(9)	60	(8)	38	(9)
3	59	(13)	70	(11)	46	(10.5)
4	49	(10)	73	(12)	46	(10.5)
5	43	(8)	79	(14)	36	(8)
6	55	(12)	74	(13)	47	(12.5)
7	30	(5)	46	(4)	30	(6)
8	18	(1)	40	(3)	8	(1)
9	26	(3)	35	(2)	22	(4)
10	62	(14)	69	(10)	59	(15)
11	29	(4)	63	(9)	19	(2)
12	65	(15)	80	(15)	58	(14)
13	42	(7)	54	(5)	35	(7)
14	50	(11)	55	(6)	47	(12.5)
15	35	(6)	58	(7)	21	(3)
		% Unjustly treated				
1	47	(4.5)	38	(3)	51	(5)
2	37	(8)	25	(7)	43	(8)
3	18	(13)	10	(14.5)	32	(9.5)
4	29	(9)	13	(11.5)	32	(9.5)
5	25	(10)	14	(10)	29	(11.5)
6	22	(11)	13	(11.5)	29	(11.5)
7	41	(6)	29	(5.5)	45	(7)
8	70	(1)	53	(2)	81	(1)
9	59	(2)	55	(1)	60	(4)
10	16	(15)	12	(13)	16	(15)
11	55	(3)	22	(8)	68	(2)
12	20	(12)	15	(9)	25	(13)
13	40	(7)	35	(4)	46	(6)
14	17	(14)	10	(14.5)	18	(14)
15	47	(4.5)	29	(5.5)	62	(3)

cross-institutional differences in sentiments about justice of treatment diminish after controlling for differential perceptions about sentencing at the institutional level, we find that they remain, and in relatively the same magnitude. Devising a complex weighting procedure, then, would have little import, since for purposes of sorting out sentence and treatment, institutional controls provide relatively redundant information.

We therefore will retain the values initially assigned to responses about the justice of prison treatment and make problematic their variability. In general, we can assume, given the skewed distribution of values on justice of sentencing in the direction of injustice, that the proportion of inmates feeling unjustly treated is somewhat inflated and the proportion feeling justly treated somewhat deflated. Inmate feelings about the justice of their sentence will be controlled in the analysis of justice and other variables, where possible, although frequently the number of other simultaneous controls render this procedure impractical.

We proceed first to a consideration of justice of treatment as an element of institutional climate, and then we move to the individual level of analysis with a perspective that considers feelings of justice as an element of inmate response to incarceration.

Justice of Treatment as an Aspect of Institutional Climate

As originally conceived in our research design, feelings about justice of treatment were considered aspects of the inmate's response to imprisonment, whose covariation with personal background, experiences within the prison, and other attitudes and behaviors would be explored. In short, it was our intent to explore these feelings from the perspective of the social psychology of the prison inmate. However, apart from these interests, we would indeed be surprised if there were no differences across prisons in the degree of justice which characterizes the treatment of their inmates.

Much of the contemporary rhetoric and normative discussion about prison justice has at its basis the assessment that prisons, though generally unjust, are differentially so. We observed in Chapters 3 and 4 that on objective measures of prison structure and climate (such indicators as architectural plan, prison policy concerning personal freedoms available to inmates, the coerciveness of the prison regime, etc.), the institutions

Table 8.4 Inmate perceptions of the justice of their treatment by institution

Institution[a]	Justly treated	Don't know	Unjustly treated	Total
1 N-D	26%	28%	47%	(51)
2 N-N	45%	18%	37%	(148)
3 N-Y	59%	22%	18%	(49)
4 S-D	49%	21%	29%	(136)
5 S-Y	43%	32%	25%	(65)
6 S-N	55%	22%	22%	(89)
7 F-N	30%	28%	41%	(272)
8 F-Y	18%	12%	70%	(84)
9 F-D	26%	15%	59%	(112)
10 F-S	62%	23%	16%	(161)
11 D-D	29%	16%	55%	(138)
12 D-N	65%	14%	20%	(173)
13 D-N	42%	19%	40%	(193)
14 D-Y	50%	33%	17%	(88)
15 D-S	35%	18%	47%	(155)
Total	42%	21%	37%	(1914)
Mean	42	21	36	
SD	14.0	6.2	16.4	

[a]Number, Country, Type (*N* = Normal, *D* = Detention, *Y* = Youth, *S* = Special)

in our sample did indeed vary. Although these attributes of the prison are quite distinct from notions of justice, they are related sufficiently to cause us to seriously ponder the possibility of institutional differences in levels of justice.

Table 8.4 demonstrates that cross-institutional differences in feelings regarding justice of treatment are indeed very large. The proportion of inmates who considered their treatment unjust ranged from 16% in the Finnish open labor colony for drunk drivers (Seutula #10) to 70% in the Finnish youth institution (Karava #8). Institutional differences in expressions of just treatment, though not as large, were certainly significant, ranging from 18% of the inmates in Karava feeling justly treated to 65% of Vrids1oselille's inmates with similar feelings. This somewhat smaller magnitude of differences may reflect the fact that "don't know" responses are more frequently found in institutions which have low proportions of feelings of injustice.

That the cross-institutional distribution of assessments of justice of treatment are widely variable is further reinforced by the standard deviation calculated for the distribution of these 15 institutional scores, reported at the bottom of Table 8.4. When we compare the standard deviation of the distribution of the proportion of inmates who consider their treatment unjust with that calculated for the other major response variables in our study—attitudinal and behavioral conformity, feelings of help or harm from incarceration, perceptions of having benefitted from a variety of aspects of the institutional regime—this standard deviation is the largest (with sd's for the other measures ranging from 9.0 for attitudinal conformity to 16.0 for behavioral conformity). In other words, the cross-institutional variance in perceptions of the injustice of institutional treatment is even higher than aspects of institutional life which are variable by design—phenomena such as classroom education, vocational training, help from staff in solving personal problems, or the allocation of conduct infractions to misbehaving inmates. It is this substantial cross-institutional variation in justice of treatment that will be made problematic in the following section.

Now it is the case that these institutional characterizations of justice are based on the aggregated individual responses of the inmates incarcerated therein. As is the case with the other measures of institutional climate considered in this volume, then, this aspect of justice does not reflect any objective assessment, but rather the subjective (and potentially variable) standards of those experiencing these climates. For those readers who feel uncomfortable with such a "methodology," it is recommended that they return to the extended discussion of this strategy presented at the beginning of Chapter 4.

How, then, can we account for variations at the institutional level in perceptions of just or unjust treatment? A cursory glance at the data in Table 8.4 notes a few obvious patterns. We observe, for example, that Finnish institutions (#7–10) tend to report higher levels of injustice than those in the other Scandinavian countries, although the institution with the lowest level of injustice is also found in a Finnish institution (Seutula #10).[3]

[3]A systematic view of national differences in justice of treatment is presented at the end of this chapter.

Furthermore, we notice that preventive detention institutions (type "D") report higher levels of felt injustice than other institutions.[4] We note that among youth institutions, where one might expect the age effect to result in higher levels of perceived injustice, the distribution is quite variable. Although the highest level of injustice (70%) is expressed in a youth institution, Karava (#3), these sentiments are very rarely expressed in Norway's youth institution, with Berg (#3) at 18%. Intermediate levels of injustice are expressed in the youth prisons in Sweden and Denmark.

Table 8.5 explores the relationship between levels of justice of treatment and other institutional characteristics that we have considered significant throughout this volume. It presents the rank order correlation (Kendall's Tau-b) summarizing the relationship between institutional level of justice (scored as the proportion of inmates feeling justly treated) and other institutional attributes, for each of the fifteen prisons. The findings are mixed, both confirming and negating our suspicions about the institutional structures and climates that covary with perceptions of justice.

We note first that justice of treatment is very weakly related to most of the aspects of prison structure contained in our data. Of all these physical and material features, only the degree of custody appears moderately correlated (−.35) with justice. Of course we would expect that this would be a fairly strong relationship, with more custodially structured institutions reflecting climates of greater injustice.[5] However, it is somewhat surprising that variables such as the level of wages paid for inmate labor are not more highly correlated with perceived justice (indeed it is correlated in a counter-intuitive direction).

We observe furthermore that there is little staffing effect on perceptions of justice, either with regard to the tradeoff of one type of staff to

[4]This very significant finding is carefully examined in the following chapter, "Legal Justice and Mental Health." Editors note: This chapter was never written.

[5]This degree of custody variable is a simple dichotomized measure which differentiates the fifteen prisons. This resulted from the absence of comprehensive data on this attribute that would have permitted more elaborate differentiation. However, we would anticipate that were these data available, the tau might have been even larger.

another or with regard to the absolute quantity of staff available for a given number of inmates. One exception, of course, is the relationship between justice of treatment and the ratio of inmates to custody staff (tau = +.33). We learn that the presence of custodial staff tends to be accompanied by greater feelings of injustice, at the institutional level.

Perhaps the most surprising finding at the structural level, however, concerns those attributes classified as "Constraints on Interaction Patterns." We note from the data in Table 8.5, that they are quite weakly related to institutional feelings of justice. Contrary to our expectation that where inmates are subject to great deprivations within the prison—in opportunities to interact with other inmates, staff, or persons outside the institution—these institutions would be characterized as unjust, but instead we find weak and inconsistent relationships. Indeed, the taus for restrictions on outside contact and limits on interaction time are in the opposite direction from that predicted, with greater restriction accompanied by higher perceived justice. The relationship between justice of treatment and the overall social deprivation index is in the predicted direction, though the magnitude of the relationship is quite weak (−.15).

Lest we despair of our attempt to explore justice as an institutional climate, let us note that our disappointments are reflective, in part, of a very small sample size. Because the tau's reflect only fifteen prisons, conflicting trends or idiosyncracities of a particular prison, often strongly diminish (or even reverse) meaningful relationships. We find, for example, that preventive detention institutions are much less likely to be characterized as just, despite their structural similarity or comparability of climate to other institutions. As we will see graphically in a moment, they tend to depress relationships that quite consistently characterize the other eleven institutions. Other institutional attributes, such as nationality, median inmate age, etc., might also serve as countervailing pressures in the operation of other relationships.

However, when we turn to attributes of institutional climate, we find some modest and predictable relationships to institutional climate of justice. We look at three aspects of the institutional regime, all of which we would expect to be related to justice of treatment: the power of prison guards, their understanding, and their coerciveness (the

Table 8.5 Relationship of institutional justice of treatment to aspects of prison structure and climate

	Tau-b
Type of institution	
Normal prison	.31
Preventive detention institution	−.38
Youth institution	.03
Physical and material features	
Date of construction	.20
Number of inmates	.10
Degree of custody	−.35
Wages	−.15
Store items	.01
Staffing policies	
Ratio of inmates to custody staff	.33
Ratio of inmates to treatment Staff	.05
Ratio of inmates to total staff	.14
Ratio of custody to treatment staff	−.20
Constraints on interaction patterns	
Restrictions on outside contact	.11
Limits on interaction time	.06
Social deprivation index	−.15
Inmate perceptions of officials	
Guard power	−.16
Treatment staff power	−.12
Total power	−.22
Balance of power	−.06
Guard understanding	.33
Treatment staff understanding	.07
Total understanding	.28
Balance of understanding	.14
Coerciveness	−.24
Relations between staff and inmates	
Staff pressure	−.41
Inmate pressure	−.31
Total pressure	−.47
Balance of pressure	.07

latter indexed by the quantity and inflexibility of rules and their enforcement, as perceived by the inmate). The taus for these relationships, as noted in Table 8.5 are −.16, +.33 and −.24, respectively. We find, then, that in institutions in which guards are considered to be low in authority, high in understanding, and less coercive, inmates are more likely to

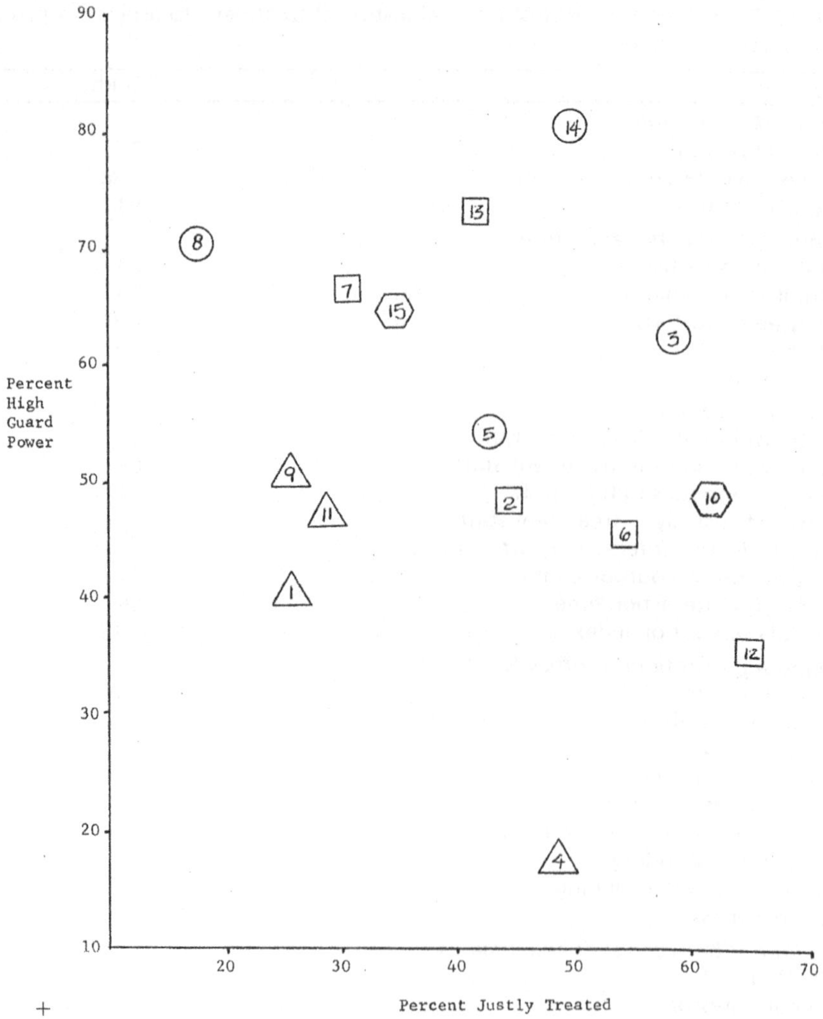

Fig. 8.1 The relationship of justice of treatment to guard authority (tau = −.16)

consider themselves justly treated. This is illustrated in Figs. 8.1 through 8.3, which plot for each institution the proportion of inmates who feel justly treated against their expressions on the other dimension. Figure 8.1, which plots justice against guard power, is not especially striking (reflected in the low tau of −.16). However, note that in the lower left-hand corner of the table we find all of the preventive detention institutions plotted (triangled #s 1, 4, 9, and 11). In an almost linear fashion, these four institutions parallel the overall relationship, but because of their unexplainably low levels of perceived justice, they are further to the left of the graph than we would have expected on the basis of the amount of power invested in custodial personnel. If we ignore these four institutions, the relation between just treatment and guard power becomes much stronger.[6]

Similarly, in Figs. 8.2 and 8.3,[7] which present the relationship of just treatment to guard understanding and coerciveness, respectively, the plotted relationships become even stronger, and nearly linear if we drop off the preventive detention institutions, especially #'s 1 and 11 which are run as psychiatric institutions.

A second aspect of institutional climate is the relationship between inmates and prison staff, and these measures are even more strongly related to perceived levels of justice. We note from Tables 8.3, 8.4, and 8.5 that the taus between felt justice and staff pressure, inmate pressure, and total pressure are −.41, −.31, and −.47, respectively. In other words, as the pressure exerted on inmates by either staff or other inmates increases, the level of just treatment reported for that institution decreases. These relationships are graphically illustrated in Figs. 8.4 and 8.5. Again we find near-linear negative relationships between these two attributes of prison climate and justice of treatment. Furthermore, exclusion of the preventive detention institutions makes the relationship even stronger.

The most obvious interpretation of these data suggests that, when inmates respond to a single question about justice of treatment, they conjure up similar experiences and sentiments when evaluating treatment as they do when evaluating pressure. An unjust institution is one in which staff members exert a great deal of pressure on inmates. The correlation of the two measures may reflect the possibility they are indicators of similar aspects of institutional climate. Since we know from our analysis of prison climates in Chapter 4 that staff and inmate pressure are complementary phenomena rather than zero-sum, in which high inmate and high staff pressure tend to manifest themselves in the

[6]Editors note: See new section at the end of this chapter, titled "Epilogue to Chapter 8" where these four institutions are removed and new regression lines are drawn.

[7]Figures 8.3 and 8.4 are shown in Appendix III.

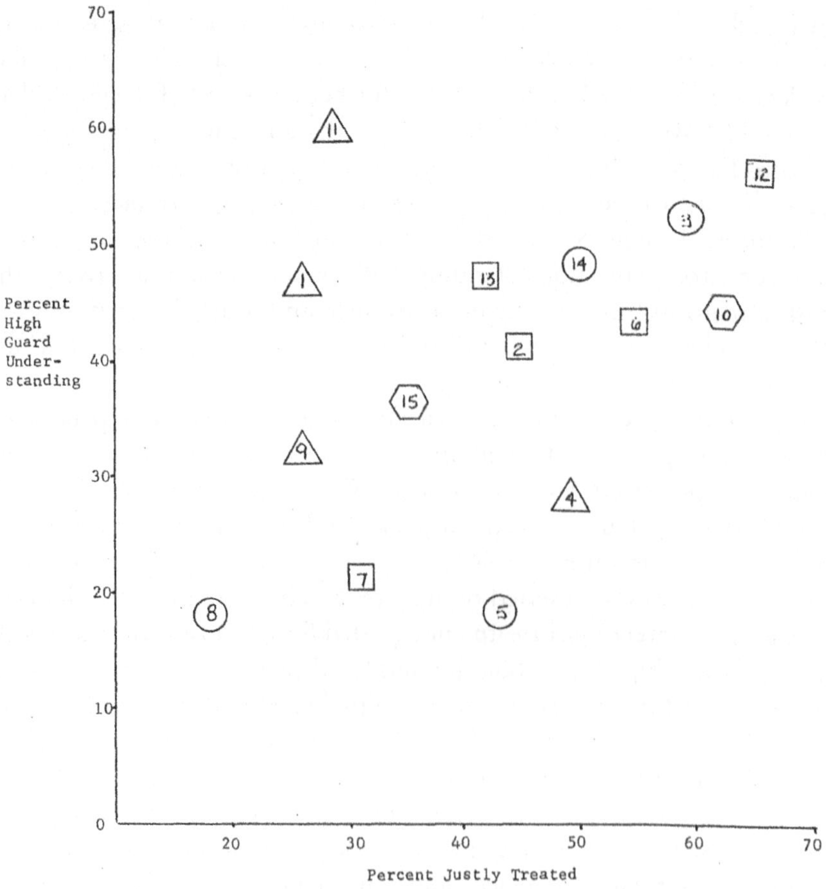

Fig. 8.2 The relationship of justice of treatment to guard understanding (tau = .33)

same institutions, the comparable taus between justice and both inmate and total pressure no doubt reflect their correlation with level of staff pressure. At any rate, we note from Figs. 8.4 and 8.5 that the institutions are arrayed very similarly on the vertical dimension, again demonstrating the fact that total pressure provides redundant information given knowledge of staff pressure.

The limitation of having only 15 institutions does not allow a careful test of our interpretation of these findings. Nonetheless, we do find

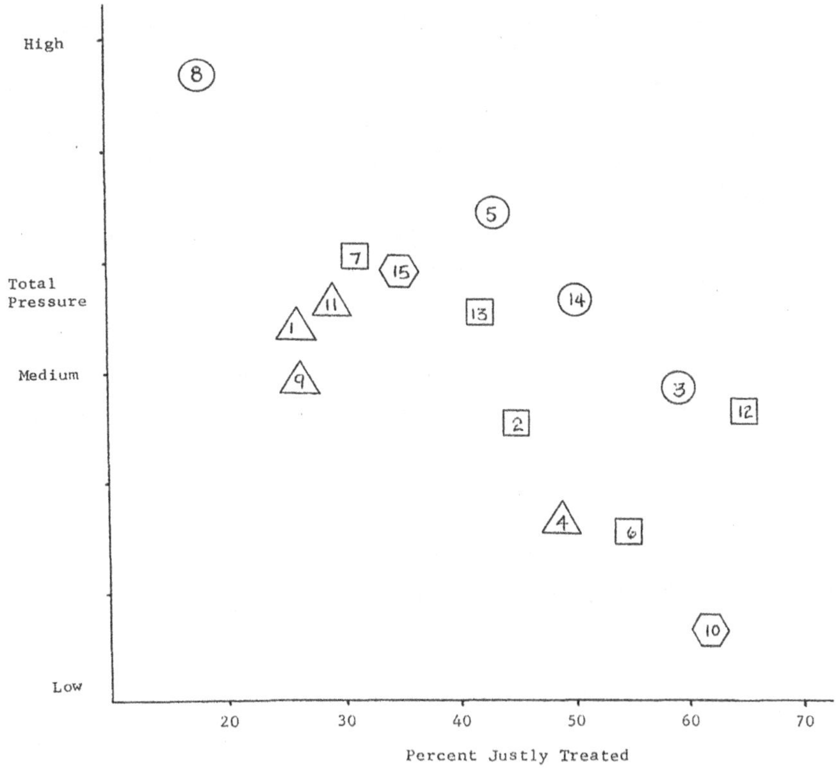

Fig. 8.5 The relationship of justice of treatment to total pressure (tau = −.47)

some consistent relationships of aspects of prison climate to perceptions of just treatment. Just prison climates tend to be those in which guards have little power, exert little pressure on inmates, are understanding, and in which institutional regimes are not considered coercive. The extent to which the idiosyncrasies of our small data set has resulted in spurious correlations (for example, the fact that Finnish institutions are considered both coercive and unjust, and that this overall relation may reflect some quality of Finland rather than the perceptions of coercive regimes) or the rejection of prior hypotheses because of weak and inconsistent relationships, is beyond our determination. However, it would be reasonable to assume that as prison officials attempt to change the climates (and probably also structures of power and privilege) in their institutions, the justice of these prisons, as perceived by their incarcerated men, will shift concomitantly. Furthermore, our data would indicate that it is unwise to relegate perceptions of justice entirely to the social psychology of the prison inmate, his values, perceptions, background, and experiences. Rather, justice appears to be more than the sum of the perceptions of those experiencing prison conditions, and an attribute of supra-individual systems which is patterned according to the variation of other supra- individual characteristics.

It is to the individual level of analysis to which our attention now turns, where we examine variations in feelings about just treatment, controlling for institutional differentiation. This analysis will consider individual and collective explanations of variability in justice of treatment.

Justice of Treatment as a Form of Inmate Response to Incarceration

Although the previous analysis demonstrated quite striking variability across institutions in the feelings of just treatment, assessments of justice are by no means homogeneous within a given prison. Indeed, we find that on our single item measuring inmate feelings about justice of treatment, the variance for the entire sample of 1937 inmates is .79, while for each of the fifteen institutions, it ranges from .56 in Seutu1a (#10) to .82 in Botsfengs1et (#2), corresponding, respectively, to a special prison with perhaps the most homogeneous group of inmates and to a normal prison with one of the most heterogeneous inmate populations. It is the case, then, that a considerable amount of the variability in feelings of justice remain after exploring differences in the structure, climate, and administration of a given prison, and it is to this within-institutional distinctions that we must now turn our attention.

In this section, we will examine individual feelings of just treatment rather than differential climates of justice at the institutional level based on the aggregation of these individualized feelings. We consider assessments of the individual inmate as an element of his response to incarceration, and our interest will be to account for the variability in these individualized perceptions and to explore the correlates of his sense of justice. We will explore the variability in inmate perceptions of justice with regard both to differentials in the social and criminal background that the inmate carries with him to the prison and to variability in his experience while in the institution. As difficult as is the task of causal analysis, particularly with cross-sectional data, it is along these lines that this first portion of the section is oriented—a concern for those characteristics and sets of influence and experience that seem to "predispose" the inmate to the adoption of a particular feeling or perception of justice. The second portion of this section has a different theoretical orientation, concerned with complimentary attitudes and behaviors that tend to vary with feelings of justice or injustice. We look specifically to other elements of inmate response to incarceration—attitudinal and behavioral conformity and perceived effect of incarceration—and explore their correlations with inmate sense of justice. We do not address the causal connection of these attributes because we lack data to disentangle what are most certainly mutually reinforcing phenomena. Rather, we will limit our exploration to the constellation of attitudes and behaviors which the inmate expresses or manifests while incarcerated, and which thus constitute his responses to this experience.

Given the large and theoretically justifiable institutional differences in feelings concerning justice of treatment which we explored above, we find it necessary to control for this variability in the following analyses, lest these individual level relationships reflect the differential allocation of inmate characteristics at the institutional level. Our method is similar to that employed in the contextual analysis of Chapter 7. We have isolated subgroups of institutions most homogeneous on inmate characterizations of justice of treatment.[8] We then look at the relationship between individual characteristics and personal feelings of justice within

[8]Institutions were ranked according to the proportion of their inmates who considered their treatment unjust and were divided into three subgroups with cutting points based on the natural breaking points of this distribution. Context 1, in which inmates felt least unjustly treated included Berg in Norway (3), Norrtalje (6) in Sweden, Seutula (10) in Finland, and Vridsloselille (12) and Sobysagard (14) in Denmark. Context 2, with moderate feelings of injustice included Botsfengslet (2) in Norway, Hall (4) and Mariefred (5) in Sweden, and Nyborg (13) in Denmark. The third context, representing those institutions whose inmates feel most unjustly

each homogeneous subgroup. We explore whether these individual level relationships (which we will also examine for the entire sample) have the same patterning and magnitude within each context.[9]

Our strategy, then, is to explore the relationship at the individual level between feelings concerning the justice of treatment and other individual attributes within institutional settings most comparable in overall climate of justice. Since both our dependent variable and the definition of context are virtually the same, cross-context comparisons in levels of justice are not meaningful: by definition, context 1 is highest overall and context 3 lowest overall in the level of just treatment.[10]

Sense of Justice and Inmate Background

Who are the inmates who feel their prison treatment is unjust? Do they differentiate themselves in social or criminal background or their conception of self? Our data indicate that indeed they do on many of the background characteristics which we have found to be important predictors in previous analyses. Not unexpectedly, we find the relationship between age and feelings of just treatment a strong one, as illustrated

treated, included Ila (1) in Norway, Konnunsuo (7), Karava (8), and Turku (9) in Finland, and Herstedvester (11) and Kragskovhede (15) in Denmark. These assignments reflect two particular biases: the preponderance of Finnish prisons in the most unjust context (a matter which we will consider in the last section of this chapter which explores national differentiation in feelings of justice) and the preponderance of preventive detention institutions in this context. (an important empirical observation specially considered in the following chapter, "Legal Justice and Mental Health.") Thirty-seven percent of the inmates in our entire sample consider their prison treatment unjust; this sentiment is shared by 19% of those inmates in context 1, 35% of those in context 2, and 50% of those in the third context.

[9]One technical consideration is in order. By subdividing inmates into contexts composed of institutions more-or-less homogeneous regarding feelings of injustice, we are potentially constraining the variance in such feelings within each context. To the extent that this variance is reduced, the magnitude of relationships between these feelings and other phenomena is thereby potentially lessened within each context. This methodological issue is not seriously problematic with our data, since the reduction in intra-context variance is not terribly significant. Whereas the overall variance in feelings of just treatment for 1937 inmates is .787, the corresponding variance in context 1 is .613, .783 in context 2, and .745 in context 3.

[10]Editor's note: Figs. 8.6 to 8.13 are found in Appendix III.

in Fig. 8.6.[11] The darkest line on the graph reflects the total sample, and this indicates that while 52% of inmates over the age of forty consider their treatment just, this sentiment is shared by only 34% of inmates under 21. There are fairly consistent increases in felt justice at each increase in age level. As reflected in the three lighter black lines, representing each of the three institutional contexts (as defined in fn. 6), both the patterning and magnitude of this relationship remain comparable: with increasing age, inmates are more likely to consider their prison treatment just, irrespective of the overall climate of the institution in which they have been incarcerated.

A similarly significant relationship is found when we look at the social background of the inmate. Figure 8.7 represents feelings of justice and marital status, with married inmates feeling most justly treated (53%), single inmates least justly treated (36%), and the feelings of widowed, separated, or divorced inmates are in between (44%). The patterning of this relationship is comparable in all three contexts and for the entire sample; although it is strongest overall (percentage difference of 17%) for Context 3. Nonetheless, it is reasonable to conclude that marital status is related to one's perception of justice, and that this relationship remains consistent when the effect of institutional differences is removed.

Our more general index reflecting social experience favorable to crime holds a similar relationship to justice of treatment, as indicated in Fig. 8.8: Inmates whose social background is least favorable to crime (those who are married, more educated and rural) are most likely to consider their treatment just (55%), while those least likely to feel justly treated (37%) are characterized by urban residence, less education, and single marital status. We note from the figure that this relationship is even stronger than for marital status alone: percentage differences range from 11% within that context moderate in feelings of justice to 24% within that context most likely to consider treatment as just.

Somewhat surprisingly, a weaker relationship obtains between feelings of justice and criminal experience, though in the predicted direction, presented in Fig. 8.9. As criminal experience increases (as indexed

[11]Editors note: Figs. 8.6–8.13 are shown in Appendix III.

by number of previous sentences, incarceration in a juvenile institution, and age at first arrest), perception of just treatment decreases. Feelings of justice drop by 11% for the overall population and for the context for greatest felt injustice; they drop off by 8% for the first context, and there is no linear relationship for the middle context.

When we examine a somewhat different indicator of criminal experience, the number of previous jail sentences, we find that a relationship comparable to that for the criminal background index. Figure 8.9a, which plots the relationship between prior incarceration and feelings of just treatment, separately for each age category (since age is highly related to the likelihood that one has been previously jailed), demonstrates that there is about a 10% difference in feelings of being justly treated between those never previously incarcerated and those inmates who have served one or more jail sentences.

It is both interesting and somewhat remarkable to find that inmate feelings concerning the justice of treatment in prison are so little affected by the extent of their prior involvement with the criminal justice system (at least as measured by our indices). It is remarkable both because one would expect somewhat more punitive or restrictive treatment for those most frequently involved with the criminal justice system and because one would expect this subset of inmates to differ from their less criminally experienced comrades by being more critical of those incarcerating them. However weak, this observation holds whether or not we control for the variability in institutional climates from which these respondents have been drawn.

Finally, we consider one aspect of inmate self-conception, an attribute theoretically quite relevant to assessments of the justice with which those in authority treat the inmates. We refer to the composite index, "sensitivity to authority," which was employed and described in Chapter 5 and in the Appendices to this volume. Our expectation that those most sensitive to authority would feel least justly treated is confirmed by our data, presented in Fig. 8.10. For our total sample of inmates, about half of those low in sensitivity to authority consider their prison treatment just, contrasted to 35% of those highly sensitive to authority. This relationship is even stronger (differences of 18%) among those inmates in institutions with unjust climates, and somewhat weaker (differences of 6%) in more just institutional climates, with the relationship in the middle context comparable to, though a bit stronger than that for the total sample. It is unclear why the magnitude of this relationship should be so variable cross-institutionally.

Our findings concerning the relationship between inmate background characteristics and sentiments about the justice of their prison treatment sound reminiscent of our findings concerning attitudinal conformity, explored in Chapter 5. As with attitudinal conformists, those inmates who evaluate their treatment as just tend to be older, with both social and criminal experience less favorable to crime, and who are less sensitive to authority.

Sense of Justice and the Experience of Incarceration

As consistent and theoretically predictable as were our findings in the analysis of the relationship between feelings concerning justice of treatment and inmate background, we are not terribly surprised by the relatively modest level of these correlations. Certainly, both theoretical considerations of justice and common sense would suggest that it is the quality of the experiences themselves more than the predispositions and characteristics of the respondent that should predict his sense of the justice of these experiences. Undoubtedly, it is the case that inmate background and predisposition are correlated with subsequent experiences—those most sensitive to authority probably behave in a manner which is responded to more punitively, those inmates coming from a background of frequent and serious crime are probably responded to differently from those incarcerated for the first time on charges of drunk driving, etc. Nonetheless, by turning our attention specifically to the nature of these prison experiences, we expect that our understanding of differentials in inmate sense of justice should improve. In the following section, we will concern ourselves with three different dimensions of the experience of incarceration: the structural conditions of incarceration, the length of incarceration, and patterns of inmate involvement and contact with other inmates, prison staff, and persons outside of the institution.

The Structural Conditions of Incarceration

In the first part of this chapter we explored institutional variation in inmate conceptions of the justice of their treatment. We analyzed the correlation of this attribute with other characteristics of the institution, one of which concerned the structural and interpersonal conditions to which the inmate was subjected. Certainly, it is the case that institutions do not provide a perfectly homogeneous set of such conditions and experiences to all of its inmates at a given point in time. Although the extent of heterogeneity of prison experience is certainly a variable phenomenon cross-institutionally, it is an issue worthy of attention. Some of the institutions in our sample contained, for example, both open and maximum custody sections, some had units for solitary confinement, others special sets of privileges and living conditions for given subgroups of inmates. To the extent that we expect that perceptions of just treatment are responsive to differential conditions of treatment, and to the extent that we consider assessments of justice to reflect relative evaluations—determinations of whether the set of conditions imposed upon other inmates, given their behaviors and backgrounds, relative to one's own conditions, with the same givens, is warranted and appropriate—experiential variability within the institution would appear a potentially valuable area of inquiry.

Unfortunately, our data set affords only the most cursory and incomplete information of this sort. The nature of our data collection procedures and our assurances of confidentiality to the respondents precluded the possibility of gathering systematic and detailed information which would have allowed us to classify each of our respondents according to such variable prison conditions. For some of the prisons, we have been able to isolate subgroups of the inmate population that had been subjected to markedly different conditions than other subgroups within the institution. In some instances, respondents were interviewed in groups according to living unit (i.e., open versus closed custody wing, the solitary confinement section versus other cell blocks), with conditions of questionnaire administration noted in each questionnaire.[12]

[12]See the Appendix on data collection procedures and Chapter 2 for further elaboration of these methods. In many cases, inmates were questioned by work group, or some other meaningless "experiential" designation, and could therefore not be meaningfully classified.

These categorizations, however, are neither exhaustive nor particularly refined. We do not know, for example, for those respondents who were exposed to a particular set of conditions about which we are aware, the length of this experience, whether they had served their full sentence in this experiential setting, or whether they had just been moved from a rather different setting. For this reason and because of the fact that we have even such cursory data on only a small proportion of our total sample, the following remarks are necessarily exploratory.

Table 8.6 presents the findings of this analysis. The proportion of inmates who feel justly treated are reported for particular experiential subgroups (described across the top row) in particular prisons. These experiential subgroups are arrayed from left to right in the order of generally decreasing restrictiveness, punitiveness, high custody or supervision. This is an ordinal scale. We assert that a set of conditions to the right of another are less harsh, but we make no statement about the degree of similarity or dissimilarity of these conditions. Furthermore, we assert that a particular category of conditions is not necessarily comparable across prisons and that, therefore, comparisons are meaningful only intra-institutionally. Nonetheless, one might expect perceptions of justice to reflect the harshness of conditions experienced by the inmates. Indeed we find in Table 8.6 that this is the case: as we move from left to right across the table, from more to less restrictive and punitive conditions, inmate perceptions of justice of treatment rise. The magnitude of this increase in these feelings is quite variable.

There is actually a drop of 2% in feeling justly treated with "improved" conditions in Herstedvester; in several of the institutions the magnitude of change is only 5–10%. However, in a few of the contrasts, differentials in perceptions of justice are rather striking. There is an increase of 30% between the closed and open units at Berg; of 24% between those subject to normal conditions of imprisonment and those in solitary confinement in Turku; of 33% between those in normal conditions of imprisonment and those restricted to their cells in Nyborg; and of 32% between normal imprisonment and imprisonment in an outside relatively open farm unit in Kragskovhede. With the minor exception of Herstedvester mentioned above, the pattern of the relationships is quite consistent.

Table 8.6 Perceptions of just treatment for varying conditions of incarceration (% justly treated[a])

Prison & #	Cell work; solitary confinement	Closed unit; custodial	Hard labor	Normal	Elites; best	Open unit	Outside unit	New arrivals
Botsfengslet #2				54% (113)	67% (9)			
Berg #3		61% (18)				90% (20)		
Hall #4		60% (78)					69% (29)	
Mariefred #5				62% (26)	64% (11)		71% (7)	
Konnunsuo #7			39% (135)	43% (46)				71% (14)
Turku #9[b]	9% (11)			33% (84)				
Herstedvester #11				35% (95)		33% (21)		
Nyborg #13	26% (39)			59% (118)				
Kragskovhede #15				36% (102)			68% (25)	

[a]Respondents expressing "don't know" were excluded, so (*N*'s) reflect only those indicating just or unjust treatment
[b]Semi-open

Because of the very small number of cases in each of the comparison groups, it is impossible to probe further the nature of differential experience within the institution and even to be confident that these findings are stable. Certainly, the magnitude of these differences in level of felt justice reflect the operation of a variety of phenomena, for example, the type of inmate that is subjected to a particular set of conditions, a topic which we are unable to explore. Nonetheless, our findings, however exploratory, confirm an important hypothesis about perceptions of justice—that as the conditions of incarceration become less restrictive, less punitive, and more open, assessments of one's treatment as just rise concomitantly, complementing the weaker and less consistent relationships observed cross-institutionally.

Length of Incarceration

A rather important perspective on the experiences of incarceration and the inmates' responses to them moves from the static to the dynamic level and probes changes in inmate response to incarceration with increasing time in prison. An entire Chapter (12)[13] will be devoted to this matter, and therefore, we will not probe these issues at length in this context. However, a significant concern is changes in inmate perceptions of the justice of their treatment over time. Hypotheses about this relationship could be advanced in two directions. On the one hand, newcomers to the prison might experience their treatment as most unjust as they are strikingly confronted by the constraints and limitations of their freedom imposed by incarceration. Such an account would predict that as the inmate becomes "acclimated" to his new environment, feelings of injustice would falloff. A contrasting hypothesis would predict that feelings of justice would rather increase over time, as the inmate accumulates instances of deprivation, punishment, and negative sanctions of many sorts, and as his distance from and aspiration for a life of freedom becomes more acute.

[13]Editors note: Chapter 12 was not written.

Table 8.7 Relationship of the length of time served to justice of treatment

Time served	% Unjustly treated	(*N*)
Under 1 month	16	(135)
1–3 months	25	(427)
3–6 months	32	(420)
6–12 months	40	(419)
Over 1 year	53	(504)
Total	37	(1905)

The prediction from the latter account receives support from our data, as shown in Table 8.7. These data do not provide a longitudinal portrait of an inmate's changing perceptions over time, since our data were collected at one point in time. Rather, they approximate this condition by contrasting various cohorts of inmates in their perceptions of the justice of their treatment. Inmates who have been in prison for only one month are compared with groups of inmates imprisoned for longer time periods.[14] The results of such a comparison are quite clear: As the inmate increases the amount of time spent in prison, he is a great deal more likely to consider his treatment unjust. Only 16% of those inmates incarcerated for less than one month feel unjustly treated in contrast to about one-third of those in prison for three to six months and over half of those imprisoned for one year or more. Greater length of exposure to imprisonment, then, appears to be accompanied by increasing feelings of injustice in the treatment received.

This phenomenon, furthermore, is consistent even when we attempt to sort out the effect of institutional climate. The relationship of increasing felt injustice with increasing length of incarceration remains within each of the three institutional contexts, at approximately the same magnitude as the relationship overall. Thirteen percent of those incarcerated in context 1 (greatest expressed justice) for less than 3 months feel unjustly treated in contrast to 40% of those incarcerated for over one year. The corresponding figures in context 3 (greatest expressed injustice) are 35 and 64%.

[14]See Chapter 12 for an extended discussion of the utilization of such an analytic strategy and the methodological difficulties of drawing such inferences.

Now there are two alternative explanations for this phenomenon that must be explored. First is the fact that sentences for the preventive detention institutions in our sample tend to be a good deal longer than those in the other institutions, and the fact that inmates in these preventive detention institutions are more likely to feel unjustly treated than their counterparts incarcerated elsewhere (a problem to which the following chapter is devoted). To ascertain that the relationship of justice to length of incarceration is not an artifact of this special quality of preventive detention, we have excluded all inmates from preventive detention institutions and reexamined the relationship. It remains fundamentally unchanged. The levels of felt injustice for each of the first four categories of time served are virtually identical for the entire sample and for the sample minus respondents in preventive detention institutions. There is a slight change in the last category containing inmates who have already served sentences of over one year. In this case, the proportion of inmates who feel unjustly treated is smaller (by about 4%) after controlling for type of institution. This difference is clearly not significant.

A second explanation argues that length of time in the institution is correlated with total length of sentence, which is correlated to perceived justice of one's sentence, which is correlated with perceived justice of treatment. This perspective argues that the relationship between length of time served and perceptions of justice of treatment simply reflect the correlation of justice of treatment and justice of sentence.[15]

Patterns of Inmate Involvement

Perhaps most importantly, we turn to the social circles and patterns of interaction in which the inmate is embedded. We would expect that differential patterns of contact between inmates and significant others (be they other inmates, prison staff, or persons outside the prison) should be related to their feelings about justice of treatment, because they expose

[15]Editors note: In the original text, there was a note "awaiting data" to test this hypothesis, which would have been put in an additional table.

the inmate to both different prison experiences as well as different normative and evaluative systems. On experiential grounds, the inmate who interacts more frequently with prison staff, experiencing commaradery with them perhaps might be more likely to consider his treatment just than the inmate whose infrequent interaction might be a matter of discipline, custody, or order maintenance. Furthermore, differential association exposes one to different normative subcultures as well as varying experiences. Thus, from the viewpoint of social learning and the transmission of social values, different involvement patterns may predispose the inmate to the adoption of differing values, attitudes, or evaluations of social phenomena. A hypothesis of differential association as related to sentiments of just treatment is worthy of exploration, then.

In Chapter 6 we introduced a number of indices which tapped various components of the interactional network of the inmate. For purposes of this analysis, we employ dichotomized measures of contact with other inmates (based on number of friends), with staff (based on quantity of informal conversation with prison guards), and with persons outside the institution (based on the quantity of letters sent and received), and the eight-fold classification of combinations of these three variables.[16] We find that there are some rather clear and significant differences in perceptions of just treatment across categories of these indices of involvement.

Table 8.8 presents the proportion of inmates who consider their treatment just across each of these three dichotomized sources of contact. Data are presented for each of the three contexts of institutional climate of justice as well as for the entire sample. The findings are relatively clear: regardless of the source of contact, inmates who have more contact feel more justly treated. This pattern is strongest for staff contact, as expected, with percentage differences in justice between 6 and 9%, and weakest for inmate contact, where perceptible differences in feelings of justice are found only in that context where institutional climates are perceived as reasonably just. This latter finding, though extremely weak, is contrary to our expectations, which would have

[16] See Appendix III for further details on the construction of these indices.

Table 8.8 Patterns of contact and feelings of just treatment

	Inmate contact		Staff contact		Outside contact	
	High	Low	High	Low	High	Low
Entire sample	45%	41%	47%	39%	47%	38%
	(691)	(1066)	(1012)	(745)	(939)	(818)
Context 1	64%	57%	63%	57%	63%	56%
	(228)	(279)	(275)	(232)	(326)	(181)
Context 2	46%	45%	49%	40%	46%	44%
	(153)	(342)	(301)	(199)	(268)	(232)
Context 3	30%	29%	33%	25%	32%	26%
	(305)	(445)	(436)	(314)	(345)	(405)

indicated that greater contact with other inmates, and most likely with anti-staff inmate subculture, would result in increased feelings of injustice, as it did in attitudinal nonconformity. That this counter- theoretical observation holds only for the first context is somewhat reassuring, though the fact that the relationship was not reversed (and strongly so) is much less so.

Since we learned in Chapter 6 that the quantity of contact with other inmates and staff is positively correlated, one might suspect that the small though reversed relationship of inmate contact to sense of justice is a reflection of the fact that inmates high in contact with other inmates are more likely to be highly involved with staff members. We explore this question and others concerning the additive and interactive effects of various combinations of contact with data provided in Table 8.9. The table provides the proportion of inmates who feel justly treated for each of the eight combinations of types of involvement for the entire sample and for each of the three institutional contexts.

Table 8.9 provides a very rich source of data from which to explore such additive and interactive hypotheses. For example, we can examine, the effect of increasing the quantity of a particular form of contact, while holding the other two sources of contact constant. Thus we note that with very few and quite trivial exceptions, the effect of additional contact with either staff or persons outside the institution is a concomitant increase in perceptions of having being treated justly. For the entire

Table 8.9 Refined patterns of involvement and feelings concerning justice of treatment

Inmate	High staff		High staff		Low staff		Low staff	
	High outside		Low outside		High outside		Low outside	
Contact	%	(*N*)	%	(*N*)	%	(*N*)	%	(*N*)
Full sample–hi	**55**	(223)	44	(188)	45	(148)	*31*	(132)
-low	46	(331)	39	(270)	42	(237)	37	(228)
Context 1–hi	**72**	(78)	71	(42)	59	(81)	*48*	(27)
-low	61	(92)	51	(63)	60	(75)	55	(49)
Context 2–hi	**55**	(53)	52	(46)	36	(28)	*32*	(31)
-low	48	(113)	45	(89)	42	(74)	44	(66)
Context 3–hi	**40**	(92)	28	(100)	*20*	(39)	24	(74)
-low	35	(126)	28	(118)	26	(88)	25	(113)

Highest percentages in bold, lowest percentages italicized

sample, for example, decreasing levels of staff contact are reflected in levels of justice of 55% versus 45%, 44% versus 31%, 46% versus 42%, and 39% versus 37%, and so on. The effect of contacts with staff and persons outside the institution, then, is a complimentary one; higher levels of contact with both sources result in higher proportions of feelings of just treatment.

Returning to our initial question concerning an explanation of the anomalous finding of increased inmate contact as a source of feelings of greater justice rather than injustice, data in Table 8.9 provide interesting insights. Had we expected a purely additive effect of inmate involvement (assuming as we found that more inmate contact resulted uniformly in more justice), we would have predicted that highest levels of perceived just treatment would be found among those inmates with high levels of involvement with staff, persons outside the institution, and with other inmates, and the lowest proportion of such feelings would be found in that subgroup reported low in contact with all three sources. Data in Table 8.9 confirm the first prediction: both overall and for all three institutional contexts, the highest proportion of feelings of justice are found among those inmates high in all three sources of contact. They disconfirm the second prediction and suggest instead that feelings of injustice are most likely to be found among those inmates who are low in contact with staff (and in most cases with persons outside the institution), but whose contacts with other inmates are high.

This is the type of inmate we found most likely to be attitudinal nonconformists, and which the correctional literature would suggest to be most immersed in inmate subculture and antagonistic to the institutional regime.

That pattern emerges because, as we find in the table, staff and inmate contact do not have an additive effect, but rather an interactive one. Where inmates report high levels of contact with prison staff, the effect of high contact with other inmates is to increase feelings of just treatment. We note that as we read down the first two columns of the table, decreasing levels of inmate contact, holding constant contact with staff and the outside world, result in lower proportions of inmates feeling justly treated. However, if we read down the last two columns of the table, where staff contact is low, decreasing levels of inmate contact generally result in greater proportions feeling justly treated.[17] The percentage differences in each of these eight comparisons sample (for the entire/and three contexts) is somewhat sporadic, but the consistency of the direction of these relationships certainly is not.

We find, then, that heavy involvement with other prison inmates does not have a consistent normative input with regard to assessments of the justice of their treatment. Rather, the nature of its normative contribution is based upon being complimentary to patterns of involvement with prison guards. Where contact with guards is high, extensive inmate contact serves to maximize feelings of justice. Where guard contact is low, the more stereotypic subcultural influences operate, making perceptions of justice more likely if one's contact with other inmates is minimal. Note, however, that it is generally the case that the next most likely subgroup to experience unjust treatment, as reflected in Table 8.9, is a group not especially likely to be involved in anti-staff inmate subcultures, that group of social isolates reporting low levels of contact with all three sources.

---

[17]The fact that overall, inmates with high levels of involvement with other inmates feel more justly treated, reflects, then, the fact that among inmates with high contact with other inmates, a greater number report high staff contact than low staff contact, thus giving greater weight to this "side" of the interactive relationship. Had these "subgroups" been weighted equally, an interactive interpretation would have predicted that the overall effect of levels of contact with other inmates on feelings of justice would have been insignificant.

Given the rather gross index of justice of treatment on which our analysis must be based and the absence of other elaborative material in our data, it is unclear what to make of these findings. On the one hand, one might suggest that differential conditions of prison treatment are experienced by this group of prison inmates whose only major form of contact is with other inmates, relative to other subgroups in the prison, and thus their lower perceptions of justice reflect this differential experience. On the other hand, one might argue that the conditions of incarceration and treatment are not substantially different for this group, and their varying perceptions reflect their exposure to a normative climate which is most critical of inmate treatment and most likely to evaluate it as unjust. In the absence of data about the quality of such treatment, the plausibility of either interpretation can be debated. However, given our earlier understanding about the distinctiveness of this subgroup in regard to another aspect of the normative climate, attitudinal conformity, it is possible that the interpretation stressing the influence of normative components has some value.

Sense of Justice and Other Inmate Responses to Incarceration

In this section, we seek to explore the concomitants of variability in perceptions concerning justice of treatment and to investigate specifically the correlations between this variable and other aspects of inmate response: attitudinal and behavioral conformity and feelings of being helped or harmed by incarceration. As we have argued earlier, our interest here is not in sorting out these relationships causally. That is difficult (1) because our data is cross-sectional and (2) because of the theoretically expected reciprocity and feedback between these phenomena. Rather, our goal is to understand some of the other attitudes and behaviors that are shared by those inmates with a particular sense of justice, as well as the variability in conceptions of justice among those sharing other attitudes and behaviors.

Attitudinal Conformity

In Fig. 8.11 we present the relationship between perceptions of just treatment and attitudinal conformity (with both considered dependent variables).[18] As was the case in the analysis of inmate background and experience, we present data in this figure for the entire sample as well as data subdivided by institutional context, therefore controlling for the possibility of spurious relationships potentially contributed by the correlation between justice and response at the institutional level.

Throughout the earlier discussion of some of the prevailing backgrounds and predispositions associated with a feeling of being justly treated, we noted that attitudinal conformists and those feeling justly treated seemed to share the same background characteristics. Though this by no means implies that the two variables are necessarily related, it would not be surprising if they were. The data presented in this figure reasonably bear out such an expectation. In general, it is the case that as conformity decreases (left graph), perceptions of being justly treated decrease (overall from 50 to 26%) and as one's sense of just treatment decreases (right graph), there is an accompanied drop in attitudinal conformity (overall from 78 to 55%). One's sense of justice and conformity with staff norms, then, are rather strongly related, reflected as well in the gamma of .37 which summarizes this relationship.

However, our understanding of the relationship between feelings about justice of treatment and justice of sentence suggests that we control for the effect of feelings about sentencing when evaluating the relationship between conformity and treatment. These data are presented in Table 8.10. As this table clearly demonstrates, the relationship between treatment and conformity is not especially colored by inmate sentiments about the justice of their sentence. Although those feeling unjustly sentenced are less likely to be attitudinal conformists (reflected in the top portion of the table) and are less likely to feel justly treated (reflected in

[18] We recall from Chapters 5 and 6 that attitudinal conformity is an index based upon inmate responses to three hypothetical situations which involve anti-staff values. See Appendix III for details of index construction.

Table 8.10 The relationship between attitudinal conformity and justice of treatment by justice of sentence

	Justly treated		Unjustly treated	
	%	(*N*)	%	(*N*)
Percent attitudinal conformists				
Justly sentenced	79	(232)	63	(98)
Don't know	83	(120)	60	(75)
Unjustly sentenced	76	(429)	52	(510)
	Attitudinal Conformists		Attitudinal Nonconformists	
Percent justly treated				
Justly sentenced	66	(280)	45	(107)
Don't know	51	(197)	26	(78)
Unjustly sentenced	44	(728)	23	(465)

the bottom portion of the table) than their counterparts who felt justly sentenced, the relationship between conformity and treatment tends to remain consistent and of approximately the same magnitude within each category of justice of sentence as it did in the overall relationship. One exception is the slightly weaker relationship where attitudinal conformity is the dependent variable among those inmates feeling justly sentenced.

More confident now about the theoretical significance of the interrelation between justice of treatment and attitudinal conformity, it is important to pose additional questions about this relationship. These concern particularly the institutional variation in justice and the interface between institutional and individual relationships. These questions are addressed by the data presented in Fig. 8.11. We note that by contrasting the slope of the line for the overall relationship (darker line) with that of the three institutional contexts (lighter lines), we can explore the diminution of the individual level relationship by controlling for institutional variation, and by comparing the slopes of each of these three lines relative to each other, we can evaluate the interaction between qualities of the institution and those of the individual in the relationship between conformity and perceptions about the justice of prison treatment. We find that some of these comparisons yield rather interesting results. First we note that regardless of whether justice or conformity is the dependent variable, the slope of the line of the overall relationship is somewhat steeper than for the institutional contexts, and that the slope of the line for each of the contexts increases as the sense of institutional injustice increases (from context 1 to context 3). These observations are stated in a different medium through exploration of the gammas summarizing the strength of each of these relationships. They suggest that the relationship between justice of treatment and attitudinal conformity is strongest overall and particularly in the third context (of greatest institutional injustice) than in the other two contexts.

The first observation, that the relationship overall tends to be stronger than those within relatively homogeneous institutional contexts, is not entirely surprising. It simply reflects the fact that some of the individual variability is accounted for by the institutional level relationship between justice and conformity (tau = .16). However, this observation is not particularly significant; there remain rather strong individual level relationships after controlling for institutional variation in climate, as we note from both the slopes of the lines for each context and the gammas summarizing these relationships. More interesting is the observation that the relationship between justice and conformity increases in strength as institutional climate reflects more sensed injustice. This finding is true where both justice and attitudinal conformity are the dependent variables.[19]

This finding of increasing slope with increasing institutional injustice is even more interesting where attitudinal conformity is the dependent variable (right graph). In this case, we note that among inmates who consider their treatment unjust, institutional contexts behave in a predictable fashion: the level of conformity is highest where institutional justice is highest and lowest where institutional justice is lowest. However, this relationship is so strong in the most unjust context that this pattern is reversed among those who consider their treatment just. That subgroup most likely to be attitudinal conformists among

[19]Where justice is the dependent variable, we note that there is almost no relationship in the first context. This finding reflects a rather peculiar distribution of "don't know" responses in this particular context. When we examine inmate perceptions of being unjustly treated, we find a modest relationship in this context, where 16% of all attitudinal conformists consider their treatment unjust in contrast to 24% of the non-conformists, producing a slope only slightly smaller than that found in the other two contexts.

this group are inmates in context 3 rather than those in context 1 as we would have predicted. We will delay an explanation of this finding until after we have explored the relationship between justice and our other response variables, for which a similar pattern is also observed.

Behavioral Conformity

The relationship between behavioral conformity and sense of justice is even stronger than that associated with attitudinal conformity, as shown in Fig. 8.12.[20] For the sample overall, behavioral conformists consider their treatment just in 48% of the cases, compared to only 22% of those individuals having received disciplinary punishment (left graph). Further, 87% of those justly treated are also behavioral conformists in contrast to 60% of those who considered their treatment unjust (right graph). These findings of a high correlation between feeling unjustly treated and having experienced disciplinary punishment (gamma overall = −.52), of course, have no clear causal interpretations: one can argue that feelings of unjust treatment result from having been treated punitively by prison staff or that perceptions of being treated unjustly precipitates deviant behavior which is subsequently sanctioned by the staff. Both arguments are consistent with these data.

As in the case of the relationship between justice of treatment and attitudinal conformity, it is necessary to control for feelings about justice of sentence. Table 8.11 presents data for the relationship between justice of treatment and behavioral conformity, controlling for justice of sentence. A first and important observation reflected in this table is the fact that justice of sentence and behavioral conformity are basically unrelated, and furthermore that their slight interrelation is not in the expected direction. The proportion of behavioral conformists in each category of justice of sentence ranges from 74% among those justly sentenced to 76% among those unjustly sentenced, with inmates who "don't know" about the justice of their sentence having the highest

[20] We recall from Chapters 5 and 6 that behavioral conformity indexed the number of conduct infractions for which the inmate received disciplinary punishment.

Table 8.11 Relationship between behavioral conformity and justice of treatment by justice of sentence

	Justly treated		Unjustly treated	
	%	(*N*)	%	(*N*)
Percent behavioral conformists				
Justly sentenced	82	(236)	56	(100)
Don't know	90	(121)	68	(76)
Unjustly sentenced	90	(437)	60	(311)
	Behavioral Conformists		Behavioral Nonconformists	
Percent justly treated				
Justly sentenced	66	(293)	42	(103)
Don't know	47	(230)	26	(47)
Unjustly sentenced	43	(911)	16	(295)

proportion of behavioral conformists (83%). Apparently, then, one's feelings about the justice of one's sentence have little import for the likelihood that one has been sanctioned for conduct infractions.

Furthermore, we find that controlling for justice of sentence leaves the relationship of justice of treatment and behavioral conformity fundamentally unchanged. For each category of justice of sentence, the direction and magnitude of the relationship of conformity and treatment is reasonably comparable relative to other categories of sentencing and relative to the relationship overall (though the relationship is slightly weaker among those inmates who "don't know" about their sentence). Thus, information about the inmate's feelings about sentencing neither alter, diminish, nor further specify the relationship of justice of treatment to behavioral conformity.

However, a second set of controls seems theoretically warranted. We recall that our measure of behavioral conformity is a query about the number of times the inmate has received disciplinary punishment while in the institution. Since this is a measure of all disciplinary punishments ever received, rather than the number per unit of time, one is likely to have more conduct infractions the longer one has been imprisoned. As demonstrated in Table 8.12, this is quite clearly the case. Ninety-two percent of all inmates incarcerated for less than three months have never been sanctioned for conduct infractions in contrast to only 58% of

Table 8.12 The relationship between behavioral conformity and length of time served

Time served	Behavioral Conformists (%)	Behavioral Nonconformists (%)	(*N*)
Under 3 months	92	8	(558)
3–6 months	84	16	(412)
6–12 months	71	28	(415)
Over 12 months	58	42	(500)
Total	76	24	(1885)

those inmates incarcerated for more than a year. Since we have already learned that perceptions of justice are correlated with length of time spent in the institution, we must control for this latter variable in assessing the relationship of behavioral conformity to justice.

Table 8.13 presents the results of this analysis. It demonstrates that the relationship between justice and behavioral conformity remains after controlling for the amount of time served: behavioral conformists are appreciably less likely to feel unjustly treated than behavioral nonconformists for each category of time served (although the relationship is somewhat weaker in each category than the overall relationship). This relationship remains strong after controlling for institutional context, though it is strongest in context 3 (reflecting most unjust climates) and weakest in the first context. Thus, with regard to the potential confounding effect of length of incarceration, the relationship between behavioral conformity and justice remains solid.

As in the analysis of attitudinal conformity, we examine institutional variations in the relationship between behavioral conformity and sense of justice. The patterning is very similar. The relationship between behavioral conformity and justice tends to be higher for the overall sample than for the institutional contexts, as reflected graphically in Fig. 8.12. Of course, this finding is not surprising. There is a strong relationship between behavioral conformity and justice of treatment at the institutional level (tau = +.50), reflecting the fact that institutions which frequently sanction their inmates are considered less just. The overall relationship is slightly stronger, then, because part of this institutional effect is removed from the individual level relationships with

Table 8.13 Relationship between behavioral conformity and justice of treatment by length of time served (percent unjustly treated)

	Behavioral Conformists		Behavioral Nonconformists	
Time Served	%	(*N*)	%	(*N*)
Under 3 months	22	(512)	39	(46)
3–6 months	26	(344)	66	(68)
6–12 months	33	(296)	57	(119)
Over 12 months	43	(289)	67	(211)
Totals	29	(1441)	61	(444)

the controls introduced by the three contexts. Furthermore, we find that the relationship increases in strength with increasing levels of injustice in institutional climates, reflected both in the slope of the lines for each context and in the magnitude of the gammas that summarize these relationships. This pattern of increasingly stronger relationships as the institutional context becomes increasingly unjust is particularly apparent where behavioral conformity is the dependent variable. However, unlike the relationship involving attitudinal conformity, we find that levels of behavioral conformity tend to remain lowest in the third and most unjust context.

Perceived Effect of Incarceration

We turn, finally, to a third form of response which has been considered in depth in this volume, that of the perceived effect of incarceration, and the inmates' judgment concerning whether they will be helped or harmed by imprisonment in their ability to cope with life outside the prison. Data in Fig. 8.13 demonstrate that indeed there is a relationship between these perceptions and those concerning the justice of one's treatment. We find in the figure a very clear relationship: feelings of justice are positively related to feelings of being helped by incarceration (gamma=.30). While 51% of those inmates who consider their imprisonment helpful also feel justly treated, only 35% of those who feel harmed share these feelings in the overall sample (left graph). Furthermore, 49% of those justly treated feel harmed, as opposed to

69% of those unjustly treated in the overall sample (right graph). Thus, feelings of injustice are quite likely to be accompanied by feelings of being harmed. Again, the causal ordering is unclear, though probably reciprocal.

Data reflecting controls for feelings about justice of sentence are more interesting here in the relationship of feelings of help or harm to justice of treatment, than they were for conformity (see Table 8.14). First, we note that justice of sentence and feelings of being harmed by incarceration are fairly strongly related. Whereas 42% of those inmates feeling justly sentenced also feel harmed, these sentiments are shared by 48 and 66% of those inmates who "don't know" or who feel unjustly sentenced, respectively. Furthermore, we find that although the direction of the relationship between perceived effect of incarceration and justice of treatment remains consistent throughout categories of feelings about sentencing, the magnitude of these relationships is quite variable. Specifically, where inmates consider their sentence just, this relationship is stronger than the overall relationship, while it is weaker than the overall relationship for inmates who feel unjustly sentenced. (This is true both where perceived effect of incarceration and justice of treatment are considered dependent variables—noted on the top and bottom of the table, respectively.) It is unclear why this differential in magnitude of the relationships is manifested. Despite this finding, however, the relationship between justice of treatment and help or harm remains strong and consistent. For any category of feelings about the justice

Table 8.14 Relationship between effect of incarceration and justice of treatment by justice of sentence

	Justly treated		Unjustly treated	
	%	(*N*)	%	(*N*)
Percent harmed				
Justly sentenced	34	(233)	60	(100)
Don't know	37	(122)	60	(76)
Unjustly sentenced	60	(438)	72	(514)
	Helped		Harmed	
Percent justly treated				
Justly sentenced	67	(229)	48	(164)
Don't know	53	(146)	34	(134)
Unjustly sentenced	43	(411)	33	(797)

of sentencing, inmates justly treated are least likely to feel harmed by imprisonment and inmates feeling harmed are least likely to feel treated justly.

Figure 8.13 also presents data on the institutional or contextual contribution to the individual level relationship of justice of treatment and help or harm. With one exception, differentiation in this relationship across contexts, a pattern observable in the data that cross-tabulated the relationship of justice and conformity, is not salient in this figure. The slope of the lines (and thus the magnitude of the relationships) is comparable across institutional contexts and between institutional contexts and the overall sample. The gammas which summarize these relationships do increase as one moves from relatively just to relatively unjust institutional contexts, though the size of the increase is much less substantial than that found for the relationship of justice of treatment to attitudinal and behavioral conformity. Thus, institutional variation in feelings of justice (and its potential correlation with help or harm) does not significantly alter the strong and consistent relationship at the individual level between perceptions of justice and those of being harmed.

The one exception to this observation is quite interesting and significant enough for us to have devoted the following chapter to its exploration. That exception is found in the right-hand graph, in which we note overall levels of feelings of having been harmed for each of the three institutional contexts. We find that increasing harm is related to increasing feelings of injustice, and hence we would have predicted that the relative ordering of overall feelings of harm by context would find those in context 3 feeling most harmed and those in context 1 feeling least harmed. This pattern is not observed in our data. It is the case that inmates in the second context consistently feel more harmed than those in the first, as we predicted. However, that subgroup of inmates least harmed is found in context 3, characterized by the highest levels of felt injustice. This anomaly is accounted for by the fact that a large proportion of the prisons in the third context are preventive detention institutions (as we noted earlier), and these institutions represent a very peculiar and interesting constellation: their inmates feel both unjustly treated, yet helped by incarceration. The reasons and implications for this phenomenon will be examined in the following chapter.[21] We simply note the pattern at this time.

We find, then, that feelings about the justice of one's treatment in prison are highly inter-correlated with other responses to and assessments of the quality of incarceration, and indeed are more highly related than they are to characteristics of the inmate or to the nature of his prison experience. We are better able to predict and appreciate the inmates perceptions about the justice of his treatment with information about his other attitudes, behaviors, and responses to the prison, than we are with information about the quality of the prison experience or the nature of the inmate's background and previous experiences. This is certainly not to argue that feelings of injustice are unresponsive to the quality of one's experience, for clearly they are. Rather it is to argue that we can better summarize the subtleties and impact of these experiences with related attitudes and responses to the prison, than we can by the gross indicators of experience available in our data set. Furthermore, it appears that data about these other attitudes and behaviors provide insights about the very complex process characterized by the transition from experience to evaluation.

We reemphasize that the findings here reported do not suggest or evaluate causal relationships. We suggest that the interplay of these varieties of response to imprisonment over time pose fascinating research questions. How do feelings of justice color the extent of an inmate's hypothetical adherence to anti-staff values and promotion of anti-staff behaviors? What is the effect of being disciplined by prison authorities on feelings of justice? These and other questions could be addressed by a longitudinal design and one which is more sensitive to subtleties of meaning and experience. They are not addressed here and any related interpretations are therefore necessarily speculative.

These analyses revealed as well that the inter-correlations between inmate response and feelings about justice of treatment remain both strong and consistent even after controlling for inmate feelings about the justice of their sentence and for institutional differentiation in climates of justice. We did find, however, that the magnitude of these inter-correlations are somewhat variable across institutional contexts. Particularly

[21]Editor's note: The following chapter, which would be Chapter 9, was not written.

with regard to attitudinal and behavioral conformity, we found that as prison climates become increasingly unjust, the relationship between feelings regarding justice of treatment and other responses to incarceration became stronger. It is unclear what to make of this finding. An account of this pattern must look to the quality of the institutional contexts that are being contrasted and query the features of these contexts, the constellations and severity of experiences, the diversity in background of their inmates, etc., that maximize the degree of relationships within them. We noted, for example, in the case of perceptions of the effect of incarceration, that the fact that so many of the prisons in the third context were preventive detention institutions (which provide a rather unique set of both therapeutic facilities yet non-universalistic conditions of therapy and treatment), resulted in a patterning of relationship within this context atypical of that in the other two contexts. Our ability to provide a theoretically meaningful and responsible account of this process with these data is limited, so we will therefore refrain from doing so at this time.

Before completing our consideration of the variability and concomitants of perceptions of justice, we will turn to one final important differentiation in these perceptions, and that concerns cross-national variability.

National Differences in Perceptions Concerning Justice of Treatment

In a later chapter (10), we will systematically consider national differentiation in our major response measures and in attributes of prison climate.[22] However, as the previous analyses have demonstrated, levels of perceived injustice are so intertwined with national distinctions that a fuller understanding of the variability in these perceptions dictates a closer and immediate examination of cross-national variation. The assessment of meaningful cross-national differentials in perceptions

---

[22]Editor's note: parts of Chapter 10 were incorporated into Chapter 7.

concerning justice of treatment and an attempt to account for them is the concern of this final section of the chapter.

We recall that when we wished to evaluate institutional variation in overall levels of felt injustice, and we attempted to control for this variability through the construction of institutional contexts, there were some sharp national biases in the assignment of institutions to particular contexts. We found that all Finnish institutions except the special open labor colony were assigned to the third context, representing those institutions with the highest overall levels of felt injustice. This third context, however, did not include any Swedish institutions, all of which were characterized as more "just."

When we shift from the institutional to the individual level of analysis, we find similar cross-national differentiation. We have aggregated the pool of all inmates incarcerated in a particular nation and report cross-national distributions of feelings concerning justice of treatment in Table 8.15. These data indicate that there are some rather sharp national differences in these feelings: While half of all Swedish inmates feel justly treated, these sentiments are shared by only 36% of the Finnish inmates, with 44% of both Norwegian and Danish samples also feeling justly treated. Although the proportion of inmates who "don't know" about the justice of their treatment is subject to a bit of national differentiation as well, differences by country in expressions of unjust treatment reflect essentially the same pattern.

We do not treat these aggregated data as an authoritative statement of differentiation attributable to national distinctions, because there are biases in the composition of the national pool of inmates in characteristics that are salient to their assessments of justice. Thus, to eliminate the possible contribution of differential inmate characteristics in overall national levels of justice, we have controlled for inmate age and social and criminal background. Inmates comparable on a combination of all of these characteristics were contrasted and national differences within these homogeneous subgroups were assessed. Although it would have been desirable to control for a variety of other characteristics of the respondents and their institutional affiliations, this was precluded by limitations in sample size. The distribution of cross-national differences assessed in each of these homogeneous subgroups was then evaluated by

Table 8.15 National differences in feelings of justice or injustice of treatment

	Norway	Sweden	Finland	Denmark
Justly treated	44%	50%	36%	44%
Don't know	21%	24%	22%	19%
Unjustly treated	35%	26%	42%	37%
Total	(248)	(290)	(629)	(747)

a sign-test, testing whether differences significantly depart from random variation.[23] A summary of these results are presented in Table 8.16.

Let us look, for example, at the comparison between Norway and Sweden. There were 36 subgroups of inmates homogeneous in age, social, and criminal background, and in 22 of these contrasts, a higher proportion of Norwegian than Swedish respondents indicated feeling unjustly treated. As evaluated by the sign-test (and the binomial distribution), this can be considered a random occurrence. We note that some of the cross-national differences are statistically significant at an acceptable level. As we would have expected from the marginal distributions reported in Table 8.15, Swedish inmates are much less likely to feel unjustly treated than Finnish inmates ($p<.001$). Other significant differences are those between Sweden and Denmark, Denmark and Finland, and Norway and Finland, in each of which inmates in the latter nation feel more unjustly treated than those in the former. We find, then, that even after controlling for differences in the personal characteristics of respondents in each of the nations, overall differences in levels of perceived injustice remain significant—Finnish inmates are much more likely to feel unjustly treated than their counterparts in any of the other Scandinavian countries, and Danish inmates feel more unjustly treated than their Swedish counterparts.

[23]The section in Chapter 10, "A Methodology for the Assessment of National Differences," presents a detailed and technical description of the process of constructing homogeneous subgroups and of evaluating the results of these analyses. The reader is strongly advised to consult this section.

Table 8.16 Homogeneous subgroup analysis for national differences in feelings about justice of treatment

	Sign test prob.
Norway vs Sweden	Not sig.
Norway vs Finland	<.05
Norway vs Denmark	Not sig.
Sweden vs Finland	<.001
Sweden vs Denmark	<.01
Finland vs Denmark	<.05

We have been concerned throughout this chapter with the confounding of feelings concerning justice of treatment with those concerning justice of sentence. In the arena of national differentiation, this interrelationship is especially critical, since it is clearly the case that principles and procedures of sentencing are nationally variable. Although it is difficult to operationalize variable sentencing systems, and unreliable to assume that prison inmates have the legal sophistication to reflect accurately on these systems, we do have data on inmate perceptions of the justice of their sentences. And whether these latter perceptions reflect the structure of national sentencing or some other phenomenon, they nonetheless have import for concomitant feelings about justice of treatment. Indeed, although differences are not as sharp as they were for perceptions of treatment, there are national differences in feelings about justice of sentence. They range from 13% of the inmates in Finland who feel justly sentenced to 27% of their Danish counterparts, with 18% of the Swedes and 23% of the Norwegians sharing these sentiments. Although the overall level of feelings concerning justice of sentence does not pattern itself cross-nationally as did feelings about treatment, it is clearly necessary to control for feelings about sentence in the assessment of national differentiation in perceptions about treatment.

Table 8.17 presents these data, which reflect differential feelings about treatment cross-nationally among inmate subgroups who share similar feelings about the justice of their sentence. Where inmates consider themselves having been justly sentenced, we note that the pattern of national differentiation previously documented remains very

Table 8.17 National differences in feelings of justice/injustice of treatment by justice of sentence

Sentence	Treatment	Norway	Sweden	Finland	Denmark
Just	Just	59%	75%	47%	61%
Just	Don't know	19%	12%	16%	14%
Just	Unjust	22%	13%	37%	25%
	Total	(68)	(52)	(79)	(199)
Don't know	Just	50%	45%	37%	48%
Don't know	Don't know	33%	33%	30%	27%
Don't know	Unjust	17%	21%	33%	26%
	Total	(18)	(42)	(108)	(113)
Unjust	Just	36%	44%	33%	36%
Unjust	Don't know	21%	25%	22%	18%
Unjust	Unjust	43%	31%	45%	46%
	Total	(157)	(196)	(439)	(429)

consistent (the differences in fact are even stronger): three-quarters of the Swedish inmates in contrast to less than half of the Finnish inmates feel justly treated, with 59 and 61% of the Norwegians and Danes, respectively, feeling similarly. These differences are much weaker when we turn to that larger portion of the sample who felt unjustly sentenced. The Swedes are still most likely to feel justly treated (44%) and least likely to feel unjustly treated (31%), but the sentiments of Finnish inmates are no longer different from those of their counterparts in Norway and Denmark, and not strikingly different even from those in Sweden.

However, one last control is warranted. We wish to eliminate respondents from the two special institutions in our sample, the open colonies of Seutula (#10) in Finland and Kragskovhede (#15) in Denmark which are subject to such variant conditions of incarceration, with no comparable institutions in the other Scandinavian countries, that they may color national aggregates in potentially very confusing ways. The elimination of the 156 respondents from Kragskovhede makes little difference in the overall responses for Denmark. The proportion of inmates who feel unjustly treated drops by 2% for that sample feeling justly sentenced and drops 5% for the group feeling unjustly sentenced. However, by eliminating the 161 Finnish inmates from Seutula, assessments of injustice in Finland become even more common: the proportion of inmates who feel unjustly treated grows from 37 to 43% among those justly sentenced, and from 45 to 58% among those unjustly sentenced.

Thus, once we take into consideration the very special institutional features of these open colonies, we find that consistent cross-national differences in feelings concerning justice of treatment remain, even after controlling for justice of sentence. Finnish inmates feel very unjustly treated; Swedish inmates feel more justly treated; and Norwegian and Danish inmates fall somewhere in the middle, despite differentials in their perceptions about the justice of their sentences.

However, our finding about the status of our special labor colony in Finland (Seutula) is significant. It warns us that there is not something characteristically "Finnish" about injustice, that indeed there are inmates in a Finnish institution who perceive their treatment at variance with fellow nationals, but not with inmates incarcerated in other countries.[24] This finding reminds us, then, that despite our assessment that the Scandinavian countries meaningfully differentiate themselves in levels of injustice experienced by their inmates, national inputs into correctional administration are still by no means consistent and homogeneous. We must explore intra-nationally the variation in the conditions of incarceration and how these feed into the perceptions of those incarcerated.

A fuller understanding of the "correctional character" of each of the four Scandinavian countries will be presented in Chapter 10, and it is somewhat premature at this point to explore the sources and correlates of differential perceptions of justice at the national level. However, we will address this issue in a very introductory manner in order to provide a flavor for the concomitants of the patterning of these perceptions cross-nationally.

Earlier in this chapter we considered justice of treatment as an element of institutional climate and explored its relationship to other attributes of prison climate. We recall that some rather significant

[24]Sixty-one percent of the inmates at Seutula felt justly treated and 16% felt unjustly treated. This contrasts with 42 and 37%, respectively, of sentiments of respondents in the entire sample.

correlations were found, suggesting that characterizations of prisons as relatively just or unjust are related to the way in which inmates experience various aspects of the institutional regime and levels of pressure that are exerted upon them both by staff members and other inmates. Since we can expect some degree of national differentiation on these related measures of prison climate,[25] findings of national differences in justice may be simple reflections of the distribution of these climate variables. The following analysis will attempt to control for several of these aspects of institutional climate. It will query whether national differences in justice of treatment remain at the institutional level, once one takes into consideration the patterning of other aspects of prison climate.

Because of the small *N* of only fifteen institutions and the *N* of only three, once national distinctions are made problematic, it is impossible to enlist a strict methodological design to evaluate these questions. Our preference would have been to contrast levels of perceived justice cross-nationally for prisons which are characterized similarly' on some salient attribute of climate. This is clearly impossible.

Given the distribution of the institutional data without regard to national distinctions, one can compute a predicted value of justice of treatment, given a particular value on another salient climate indicator. Specifically, since all of our climate variables are measured at the interval level we can state these predictions in terms of the intercept and slope of the regression equation which characterizes the relationship of justice to other attributes of institutional climate.[26] One might then explore the "residuals" of this regression, the pattern of institutions that depart from these predicted values and the magnitude of these departures. To the extent that national differences in levels of justice are hypothesized to be non-spurious, and hence not accountable by the relationship between

[25]See Chapter 10 for a more systematic evaluation of this hypothesis.

[26]We recall that climate values were based on the percentage of inmates in a particular institution who expressed a particular sentiment about the character of their prison on a given dimension.

justice and other aspects of institutional climate, we would expect to find national differences salient in the distribution of these residuals.[27]

This method has been employed in the analysis of some of the major institutional level predictors of justice which we considered earlier in the chapter: guard authority, guard understanding, coerciveness, staff pressure and total pressure. The figures which initially illustrated these relationships are again provided. This time, however, we direct our attention to the nationality of the prison, characterized by their numbers: 1, 2, 3 for Norway; 4, 5, 6 for Sweden; 7–10 for Finland; and 11–15 for Denmark. An additional piece of information is added to these figures. That concerns the regression equation for each of these relationships and the line representing the predicted value of justice for various values of the independent variable, superimposed on the graph.

We begin our analysis with Fig. 8.1′, which considers the relationship of justice of treatment and guard authority.[28] Look, for example, at the three Norwegian prisons (1, 2, and 3). Institution #2, Botsfengslet, falls exactly on the regression line; the other two institutions fall at almost equal intervals on either side of the line. In this case, it would appear that nationality was not especially relevant in accounting for levels of justice manifested in these prisons. However, the Finnish institutions behave differently, particularly if we disregard the rather unique special open labor colony, Seutula (10). The Finnish prisons (7, 8, and 9) all fall significantly to the left of the line (in the direction of greater injustice), indicating that values of institutional justice are a good deal lower than we would have predicted on the basis of levels of guard power. Similarly, institutions in Denmark and Sweden tend to fall a little bit further to the right of the regression line (indicating greater justice) than we would have predicted.

This pattern of national differentiation reflected in the residuals of the predicted relationship between justice and other attributes of climate is even more apparent with regard to guard understanding and

[27]We will not analyze these residuals systematically or statistically. We feel our data do not warrant such attention. Rather our assessment will rely on visual contrasts derived from graphical materials.

[28]Editor's note: See Appendix III for modified Figs. 8.1′–8.5′ with fitted regression lines.

coerciveness, illustrated in Figs. 8.2′ and 8.3′, respectively. In both of these figures it is clearly the case that Finnish institutions fall considerably to the left of the regression line and Swedish institutions significantly to its right. Norwegian and Danish institutions tend to be divided on either side of the line, and we will not concern ourselves with the overall weighting of these institutions toward greater justice or injustice. Indeed, then, our finding that Finnish inmates are most likely to consider their treatment unjust and that Swedish inmates are least likely to have these sentiments, is not accounted for by differences in these nations in other aspects of institutional climate. We note, for example, the youth institutions in Finland (8) and Sweden (5). As illustrated in Fig. 8.2, they are both characterized by comparable levels of guard understanding (about 17% of their inmates find guards understanding). Yet levels of justice of treatment range from less than 20% in the Finnish institution to over 40% in its Swedish counterpart.

Our figures evaluating the relationship between levels of justice and pressure exerted between staff and inmates (Figs. 8.4′ and 8.5′) provide greater insights concerning national differentiation in perceptions of just treatment. Although the residuals still reflect some national differences, we find that Finnish and Swedish institutions are moving closer to the regression line. Furthermore, Finnish institution #7 has moved to the right of the line, indicating higher levels of perceived justice and Swedish institution #6 has moved to the left of the line, indicating lower levels of just treatment than would be expected on the basis of levels of staff pressure (Fig. 8.4′). In the case of total pressure (Fig. 8.5′), the institutional differences with regard to Sweden have entirely disappeared, and with regard to Finland, they have been somewhat reduced.

We realize that this visual technique of data analysis is far from rigorous. However, given the small number of institutions, our inability because of the small N to employ multiple regressions to sort out the effects of nationality controlling simultaneously for a variety of aspects of institutional climate, and the noncomparability of some of the special institutions in the sample, a more systematic method would have been unreliable and quite pretentious.

In summary, it would be fair to say that national differences in justice of treatment, particularly with regard to Finland relative to the other Scandinavian nations, cannot be accounted for entirely by national differentiation in these other elements of institutional climate. However, consideration of these institutional climates in large part diminishes the differences observed cross-nationally. We get a sense, then, that national differentiation in perceptions regarding the justice of institutional treatment is not an entirely new insight or explanatory system in our search for an accounting of the observed variability in feelings about institutional injustice. Indeed justice is a reflection of other attributes of the prison climate and experience, and an understanding of national differences in justice must consider the nature and sources of national differentiation in these attributes of prison experience (see Chapter 10). Our conclusion, then, is that national insights may be providing us with somewhat redundant information in our exploration of the sources of variable perceptions of justice. This is not to say that these distinctions are not meaningful to those concerned with the quality of a particular correctional system. Nor is it to say that our finding of such widespread national differences, even after controlling for the divergent background of those characterizing their experiences is not important. It simply redirects our attention to national inputs into the structuring, staffing, and, in other ways, the construction of the prison experience.

Conclusion

The foregoing has provided a rather lengthy consideration of sources and concomitants of the variability in inmate perceptions of justice and in the distribution of these perceptions across various aggregations of the pool of inmates. Perhaps it has been too lengthy and detailed, given the fact that the relationships evaluated in this chapter were based on responses to a single questionnaire item. Nonetheless, the quite dramatic and consistent patterning of its interrelation with other variables and at varying analytic levels, assures us that we have isolated a concept of importance in the consideration of variable prison systems and inmate responses to incarceration. Furthermore, our consideration of its interrelation with inmate sentiments about the justice of other encounters with the criminal justice system prior to incarceration assured us that sentiments about the justice of treatment, though certainly related, were distinct phenomena subject to their own patterns of variability.

Our findings have been varied. We considered institutional variability in perceived justice of treatment, and found that other elements of institutional climate, particularly the level of staff pressure exerted on inmates and other elements of the institutional regime, such as the understanding, power, and coerciveness of guards, were modestly to strongly related to institutional differentials in justice.

However, a considerable variability in perceptions about justice of treatment remained after consideration of institutional phenomena. Several sources and correlates of assessments of justice were considered. They included inmate background characteristics (age, social and criminal experience, and sensitivity to authority); differential prison experience, highlighted by the structural conditions of incarceration, length of time served, and patterns of involvement with other inmates, staff, and persons outside of the institution; other responses to incarceration concerned with attitudinal and behavioral conformity and perceptions of being helped or harmed by imprisonment; and finally national differences in perceptions of justice at both the institutional and individual level. In general, we found that the strongest relationships occured between justice of treatment and other forms of inmate responses to incarceration, and the weakest from its relation to inmate background characteristics. Although some national differences in levels of perceived justice were found quite striking, they seemed largely accountable for by other qualities of institutional life which also varied cross-nationally rather than by some unique feature of the treatment of prison inmates which was distinctively "national."

The variable of justice of treatment, at least as conceptualized in this study, is a fascinating issue for a sociological evaluation of the prison, because it clearly calls into focus analytically qualities both of social systems and of the individuals within then and of their interaction. We found that variability in justice could be meaningfully approached at the institutional and the individual level, and that the insights from one level of analysis tended to complement and expand rather than diminish the insights obtained from the other. Where sources of individual variability in feelings of justice were considered problematic, institutional affiliations were controlled, and we recall that the general result was only a very slight diminution of the overall relationship across institutional contexts.

Rather we found that relationships overall were patterned similarly within various institutional settings, but that often institutional settings characterized by greater perceived injustice tended to magnify the differences in perceptions of justice between inmates who varied in background, experience, or other attitude. It is indeed our interest in the contribution of variable institutional settings to an understanding of the manifestation of feelings of justice or injustice of treatment that sparked the following chapter which takes a closer look at the preventive detention institution.

The breadth of our understanding about justice of treatment in correctional regimes has been only whetted by the previous analyses. Although it serves as a rather powerful introduction to some of the major correlates of perceptions of justice in our sample, it also highlights many of the limitations of our data set and research method analytically. Perhaps most lacking is a closer conceptualization and measurement of the subtlety and intricacies of perceptions of justice. Secondly, we sorely lack a longitudinal design, which explores not only differential experience across a pool of inmates from a static perspective, but which queries differential experiences encountered by the single respondent over time and the dynamics of perceptual change. Finally, sociometric data, which explore the inmate's perceptions of the experiences of others and interactions with them, would better accommodate the traditional social science questions about distributive justice, which treat feelings of justice as explicitly social, relative, and comparative.

Epilogue: The Fate of Prevention Detention Prisons

By David Armor, Thomas Mathiesen, Fleming Balvig, Henrik Tham, and Aarne Kinnunen

Earlier in this chapter, Wheeler and Cline made the observation that the preventive detention prisons Ila (1), Hall (4), Turku (9) and Herstedvester (11) tended to have lower rates of perceived justice of treatment, relative to other prison characteristics indicating strong perceived guard power & coerciveness. This was especially true for Ila and Herstedvester, which were consistently in the lowest quadrant of perceived justice and institutional pressures. The authors planned to take up this issue in Chapter 9, which was to discuss the issue of psychiatric treatments in prisons. Unfortunately, that chapter was never written.

While we can never know what their conclusions might have been, we do think it is useful to make a few observations in light of what happened to these institutions following writing their SPS report. To emphasize the importance of their observations, Fig. 8.1 has been revised below to show separate regression lines for the preventive detention prisons as compared to all other prisons. The overall relationship for all 15 prisons is $r = -.26$, but when the preventive detentions are separated out, the r for all other prisons is much stronger ($r = -.58$) and the intercepts differ by more than 20 points, indicating two different populations.

The most important implication of these results might be the fact that within 10–20 years after the SPS data was collected, all of the preventive detention prisons were converted to other types of prisons.[29] The reason for the low feelings of just treatment might be related to the fact that most of the prison sentences were of indeterminate length, and also that inmates were being held for "psychopathic" disorders. At any rate, prison reform in these Nordic countries appear to be the main reason these types of prison sentences have either been eliminated or severely limited. It might be said that the low levels of prisoner feelings of just treatment that the SPS found in these prisons presaged their ultimate demise.

[29]T. Lappi-Seppala, "Penal Policies in the Nordic Countries 1960–2010," *Journal of Scandinavian Studies in Criminology and Crime Prevention*, 2014, 13 sup 1: 85–111.

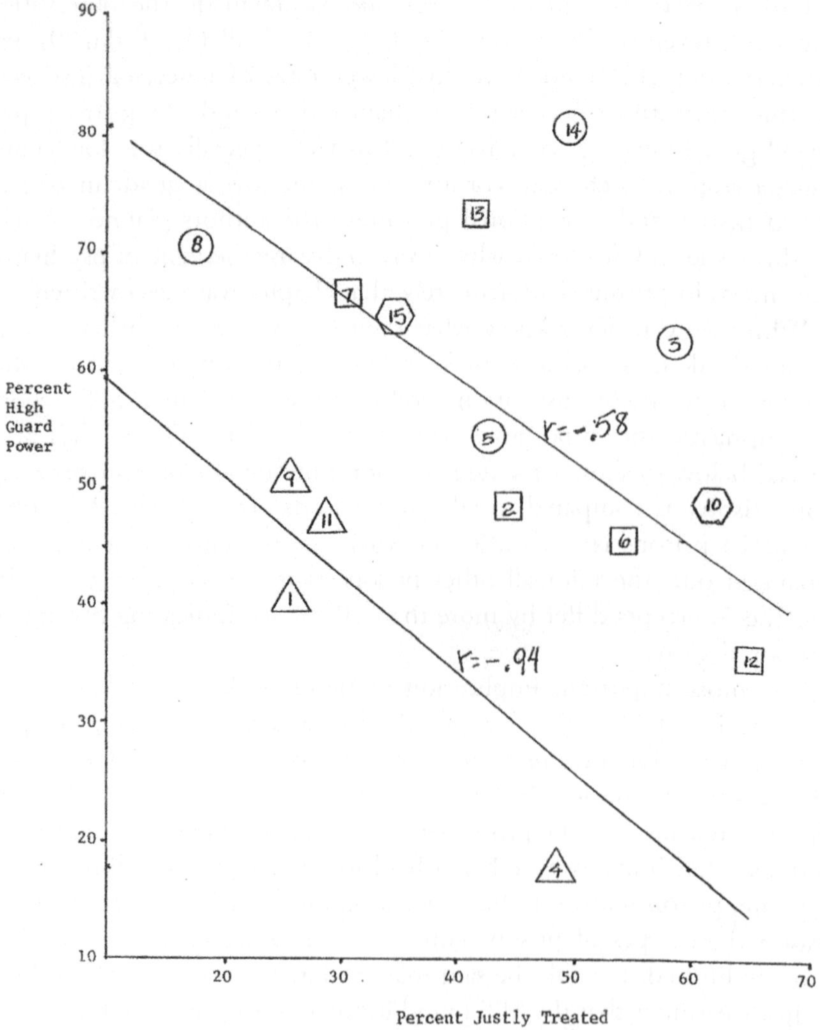

Figure 8.1 revised with regression lines fit separately for preventive detention prisons vs. all other prisons ($r = -.26$ for all 15 prisons combined).

Afterword

By Thomas Mathiesen, professor emeritus at the University of Oslo, and Member of the Political Committee of KROM—the Norwegian Association of Penal Reform. In Cooperation with professor emeritus Flemming Balvig (Copenhagen), Chairman of the Scandinavian Research Council for Criminology Aarne Kinnunen (Helsinki) and professor emeritus Henrik Tham (Stockholm).

The Beginning

Stanton Wheeler visited the three Scandinavian countries and Finland in the early 1960s, and, with his colleague Hugh F. Cline, launched his impressive sociological study of 15 penal establishments and close to 2000 inmates.

Much in terms of politics in general and criminal justice in particular has taken place in Norway and in the other Northern European countries since then. For one thing, both Stanton Wheeler and I were young: Stanton Wheeler was a little over 30 years old, and I was 27. For another, Stanton Wheeler died at the age of 77, in 2007, while I am still

S. Wheeler and H. F. Cline, *The Scandinavian Prison Study*, Palgrave Studies in Prisons and Penology, https://doi.org/10.1007/978-3-030-26462-8

alive but close to 85 and an old man. A few words about the very start of the study, which I witnessed at close quarters, are probably in order.

Stanton Wheeler was not only young at the time, he was also a very promising and upcoming sociologist. Among other things, he was about to publish a large and very noteworthy article in one of the major sociological journals in the US.[1] He had just received a Fulbright scholarship and planned to stay for a year in Norway. He was one of the many social scientists who visited Norway and other Nordic and European countries at the time, during the aftermath of World War II. He was well received in Oslo, the capital city of Norway, where he settled down with his family.

After a short while he established close contact with Norwegian sociologists such as Nils Christie, at that time associate professor of criminology, and myself who was about to start a research project in a Norwegian penal institution. He also met with other Scandinavian researchers. Wheeler soon proposed a joint research design for us: Would we, together with him, embark on a research study of Norwegian prisoners, perhaps with his own article from the US as a model? We certainly would, and we constructed a long questionnaire with a number of questions to be answered by inmates. I administered the questionnaire (read it out loud) at Ila Security Institution outside Oslo, where I by now had begun my own study. Two other Norwegian institutions later became Norwegian targets of the large Nordic study which was now under way.

Wheeler also visited Sweden, Denmark and Finland, where 12 further institutions were selected, reaching altogether 15 penal establishments. The study was even given a name—it was called the SPS—the Scandinavian Prison Study—even though Finland of course was and is located outside the three Scandinavian countries. The selection of countries was sociological rather than purely geographical, and as we shall see later, there was good reason to also include Finland.

[1]Wheeler, Stanton (1961): "Socialization in Correctional Communities," *American Sociological Review*, Vol. 26 No. 5, pp. 697–712.

Eventually, when the data had been collected Stanton Wheeler went back to the United States. As far as I know, he visited the four Nordic countries several times, and cooperated with several social scientists,[2] but a full study of the fifteen penal institutions for a very long while remained unfinished. While the Scandinavian Prison Study took place over 50 years ago, much of the writing was done over a 15 year period, including some chapters during the time that Wheeler and Cline were at the Russell Sage Foundation in New York. The final round of editing has been diligently done by professor emeritus David Armor of George Mason University. Wheeler's widow, Marcia Chambers, who unfortunately also passed away as this project was being finished, was responsible for asking David to edit the SPS and asking me to write this Afterword.

Due to its long history prior to publication, the study may be best seen as a historical study of the opinions, views, feelings, and activities of inmates who lived their lives in 15 Nordic penal institutions half a century ago. As such, they might be compared with inmates' views, feelings, and activities today—a major piece of research in itself. Rather than carrying out such a project, I will focus on several issues relevant to Scandinavian society and penology in general.

Purpose of This Afterword

First, I will discuss the NGO movements (such as KROM in Norway) which were influential in shaping prison policies, especially in Norway. In a final section, I will discuss the issue of Scandinavian "exceptionalism," a concept applied by several European criminologists to explain low rates of incarceration in these countries.

[2]See for example Balvig, Flemming et al. (1969): *Fængsler og fanger* (Prisons and Prisoners). Paludan. The Danish sociologist professor Preben Wolf, who died in 2018 nearly 100 years old, also had a close relationship to Stanton Wheeler. Wolf was also important in securing that Wheeler's Danish data were thoroughly analyzed and used.

Norway, Sweden, and Denmark Got Their NGOs

In Scandinavian countries inmates, researchers and others started a struggle in the late sixties for better conditions for prisoners. An important NGO (a "Non-Governmental Organization") was founded in Norway in 1968 named KROM, Parallel NGOs were established in the other three Nordic countries mentioned earlier. The other NGOs did important work,[3] based on major unrest and modes of alternative thinking regarding criminal policy among a large number of young people. Wide spread hunger strikes among inmates in Sweden, and so-called negotiations with prison authorities there, took place during the late 1960s and 1970s. The prison strikes were widely covered in national and the international press at the time. The NGOs viewed the Scandinavian criminal justice systems in a different way than most people—as rather bureaucratic systems where much should—and could—be done in terms of opening the prisons and make the ties between prisoners and the world outside less restrictive.

But in the other three countries the NGO movements more or less ended their lives in the late 1970s and later, while the Norwegian NGO continued its work, in fact until this day.[4] Replicas were founded in Germany and England, and had similar names.

The Formative Years of KROM in Norway

During the first formative years, the Norwegian NGO concentrated on having four major so-called "special measures" in criminal policy in Norway abolished—the system of forced labor for vagrants and alcoholics; the detention center system (a British model); the youth prison system (the borstal system, also a British model); and the security system

[3]See Mathiesen, Thomas (1972):, *Det ofullgågna* – Bidrag till politisk aktionsteori (The Unfinished—Contributions to Political Action Theory). Stockholm: Wahlström & Widstrand. Note that Finland also had her NGOs, in fact two of them. One was quite revolutionary, the other one less so. They both ended their lives early.

[4]For details, see Mathiesen, Thomas (2017): *Cadenza—A Professional Autobiography*. European Group Press, English ed. The book will probably also be published in Norwegian.

(designed for preventing future crimes). They all had "treatment" as major ideological slogan, and the inmates received much longer sentences than similar crimes under normal circumstances would allow for. After years of struggle the Norwegian NGO was in fact successful (in cooperation with others[5]) in abolishing the first three of these four systems, but "security"—which meant incarceration for more or less minor crimes—was reduced in use but maintained and in fact changed into a much harder preventive detention system.[6] Through the years KROM has published a number of books and countless newspaper articles, for a long while it published a journal written by inmates and academics, they have held almost 50 large yearly criminal policy conferences with 120–150 participants and continue to do so (the last one was held in 2018), during the first years they held 5 large so-called "teach ins" with hundreds of people attending on a number of topics, and so on. They live off membership fees and some gifts, no government money.

Political Changes 2010–Present

The government of Norway has for years been set up by the Social Democratic Party (SDP), and sometimes by the Conservative Party and sometimes by a mixture of coalitions between parties. In 2011, a Norwegian terrorist exploded a bomb in the government building, killing 8 people, and then he shot 69 persons at a SDP Youth Group meeting before being arrested. The event of course created a major public outcry. Ensuing trials found him not insane but mentally disturbed

[5]On *the forced labor system*, see for example Christie, Nils (1960): *Tvangsarbeid og alkoholbruk* (Forced Labor and the Use of Alcohol). Universitetsforlaget. On *the Youth Prison System*, see for example two books by Bødal, Kåre (1962, 1969): *Arbeidsskolen og dens resultater* (The Borstal and Its Results), and *Fra Borstal til ungdomsfengsel – klientel og resultater* (From Borstal to Youth Prison—Clientele and Results), both with Universitetsforlaget. Kåre Bødal was director of the Youth Prison, and found recidivism there to be dangerously high. He passed his Ph.D. on the two books. On *the security system*, see Mathiesen's doctoral dissertation in Mathiesen, Thomas: *The Defences of the Weak. A Sociological Study of a Norwegian Correctional Institution*. Tavistock Publications (reprinted by Routledge in 2012).

[6]See Mathiesen 2017 op.cit. Chapter 9.

according to psychiatric criteria, and the court convicted him to life detention (21 years, in practice Norway's equivalent to a life sentence).

The ensuing national political debates were followed by several years of election turmoil, with the SDP being replaced by various coalitions of more conservative parties. The conflicts concentrated on a variety of political matters, including the serious migration issues emanating from the major war in Syria and other places in the Middle East. It has also resulted in deep-seated conflicts between the right-wing Progressive Party in Government and the NGO KROM.

The conflicts have gone through several phases, corresponding to reforms attempted by three successive ministers of justice to change various aspects of prison policies.

Phase 1: Overcrowding Due to lack of prison space, Norway has for years had a queue of prisoners waiting to serve sentence. After his appointment, the Minister of Justice from the Progressive Party proposed to export prisoners waiting for cells by renting cells in other countries. Sweden said "no" but the Netherlands said yes, and after signing a contract 242 Norwegian prisoners were in fact sent to the Dutch prison of Norgerhaven.

Criticism of the plan was immediate. How could rehabilitation be successful in a country far away from home with a foreign language? The government defended the contract by pointing to the fact that some prisoners were themselves foreigners in Norway, they were asylum seekers who would be sent home after their sentences had been served. However protests continued, and the policy continued to generate debate and criticism.

In 2018 the question of renewal of the contract came up, but by then the number of prison cells in the country had gone down abruptly and significantly. The Director of Prisons did not renew the contract with the Netherlands,[7] so the battle over exporting prisoners was ended.

[7]On March 1, 2018, the Director of Prisons said that the Crime Directorate would not recommend a renewal of the contract with the Netherlands. From the Internet.

It was still a fact that Norwegian prisons were old, cramped and in bad shape, internally and in terms of architecture. Of the three penal establishments included in Wheeler's study, Botsfengslet is today empty and not in use, and in fact protected by law; Berg is no longer a borstal or youth prison but a regular prison for ordinary criminals; Ila is no longer a security institution for minor offenders but a long term preventive detention institution for serious criminals.[8]

The Minister of Justice's second idea was to build new prisons, and to build them very cheaply. He proposed to build "container prisons," "modular prisons" which may be built almost anywhere, according to standard models, and even be placed inside old cells which are already there so that new buildings do not have to be constructed. Containers may be designed for military camps, schools, kinder gardens, places where workers can live for long periods while performing construction work, and so on.

The idea received positive reviews from the Criminal Justice System, and construction was planned at the old prison of Ullersmo (opened in 1970) and several other places, altogether with several hundreds of cells. However, KROM opposed the proposal generally, but since there is no longer a queue of prisoners waiting for a cell, the issue is not a pressing one today.

Phase 2: Inmate Leaves, Closing Prisons, and Special Arragements. For over 20 years, KROM has had a small extra number of very short-term leaves (a few hours) for inmates to attend KROM board meetings. Similar arrangements allowed for participation as speakers and moderators at KROM's conferences. Recently, the Directorate of Corrections deleted the section on special leaves which created a great deal of concern in KROM. After several letters and a threat to bring the case before the Parliamentary Ombudsman, the Directorate gave in and KROM was granted further short-term leaves for inmates.

There is now a movement to close "open" prisons, presumably because of cost. Osterøy prison, which is a section of Bergen prison,

[8]The change of clientele in effect signals a change away from prevention and rehabilitation.

is an open prison with a rather liberal culture. It is located on an island near the city of Bergen, and presumably it has to be shut down. The reason is presumably that the prison system is unable to buy the island when the contract is terminated. Journalists and staff are protesting vehemently, and KROM has reviewed the case at a recent board meeting.[9] At the moment, the shutting down of Osterøy is a bit uncertain.

Hassel prison in Buskerud is a unit with low security, primarily a "release prison," which also receives ordinary prisoners upon application from male prisoners in maximum security prisons. The rumor (NB!) among convicts on KROM's board is that Hassel also stands in danger of being shut down. There is a constant discussion among inmates on the board on the tendency toward the dwindling of constructive contents of Norwegian prisons.

Finally, Per-Willy Amundsen, the second Minister of Justice after Anundsen proposed to place fetters (fotlenker) on men in "very clear" cases of violence in close relationships. Fetters were recommended by Minister of Justice Per-Willy Amundsen in cases when the possible offender is reported to the police and not yet followed by a final court sentence.[10] This directly challenges the presumption of not guilty until tried, which is a basic premise in Norwegian criminal justice. Per-Willy Amundsen has also voiced the opinion that convicted pedophiles should be physically castrated.[11]

---

[9]On the Internet, Wikipedia: "Unique island for a prison will be shut down. A great loss. The special prison on the idyllic Ulvenæs island has animal farming and open custody, Staff is angry at its disappearance." Also on the Internet, Wikipedia: "All the small prisons are to be shut down. They are inefficient". This came up as a slogan as early as during the social democratic period in 2011.

[10]Noted after listening to a Norwegian televised radio talk (Dagsnytt 18). Also in a news report from the newspaper Verdens Gang (The World News), On the Internet, Wikipedia undated.

[11]«Justisminister Per-Willy Amundsen vil tvangskastrere pedofile» ("Minister of Justice Per-Willy Amundsen wants to castrate pedophiles by force". From Verdens Gang (The World News), Wikipedia 2–4 March 2017.

Developments in Sweden

A few words about Sweden are also in order. Henrik Tham has very recently written an excellent book on recent developments in Sweden.[12] He. presents a content analysis of legal proposals of penal law handled by the legal committee of the Swedish Parliament. The point is whether the proposals constitute a widening or a restriction of the law. The data are set up according to whether they are presented by a social democratic or a right-wing government—between 1965 and 2017. This means that a differentiation between 8 political periods are presented.

During the first period, which was social democratic and contained 17 proposals between 1968 and 1975, about half were widening and the other half contained restrictions on their use. Tham inspects all of the remaining periods, ending with the 7th and the 8th period (2006–2014 and 2014–2017 respectively), and finds that 30 proposals are widening during the two periods, and 2 proposals containing restrictions on their use. There are of course differences between laws, from drunk driving to murder and so on. But the overall relationships are extremely clear. Sweden is moving in a widening right-wing direction.[13]

The Swedish welfare state is a famous aspect of Sweden. In 2015, in an attempt to extend this principal, its borders were opened to 163,000 asylum seekers who had escaped the war in Syria. Six months later it was over; on 4 January 2016 Sweden again closed its borders, together with Denmark. There has been much debate about the reasons for this turnaround, but it does suggest that the welfare state concept has its limits.

New and Different Values

The advent of rather different political times in the Scandinavian countries today, with new and rather different values and views than 55 or

[12]Tham, Henrik (2018): *Kriminalpolitik - Criminal Policy – Crime and Punishment in Sweden Since 1965*. Norstedts juridik.

[13]See Tham, p. 35.

60 years ago, are quite similar to the situation we tend to find in various other parts of Europe. Norway, Sweden and Denmark pride themselves of being very distant from many other (Eastern) European countries, and more in line with the old Norwegian notion of "giving a second chance" to people who have failed—such as offenders. Presumably we uphold principles of legal values and human rights, and probably we do in fact uphold these legal values—but only to an extent. The difference is not as great as we like to think between the Scandinavian countries and other countries in Europe.

In Norway, Sweden and Denmark there are also streams of populism, which is a difficult term but which at least involves tougher measures toward people engaged in crime and other groups like migrants and asylum seekers. Migrants and asylum seekers have recently (2015) arrived in great numbers to our cities and towns, and created a new situation. We were friendly countries, and we are friendly but the friendliness stops at a certain point and alters into distance and a chillier attitude. The ultra-right Progress Party of Norway, which presently is part of a government coalition running the country, finds these values more to their liking, and finds the closure of borders as a fully sensible political line today. Such values and views may trickle down also to the inmates and staff in our various prisons.

Finland deviates a little from this picture. The country's closeness to Russia makes this understandable. But the country's deviance may also be temporary and not fostered by deeper differences.

A relatively new Norway, and a new Sweden and a new Denmark, which seem at least in part to be coming up, becomes a part of the lore of the prisoners, and possibly makes the prisoners less amenable to whatever attempts at rehabilitation and thinking away from crime and prisonization (to use Donald Clemmer's old term),[14] which the staff tries to inculcate in them.

In terms of prisons (and in terms of other institutions as well) the countries in question are at least different societies today compared to the ones prisoners knew when the prisoners of the past answered

[14]Clemmer, Donald (1940): *The Prison Community*. Holt, Reinhardt and Winston.

Stanton Wheeler's very carefully designed questionnaire. The prisoners of today should be aware of this. Other readers of this book, which is a very important study of our own criminal justice system of the past, are also well advised to keep this in mind.

The Fourth Minister

Tor Mikkel Wara was installed as Minister of Justice on April 4, 2018. The right-wing party in Government, the Progress Party, has kept an emphasis on upholding welfare state ideas and policies on Norwegian citizens, and rather concentrated its populist efforts on a range of deportation policies and penal projects toward foreigners. Rules governing immigrants wanting to come to Norway are very strict, and concentration on a series of penal populist policies, including a warehouse prison regime and a targeting of petty offenders for the double punishment and imprisonment and deportation, is strong. This is done in a context where the penal welfare consensus with respect to Norwegian citizens remains relatively stable. It "is easier for the Progress Party to 'do populism' by focusing on non-citizens."[15]

It may also be said of the populism of Norway that it is developing a "Janus Face"—a relatively mild and relatively humane aspect when it comes to "ordinary," more or less petty Norwegian offenders, versus a harsh, punitive and "prisonlike" policy when it comes to unfortunate foreigners who try to enter the Norwegian welfare state. The vision of a Janus-faced criminal policy is taken from an article by Vanessa Barker.[16] There may of course be exceptions to this, but it is a notion which may be advanced in further research as time goes on.

---

[15]The quoted statement is from the abstract of the article. See Todd-Kvam, John (2018): "Bordered Penal Populism: When Populism and Scandinavian Exceptionalism Meet," *Punishment and Society*), pp. 1–20, 1.

[16]Barber, Vanessa (2013): "Nordic Exceptionalism Revisited: Explaining the Paradox of a Janus-Faced Penal Regime": *Theoretical Criminology*, Sage.

A Brief Summary: Will Scandinavian Exceptionalism Survive?

Where do we stand now, in the middle of 2018, regarding criminal justice and policy in Scandinavia? I leave Finland out, because the language, and partly the culture, is quite different from the fairly unified Scandinavian setting. A vast amount of time and cultural, political and technological change has taken place during the almost 60 years which have passed since Stanton Wheeler did his study. Where are we heading?

I will briefly make a few guesses at the end of this Afterword. My guesses are guided by an understanding of a general development in Scandinavia, from a relatively quiet period after World War II where we were rebuilding and restructuring our lives, until Scandinavia was more or less integrated in the economies and influences of the world, participating in a wide range of political developments. It includes a right-wing populist way of thinking, at least in Europe.

First of all, do penal sentences become longer and punishments stiffer under a populist rule which we now experience in the three Scandinavian countries? My prediction moves into a period of say 10 years from now, until about 2030, and assumes that the culture of training guards and other staff remains largely unchanged. The prediction is that sentences will become somewhat longer and stiffer if the present political regime continues. The curves will bend upwards.

The Scandinavian training schools for staff members uphold a humane touch, they are among the best at least in Europe, the very important slogan still exists that the planning of release begins on the day you enter the prison, ideas concerning the rights of prisoners are in the forefront, protective institutions for this do exist (the Civil Ombudsman is one of them), KROM as an important NGO does exist, and so on. The counter-forces are certainly also there, younger generations of staff who support firmer and less forgiving methods of treating prisoners.

If the first prediction contains a truth—more prison sentences and stiffer sentences—we will have more prisoners behind the walls. According to Tham, the number of penal sanctions in Sweden has clearly dwindled and moved in the direction of limiting people's actions rather than expanding them. The Scandinavians, at least in Norway, are building prisons.

We have presented evidence in this Afterword the prisons are built without the space and intricacies which probably are necessary for giving worn-out prisoners a quest for a new and better life. We know now that "container prisons" are built, standardized buildings for standardized prisoners, not for humans in growth. We also know that new technology is entering our prisons. Fetters are increasingly used, sometimes wanted by prisoners for visits to family and so on, but not necessarily humane. Surveillance techniques are developing by leaps and bounds; in due time—say 10 years from now on—surveillance techniques may empty some of our prisons.

The building of highly standardized prisons (see above), the advent of complex surveillance techniques of various sorts (again see above) and other contrivances will pave the way for a "modern life." Prisons would not be so bad if we had many more of these "small places."

Scandinavia is said to contain an important exception to much of the rest of the Western anglophile world. The exception is its humane traditions in criminal justice—short sentences, not so stiff punishments, few people in prisons, quite a few open or half-open prisons. Is this still true?[17] We have more prisoners and stiffer sentences now than in the early 1960s, but the difference is not drastically large. This may be said to be in favor of a continued Scandinavian exceptionalism. But when we come to the question of more people in prison and small half-open prisons, things become more doubtful. Open prisons are struggling for existence, and do not seem to be in with the times. They seem to be lower on the political agenda. Perhaps we end up with a relatively large criminal population group which in this sense is more or less invisible, and a smaller criminal population group which is more or less dangerous and which is kept behind something called walls?

---

[17]See John Pratt: "Scandinavian Exceptionialism in an Era of Penal Excess", *British Journal of Criminology*, Part I and II, op. cit.

A Classic

As we have seen in this Afterword, Scandinavian politics in a wide sense changed substantially while Stanton Wheeler's great study of prisoners' views from the 1960s laid waiting for publication. Politics changed more or less from a social democratic period in Wheeler's time, where things were fairly stable and peaceful (though there were exceptions), to a time where things were relatively unstable, with political struggles of various sorts and hatred, threats of the involved, terroristic attacks and much else. The number of people is of course limited, but they have reached public recognition and notice. The struggles most often turn out to be between a losing Social Democratic platform on the one hand and growing of alternative political wings on the other.

In the long run, bringing our vision from say 2020 and up 10 years or more, to 2030 or more, the world in fact is also changing or has also been changed quite a bit, to put it mildly. It may therefore also have influenced the criminal policies in a narrow sense of the countries concerned. The data from the 1960s may therefore, in a long run, be somewhat out of date. Prisons and policies of crime are after all not outside the political order. But we may envisage a future where the values of humanity and well-being also for prisoners requires much more hard work to uphold as values. The image of "Scandinavian exceptionalism" is at present a kind of rumor which is upheld by Scandinavian criminalists and some others. It may become even less of a truth when time in the new political era becomes a closer part of our everyday life. The struggle for Scandinavian exceptionalism must learn to be much harder and stronger than today.

The Wheeler and Cline study, though it may not tell us entirely what goes on now in Scandinavian prisons today and how prisoners react today, is a complex historical work in a genuine sense of the word. As an historical work, Stanton Wheeler's work was the first study—not of a single group or prisoners, not of a few single groups of prisoners, not of one or maybe a few institutions, not of prisons in a couple of countries—all of which there are many in present-day criminology, but it was the first detailed study of prisoners in altogether 15 main and very different prisons, in four significant countries, in a whole region of the European continent involving close to two thousand prisoners. Wheeler's study has a breathtaking magnitude which hardly is matched by any other study in our field, barring that there may be some which I am not aware of.

In this Afterword I have looked at some of the political trends from Wheeler's time in the past to our situation today. But this is not the main point if our wish is to evaluate his study. The study is above all the first study of such a uniquely encompassing character, designed and carried out with such ingenuity and forcefulness, that it deserves the status of a true classic.

Stanton Wheeler used all of the techniques available to him at the time in his attempt to unravel the many details and probe the many questions raised by his unusually extensive material. As a classic you have to read it, and become immersed in it, if you are at all interested in prisons and prisoners.

Appendix I: Prison-Level Data Collection Methods

In each of the 15 institutions either the warden or another official designated by the warden participated in a structured interview designed to collect information about each institution, its history, operating procedures, daily schedules, personnel, and the like. Listed below are the instructions given to the interviewee together with the structured interview schedule.

General Questions of Chief Informant

1. What are the chief purposes or goals of the institution? Probe for balance between punishment, custodial, and treatment programs, and whether treatment is seen largely through programs of education and training, such as work and education programs, or through more psychologically oriented programs designed to change the personality or values of the inmates. This is clearly a broad and general question.
2. Problems in accomplishing major purposes or goals? What does the director see as the major problems standing in the way of his

S. Wheeler and H. F. Cline, *The Scandinavian Prison Study*,
Palgrave Studies in Prisons and Penology,
https://doi.org/10.1007/978-3-030-26462-8

accomplishing his goals for the institution? A special question you might ask is the following: if the director were free to make any one major change in the institution and its operations, what would he most want to change?

3. Probe for particular problems regarding the following possible sources of inability to achieve goals:

    a. The characteristics of the inmates—they are seen as not able to change, as too severe or difficult, and the program does about as much as can be expected for the type of. inmate the institution receives.
    b. Characteristics of staff: problems of low pay. lack of training, etc., if these are mentioned as possible sources of failure to achieve goals.
    c. Problems of facilities: lack of funds to implement programs. old buildings, lack of money for staff, etc.
    d. Relations between the institution and the surrounding environment.. Any special problems in the perceptions or feelings about the institution from persons in nearby local communities? In the newspapers? Government bodies?

4. Ask about any major "incidents" in the life of the institution over the past one, and then past three, years. Major disturbances, problems, or accomplishments, major changes in program if any, additions of new programs, etc.
5. Background of institution director: level and type of education, length of experience in corrections, background prior to becoming director.

Institutional Characteristics

I. General characteristics:

1. Size (number of inmates in the institution at time of study):
2. Maximum size: number of inmates the institution can hold at full capacity. (1 may be greater than 2 in cases of overcrowding.)

3. Year institution was first opened (as rough index of the age of the physical plant):
4. Cost (figures on the daily per capita cost of the institution, if any available, or if not on the total budget for the institution per year):
5. Size (amount of space covered by the institution—square yards, meters, or standard unit of measurement used):
6. Meal arrangements: Do inmates eat in own cell or room, or in a larger dining area?
7. Housing arrangements: Do inmates have single rooms, or are there two (or more) individuals in each room. If both types, how many inmates in single rooms, how many in rooms with others?

II. Staff characteristics:

1. Total number of employees at time of study
2. Number of custody employees—guards
3. Number of specifically treatment staff employees, and the positions they hold: social workers, psychiatrist, if any, education or teachers, medical personnel, priests
4. Other personnel, by type of position: secretaries, clerks, work supervisors, etc.
   (The figures listed under 1 should equal the total of 2, 3, 4. But it is important here to get, where possible, actual descriptions of what the people do, for the various institutions sometimes use different words for persons who perform the name function.)
5. Persons "available" but not "in" the institution: visiting teachers, therapists, doctors, etc. (There may be no persons in this category, but we should ask to be sure)
6. Staff background characteristics: We would like to have information on the. characteristics of staff members average age, length of employment in the institution, educational background, etc. This information is probably lacking in precise form, but we should ask to find out if it is available. If no specific figures available, should ask informant to estimate the average age of the custodial staff, the proportion who'have held their jobs for more than three years, and the proportion who have education beyond a certain minimum level of schooling in your system.

III. Program characteristics:

This is to provide indicators of the kinds of programs and events within the institution as they may relate to institutional functioning. In each case ask if there is a program, and then how many inmates are directly involved in it.

1. An organized athletic program?
2. An organized school program?
3. Band, choir, or other musical events?
4. An institution newspaper?
5. A hobby shop or craft program?
6. An organized religious program?
7. Other special programs—Alcoholics Anonymous, etc.

IV. Rules and privileges for inmates:

1. Number of visits allowed per week (or per month if this is the form of the rule):
2. Length of visits allowed:
3. Number of letters the innate is allowed to write (letters or brev-corts):
4. Number of letters allowed to receive
5. Amount of money the inmate may spend for purchase of goods within the prison
6. Type of goods that can be purchased (cigarettes, candy, etc.)
7. Amount of payment for work assignments. Indicate min. & max. amounts, by day or week whichever is used as the basis for payment
8. Are furloughs or weekend leaves allowed? Aproximately how may inmates receive such privileges if allowed? What percentage of inmates are allowed furloughts?

V. Typical daily schedule for inmates

This information used to characterize the daily routine of the inmates, and to get an estimate of the amount of time for free interaction with other inmates. Should get this separately for a weekday, Saturday, and Sunday. And done by hours or blocks of times: for example, awakened at 6:30 a.m. in room for cleaning and breakfast until 8 a.m., work from 8 to 11:30, etc. Pay particular attention to hours between end of work and lock-in at night. Are the times in between open for interaction and contact between inmates, or are the inmates in their own rooms?

VI. Inmate Behavior

This is to give a crude index of possible differences between institutions in the extent to which inmates have behaved in certain ways, Each one should be asked separately for (a) the past one-year period, and (b) the past three-year period. Must ask them to remember as accurately as they can, though recognizing that they may only be able to give an approximate figure.

1. Number of "successful" escapes. Success here means that the inmate did get outside the institution, even though he may have been caught and hour or two later.
2. Number of attempted but unsuccessful escapes. Inmates who tried to escape but did not get outside the institution. (Both here and in number 1 it is the number of inmates who have done this, counting one escape attempt by a group of three inmates as three escape attempts. etc).
3. Number of fist-fights, physical attacks, or assaults of one inmate against another. Count as physical attack any serious fist-fight or any attack involving use of a weapon knife, piece of metal, wooden stick, etc.
4. Number of physical attacks by inmate(s) against one or more staff members.
5. Number of times inmate destroyed or seriously damaged the fixtures, chairs, etc., in his own room.
6. Number of attempted or completed suicides, if any.

VII. Staff sanctions for inmate misconduct

List the disciplinary actions that may be taken by the staff against inmates who violate institution rules. From least serious disciplinary action to most serious. Indicate how frequently used (estimate) for each type of disciplinary action. The major types will probably be withdrawal of privileges (visiting, furloughs, etc.) perhaps use of the radio, restriction on work-pay, up to segregation or solitary confinement. Try to find out how many inmates have been given these various disciplinary actions during the last month prior to study, and, if figures are available, the previous year.

Appendix II: Inmate Data Collection Methods

This appendix presents and briefly discusses the major data collection procedures for inmates. Detailed instructions were prepared for administering the questionnaire. These instructions are below. Following these instructions, and a brief description of coding conventions, the inmate questionnaire is provided along with marginal totals for the responses to each question.

The following notes provide a rather detailed statement of the procedures to be used in the gathering of data for the comparative study of prisons in Scandinavian countries. They should be followed as closely as possible, although there will of course be some slight differences that are necessary because of the differences in institutions, in the procedures which governors will approve, etc.

Once approval has been given to study a particular institution, the following procedures should be used:

1. The researchers work out a feasible way of dividing the institution into units for the purpose of administering the questionnaire. If possible, the groups should be about 20 in size, although they may

S. Wheeler and H. F. Cline, *The Scandinavian Prison Study*, Palgrave Studies in Prisons and Penology, https://doi.org/10.1007/978-3-030-26462-8

be smaller or larger if necessary. Also, probably the most convenient way of dividing them is in terms of housing unit, or cell unit. Most of the institutions will have separate cell blocks, dormitories, etc., each of which houses a certain number of men. If they are large units, they can be divided by tier, or section, so that about 15 to 25 are present for each group.

2. Time of scheduling. We allow at least one and a half hours per unit, collect then, and discuss tee research. Typically the introduction. will take from 3 to 5 minutes, reading it from 30 to 35 minutes, collection 2 or 3 minutes, and then from 15 to 4-0 or so minutes for discussion. But the groups should be scheduled if possible.at about one and a half hour intervals, The order of the groups can be arranged according to administrative need, if necessary. If there is no particular administrative reason for choosing one before another, then begin with the minimum custody. units, working up to the close or maximum custody units. The choice of day can again be left to the warden, if he has strong feelings about it.
3. Place of Administration. The choice of a room in which to administer the questionnaire is dictated largely by the facilities at the institution. Where possible, if there is an education room with desks, etc., it can be used. If not, one may use either a cafeteria or an auditorium. The central room requirement is that it be large enough to hold the largest group of inmates that will be coming at one time, and that there is enough light and enough tables, chairs, or benches to accommodate the group. We try to have them sitting about one and a half meters apart, and in any case no closer than one meter, so they are not forced or tempted to see what the next inmate is writing. Within these limits, they should be seated close enough to the administrator of the questionnaire so that all can hear the questions as they are read.
4. Announcement about the research. Provide a brief mimeographed statement about the research which the inmates each receive prior to the visit. This simply lets them knew that we are coming, and explains very briefly why we are coming. Typically, this letter announces the day on which we will be coming (or the week in which we'll cane), tells them that the purpose of the project is to get a better understanding of the reactions of inmates to their prison

experience, and especially points out that this project includes institutions in other Scandinavian countries and also in the US. It also indicates that we do not want or need to know the individual name or number of the inmate, and do not ask for this information. Also, that no institution official will see their responses. We also point out that participating inmates will receive one pack of twenty cigarettes as part payment for the inconvenience we cause. Finally, the statement indicates that they nay raise further questions, if they have them, with the researchers when they cone to the institution. The researcher should see to it that these mimeographed statements are in the hands of prison officials so that they may be distributed to the inmates at least a day in advance of the arrival of the research team. If the time for scheduling each unit has bean clearly established ahead of time, the time and place of meeting for each group may appear on this advanced statement. If not, the warden may be asked to issue such a statement and have it posted wherever necessary.

5. <u>Getting the men to the research room</u>. The most crucial task for the researchers is to get a large proportion of the men to show up for the res arch. It is clear that participation is voluntary, but most the wardens will be willing to get the men to the testing room, and once there, they almost always stay. to participate. The researcher should simply see to it that all is done to assure the inmates, guards, etc., that participation is important, but that the study is done for scientific purposes and can in no way be used for or against a particular inmate. You will probably get full cooperation from both inmates and staff, as we have gotten so far.
6. <u>Administration</u>. When the group is assembled, the chief administrator begins by introducing the research team and then giving introductory comments about the research (described further below). The assistant waits until the introduction is over, and then the two of them pass out questionnaires and pencils (with erasers). The chief administrator explains that he or she will read the questions out loud, so that there will be no misunderstanding, and that he will pause briefly for them to give their response, then move on to the next question. He should begin by reading the title page, then turn

quickly to the first question. The researcher should read the content categories for the answers as well as reading the question, should also announce when turning to the next page. After the first five questions or so, he may pause briefly to ask if he is going too fast or too slow, and then adjust speed accordingly. Also just prior to the beginning of the questions, you should tell the group that you will appreciate it if they will hold their comments to the end of the questionnaire, except when they have a particular question that they don't understand. You want to cut down interruptions since they interfere with the administration for others. You read all questions up to the last page, which contains the self concept statements. At that point you read the introductory statement, but then say that they can read tee items themselves. Then wait until nearly all persons have put down their pencils, and you may then indicate that you will collect the pencils and questionnaires, pass out the cigarettes, and then can have a discussion about the questionnaire, the prison, etc. The two researchers collect the questionnaires, but in no particular order, You may ask the men to pass the questionnaires to one aisle, or it may be easier to simply go by the desks to pick them up. But the order is unimportant. Discussion will be described further below.

7. <u>The Introductory statement</u>. The general points in the introduction are as follows:

    a. Background. The general purpose of the research program being conducted in the institutions is to provide greater understanding of inmates reactions to imprisonment. We are interested in the response of different types of inmates, in different types of institutions, in different countries. With this interest in mind Scandinavian and American researchers have been working together in the US, and in Norway, Denmark, Sweden, and Finland.
    b. We would prefer to talk individually with both inmates and staff, but this unfortunately takes more time and money than are available. So we are doing the next best thing, which is to ask a standard set of questions of inmates in each of the institutions.

c. The prison officials have given us permission to ask these questions, but they will not see any of the individual questionnaires. After they are filled out they will go directly to the university, where they will then be prepared for a statistical analysis. We are not interested in the response of any particular inmate, so you are asked not to put your name or number on the questionnaire. After you have completed the questionnaire, you will each receive a pack of cigarettes as part payment for the inconvenience we cause and for your help.
d. The questions cover several different aspects of institutions. We ask about how much contact you have with the officials, with other inmates, and so on, how you feel about various conditions in the institution, and a bit about your own background.
e. After this brief and informal introduction (and you may of course choose your own words, but try to stay fairly close to the topics above), the researcher asks if there are any questions before we begin. As he says that, the assistant begins to pass out pencils, followed by questionnaires, and the researcher announces that he would prefer that they go through the questionnaire along with the researcher, rather than moving ahead on their own. Usually, there are no questions, but some items that sometimes arise are discussed under the "discussion" section below.

8. Conduct of the administration . There will usually be no problems at all, at least judging from past experience. In some of the youth institutions, the boys may talk with each other a bit. When they do you can ignore minor passing remarks, but ask them to keep comments to themselves until after the questionnaire, if necessary. One or two inmates may be abnormally slow in filling out the questionnaire. It would be well to get one or two of the slowest ones on the top or bottom when you collect the cases, so that we may consider separating out their questionnaires if they seem not to have understood. If someone does not want to participate, you may try to encourage them, but if that fails you can quietly lot then leave and proceed without them.

9. Discussion. You first ask if they have any questions, and you can answer them as best you can. If they don't volunteer any, you can say that you are concerned whether the questions, some of which were developed from experience in other countries, seem meaningful to then, and get them to talk about it. Typically they will volunteer some aspect of their own institution which they don't like, and you should bring out their comments and let them talk so that we learn a bit more about their reactions. Remember only that the researcher is identified neither with the inmates, nor with the prison administration, but stands apart from both groups. If they ask about the experience in other countries, you can tell them that we are just now analyzing the results, but that the inmates seemed to enjoy and take an interest in the research. We hope eventually to write a report summarizing the findings, but it will be some time before such a report is ready. The discussion may go on for as long as you have time, but when you see that they have no more questions or are getting restless, you may thank them for their cooperation and let them leave the room. If they indicate during the administration that they don't understand a question, you can first slowly read it to them again, and usually that will do. If not you can ask them to fill it out as best they can, or clarify it when it is obvious where they are misinterpreting it. One example here concerns the first three questions, where they may ask what you mean by a "little longer talk…" etc. You indicate that you mean something more than a passing hello or greeting, although the conversation may be about institution business, and need not be purely informal. Alto, and this is important, you should mention before passing out the questionnaires that some of the items were developed for use in other correctional systems and may not be so meaningful in their own.
10. The sample: We want an accurate statement of the population in the institution and of the persons we actually get. The following categories are relevant:

   a. The total population. This is the total number of inmates officially assigned to the institution, including those momentarily on leave, at court, or elsewhere. The total number on the day the research begins.

b. The "target" population. This is the total number of inmates we actually try to reach, and differs from the total population as follows:
    1. We exclude inmates on leave, or those on work assignments that make it impossible for them to appear for the research.
    2. We exclude all inmates in the prison infirmary or hospital.
    3. We exclude inmates, if any, who are in isolation cells for punishment, unless the staff will permit them to be included.
    4. We exclude any persons deemed by staff to be so mentally abnormal or incompetent that they cannot fill out the questionnaire, including those in some institutions who nay be senile.
    5. The resulting number constitutes the target population, and each researcher should record the target population figure for each institution.

c. The sample includes all those inmates who show up for the research. If you become aware of inmates whom we fail to get because of some feature similar to those listed above, they should be removed from the figures for target population. Examples: inmates with very poor eyesight, inmates who cannot come to the testing room because of a physical injury but who are not in the hospital, etc.

   Typically, the difference between sample and target population is composed of those who don't hear about the testing for some reason, who simply aren't interested, or who directly refuse.

   The assistant researcher should count the number of inmates in the research room, and also count the total number of questionnaires received, separately for each testing group. He should have a figure for the target population and the final sample for each testing group as well. If the number seems unusually low when you are preparing to begin, you may ask one of the guards if you have the correct figures, and if more men are or are not coming. But your final figures for each institution will include: (these figures for example only)

Testing group	Target population	Sample
1	20	18
2	24	21
3	17	13
Etc.		
Total	61	52

11. Each questionnaire should be given an identification code number. The code we are using is as follows, and will appear in the upper left-hand corner of the front page of the questionnaire:

    a. The first two digits refer to the institution studied, numbered in the order in which the data are collected.
    b. The second two digits refer to the testing group within the institution, again in order tested. These will go from 01 up to the highest number of groups tested within that institution.
    c. The last two digits refer to the number of a particular questionnaire, again from 01 to the highest number for that particular testing group.

Once all questionnaires were assembled, the responses were coded on data sheets. Any questionnaire that had more than 15% no responses or widely varying response patterns (such as representing a very young age and a very large number of previous convictions), or written comments which indicated that the respondent was not taking the questionnaire seriously were all eliminated from the analyses. This resulted in 103 inmates were excluded from the study (about 5%). In coding non-responses to individual items, a uniform code of BLANK was used. Throughout all analyses, cross-tabulations, correlations, and regressions, missing observations were unifrmly excluded.

Reproduced below is the inmate questionnaire (starting with the cover sheet) and marginal totals for each question. this is the English version of the questionnaire which was originally administered in Norwegian, Swedish, Danish, or Finnish. In both Norway and

Denmark certain unique questions were included at the request of our Scandinavian colleagues. These unique items have not been included in our analyses and are omitted from the English version of the questionnaire.

Cover Sheet

There are many people today who think that they understand prison life. Those who are really able to express an opinion on it, however, are naturally those who are in an institution day after day. Therefore it is important to find out how both inmates and personnel feel about prisons. The following questionnaire has been worked out cooperatively by both American and Scandinavian sociologists. This institution is only one of several where these questions are being asked. The study is being carried out for scientific purposes only. No correction officials (reformatory, department of institutions, or parole board) will see any of these questionnaires after you have filled them out.

We are not interested in the response of any particular individual to these questions. Everything is anonymous. Therefore DO NOT PUT YOU NAME OR NUMBER on the questionnaire. We hope that you will answer the questions as honestly as possible, and we are very grateful for your cooperation.

KNUD WAABEN
University of Copenhagen
Denmark

INKERI ANTTILA
University of Helsinki
Finland

NILS CHRISTIE
University of Oslo
Norway

STANTON WHEELER
Harvard University
U.S.A

BRITT-MARIE PERSSON-DLEGVAD
Uppsala University

Mark an "x" in the square next to the answer which comes closest to describing your own response to the question.

1. How often do you talk informally with the guards here in the institution?

		%	(N)
Several times a day	☐	19	(358)
At least once a day	☐	23	(436)
At least once a week	☐	16	(313)
At least once a month	☐	9	(165)
Less than once a month	☐	12	(228)
Never	☐	22	(423)
(No Response)			(14)

2. How often do you talk informally with persons such as psychiatrists, psychologists or social workers in the institution?

		%	(N)
Several times a day	☐	1	(16)
At least once a day	☐	3	(50)
At least once a week	☐	15	(287)
At least once a month	☐	19	(366)
Less than once a month	☐	35	(667)
Never	☐	27	(510)
(No Response)			(41)

3. How often do you talk informally with other inmates?

		%	(N)
Several times a day	☐	71	(1362)
At least once a day	☐	16	(316)
At least once a week	☐	5	(104)
At least once a month	☐	2	(34)
Less than once a month	☐	2	(38)
Never	☐	4	(67)
(No Response)			(16)

4. Have you made any good friends among the other inmates in the institution?

		%	(N)
Yes, many (more than 5)	☐	22	(422)
Yes, some (3 to 5)	☐	18	(339)
Yes, one or two	☐	37	(708)
No, none	☐	23	(449)
(No Response)			(19)

5. Think back on your past month in this institution. How would you say you spent most of your free time, when you were not locked in your cell?

		%	(N)
Mostly with a group of inmates who are together quite a lot	☐	16	(296)
With one or two inmates	☐	21	(394)
With several different inmates, but not in any group	☐	31	(582)
Mostly by myself	☐	33	(615)
(No Response)			(50)

6. How do you usually find out about rules and regulations in this institution?

		%	(N)
Usually from other inmates	☐	52	(968)
Usually from the staff	☐	48	(882)
(No Response)			(87)

7. Would your life in the institution be easier if there were more rules, or would it be easier if there were fewer rules?

		%	(N)
It would be easier if there were more rules	☐	10	(201)
It would be easier if there were fewer rules	☐	63	(1213)
It is all right as it is now	☐	26	(499)
(No Response)			(24)

8. Institution staff members sometimes try to get inmates to act in certain ways. How often do staff members in this institution try:

To get inmates to work harder than they otherwise would?

		%	(N)
Often	☐	36	(683)
Sometimes	☐	33	(636)
Almost never or never	☐	31	(595)
(No Response)			(23)

9. Similarly, inmates sometimes try to get other inmates to act in certain ways. How often do inmates in this institution try:

To get other inmates to stay away from the staff?

		%	(N)
Often	☐	16	(312)
Sometimes	☐	33	(627)
Almost never or never	☐	51	(976)
(No Response)			(22)

To get other inmates to work less hard than they otherwise would?

		%	(N)
Often	☐	14	(268)
Sometimes	☐	31	(594)
Almost never or never	☐	55	(1037)
(No Response)			(38)

To get other inmates to support those inmates who oppose the staff?

		%	(N)
Often	☐	15	(280)
Sometimes	☐	32	(599)
Almost never or never	☐	54	(1017)
(No Response)			(41)

10. If you yourself could decide, would you prefer to have more opportunity to be alone, or would you prefer to have more opportunity to be together with other inmates?

		%	N
More opportunity to be alone	☐	18	(356)
More opportunity to be together with others	☐	47	(900)
It is all right as it is now	☐	35	(672)
(No Response)			(9)

11. If you had a personal problem you wanted to talk over with someone, would you prefer to talk it over with one of the inmates or with one of the staff?

		%	N
With one of the inmates	☐	46	(823)
With one of the staff	☐	54	(957)
(No Response)			(157)

12. During the past month, have you received any letters or postcards from relatives or friends outside the institution?

		%	N
No, None	☐	28	(505)
Yes, 1	☐	10	(185)
Yes, 2	☐	13	(239)
Yes, 3	☐	9	(156)
Yes, 4	☐	13	(236)
Yes, 5-7	☐	13	(238)
Yes, 8-10	☐	8	(154)
Yes, 11-15	☐	4	(64)
Yes, 16 or more	☐	2	(46)
(No Response)			(114)

13. During the past month, have you written any letters or postcards to relatives or friends outside the institution?

		%	N
No, None	☐	24	(441)
Yes, 1	☐	10	(189)
Yes, 2	☐	16	(285)
Yes, 3	☐	10	(178)
Yes, 4	☐	16	(291)
Yes, 5-7	☐	13	(243)
Yes, 8-10	☐	7	(122)
Yes, 11-15	☐	2	(46)
Yes, 16 or more	☐	2	(37)
(No Response)			(105)

14. During the past month, have you had any visits from relatives or friends outside the institution?

		%	N
No, None	☐	64	(1196)
Yes, 1	☐	18	(332)
Yes, 2	☐	8	(157)
Yes, 3	☐	2	(42)
Yes, 4	☐	5	(89)
Yes, 5-7	☐	2	(36)
Yes, 8-10	☐	1	(14)
Yes, 11-15	☐	*	(5)
Yes, 16 or more	☐	*	(7)
(No Response)			(59)

		%	(N)
15. Which of the following, would you say, is the major purpose of this institution, as it is now being run?			
To punish persons who have violated the law.........	☐	44	(800)
To provide treatment for persons who have violated the law....................................	☐	16	(282)
To protect society from persons who have violated the law..	☐	17	(316)
To serve as a way of warning others of the consequences of violating the law..................	☐	23	(420)
(No Response)			(119)
16. How much influence do the guards have over inmates in the daily life of the institution?			
Very much influence................................	☐	35	(683)
Much influence.....................................	☐	18	(350)
Some influence.....................................	☐	18	(355)
A little influence.................................	☐	11	(217)
Almost no influence................................	☐	17	(322)
(No Response)			(10)
17. How much influence do persons such as the psychiatrists, psychologists and social workers have over inmates in the daily life of the institution?			
Very much influence................................	☐	25	(473)
Much influence.....................................	☐	14	(264)
Some influence.....................................	☐	20	(376)
A little influence.................................	☐	15	(284)
Almost no influence................................	☐	26	(498)
(No Response)			(42)
18. Do the guards usually give a straight answer when questions arise?			
Usually..	☐	26	(509)
Fairly often.......................................	☐	21	(407)
Seldom...	☐	20	(386)
Almost never.......................................	☐	32	(624)
(No Response)			(11)
19. Do persons such as the psychiatrists, psychologists and social workers usually give a straight answer when questions arise?			
Usually..	☐	31	(593)
Fairly often.......................................	☐	20	(372)
Seldom...	☐	16	(313)
Almost never.......................................	☐	33	(623)
(No Response)			(36)

20. Are the guards usually able to understand the inmates' point of view?

		%	(N)
Usually	☐	14	(278)
Fairly often	☐	24	(473)
Seldom	☐	26	(491)
Almost never	☐	36	(685)
(No Response)			(10)

21. Are persons such as the psychiatrists, psychologists and social workers usually able to understand the inmates' point of view?

		%	(N)
Usually	☐	24	(452)
Fairly often	☐	32	(601)
Seldom	☐	22	(412)
Almost never	☐	22	(420)
(No response)			(52)

22. To what extent do the guards "look the other way" when an inmate commits a minor rule infraction?

		%	(N)
Quite often	☐	12	(237)
Sometimes	☐	39	(751)
Very seldom	☐	49	(938)
(No response)			(11)

23. If it were up to you, would you prefer the guards to have more informal contact or less informal contact with the inmates?

		%	(N)
They ought to have more informal contact	☐	46	(879)
They ought to have less informal contact	☐	21	(406)
It is all right as it is now	☐	33	(638)
(No response)			(14)

24. If it were up to you, would you prefer persons such as: the psychiatrist, psychologist or social worker to have more informal contact or less informal contact with the inmates?

		%	(N)
They ought to have more informal contact	☐	66	(1257)
They ought to have less informal contact	☐	11	(202)
It is all right as it is now	☐	24	(455)
(No response)			(23)

25. Who has the most influence on the outcome of a criminal case?

		%	(N)
The police	☐	17	(291)
The court psychiatrist	☐	11	(195)
The judge	☐	21	(356)
The psychologist	☐	3	(50)
The defense attorney	☐	4	(64)
The state prosecutor	☐	34	(579)
The case examiner (probation officer)	☐	7	(128)
The welfare agent	☐	2	(26)
Other	☐	2	(39)
(No response)			(209)

26. Who has the greatest influence in the daily routine of the inmates in the institution?

Psychiatrist	☐	6	(102)
Warden or Assistant Warden	☐	48	(875)
Guard	☐	29	(526)
Teacher	☐	3	(47)
Psychologist	☐	*	(9)
Chaplain	☐	1	(14)
Social Worker	☐	*	(8)
Work Foreman	☐	12	(224)
Other	☐	2	(31)
(No response)			(101)

27. If you, as an inmate, had a personal problem that you wanted to talk over with one of the staff, which one of them would you prefer to go to?

Psychiatrist	☐	7	(121)
Warden or Assistant Warden	☐	37	(646)
Guard	☐	6	(101)
Teacher	☐	9	(163)
Psychologist	☐	5	(78)
Chaplain	☐	13	(233)
Social worker	☐	19	(344)
Other	☐	3	(53)
(No response)			(208)

28. Do you think that your sentence was a just one in relation to what you did?

Yes	☐	21	(402)
Don't know	☐	15	(283)
No	☐	64	(1234)
(No response)			(18)

		%	(N)
29. Compare yourself with others who have been sentenced for the same thing as you. Do you think that your sentence was lighter or heavier?			
Lighter than most of the others....................	☐	9	(173)
About the same as most of the others...............	☐	35	(657)
Heavier than most of the others....................	☐	56	(1066)
(No response)			(41)
30. Do you think that you have been justly treated here in the institution?			
Yes..	☐	42	(810)
Don't know.....................................	☐	21	(402)
No...	☐	37	(702)
(No response)			(23)

Described below are some situations which occasionally come up in institutions. They concern no particular person or institution--they could happen anywhere. In each case, we would like to know how you <u>personally</u> feel about what happens, and in addition, how you believe <u>most of the others</u> in this institution would feel.

31. An inmate, without thinking, commits a minor rule infraction. He is given a "write-up" by a correctional officer who saw the violation. Later two other inmates are talking to each other about it. One of them criticizes the officer. The other inmate, Hansen, defends the officer, saying the officer was only doing his duty.

How do you personally feel about Hansen defending the guard?

		%	(N)
Strongly approve................................	☐	35	(678)
Approve...	☐	30	(571)
Disapprove......................................	☐	12	(230)
Strongly disapprove.............................	☐	23	(439)
(No response)			(19)

How many inmates in this institution do you think would <u>approve</u> of Hansen defending the guard?

		%	(N)
Almost all would approve........................	☐	12	(234)
About three-fourths would approve...............	☐	11	(204)
About half would approve........................	☐	23	(439)
About one-fourth would approve..................	☐	19	(361)
Almost none would approve.......................	☐	35	(665)
(No response)			(34)

32. Inmates Jansen and Lund are very good friends. Jansen has some money that was smuggled into the institution by a visitor. Jansen tells Lund he thinks the officers are suspicious, and asks Lund to hide the money for him for a few days. Lund takes the money and carefully hides it.

How do you personally feel about Lund hiding the money?

		%	(N)
Strongly approve..............................	☐	39	(753)
Approve..	☐	11	(218)
Disapprove.....................................	☐	11	(211)
Strongly disapprove............................	☐	38	(734)
(No response)			(21)

How many inmates in this institution do you think would approve of what Lund did?

		%	(N)
Almost all would approve.......................	☐	47	(891)
About three-fourths would approve..............	☐	12	(236)
About half would approve.......................	☐	16	(300)
About one-fourth would approve.................	☐	9	(163)
Almost none would approve......................	☐	16	(314)
(No response)			(33)

33. Inmate Olsen goes before a committee that makes job assignments. He is given a choice between two jobs. One job would call for hard work, but it would give Olsen training that might be useful to him on the outside. The other job would allow Olsen to do easier time in the institution, but it provides no training for a job on the outside. Olsen decides to take the easier job.

What do you personally think about Olsen taking the easier job?

		%	(N)
Strongly approve..............................	☐	23	(449)
Approve..	☐	8	(147)
Disapprove.....................................	☐	16	(312)
Strongly disapprove............................	☐	53	(1012)
(No response)			(17)

How many inmates in this institution do you think would approve of what Olsen did?

		%	(N)
Almost all would approve.......................	☐	32	(606)
About three-fourths would approve..............	☐	14	(271)
About half would approve.......................	☐	26	(493)
About one-fourth would approve.................	☐	12	(224)
Almost none would approve......................	☐	17	(319)
(No response)			(24)

34. How long have you been here on your present sentence?

		%	(N)
Less than 1 month	☐	7	(136)
1 to 3 months	☐	22	(429)
3 to 6 months	☐	22	(425)
6 to 12 months	☐	22	(426)
12 to 18 months	☐	10	(185)
18 months to 2 years	☐	5	(101)
2 to 3 years	☐	5	(93)
3 to 5 years	☐	3	(57)
Over 5 years	☐	4	(76)
(No response)			(9)

35. When do you expect to be released?

		%	(N)
Within a month	☐	13	(237)
In 1 to 3 months	☐	22	(410)
In 3 to 6 months	☐	22	(422)
In 6 to 12 months	☐	19	(361)
In 12 to 18 months	☐	9	(165)
In 18 months to 2 years	☐	4	(69)
In 2 to 3 years	☐	5	(97)
In 3 to 5 years	☐	2	(42)
In over 5 years	☐	4	(69)
(No response)			(65)

36. For what offense are you now serving time?

		%	(N)
Offense against property	☐	62	(1127)
Offense against person	☐	13	(240)
Sex offense	☐	8	(149)
Crimes involving alcohol	☐	8	(147)
Fraud, bankruptcy, perjury	☐	1	(22)
Other	☐	7	(134)
(No response, combination)			(118)

37. Have any disciplinary actions been taken against you since you have been here?

		%	(N)
More than 5 times	☐	4	(78)
3 or 4 times	☐	4	(69)
1 or 2 times	☐	16	(306)
Never	☐	76	(1463)
(No response)			(21)

38. Were you ever committed to a juvenile institution?

		%	(N)
Yes, two or more times	☐	14	(258)
Yes, once	☐	14	(259)
No, never	☐	73	(1381)
(No response)			(39)

		%	(N)
39. Have you ever served a jail sentence?			
Yes	☐	63	(1185)
No	☐	37	(710)
(No response)			(42)
If yes, how many times have you served a jail sentence?			
10 or more times	☐	9	(105)
5 to 9 times	☐	25	(294)
3 or 4 times	☐	21	(246)
Twice	☐	20	(236)
Once	☐	26	(304)
(No response, inappropriate)			(752)
40. Prior to the offense for which you are now serving your sentence, have you ever been committed to a reformatory, penitentiary, or other adult institution?			
Yes	☐	66	(1266)
No	☐	34	(653)
(No response)			(18)
If yes, how many times?			
Once	☐	58	(735)
Twice	☐	30	(383)
3 times	☐	9	(113)
4 or more times	☐	3	(35)
(No response, inappropriate)			(671)
41. How old were you when you were arrested for the first time?			
Under 14	☐	9	(174)
14 to 17	☐	22	(412)
18 to 20	☐	23	(424)
21 to 24	☐	17	(325)
25 to 29	☐	12	(215)
30 to 39	☐	11	(202)
40 to 49	☐	4	(75)
50 or over	☐	2	(39)
(No response).			(71)
42. How old are you now?			
Under 18	☐	4	(70)
18 to 20	☐	10	(193)
21 to 24	☐	14	(277)
25 to 29	☐	17	(333)
30 to 39	☐	32	(604)
40 to 49	☐	15	(296)
50 to 59	☐	6	(116)
60 to 69	☐	1	(27)
70 or over	☐	*	(1)
(No response)			(20)

		%	(N)
43. Where were you living when you were last sentenced?			
In the capital city	☐	46	(877)
In another city	☐	34	(652)
In a smaller town	☐	6	(119)
In the country	☐	13	(252)
(No response)			(37)
44. What is your marital status?			
Married	☐	23	(445)
Single	☐	51	(973)
Divorced, separated, widower	☐	26	(491)
(No response)			(28)
45. How many years, if any, did you attend school beyond Fokleskole? #			
None	☐	61	(1144)
One year	☐	9	(175)
Two years	☐	10	(193)
Three or more years	☐	20	(373)
(No response)			(52)
46. What effect do you think your stay in the institution will have on your ability to get along successfully when you are outside?			
It will help me a lot	☐	10	(183)
It will help me a little	☐	8	(151)
It will neither help nor harm me	☐	24	(461)
It will harm me a little	☐	23	(446)
It will harm me a lot	☐	35	(674)
(No response)			(22)
47. Have you benefitted from your stay here in any of the following ways:			
Vocational training			
Yes	☐	24	(433)
No	☐	68	(1208)
Don't know	☐	8	(148)
(No response)			(148)

"Folkeskole" literally means "folk school," after completion of which students are roughly 13-14 years of age.

Classroom education

Yes..	☐	25	(420)
No...	☐	70	(1187)
Don't know...................................	☐	6	(102)
(No response)			(228)

Understanding of myself by having had time to think problems through.

Yes..	☐	52	(957)
No...	☐	37	(690)
Don't know...................................	☐	11	(206)
(No response)................................	☐		(84)

Understanding of myself as a result of help from someone on the staff.

Yes..	☐	15	(271)
No...	☐	76	(1336)
Don't know...................................	☐	9	(162)
(No response)			(168)

Better physical condition

Yes..	☐	23	(408)
No...	☐	68	(1197)
Don't know...................................	☐	9	(165)
(No response)			(167)

Better relationship with my family.

Yes..	☐	22	(396)
No...	☐	66	(1197)
Don't know...................................	☐	13	(235)
(No response)			(109)

48. We all make statements about ourselves, and what kind of person we are. A number of statements made by men in institutions are listed below. Before the number of each statement are three sets of letters: T, NT, and DK. If you feel that the statement is True of you, circle T. If you feel that the statement is Not True of you, circle NT. If you Don't Know whether the statement is true of you or not true of you, circle DK.

There are no "correct" answers. Work quickly and do not spend much time with any one statement. Please describe yourself as you really are, not as you want to be.

1. When I am outside the institution, I like to be together with lots of people.

		%	(N)
True	☐	56	(1044)
Not true	☐	33	(618)
Don't know	☐	12	(220)
(No response)			(55)

2. My family and friends outside the institution have confidence in me.

		%	(N)
True	☐	56	(1055)
Not true	☐	15	(278)
Don't know	☐	30	(560)
(No response)			(44)

3. Inmates often come to me for advice.

		%	(N)
True	☐	35	(644)
Not true	☐	39	(714)
Don't know	☐	26	(477)
(No response)			(102)

4. I'm the kind of person who doesn't like to be told what to do.

		%	(N)
True	☐	46	(859)
Not true	☐	39	(725)
Don't know	☐	14	(269)
(No response)			(84)

5. I don't have much in common with law-abiding people.

		%	(N)
True	☐	19	(351)
Not true	☐	64	(1169)
Don't know	☐	17	(318)
(No response)			(99)

		%	(N)
6. It is not important to me to have many friends.			
True	☐	36	(670)
Not true	☐	48	(902)
Don't know	☐	16	(289)
(No response)			(76)
7. People outside the institution do not respect me.			
True	☐	21	(385)
Not true	☐	47	(866)
Don't know	☐	32	(592)
(No response)			(94)
8. I am definitely not a leader among the inmates.			
True	☐	64	(1164)
Not true	☐	23	(429)
Don't know	☐	13	(239)
(No response)			(105)
9. I don't mind taking orders from people.			
True	☐	53	(972)
Not true	☐	32	(581)
Don't know	☐	15	(275)
(No response)			(109)
10. I am not really a criminal.			
True	☐	64	(1184)
Not true	☐	17	(311)
Don't know	☐	20	(361)
(No response)			(81)
11. People outside the institution think that I am a bad person.			
True	☐	22	(405)
Not true	☐	50	(904)
Don't know	☐	28	(516)
(No response)			(112)
12. I am very well liked by other inmates.			
True	☐	26	(477)
Not true	☐	20	(373)
Don't know	☐	53	(971)
(No response)			(116)

			%	(N)
13.	I am more "prison-wise" than the average inmate.			
	True	☐	27	(501)
	Not true	☐	64	(1174)
	Don't know	☐	9	(164)
	(No response)			(98)
14.	It irritates me when people tell me what to do.			
	True	☐	39	(719)
	Not true	☐	46	(850)
	Don't know	☐	14	(264)
	(No response)			(104)
15.	When I'm outside, I would rather work alone than together with other people.			
	True	☐	49	(915)
	Not true	☐	42	(790)
	Don't know	☐	9	(165)
	(No response)			(67)

Appendix III: Figures for Chapter 8 (Figs. 8.6–8.13 and Figs. 8.1'–8.5')

S. Wheeler and H. F. Cline, *The Scandinavian Prison Study*, Palgrave Studies in Prisons and Penology,
https://doi.org/10.1007/978-3-030-26462-8

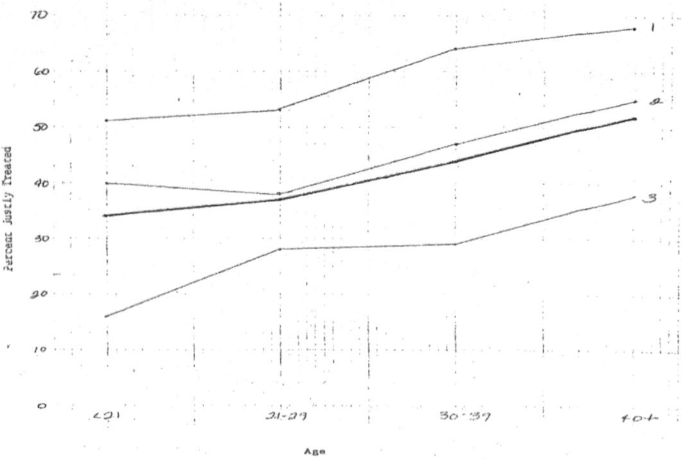

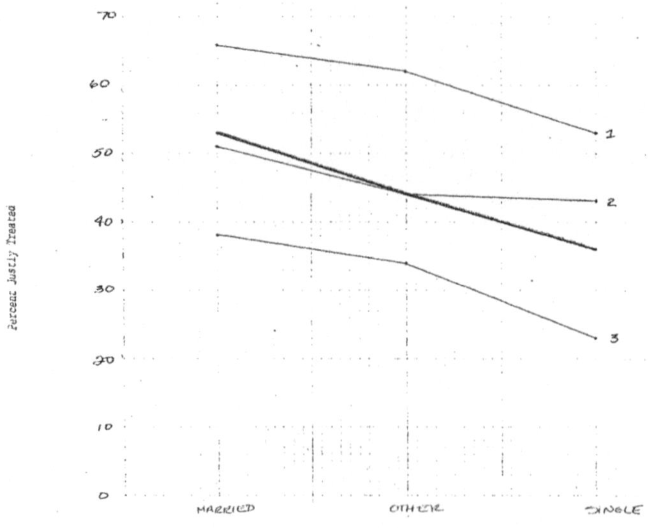

Figs. 8.6 and 8.7 Relationship of justice of treatment to age and marital status

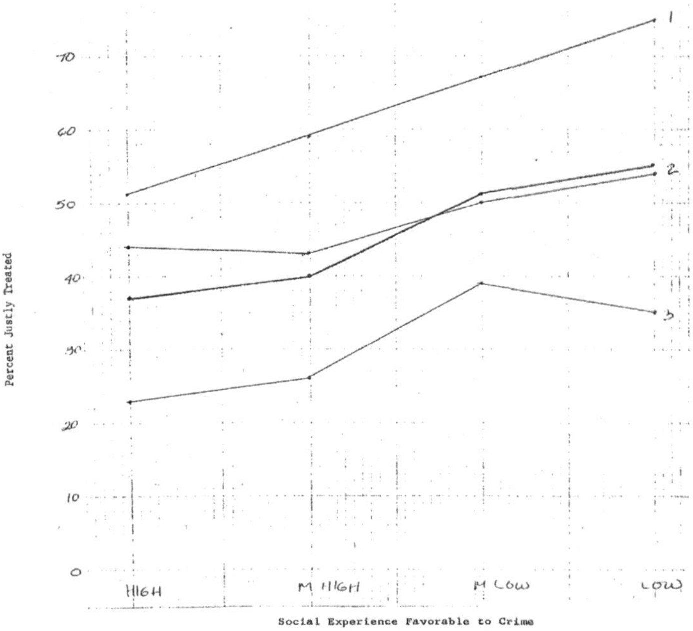

Fig. 8.8 Relationship of justice of treatment to social experience favorable to crime

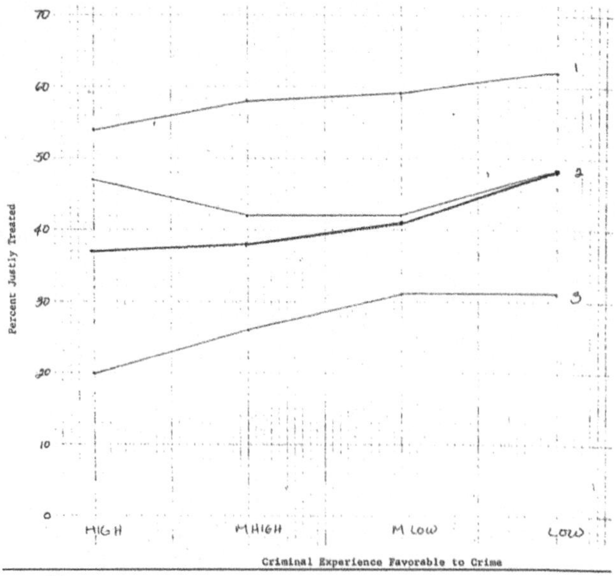

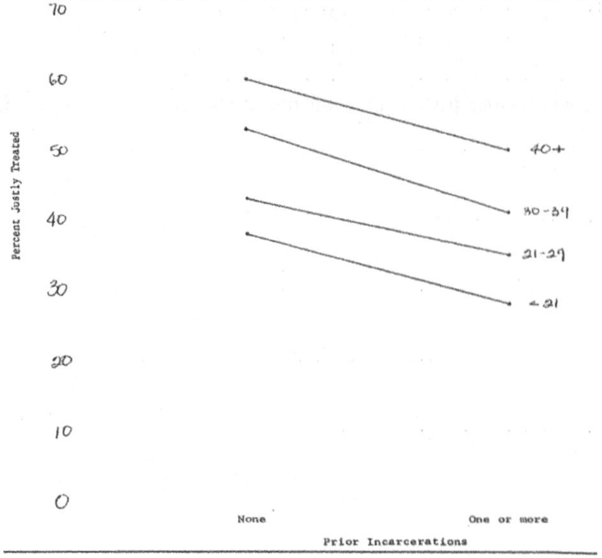

Figs. 8.9 and 9a Relationship of justice of treatment to criminal experience and prior incarcerations

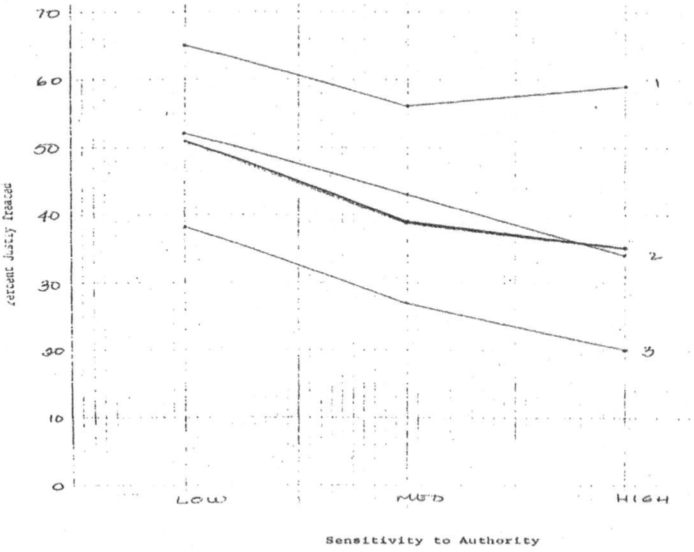

Fig. 8.10 Relationship of justice of treatment to sensitivity to authority

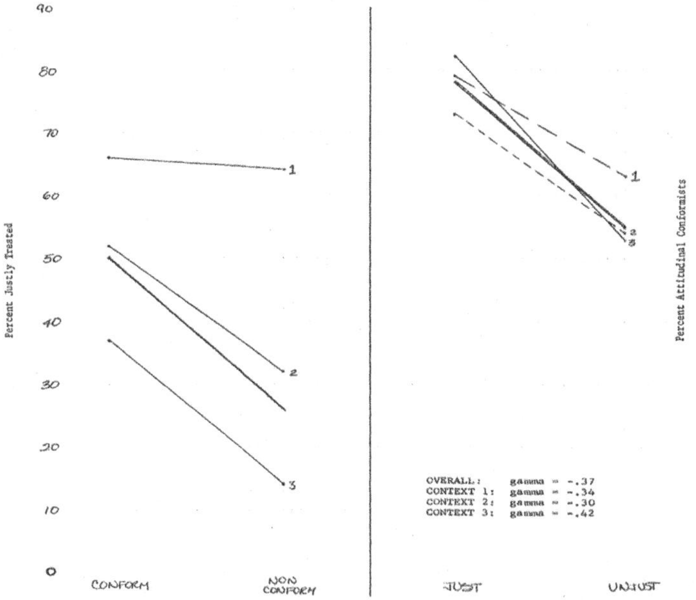

Fig. 8.11 The relationship between attitudinal conformity and justice of treatment

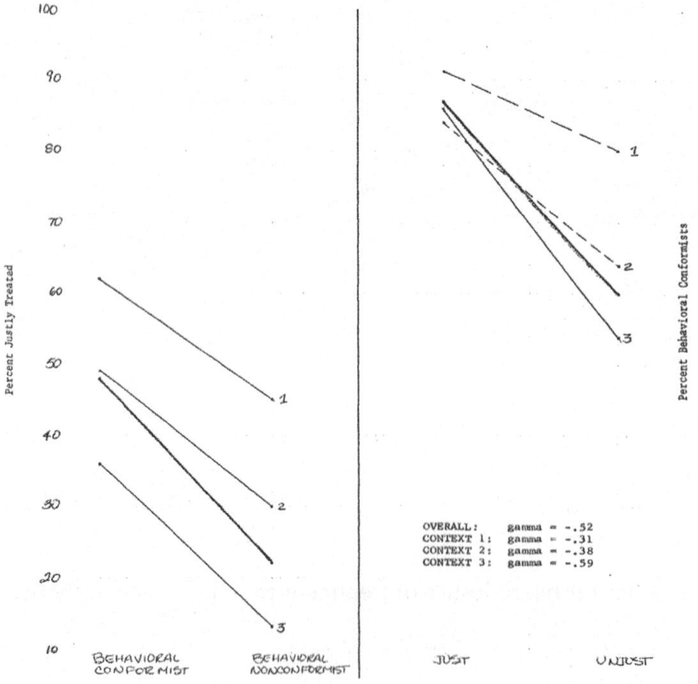

Fig. 8.12 The relationship between behavioral conformity and justice of treatment

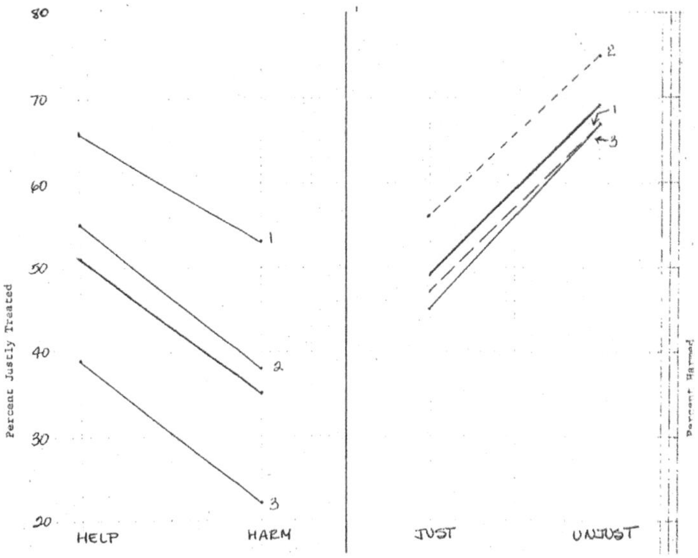

Fig. 8.13 The relationship between perceived effect of incarceration and justice of treatment (Gammas: Overall −.30; Context 1 −.26; Context 2 −.30; Context 3 −.31)

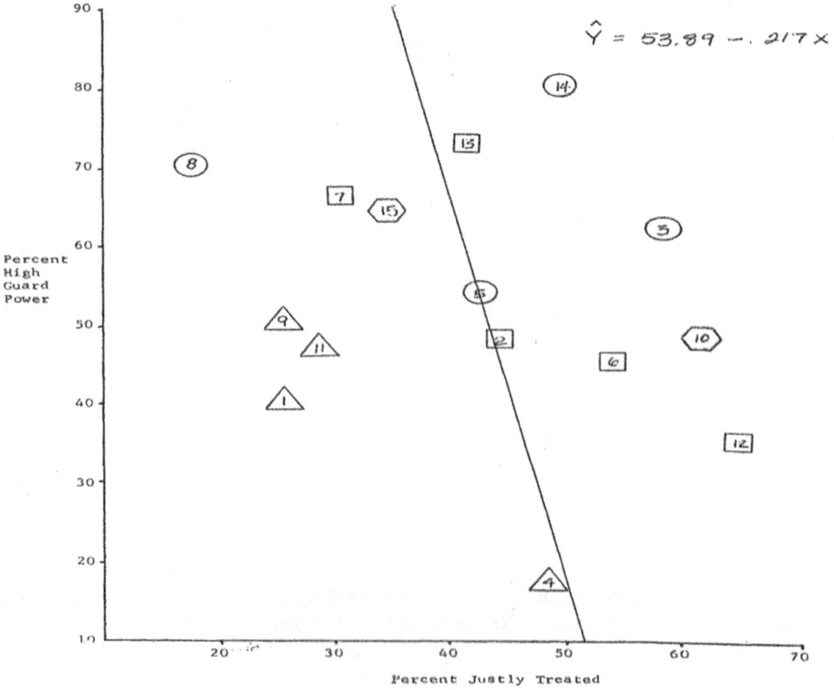

Fig. 8.1' The relationship of justice of treatment to guard authority ($r = -26$)

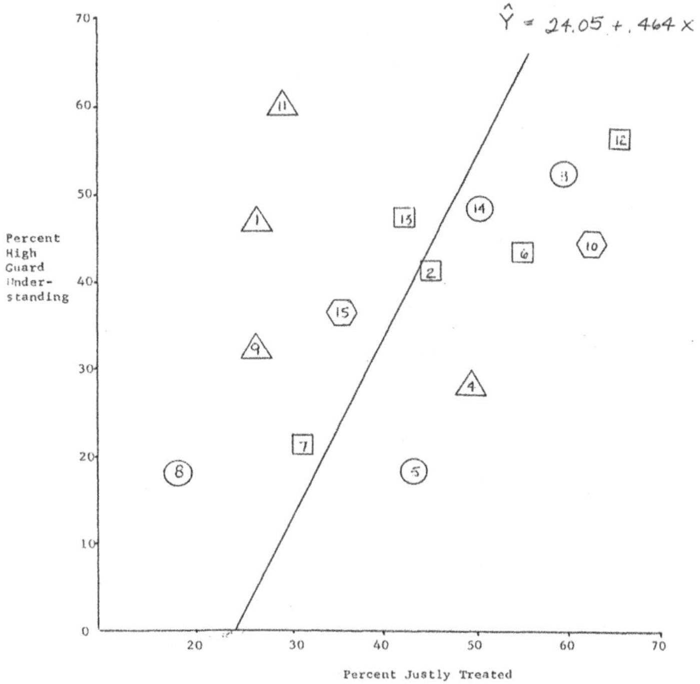

Fig. 8.2' The relationship of justice of treatment to guard understanding ($r = +.42$)

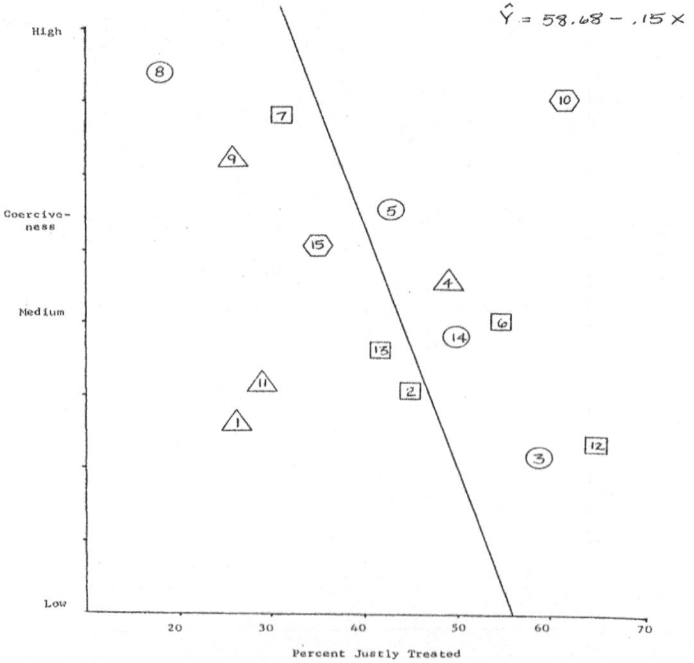

Fig. 8.3' The relationship of justice of treatment to coerciveness ($r = -.38$)

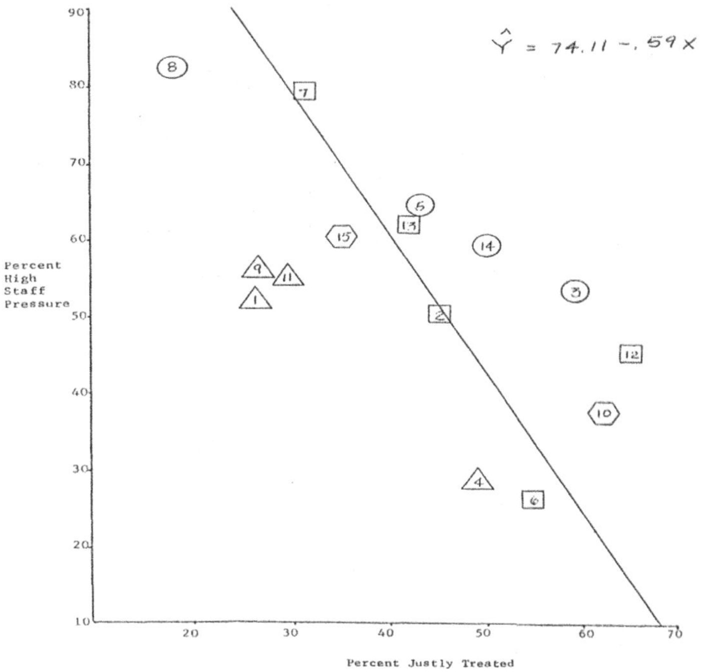

Fig. 8.4' The relationship of justice of treatment to staff pressure ($r = -.65$)

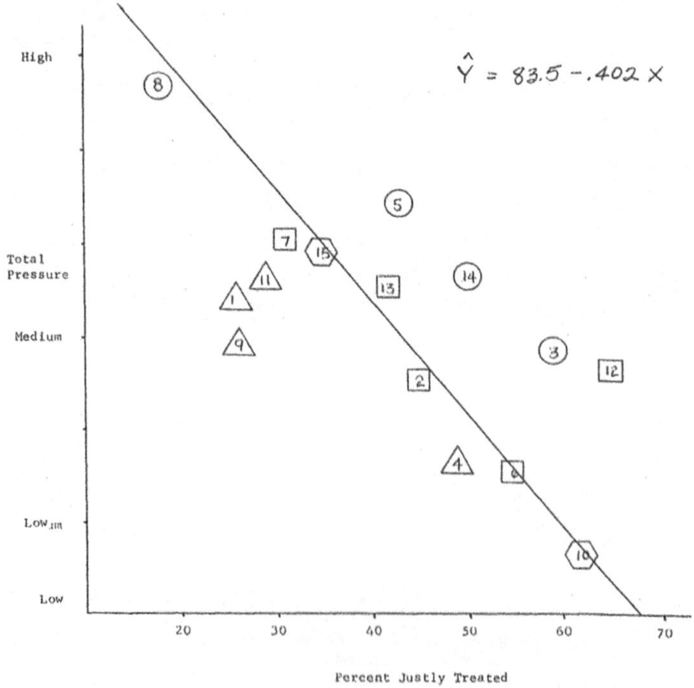

Fig. 8.5' The relationship of justice of treatment to total pressure ($r = -.70$)

Index

A
administration 3, 6, 23, 33, 35–38, 47, 51, 68, 82, 109, 238, 244, 302, 303, 305, 306
  correctional 211, 221, 270
adult offenders 48, 211
adult prisons 28, 31, 73
Afterword xii, xvii, xix, 279, 281, 290–293
age vii–x, xiii, 1, 11, 14, 21, 25, 62, 63, 66, 68, 70, 72–76, 106, 112, 125–142, 144, 147, 150–153, 155, 156, 172, 193–203, 210, 211, 231, 240–242, 267, 275, 279, 297, 308, 326
  average 48, 51, 62, 297
  effect of 74, 127, 134, 135, 139–142, 155, 156, 174, 192, 194, 199, 201, 202
  years of 139, 140, 147
age categories, major 152
age differences 129, 140, 142, 196
age groups 14, 49, 134, 141, 142
age level 141, 241
alcohol 29, 282, 298
alienation 149–151, 154
Alport, Floyd H. 101
American prison inmates 136
American prisons 65, 82, 95
American values xxv
analysis
  contextual 239
  individual level 21
  individual level of 20, 21, 26, 27, 39, 112, 113, 228, 238, 266, 275
  multiple regression 39, 128, 144, 215, 217
  national 206
  previous 177, 238, 240, 265, 276

S. Wheeler and H. F. Cline, *The Scandinavian Prison Study*, Palgrave Studies in Prisons and Penology,
https://doi.org/10.1007/978-3-030-26462-8

subgroup 210, 220, 267
Anglophone xxv
anomie xiii
anti-staff 104, 106, 107, 251, 253, 255, 264
anti-staff feeling 106
anti-staff orientations 106
Appendices 208, 242
approach, ethnographic xxii–xxiv
Arbeidsskolen 283
architecture 29, 30, 37, 42, 45, 47, 69, 228, 285
arrest 137–139, 141, 148, 150
artifact 142, 208, 249
assault 139, 140, 299
association 71–77, 122, 136, 137, 150, 154, 160, 250
asylum xxiii
asylum seekers 284, 287, 288
Attica Commission Report 4
Attica prison riot in New York xiv
attitudes 37, 52, 74, 124–126, 129–131, 139, 145, 149, 151–153, 156, 160, 172, 178, 180, 186, 203, 239, 264
  criminalization xix
  inmate's 23, 71, 101, 103, 105, 115, 123, 127, 134, 154, 162, 173, 174, 197, 228, 239, 250, 254, 276
  political xx, 125
attitudinal 112
attitudinal conformists 121–123, 139, 152, 171, 173, 175, 176, 178, 202, 203, 214, 216, 243, 255–257
attitudinal conformity xiii, xiv, 24, 114, 121, 123, 124, 126–130, 135, 137, 140, 141, 151, 152, 154, 158, 170–172, 176, 182, 188–190, 198, 201–203, 205, 213–217, 230, 239, 243, 254–258, 260, 261, 263, 265, 275, 329
attitudinal nonconformists 122, 154, 253, 256
attitudinal nonconformity xiii, 152, 153, 251
authoritarian 46, 80
authority 5, 23, 30, 64, 86, 95, 100, 112, 127, 130, 146–148, 151, 152, 155, 242, 243, 264, 275, 329
  formal 98, 167
  guard 153, 154, 209, 210, 212, 213, 233, 234, 272, 332
  official 80, 98, 152, 154, 211
authority figures 154
authority patterns 147

B

background characteristics 112, 154, 198, 201, 203, 213, 255, 297
  social 25, 129, 156, 217, 240, 275
background factors 132, 155, 198
background items 38, 124, 126, 129, 137
background measures, social 129, 134
backgrounds, inmate's 126, 192, 264
background variables 106, 126–130, 155, 215
balance, changing 100
balance of understanding 87, 89, 90, 233
Balvig, Flemming xix, 276, 279, 281

Barker, Vanessa 289
Baum, Martha 183
Baumhart, Raymond C. 105
behavioral conformity 123, 151–154, 171, 182, 187–189, 230, 239, 254, 258–261, 263, 265, 275, 330
behaviors, social psychological xiv, 228
beliefs 24, 27, 30, 31, 95, 101, 103, 107, 108, 119, 120, 124, 133, 161, 194
benefits 60, 79, 160, 172, 190, 206, 218–220
Berg 29, 56, 231, 239, 245, 246, 285
Bergen prison 285
block 37, 46, 47, 63, 244, 299, 302
Blomberg. T.G. xxv
Blumstein, A. xxii
Bødal, Kåre 283
Bondeson, Ulla xix, xx, xxiii, xxiv, 6, 136, 161, 191
Botsfengslet xix, 44, 45, 61, 65, 66, 71, 238, 239, 246, 272, 285
British model 282
Burgess, Ernest W. 145
Buskerud 286

C

captives 58, 105, 158
cases 5–7, 20, 21, 26, 30, 38, 42, 61, 64, 65, 67, 69, 80, 81, 86, 91, 95, 100, 103, 112, 121, 129, 134, 142, 149, 150, 152, 153, 167, 173, 179, 185, 189, 193, 194, 196, 199, 203, 206, 207, 211, 213, 219, 220, 224–226, 230, 238, 243–245, 247, 249, 252, 253, 255, 257–259, 263, 265, 268, 272, 273, 296, 298, 302, 305
cells 37, 44, 46–49, 51, 52, 61, 62, 65, 66, 75, 82, 141, 244–246, 284, 285, 297, 302, 307
Chambers, Marcia xi, 281
changes, social 11, 41, 59
characteristics
  aggregate xiii, xiv
  institutional 32, 33, 231, 296
  national 207, 211, 221, 266
  personal 25–27, 112, 198, 203, 267
  socioeconomic 8
Chessman, Caryl 4
Christie, Nils 29, 36, 280
cigarettes 35, 60, 298, 303–305
cities 14, 45, 46, 127, 128, 131, 143, 144, 168, 280, 286, 288
Cleaver, Eldridge 4
Clemmer, Donald xiii, xxii, xxiii, 5, 145, 160, 288
climate 22, 77, 79, 82, 83, 88, 92, 108, 206, 209, 211, 221, 228, 230–232, 235, 237, 238, 240, 241, 248, 250, 257, 260, 264, 270–275
  anti-staff 108, 109
Cline, Hugh F. v, vi, ix, x, xvii, xviii, 212, 277, 279, 281, 292
Cloward, Richard A. 161
coalitions 11, 18, 283, 284, 288
coerciveness xv, 22, 23, 80, 81, 91–94, 99, 108, 228, 232, 233, 235, 272, 273, 275, 277, 334

Cohen, Albert K. 160
Coleman, James S. 7, 21
communication 23, 56, 57, 76, 121, 178, 180, 181, 194
comparative research xxv, 206
comparative studies 21, 212, 301
concept xiii, xiv, xix, xx, xxiii, 20, 22, 60, 69, 75, 95, 124, 136, 150, 204, 274, 281, 287, 304
conceptions 6, 24, 25, 113, 149, 150, 170, 240, 244, 254
conceptualization 208, 276
conduct 2, 4, 6, 23, 28, 33, 36, 37, 82, 88, 101, 114, 119, 122, 145, 152, 154, 156, 171, 188, 190, 191, 210, 230, 258, 259, 304, 305
confinement xii, 2, 38, 42, 45, 54, 55, 105, 118, 133, 159, 194
  solitary 52, 65, 244–246, 300
conflict 56, 82, 105, 112, 119, 232, 284
conflict situations 95, 102
conformists 104, 106, 127, 129, 135, 138, 141, 161, 171, 201, 202, 209, 212–214
  behavioral 122, 153, 178, 190, 258–261
conformity
  attitudinal and behavioral 123, 151–153, 171, 182, 187, 189, 230, 239, 254, 258, 261, 263, 264, 275
  measure of 123, 126, 141, 152, 155, 171, 182, 188, 201, 259
  perceived 104, 106, 124
conservatives 10, 17, 18, 125, 160
constraints 28, 63, 65, 69, 70, 75–77, 92, 109, 131, 153, 158, 232, 233, 247
construction 41, 47, 60, 103, 175, 250, 255, 266, 274, 285
  date of 45, 59, 62, 64–68, 73, 75, 112, 233
contacts
  amount of 61, 71, 72, 159, 165, 167, 183–186, 189–191, 196, 198
  high amount of 169, 176, 177, 183, 197
  patterns of 72, 157, 170, 171, 173, 174, 176, 177, 183, 185, 186, 192, 193, 195, 196, 202, 203, 243, 249, 251
  quantity of 171, 173, 175, 198–200, 251
  social 61, 157, 159, 160, 204
contacts inmates xiv, 45, 67, 71, 73, 243, 249–253
context xviii, 8, 26, 58, 114, 133, 159, 211, 217, 221, 239–243, 247, 250–253, 255, 257, 260, 261, 263, 265, 266, 289
control/controlling xxiii, 11, 12, 22, 37, 42, 50, 52, 59–62, 86, 92, 98, 100, 105, 134, 152–155, 199, 210, 218–220, 225–228, 238, 239, 242, 249, 255–262, 264, 266–271, 273, 274, 276
convicts 30, 44, 45, 125, 166, 284, 286
cooperatives, consumer 12
Copenhagen 45, 51, 127, 279
Correctional Communities 100, 101, 161, 162, 280

correctional ideology 43, 44, 53, 61, 65, 69, 76, 100
correctional literature, contemporary 223
correctional systems 3, 43, 46, 48, 52, 65, 97, 274, 306
corrections xv, 31, 40–43, 50, 53, 54, 58–60, 62, 64, 65, 67–69, 75, 102, 157, 162, 253, 270, 276, 296, 309
correlation 39, 62, 64, 71, 74, 83, 85, 90, 92, 97, 98, 100, 111, 134, 140, 201, 231, 235–237, 239, 243, 244, 249, 254, 255, 258, 263, 271, 308
  multiple 128, 129, 139, 144, 145, 215–217
courts 50, 52, 58, 307
Cressey, Donald R. 101, 160, 161
Crewe, B. xxiv
crime vii, xi, xx–xxii, xxv, 8, 25, 45, 46, 54, 115, 125, 126, 131, 134–136, 139–144, 146, 148–151, 154, 197, 202, 224, 225, 241, 243, 283, 288, 292, 327
criminal activity 115, 136
criminal background 113, 135, 138–145, 148–151, 153, 155, 156, 197, 210, 239, 240, 266, 267
criminal background characteristics 25, 137, 139, 156, 217
criminal background index 137, 140, 141, 145, 148, 150, 197, 242
criminal experience 126, 137, 140–144, 149, 155, 197, 202, 203, 241–243, 275, 328
  prior 135, 156, 204
criminalization xix
criminal justice xviii, xxv, 148, 279, 286, 290, 291
criminal justice system xxi, 8, 24, 38, 125, 142, 146, 148, 150, 207, 214, 224, 242, 275, 282, 285, 289
criminal policy xviii, 282, 283, 289, 290, 292
criminals xix, xx, 45, 50, 57, 64, 69, 125, 133, 135–137, 142–144, 146, 149–151, 154, 155, 160, 170, 204, 285, 291
criminal subcultures 131
criminologists xii, xviii, xix, xxi, xxii, 139, 281
criminology x, xi, xvi, xx, xxv, 125, 136, 279, 280, 292
Cross-Cultural Survey Research 206, 208
cross-national differences xvi, 2, 114, 208, 210, 219, 266, 267, 270
cultural context 121
culture xxiii, 2, 5, 27, 58, 107, 111, 130, 153, 286, 290
custodial 23, 60, 63, 67, 75, 83–86, 88, 89, 92, 93, 99, 213, 232, 246, 295, 297
custodial control 47–49, 59, 60, 63, 64, 118
custodial personnel 64, 167, 235
custodial prison xv, xix, 2, 45
custody 6, 46, 53, 55, 56, 58–60, 63, 67, 68, 81, 87–90, 94, 96, 100, 108, 119, 231, 233, 244, 245, 250, 297, 302

custody staff 68, 85, 87–89, 92, 100, 108, 165
ratio of inmates to 60, 63, 64, 68, 232, 233

D

Danes 13, 55, 218, 220, 269
Danish inmates 31, 210, 213, 217–220, 267, 270
Danish institutions 31, 49, 273
Danish prisons and prisoners xix
Danish youth institution 31, 72, 85
data collection xiv, xviii, 32, 56, 110, 207, 295, 301
data collection procedures 19, 244, 301
date of origin 41, 43, 59, 64, 68, 72–74, 76
David Street 6, 21
Davis, James A. 21
delinquent 131, 136, 140
Denmark xxv, 2, 9–18, 28, 30, 31, 48, 50–53, 55, 57, 61, 64, 69, 71, 86, 98, 114, 142, 172, 209, 211, 213–215, 217, 219, 231, 239, 240, 267–269, 272, 280, 282, 287, 288, 304, 309
Densiovich, Ivan 4
density 13, 159, 160, 191, 207
deprivation measures, social 67, 76
design 1, 3, 6, 7, 19, 29, 35–37, 39, 44, 47–49, 53, 55–57, 60, 65, 69, 76, 92, 118, 179, 211, 228, 230, 264, 271, 276, 295
physical 41, 43, 76, 111
de Tocqueville, Alexis 43, 74
development xviii–xxi, 4, 6, 7, 12, 20, 29, 31, 41–43, 69, 75, 82, 95, 137, 164, 206, 208, 287, 290
deviants 65, 69, 105, 119, 149, 153, 170, 189, 258
Dickson, W.J. 159
differences, cross-institutional 227, 229
differential association theory 136, 137, 160, 161, 204
differentials, institutional 275
differentiation 48, 52, 53, 211, 219, 221, 231, 238, 240, 263–266, 268, 271–274, 287
director viii, 33, 37, 49, 50, 52, 53, 56, 70, 86, 284, 295, 296
Director of prisons 284
discipline 33, 49, 122, 206, 250, 264
discipline actions 123
disruptions 37, 116
distribution 116, 121, 122, 187, 209, 216, 218, 224, 229–231, 239, 257, 266, 271, 272, 274
marginal 138, 199, 201, 202, 267
skewed 167, 228
diversity 53, 58, 140, 265
dormitories 37, 49, 55, 56, 61, 65, 302
Drake, D.H. xxiv
drunk/drunken drivers 30, 54, 64, 69, 90, 138, 209, 229, 243, 287
Durkheim, Emile 111, 158, 159, 170, 171, 174
Durkheim hypothesis 170
Dutch prison of Norgerhaven 284

E

earnings 15, 16, 55
ecology 76
economic indicators 15
economy 8, 11, 16, 290
education 50, 55, 60, 126, 129, 134, 135, 143, 148, 219, 220, 230, 241, 295–297, 302
  public 8, 12
educational attainment, higher 131
Edwin Sutherland's theory xiii, xiv, 136, 160, 204
effect
  joint 143, 144, 198, 201
  little 101, 149, 196, 217, 231
  positive xx, 116, 130, 179
  total 65, 68, 134, 194
effectiveness xxi, xxii, 6, 21
employment 58
  stable 125
enforcement 92, 94, 109, 233
environment xxii–xxiv, 27, 76, 81, 92, 94, 95, 99, 110, 157, 159, 162, 164, 165, 183, 189, 201, 247, 296
Erikson, Thorsten 56
escape 42, 43, 54–56, 91, 92, 118, 299
ethnographic research xxiv
ethnographic studies xxii–xxiv
ethnography xxiii, xxiv
Europe xxii, 8, 10–15, 17, 43, 61, 111, 288, 290
European countries xxv, 44, 111, 279, 280, 288
European criminology xxii
evaluations xvii, 51, 224, 244, 250
exceptionalism xxv, 281
  carceral xxii
excess, penal xxv, 291
expenditures 18
experience 4, 5, 20, 23–25, 27, 30, 32, 36, 42, 61, 62, 67, 79, 81, 105, 111, 114, 118, 124–126, 132–137, 139, 140, 143–146, 149–151, 195–197, 200, 202, 203, 211, 218, 221, 224, 228, 235, 238, 239, 241, 243–245, 247, 250, 253–255, 264, 265, 271, 274, 276, 290, 296, 303, 305, 306
experts xx, xxi, 65
explanatory power 143, 144, 154, 192
explorations 27, 210, 220
exposure 141, 142, 148, 154, 160, 170, 248, 254

F

facilities 29, 42, 46, 47, 49, 54, 56, 64, 265, 296, 302
factories 133
Fængsler 281
family ix, x, xii, 12, 61, 117, 125, 131, 133, 158, 178, 179, 182, 196, 197, 220, 280, 291
family relationships 178, 182, 219
family ties 159, 182
Fangen 161
father's occupation 125
favorable social backgrounds, least 154
features 3, 6–8, 10, 21–24, 27, 33, 44, 45, 58, 60, 61, 67, 68, 70, 72–76, 112, 151, 156, 178, 183, 219, 220, 307
  material 59, 62, 63, 65, 231, 233

physical 42, 43, 59, 62, 63, 65, 231, 233
Feeley, M.M. xxi
feelings of being harmed xiv, 116, 129, 134, 137, 141, 142, 160, 174–177, 182, 198–200, 203, 205, 213, 217, 262
feelings of help 124, 128, 131, 133, 174, 182, 198, 202, 203, 215, 217, 230
feelings of help and harm 116, 118, 144, 182, 217, 262
feeling tone 22, 23, 52, 58, 79–81, 97, 98
fetters 286, 291
findings
earlier 213, 214, 216, 217
general 125, 174
main 62, 131
significant 231, 270
Finland 2, 9, 10, 12–18, 28, 30, 31, 46–48, 54, 55, 69, 90, 97, 111, 114, 193, 200, 209, 214, 215, 217–220, 237, 239, 240, 267–270, 272, 273, 279, 280, 282, 288, 290, 304, 309
Finnish inmates 210, 219, 220, 266, 267, 269, 270, 273
Finnish institutions 30, 46, 48, 55, 84, 86, 88, 98, 111, 230, 237, 266, 272, 273
Finnish prisons 46, 210, 240, 272
first arrest 112, 137, 139, 140, 150, 197, 242
Foner, Anne 131
foreigners 284, 289
format xv, xvi, 32, 116, 137, 138
France 10
freedom of movement 42, 43, 61, 65
free time 49, 71–75, 163–165, 184, 189
Frey, Frederick W. 206, 208
friendship formation 70, 71, 76
friendships 164, 185

G

generalizations 2, 58, 203
Geneva 17
George Mason University 281
Germany 10–12, 111, 282
Gillespie, W. xxiv, xxv
Glaser, Daniel 4, 6, 21
Goffman, E. xxiii
government xxi, 3, 9–12, 18, 95, 283, 284, 287–289, 296
Greenwood, P.W. xx
Gross National Product (GNP) 10, 15, 17, 18
groups
small 14, 56, 64
social 37, 145
growth xx, 14, 15, 73, 291
guard power xv, xvii, 233–235, 272, 277
guards 36, 48, 51, 54, 56, 57, 63, 83–85, 119, 158, 165–167, 170, 172, 184, 210, 212, 273, 275, 297, 303, 307

H

Hall 29, 30, 48, 52, 53, 71, 85, 86, 98, 246, 277
Hallsworth, S. xxii
Hansen 103, 120

harm 116–118, 121, 124, 126, 135, 145, 171, 172, 217, 262, 263
  best predictor of 129, 139
  feelings of 124, 128, 131, 133, 142, 174, 198–200, 213, 263
Harvard ix, x
Harvard University ix, xxi, 80
Harvard University Press xxi, xxii, 159
Hassler, Alfred 4
Helsinki 17, 30, 46–48, 54, 127, 279, 309
Herstedvester 30, 31, 48, 50–52, 86, 88, 98, 240, 245, 246, 277
Heydebrand, Wolf 7
High inmate contact Low inmate 176
Hinton, E. xxii
history 12, 14, 42, 45, 61, 69, 70, 75, 79, 95, 97, 145, 204, 295
  correctional 41, 59
homogeneous 58, 75, 152, 238, 239, 244, 267, 270
  relatively 125, 210, 220, 257
homogeneous subgroup analysis 210, 268
homogeneous subgroups 240, 266
hospital, mental xxiii, 51, 132
housing 16, 31, 51, 52, 57, 61, 65, 75, 211, 297
housing units 49, 50, 54, 66, 302
Hsu, Francis 207
hypotheses 6, 19, 20, 158, 170, 171, 206, 207, 237, 247, 251
  major 177
  particular testable 27

I

Iceland 9
ideology 41, 43, 48, 53, 58, 64, 65, 69, 70, 75, 76, 211, 221
ideology of imprisonment 41, 132
Ila xviii, xix, 29, 30, 48, 51–53, 86, 88, 89, 98, 277, 280, 285
image 48, 169, 292
impact xiv, xx, 25, 26, 114, 115, 175, 201, 207, 264
implications xv, xvii, xxi, 149, 152, 226, 263
imprisonment 1, 3–5, 7, 20, 25–28, 36, 42, 47, 58, 60, 61, 63, 115, 118, 132, 134–136, 139, 144, 155, 156, 158, 159, 178, 190, 198, 204, 218, 228, 245, 248, 261, 263, 264, 275, 304
incapacitation xx, xxi, xxv
incarceration
  conditions of 246, 247, 254, 269, 270
  effect of 115, 118, 124, 128, 196, 239, 260–262, 265, 331
  inmate responses to 178, 254, 274, 275
  structural conditions of 243, 275
incarceration rate xxv
indices 61, 70, 94, 97, 106, 108, 143, 144, 155, 156, 165, 167, 174, 175, 179, 183, 185, 195, 198, 215, 221, 242, 250
influence, significant 83, 85
informal contacts 32, 73, 164, 184
injustice xvii, 226, 228, 231, 239, 240, 248, 249, 257, 266, 269, 270, 272–274

- feelings of 223, 229, 232, 239, 247, 248, 251, 252, 262–264, 276
- perceived 231, 265, 267, 276

Inkeles, Alex 207
inmate age 232, 266
inmate background 219, 240, 243, 255
inmate background characteristics 243, 275
inmate balance 108
inmate contact 164, 165, 167, 184–187, 190
- low 170, 171, 176, 188, 202, 203
- patterns of 188, 193, 201

inmate culture 5, 101, 109, 112, 136
inmate experience 20, 114, 198
inmate feelings 23, 71, 190, 228, 238, 242, 264
inmate involvement 163, 172, 187–189, 191, 194, 202, 243, 252
inmate life 2, 5, 29, 61, 62, 101, 155, 156, 163, 166, 184, 187, 189, 221
inmate perceptions 80, 87, 93, 95, 128, 179, 223, 224, 229, 233, 239, 245, 247, 268, 274
inmate population 33, 35, 36, 39, 45, 48, 50, 52, 55, 57, 59, 100, 194, 221, 238, 244
inmate pressure 97–99, 209, 210, 213, 233, 235
inmate responses 2, 83, 94, 190, 214
inmates, youthful 31, 48, 57, 198
inmates feeling 226, 228, 231, 241, 253, 256, 262, 263
inmates report 80, 98, 162, 164, 166, 168, 253
institutional climates 211, 221, 242, 243, 250, 261, 274
institutional contexts xiv, 241, 248, 251, 252, 256, 257, 260, 263–266, 276
institutional differences xiv, 71, 205, 211, 212, 214, 229, 239, 241, 273
institutional features 82, 270
institutionalize 51
institutional level 20, 112, 114, 165, 227, 230–232, 238, 239, 255, 257, 260, 271, 272
institutional treatment xx, 224, 225, 230, 274
institutional variations 123, 260
institutions
- correctional 31, 48
- newer 62–65, 69–72, 74
- older 65, 69
- single 5–7, 81, 104, 135, 156

integration, social xiii, 158, 159, 190, 200
interaction
- amounts of 65, 68, 157
- interpersonal 211, 215

interaction patterns 24, 63, 70, 73, 74, 217, 232, 233
interrelationships 26, 27, 76, 94, 143, 165, 224, 268
interviews xix, xxiii, xxiv, 32, 33, 38, 177, 244, 295
involvement 9, 95, 144, 160, 163–168, 170, 176, 177, 185, 188–191, 218, 242, 250–253
- patterns of 27, 28, 158, 162, 171–175, 183, 187, 192, 195, 197, 198, 201–204, 213, 250, 252, 253, 275

social 157, 159, 172, 198
isolation 42, 45, 47, 58, 62, 67, 71, 116, 132, 165, 307

J

Jansen 102, 120
Janus face 289
job vi, xii, 47, 79, 103, 120, 125, 131, 297
judgments 21, 81, 135, 153, 160, 208, 261
justice
assessments of 229, 238, 242, 244, 253, 266, 275
feelings of 226, 228, 229, 232, 238, 239, 241, 242, 247, 249, 250, 252, 253, 255, 258, 261–270, 276
perceptions of 223, 224, 229, 231, 238, 239, 241, 245, 247–249, 253, 254, 256, 260, 263–266, 268, 270, 274–276
sense of 115, 239, 240, 243, 251, 254, 255, 258, 260
justice of sentence xvii, 225–227, 249, 255, 256, 258, 259, 262, 268–270
justice of treatment xvii, 225, 227, 228, 230–243, 248, 249, 252, 254, 256–263, 265, 267, 269–273, 275, 276, 326–336
Jutland 31, 53, 54

K

Kakola 46
Karelia 47
Kassebaum, Gene G. 4, 5
Kerava 30, 48–50, 55, 97, 229, 231, 240
Kinnunen, Aarne 276, 279
knowledge 64, 88, 111, 174, 207, 211, 213, 221, 236
Konnunsuo 30, 46, 47, 55, 88, 106, 240, 246
Kragskovhede 31, 53, 54, 56, 71, 91, 92, 209, 240, 245, 246, 269
KROM xvii, 279, 281–283, 285, 286, 290

L

Langholmen prison in Stockholm 57
languages x, 9, 13, 32, 36, 38, 87, 136, 284, 290
Lappi-Seppala, T. 277
law vii, xxi, 133, 285, 287
leadership 79, 80, 210
letters 168–170, 177–180, 182, 183, 186, 194, 250, 285, 298, 302
life 2, 4–6, 13, 14, 23, 35, 58, 60, 64, 69, 76, 88, 102, 105, 116, 132, 133, 136, 146, 151, 154, 156, 157, 163, 167, 172, 180, 188, 195, 201, 203, 247, 261, 296
daily 42, 43, 70, 80, 83, 85, 87, 119, 210
institutional 61, 81, 82, 230, 275

limitations xii, xiv, 6, 81, 110, 111, 156, 177, 236, 247, 266, 276
Litwin, George H. 80
Lund 102, 120

M

Mariefred 30, 56, 57, 65, 66, 86, 98, 239, 246
marital status 25, 112, 125, 127–129, 192–194, 197, 199, 200, 203, 241, 326
  inmate's 127
Mathiesen, Thomas iv–vi, xii, xviii, xix, xxi, xxii, 276, 279, 282, 283
maximum security prison 286
Merton, Robert K. 159, 208
methods xix, 4, 39, 40, 208, 239, 244, 272, 273, 276, 290, 295, 301
  ethnographic xxiii
  quantitative xxiii
migrants 14, 288
Minister of Justice 284–286, 289
Mitford, Jessica 3
money 60, 102, 120, 121, 296, 298, 304
multiple correlation coefficients 128, 129, 216
Myrdal, Gunnar 209

N

national character 207
national differences 111, 114, 206–209, 213, 214, 219, 220, 230, 265–269, 271–275
nationality 207, 211, 232, 272, 273
nature 2, 3, 5, 6, 8, 26, 27, 33, 143, 144, 156, 162, 163, 166–168, 177, 183–185, 195, 198, 209, 218, 243, 244, 247, 253, 264, 274
Netherlands 284
New Punitiveness xxii
New York's Auburn State Prison 47
NGO KROM 284
nonconformists, behavioral 122, 154, 260
nonconformity 106–109, 119, 121–123, 131, 153, 158, 189, 251
Nordic countries xviii, xxv, 10, 277, 281, 282
Norfolk Prison Experiment 92
Norgerhaven 284
normal prisons 21, 28, 29, 31, 53, 55, 69, 88, 164, 172–174, 209, 211, 212, 233, 238
normative climate 80, 101, 106, 108, 109, 254
normative order x, 100, 105–108, 112, 120, 221
norms xiii, 24, 30, 31, 47, 55, 95, 101, 104–108, 110, 112, 119, 130, 133, 155, 204, 213, 215, 217, 245, 246, 283
Norrtalje 29, 56, 57, 65, 66, 86, 98
Norway v, xxi, xxiv, xxv, 2, 9–17, 28–31, 44, 45, 51, 52, 55, 57, 61, 64, 71, 86, 98, 111, 114, 209, 214, 215, 217–220, 231, 239, 240, 267–269, 272, 279–284, 288, 289, 291, 304, 308

Norwegian prisons xix, 28, 29, 272, 285, 286
Nyborg 31, 46, 47, 53, 71, 239, 245, 246

O

offenders 29–31, 44–50, 53, 54, 56, 57, 62, 64, 69, 75, 97, 115, 116, 131, 132, 136–140, 142, 148, 166, 285, 286, 288, 289
  dangerous xx
Olsen 103, 120
open colony 31, 53, 54, 69, 91, 97, 209
open labor colony 30, 192, 193, 200, 209, 229, 266, 272
Oslo xii, xviii, xxiv, 29, 36, 44, 51, 56, 127, 279, 280
Osterøy prison 285

P

penal establishments 279, 280, 285
penal leap backward, great xxii
Pennsylvania system 42, 44, 45, 47, 65
penology xii, xviii, 7, 42, 45, 69, 281
perceived justice xvii, 231, 232, 235, 249, 271, 273, 275, 277
perceived justice of treatment xiv, 223, 225, 227, 249, 275, 277
personal background 25, 112, 114, 158, 192, 203, 228
personnel, non-custodial 60, 86, 100, 109
physical plant 6, 48, 53, 69, 75, 297
policy-oriented studies 3
populism 288, 289
power, balance of 23, 84–87, 89, 90, 92–94, 99, 100, 108, 233
predictors 129, 136, 145, 155, 240, 272
President's Crime Commission 3
pressure, balance of 97–100, 108–110, 112, 233
preventive detention institutions 21, 28–31, 50–52, 67, 71, 86, 164, 172, 174, 209, 211, 212, 214, 215, 217, 231–235, 240, 249, 263, 265, 276, 285
  primary 30
prison administrators 135
prison architecture 29, 42
prison cells 284
prison characteristics xiii, 277
prison climate 92, 207, 209, 211, 212, 221, 235, 237, 265, 270, 271, 274
prison community 48, 136, 177
prison context 153
prison design 29, 30, 42, 63
prisoners ix, xii–xv, xvii, xx, xxi, xxiv, 2, 4, 43, 44, 46, 47, 51, 77, 97, 105, 280, 282, 284–286, 288–293
prison experience, differential 220, 243, 275
prison guards xv, 232, 250, 253
prison inmates 30, 126, 145, 165, 210, 253, 254, 268, 275
prisonization xiii, xiv, xix, xxiv, 160, 288
prison life 2, 3, 5, 59, 71, 82, 131, 133, 160, 184, 185, 219, 220, 309
prison officials 4, 221, 237, 303, 305
prison policy xiii, 2–4, 220, 228
prison research xvii, xviii, xxiv, xxv

prisons
central 6, 24, 44, 47, 88
federal 6
largest xxiv
modern 1, 29, 30, 88
normal adult 31, 57, 174
preventive detention xv, xvii, xviii, 277, 278
supermax xxiv
prison setting 6, 42, 105, 122, 160, 177, 180
prison staff 24, 94, 158, 161, 191, 235, 243, 249, 250, 253, 258
prison studies xiii, xiv, xviii
prison treatment 223, 228, 240–243, 254, 256
prison type 34
psychiatrists 54, 166
punishment xxi, xxiv, 3, 166, 211, 221, 247, 258, 259, 289–291, 295, 307

Q
questionnaire xix, xxiii, xxiv, 33, 35–38, 80, 81, 115–118, 122, 146, 177, 223, 244, 274, 280, 289, 301–309

R
Rand Corporation xx, xxi
ratio of inmates 21, 64, 68
recidivism/recidivists xix, 4, 31, 46, 53, 69, 91, 115, 135, 136, 209, 211, 283
regression equations 128, 144, 215, 216
regulations 21, 80, 100, 167, 184
rehabilitation v, xx, 31, 87, 211, 218, 221, 284, 285, 288
research methods 19, 208
Rinehart xxiii, 5, 101, 145, 160, 161
rules xxiii, 6, 9, 22, 33, 36, 41, 61, 75, 76, 80, 92, 94, 95, 100, 109, 111, 112, 119, 167, 184, 185, 188, 209, 210, 212, 233, 289, 298, 300
Russell Sage Foundation vi, ix, xi, 131, 146, 281
Russia xxiv, 12, 13, 288

S
sampling 19, 28, 31, 81, 122, 142, 208, 216
Scandinavian countries ix, 1, 3, 8, 9, 10–16, 18, 27, 28, 43, 45, 48, 52, 56, 59, 75, 100, 111, 114, 127, 133, 207, 214, 218, 230, 267, 269, 270, 279, 280, 282, 287, 288, 301, 303
Scandinavian Exceptionalism xxv, 289, 291, 292
Schrag, Clarence C. 5
self-conceptions 146, 147, 153, 156
Selvin, Hannan C. 210
sentence/sentencing vii, xiv, xvii, xx–xxii, 51, 54, 59, 133, 135, 137–140, 160, 196, 197, 209, 211, 224–228, 242, 245, 249, 255, 256, 258, 259, 262–264, 268–270, 277, 283, 284, 286, 290, 291
sentencing and treatment xiv, 224–226, 228

Seutula 30, 31, 53–56, 64, 97, 103, 104, 106, 172, 192, 193, 200, 209, 239, 269, 270, 272
sex offenses 45, 50, 51, 139
Siegel, Sidney 39
Simon, J. xxi
Simpson, George 158
Sloan, J. xxiv
Sobysogard 48–50, 53, 71, 73, 85
social background 25, 124–126, 128, 129, 134, 135, 138, 140, 141, 143–145, 148, 150, 151, 153, 155, 241
social climate xiii, xviii, 1, 22–24, 27, 28, 77, 79, 80, 82, 91, 95, 98, 100, 108–110, 205, 212, 213
social deprivation xiii, 61, 63, 65–67, 72–74, 232, 233
Socialists 11, 17
socialization xx, 2, 5
socialization processes xviii
social psychology xiii, 19, 25, 26, 101, 113, 114, 155–158, 238
society xi, xxiii, 12, 32, 75, 97, 105, 118, 119, 125, 149, 150, 154, 155, 160, 161, 189, 196, 197
Solzhenitsyn, Aleksandr 4
Speer, Albert 4
staff contact 175, 184–187, 193, 195, 250, 252, 253
staff members 21, 80, 83, 87, 88, 96, 235, 251, 271, 290, 297, 299
staff norms 80, 103, 104, 122, 127, 151, 155, 156, 171, 255
staff pressure 97, 98, 209, 210, 233, 235, 236, 272, 273, 275, 335
Stockholm x, 13, 15, 17, 29, 30, 45, 52, 57, 127, 279, 282
study design 29, 207, 208
Sturup, Georg 50, 86
suicide xiii, 111, 158, 159, 299
surveillance techniques 291
Sutherland, Edwin H. xiii, 136, 137, 142, 150, 160, 170, 171, 174
Sweden ix–xix, xxv, 2, 28–31, 51, 52, 55, 56, 64, 71, 85, 86, 98, 114, 209, 214, 215, 217–220, 231, 267–269, 272, 273, 280, 282, 284, 287, 288, 290, 304
Swedish system 52, 56
Sykes, Gresham M. xxii, xxiii, 5, 161

T

Tham, Henrik 276, 279, 287, 290
theory x, xiii, 19, 31, 38, 158, 160, 190, 200, 203, 206
total power 89, 90, 92, 94, 233
training, vocational 55, 60, 117, 219, 230
treatment ideology 51
treatment orientation 64
treatment personnel 64, 67, 94
treatment programs 4, 295
treatment staff 36, 52, 54, 60, 63, 64, 67, 68, 81, 83–90, 92–94, 96, 108, 166, 167, 184, 185, 209, 213, 233, 297
treatment staff personnel 166
Trow, Martin 7
trusties 49
Turku 30, 46, 55, 88, 106, 240, 245, 246, 277
Tvangsarbeid 283
type institution 197, 205, 213, 215–217

U

Ugelvik, T. xxiv
United States v, 11, 13–16, 18, 28, 31, 36, 42, 44, 45, 53, 59, 62, 101, 111, 127, 135, 161, 162
Universitetsforlaget xviii, 283
unjust treatment xv, 225, 246, 253, 258, 266

V

validity 117, 118, 149, 155, 172
values x, xxiii, xxv, 15, 101, 103, 105, 106, 108, 160, 161, 202, 217, 228, 238, 250, 254, 255, 264, 271, 272, 287, 288, 292, 295
Vridsloselille 31, 44, 45, 47, 53, 71, 86
Vridsloselille's inmates 229

W

Wacquant, Loïc xxii, xxiv
Ward, David A. 4, 5, 8
Warwick, Donald P. 206
welfare state xxv, 8, 9, 11, 287, 289
Wheeler, Stanton v, ix, xvii–xix, 101, 161, 183, 277, 279–281, 285, 289, 290, 292, 293
work v–ix, xi, xii, xvi, xvii, 3, 5, 21, 24, 25, 37, 38, 42, 44, 47, 48, 52–55, 57–62, 70, 79, 80, 101, 103, 105, 119, 120, 127, 129, 135, 159, 170, 191, 244, 282, 285, 292, 295, 297–299, 301, 307
workers 12, 16, 54, 105, 166, 285, 297
work program 54, 55, 57
world viii, x, xvii, xviii, 2, 8, 9, 10, 13, 14, 27, 36, 38, 45, 55, 61, 73, 82, 86, 100, 101, 106, 108, 119, 137, 149, 157, 161, 162, 167, 169–172, 174–180, 186, 192, 194–198, 201, 202, 210, 220, 253, 280, 282, 290–292
  outer 68, 131, 182, 183
  western 50, 58, 75, 91, 125, 135, 191

Y

youth institutions 55, 62, 74, 88, 105, 133, 141, 164, 172–174, 209, 211–214, 217, 231, 273, 305
youth prisons 172, 231

Z

Znanieki, Florian 159

The manufacturer's authorised representative in the EU is Springer Nature Customer Service Centre GmbH, Europaplatz 3, 69115 Heidelberg, Germany. If you have any concerns regarding our products, please contact ProductSafety@springernature.com

Printed and bound by CPI Group (UK) Ltd, Croydon, CR0 4YY
30/09/2026
02225693-0001